UNIVERSITY OF NORTH CAROLINA AT CHAPEL HILL
DEPARTMENT OF ROMANCE LANGUAGES

NORTH CAROLINA STUDIES
IN THE ROMANCE LANGUAGES AND LITERATURES

Distributed by:

UNIVERSITY OF NORTH CAROLINA PRESS

CHAPEL HILL
North Carolina 27515-2288
U.S.A.

NORTH CAROLINA STUDIES IN THE
ROMANCE LANGUAGES AND LITERATURES
Number 295

ENCOUNTERS WITH BERGSON(ISM) IN SPAIN

RECONCILING PHILOSOPHY, LITERATURE, FILM AND URBAN SPACE

ENCOUNTERS WITH BERGSON(ISM) IN SPAIN

RECONCILING PHILOSOPHY, LITERATURE, FILM AND URBAN SPACE

BY

BENJAMIN FRASER

CHAPEL HILL

NORTH CAROLINA STUDIES IN THE ROMANCE LANGUAGES AND LITERATURES

U.N.C. DEPARTMENT OF ROMANCE LANGUAGES

2010

Library of Congress Cataloging-in-Publication Data

Fraser, Benjamin

Encounters with Bergson(ism) in Spain : reconciling philosophy, literature, film and urban space / Benjamin Fraser.

p. cm. – (North Carolina studies in the Romance languages and literatures ; 295)

Includes bibliographical references and index.

ISBN 978-0-8078-9299-2

1. Spain – Civilization – 20th century. 2. Spain – Intellectual life – 20th century. 3. Bergson, Henri, 1859-1941 – Influence. I. Title.

DP233.5.F753 2010
194-dc22 2010014283

ISBN 978-0-8078-9299-2

IMPRESO EN ESPAÑA

PRINTED IN SPAIN

Artes Gráficas Soler, S. L. - La Olivereta, 28 - 46018 Valencia
www.graficas-soler.com

TABLE OF CONTENTS

ACKNOWLEDGEMENTS

PORTIONS of this work are based upon ideas originally explored in the following journal articles "Unamuno and Bergson: Notes on A Shared Methodology" (*Modern Language Review 102.3* [2007]: 753-67), "Baroja's Critique of Traditional Medicine" (*Bulletin of Spanish Studies* [2008]: 29-50), "On Mental and Cartographic Space: Belén Gopegui's *La escala de los mapas*, Bergson and the Imagined Interval" (*España Contemporánea 18.1* [2005]: 7-32), "The Space in Film and the Film in Space: Madrid's Retiro Park and Carlos Saura's *Taxi*" (*Studies in Hispanic Cinemas 3.1* [2006]: 15-33), "Madrid's Retiro Park as Publicly-Private Space & the Spatial Problems of Spatial Theory" (*Journal of Cultural and Social Geography 8.5* [2007]: 673-700), "Manuel Delgado's Urban Anthropology: Multidimensional Space & Interdisciplinary Spatial Theory" (*Arizona Journal of Hispanic Cultural Studies* 11 [2007]: 57-75), and "Toward a Philosophy of the Urban: Lefebvre's Uncomfortable Application of Bergsonism" (*Environment and Planning D: Society and Space* 26.2 [2008]: 338-58). The content of these articles has been significantly recast, reorganized and expanded upon.

In addition, the appendix consists of a translation from the Spanish of Bergson's speeches at the Ateneo in Madrid on May 2nd and 6th, 1916. The speeches were published in Spanish as *El alma humana. Precedido de un estudio de Manuel García Morente*. Trans. Manuel García Morente. Madrid: Biblioteca "España", 1916 and appear here for the first time in English.

LIST OF FREQUENT ABBREVIATIONS

Books by Henri Bergson (1859-1941)

TFW	*Time and Free Will*
MM	*Matter and Memory*
L	*Laughter*
CE	*Creative Evolution*
CM	*The Creative Mind*
ME	*Mind-Energy*
DS	*Duration and Simultaneity*
MR	*The Two Sources of Morality and Religion*

Gilles Deleuze (1925-1995)

B	*Bergsonism*
MI	*Cinema 1: The Movement-Image*
TI	*Cinema 2: The Time-Image*

Henri Lefebvre (1901-1991)

UR	*The Urban Revolution*
PS	*The Production of Space*
CEL	*The Critique of Everyday Life* (v. 1, 2, or 3 as noted)
R	*Rhythmanalysis*

INTRODUCTION: BERGSON(ISM) IN SPAIN

> A "return to Bergson" does not only mean a renewed admiration for a great philosopher but a renewal or an extension of his project today, in relation to the transformations of life and society, in parallel with the transformations of science. Bergson himself considered that he had made metaphysics a rigorous discipline, one capable of being continued along new paths which constantly appeared in the world.
>
> –Gilles Deleuze (*Bergsonism*, 1966, p. 115)

> We gauge the significance of a doctrine of philosophy by the variety of ideas which it unfolds.
>
> –Henri Bergson (quoted in Chevalier 1969, p. 74)

THIS book is driven by a dual analysis. It is a look at French philosopher Henri Bergson (1859-1941) in Spain–his more or less direct influence on Spanish letters–, and also at Bergsonism in Spain–the more indirect resonance with his methodological posture articulated through explorations of Spanish texts as well as theoretical approaches to films and urban space. Through this twin investigation, one part historical and the other part methodological, this work is meant to broaden the scope of interest in Bergson's philosophy, to emphasize the interdisciplinary nature of his thought, and to insist upon the relevance of his methodological premise to two of the disciplines most important to cultural studies today–film studies and urban geography. This is ultimately to recover the call made by Gilles Deleuze for a "return to Bergson."

This work is also corrective. Previous research on Bergson's influence in Spain by Hispanists has been all-but-completely overlooked by important book-length studies, limited to a small number of journal articles that only hint at the breadth of the philosopher's influence, or buried in larger volumes with a much wider scope.[1] The scant attention paid to Bergson in Hispanism is, perhaps, the direct consequence of the traditional lack of interest in Bergsonism in the realm of philosophy. Nevertheless, interest in Bergson's philosophy is now on the rise as there is, not only in philosophy but also in film studies and urban theory, a recent and significant attempt to acknowledge his contribution.[2]

In correcting this unfortunate error of Hispanist scholarship, this work does not seek to compile an encyclopedic listing of Bergson's appearances in Spanish letters, as Gonzalo Sobejano so wonderfully has done with the influence of Nietzsche in his impressive *Nietzsche en España* (1967). Instead, far from an attempt at a totalizing reference work, the present volume recovers the very interdisciplinary thrust central to Bergson's own work, pursuing intriguing case studies of select Spanish figures who engage Bergsonism (both directly and indirectly) in philosophy, literature, film studies and urban theory. In this way I hope not only to explore Bergson's relevance to Spanish thought but also to outline a more general case for a return to his philosophy and method in the investigation of cultural and urban production. I have no doubt that the philosopher

[1] While there are many now classic texts on the influence of philosophers in Spain, none have taken on Bergson's legacy as their primary area of interest. Roberta Johnson's *Crossfire: Philosophy and the Novel in Spain, 1900-1934* (1993), while superb, mentions Bergson only in passing. The best example of a work that delves into Bergson's influence is Sherman Eoff's *The Modern Spanish Novel: Comparative Essays Examining the Philosophical Impact of Science on Fiction* (1961). While Eoff's text is far from being exclusively focused on Bergson, he manages to treat the latter's ideas both frequently and in appropriate detail, rivaling his presentation of Nietzsche's philosophy in his own volume. This introduction will mention other important essays where appropriate.

[2] This resurgence can be traced through the works of Deleuze (1966, 1983, 1985, 2004), Guerlac (2004, 2006), Hanna (1962), Kennedy (1987), Kumar (1962), Mullarkey (1999a, 1999b), Olkowski (2002), Pearson (2002) and especially the recent reissues of his classic texts by Clinamen Press, Dover Publishers and others. The journal *Culture and Organization* also features a number of interesting readings and applications of Bergson's philosophy: see Hatzenberger (2003), Linstead (2003), Linstead and Mullarkey (2003), Power (2003), Styhre (2003), and Watson (2003). See also volume 15 (2004) of *Pli: The Warwick Journal of Philosophy*, which includes a special section on Bergson titled "Lives of the Real: Bergsonian Perspectives."

himself would have enjoyed the interdisciplinary research environment that increasingly characterizes contemporary academic life. Appropriately, this book returns to his philosophy in this eclectic context–from which it necessarily draws its strengths and limitations.

As a group of encounters with Bergson(ism) in Spain, the present work–while it may not be traditional study of historical influence–is nevertheless faithful to Bergson's conception of thought as an interdisciplinary unfolding. It should thus be held to his own standard–that is, it should be judged "by the variety of ideas which it unfolds." As a way of preparing the ground for the following chapters' varied subject matter–and an interdisciplinary method which reconciles philosophy, literature, film and urban studies–it is first necessary to relate the important details of Bergson's life and work. Afterward, a concise presentation of the notable encounters with Bergson(ism) there have been in Spain will prepare the reader for the more strikingly interdisciplinary chapters to follow.

Henri Bergson (1859-1941) was born in Paris, of a Polish-Jewish father and an Anglo-Irish mother who spoke to him frequently in English. In 1891, he married the second cousin of Marcel Proust–Louise Neuburger, with whom he fathered a daughter.[3] Although fascinated by mathematics early on, he soon became intrigued by philosophy with an intuition he had regarding the fluid nature of time. A professor at various provincial and Parisian lycées before joining the esteemed Collège de France in 1900, his work was undoubtedly appreciated in his day–Bergson became a prominent member of many learned societies and, in fact, enjoyed the status of an international celebrity of sorts. He was a member of the Academia de Ciencias Morales y Políticas de Madrid from 1925 on, and of the French Academy of the same name in Paris starting in 1901. In 1913, he was named President of the British Society for Psychical Research; in 1914, a member of the Académie Française; and from 1921 to 1926 he was president of the Commission for Intellectual Cooperation of the League of Nations. In 1919 he was awarded the French Legion of Honor and in 1920 Cambridge bestowed upon him the Doctor of Letters. His notoriety led to his traveling frequently throughout Europe and also to the United

[3] Born in 1893, Jeanne was deaf from birth. Marcel Proust was in fact an attendant at Louise and Henri's wedding (R. Richardson 2006: 427).

States. He even visited Spain in 1916 as part of a diplomatic mission in the midst of World War I, giving lectures at the Ateneo in Madrid and also at the Residencia de Estudiantes, the latter having been formed in 1910 as a product of the earlier Institución Libre de Enseñanza (1876).[4] In 1927 he was awarded one of the world's greatest honors–the Nobel Prize for Literature.

The interdisciplinary impact of Bergson's legacy has been truly astounding, a fact of which he would have been quite proud given his own wide-ranging interests. Bergson was intrigued not merely by philosophy proper but also mathematics, poetry, biology, mysticism, music, experimental medicine, dreams... It is thus no surprise that critics have reconciled his work with the ideas of many of the great artistic movements, literary minds, and philosophers of our time. To wit: Mark Antliff (1993) looks at the role of Bergsonism in the Fauvist, Rythmist, Cubist, Symbolist, Fantaisiste and Futurist movements; Paul Douglass (1986) explores the significance of Bergson for literary figures T. S. Eliot and William Faulkner in depth and touches on F. Scott Fitzgerald, Robert Frost, Willa Cather, William Carlos Williams, Gertrude Stein, Henry Miller and T. E. Hulme along the way; Tom Quirk (1976) deals with his influence on Willa Cather and Wallace Stevens in compelling depth; Shiv Kumar (1962) examines Bergson's impact on James Joyce, Virginia Woolf and Dorothy Richardson in the context of the stream of consciousness novel; Mary Ann Gillies (1996) expands substantially on Kumar's work adding Joseph Conrad and John Middleton Murry to the list of Bergsonian writers; the essays collected in Frederick Burwick and Paul Douglass's edited volume (1992) take on Bergson's resonance with Mikhail Bakhtin, Samuel Taylor Coleridge, Sir Charles Bell, Nietzsche, Charles Sanders Peirce, Jean-Paul Sartre, Gilles Deleuze and numerous aspects of modernism and vitalism; and Anthony E. Pilkington (1976) explores connections between Bergson and Charles Péguy, Paul Valéry, Marcel Proust and Julien Benda.[5] Bergson was himself in a position to directly influence a

---

[4] These lectures were published by the journal *España* and later republished in a study of Spanish philosopher Manuel García Morente. The latter was documented in the journal of the Residencia. See: Bergson, Henri. "Bergson en la Residencia," *Residencia* 2 (1926), 174-76. The Institución Libre de Enseñanza was itself notable for its influence on and connections with both Machado and Unamuno (see de Jongh-Rossel 1986 and Tuñón de Lara 1975).

[5] Some of the notable but less well-explored engagements with Bergsonism

number of the most well-known intellectual figures of the twentieth century: among those who attended his classes in Paris were the French theorist Michel Foucault, the Greek novelist Nikos Kazantzakis, the Hungarian filmmaker Béla Balázs and the great Spanish poet Antonio Machado. His personal connections extended perhaps most notably to William James, who promoted the philosopher seventeen years his junior and was influential in disseminating Bergson's philosophical ideas.[6]

Although most well-known for his connections to philosophy, literature and art, Bergson was no less interested in science. He envisioned his philosophy not as a replacement for scientific thought –not as the antidote to some scientific disease–but as its complement. His explicit desire to reconcile metaphysics and science appears in a number of his works and even constitutes the methodological base for his thought. The early essay "Introduction to Metaphysics" (1903) most explicitly presents his very understanding of philosophy as a complement to, and not an attack on, science, insisting succinctly that "metaphysics cannot get along without the other sciences" (168).[7] Although Albert Einstein did not indulge the attempt, Bergson even took steps to connect his own philosophical ideas with those of the great relativity theorist in the work *Duration and Simultaneity* (1922).[8] Similarly instructive in this regard is the essay "The Philosophy of Claude Bernard" (*CM*) where Bergson expresses admiration for the latter's classic text *Introduction to Experimental Medicine* (1865). A relatively recent reexamination of the connection between Bergson's philosophy and science has even led to a number of published volumes including *Bergson and the Evolution of Physics* (ed. Gunter 1969a), Milič Čapek's *Bergson and Mod-*

include the American Personalist Ralph Tyler Flewelling's book *Bergson and Personal Realism* (1920) and a work by Olive A. Wheeler on *Bergson and Education* (1922).

6 See Robert D. Richardson (2006), where the author documents James's opinion that Bergson was "For me, a magician" (427) as well as his "excited notes and underlinings in his copies of Bergson's works" (426). On the latter, see J. Alexander Gunn (1920, 5).

7 Also "But if metaphysics demands and can obtain here an intuition, science has no less need of an analyisis. And it is because of a confusion between the roles of analysis and intuition that the dissentions between schools of thought and the conflicts between systems will arise" (169). It would surprise many to hear that Bergson's view of science was in fact quite nuanced: "Modern science is neither one nor simple" (197).

8 See Bergson 1922, Murphy 1999, Durie 1999.

ern Physics: A Reinterpretation and Re-evaluation (1971) and *Bergson and Modern Thought: Towards a Unified Science* (eds. Papanicolaou & Gunter 1987). Notably, the selective theory of memory Bergson outlines in *Matter and Memory* (1896) still holds its own in neuroscience against models of memory that argue memories are 'stored' in the brain (McNamara 1996).

Significantly, in recent years Bergson's interdisciplinary thought has been revisited by contemporary scholars working across the humanities and social sciences. Donald Maxwell (1999) examines in depth the commonly acknowledged interchange between Bergson and the literature of Marcel Proust and John Mullarkey's edited volume *The New Bergson* (1999b) goes further incorporating essays that infuse not only the philosophical, but also the musical, the cinematic and the artistic with consistent Bergsonian inflections. Similarly, Antliff (1993) explores the connection of Bergsonism with the artists of the Parisian Avant-Garde. Of course, much of this interdisciplinarity is indeed to be found in Bergson himself. In addition to the pervasive phenomenological, ontological and epistemological concerns of his work (Lawlor 2003), Bergson's thought takes on biology, the comic, morality/ethics and mysticism directly (Lacey 1989). It is perhaps this characteristic that made his ideas resonate not only with philosophers and visual artists, but also, as Chevalier (1969) argues, with syndicalists and musicians (66). In fact, recognition of the importance of Bergson's philosophy has increased exponentially in recent years–due in large part to what it offers to the growing interest in interdisciplinary questions of cinema, methodology and embodiment.[9] In urban geography, too, Bergsonism has an important role to play, as the final chapters of this work explore.

On the whole, however, appreciation of Bergson's philosophy and its interdisciplinary character has been contentious to say the very least. Over the years there have been at least as many negative appraisals of his work as positive, resulting from the curious power of Bergsonism to provoke controversy. To wit, Bergson's works were placed on the Index of Prohibited Books by the Holy Office of the Roman Catholic Church (in 1914),[10] his election to the

[9] This growing interest is greatly indebted to key works by Gilles Deleuze (1966, 1983, 1985, 2004), Elizabeth Grosz (1994, 1995, 2001, 2004, 2005), John Mullarkey (1999a, 1999b), and Keith Ansell Pearson (2002).

[10] Bergson was connected with the occult revival in early twentieth-century France (Grogin 1988).

Académie Française (although successful) was vociferously opposed by the right-wing Action Française, and "the anarcho-syndicalist Georges Sorel had provoked a controversy of a different sort by utilizing Bergson's ideas to justify class warfare in his book *Reflections on Violence* (1908)" (Antliff 4-5). Bergson's popularity seemed to demand that his work be quite publicly debated, and eventually the tide turned from admiration to denunciation.[11] This shift is evidenced in the strident rejection of his philosophy over the years by a number of figures such as Hugh Eliott, Julien Benda, Bertrand Russell, George Santayana, Wyndham Lewis, Jean-Paul Sartre, Gaston Bachelard, former student Ralph Tyler Flewelling, and even urban philosopher Henri Lefebvre, who, according to one source, "hated Bergson's guts" (Merrifield 2006: 27).[12] The ongoing open opposition and even hostility to his ideas was so severe that, in addition to costing Bergson more than one prestigious academic position, it has predisposed even many contemporary critics to reject his philosophy out of hand. Nevertheless, Bergson was willing to face marginalization not only in his professional life, but in his political life as well. He opposed the Vichy regime in France and, although he was offered exemption due to his notoriety, he registered as a Jew during the German Occupation of Paris in solidarity with the regime's victims. Ultimately, he was debilitated by arthritis and died in 1941 of pneumonia, weeks after having stood in line to register as a Jew (Burwick and Douglass 1992). Sadly, soon after his death, even the controversy surrounding his work was "almost entirely forgotten" (Lorand 1999: 400).

In the main, critics of Bergson's work and method have tended to respond to the popular conception of his ideas rather than to his ideas themselves.[13] One cause of this, perhaps, may be found in his

[11] See the sections titled "Bergson's Fall from Popularity" (Gillies 1996: 25-27) and "The Damnation of Bergson" (Douglass 1986: 13-17).

[12] Flewelling later recanted his dismissal of Bergson (Douglass 1986: 15). Lefebvre's explicit hatred of Bergson is belied by his pervasive, if unacknowledged and even unconscious, incorporation of Bergson's ideas, as will be discussed in chapter eight of this book.

[13] Gillies (1996) puts it well, "Bergson's difficulties can be traced, ironically, to the huge popularity of his philosophy. Despite the fact that it was based on a thorough understanding of previous philosophers and philosophical traditions, Bergson's own writings seem to pose fewer difficulties to non-expert audiences than other philosophical works. This is deceptive, for although one does not need to have a sound philosophical background to understand Bergson's theories, the clarity of his language and the power of his rhetoric often led the general public to believe they

deceptively straightforward writing style. Bergson's charming and unadorned prose, certainly anathema to the more recent baroque style of some poststructural and postcolonial theoretical writings, is defiantly at odds with its complex content. Yet characterizing his writing as simple vastly underestimates Bergson's achievement–an eloquent fusion of form and function. Here, the medium is the message. His words are carefully chosen and his pacing is best described not as slow, but instead as cautious, even deliberately hesitant. He is wary of language, which, he notes, is heavily informed by the tendency of intellect, an idea he deals with most directly in the later pages of *Creative Evolution* (1907). This intellectual tendency of thought partitions the world into qualities (adjectives), things (nouns) and actions (verbs) where there is only movement (*CE*, 298-304). Instead, Bergson's work is meant to be grasped as a whole, not dealt with in pieces. Accordingly, the reader who uproots an isolated page or chapter of his *Matter and Memory* (1896) from its context, for example, is likely to take away only a fragmented and thus incomplete grasp of the title pair's relationship to one another. Even the latter book's title is a challenge to the intellect's partitioning of the world through language–for matter and memory are not, for Bergson, the two completely discrete things language frames them to be. In short, it is not Bergson's simple unadorned prose, but rather its simplistic reception that has caused his works to be misunderstood–the very thing his complex philosophical method critiques.

Bergson's method is certainly complex enough for its thorough explanation to warrant an entire book.[14] Moreover, the subject mat-

---

had grasped the nuances of his theories" (26). I believe this to be the case not only with the general public, but also with experts in the field, both present and past, who have rushed to conclusions regarding Bergson's work all too quickly.

[14] Most recently, Guerlac 2006 has done an admirable job of this. Deleuze's early work *Bergsonism* (1966) also stands out in this regard, although critics unfamiliar with Bergson's work have tended, short-sightedly, to see this more as a product of Deleuze's originality. Other books dedicated to studies of his philosophy (roots and legacy) include Stewart (1911), Elliot (1912), Dodson (1913), Le Roy (1913), A. Mitchell (1914), Russell (1914), Flewelling (1920), Gunn (1920), Stephen (1922), Scharfstein (1943), Hanna (1962), Deleuze (1966), A. E. Pilkington (1976), Herman (1980), Kolakowski (1985), Moore (1996), Pearson (2002), Lawlor (2003), and even Grosz (2004, 2005). Regarding Spain, the interested reader should see the bibliography of translations and criticism in Hernández García's *La vitalidad recobrada: Un estudio del pensamiento ético de Bergson* (2001). In addition, studies of Bergson in Spanish include Benito y Durán (1969), Elosegui Itxaso (1990), Muñoz-Alonso

ter through which he articulates his ideas is so varied that a concise summary of his diverse philosophical topics is difficult if not misleading. For these reasons, as is appropriate given the interdisciplinary approach of the present book, I have chosen to undertake a more thorough discussion of the relevant aspects of Bergson's philosophy in each of the chapters that follow as they pertain to the topics at hand. For the moment, a provisional characterization of his method should suffice to orient the reader who is relatively unfamiliar with Bergsonism.

Bergson's philosophical method is based on a deceptively simple central idea concerning the relation of space and time, and figures in one way or another into all of his works.[15] His goal was not merely to produce a philosophy of time but rather a new way of thinking, to create a thought more closely attuned to the movement of life. In accomplishing this, he rejected traditional philosophical postures, drew attention to the insufficiency of intellectual models for experience, and grappled with relationships while disdaining the static and apparently discrete divisions suggested to thought through the perception of things. His writings thus underscored the *relations* between space and time, between matter and memory, between intellect and instinct, between consciousness and things, and between life and representation. In a way, his works mimicked the spatialization characteristic of the human intellect in order to expose thought's own method to itself. Certainly he explored simple

López (1996), González Bedoya (1976), González Umeres (2001), Izuzquiza Otero (1986), Osegueda (1949), Sator Ros (1975), Suances Marcos (1974), Uscatescu (1991), Zaragüeta (1941) and of course García Morente (1917).

[15] Bergson is the author of: *Essai sur les données immédiates de la conscience* (1889, Trans. *Time and Free Will/TFW*), completed in partial requirement for the docteur des lettres along with another essay on Aristotle's sense of place–*Quid Aristoteles de loco senserit*; *Matière et Mémoire: Essai sur la relation du corps avec l'esprit* (1896, Trans. *Matter and Memory/MM*); *L'Evolution créatrice* (1907, Trans. *Creative Evolution/CE*); *Le Rire* (1900, Trans. *Laughter*); *L'Energie Spirituelle* (1919, Trans. *Mind-Energy*); *Durée et Simultanéité* (1922, Trans. *Duration and Simultaneity/DS*); *Les Deux Sources de la Morale et de la Religion* (1932, Trans. *The Two Sources of Morality and Religion/MR*); and *Le Pensée et le Mouvant* (1934, Trans. *The Creative Mind/CM*). Two other works, although they have been translated into English, are seldom mentioned in contemporary and more recent studies of his ideas: 1) an annotated edition of the poem *De Rerum Natura* by Lucretius published in 1884 under the title *Extraits de Lucrèce* (and later in English as *Philosophy of Poetry*, 1959), and 2) an address given as President of the Académie des Sciences Morales et Politiques published as *The Meaning of the War* (1915), including a short article on the same theme originally published in the *Bulletin des Armées de la République*.

oppositions, but these are best understood as the raw materials for what are really

> [...] two very different kinds of multiplicity. When we speak of material objects, we refer to the possibility of seeing and touching them; we localize them in space. In that case, no effort of the inventive faculty or of symbolical representation is necessary in order to count them; we have only to think them, at first separately, and then simultaneously, within the very medium in which they come under our observation. The case is no longer the same when we consider purely affective psychic states, or even mental images other than those built up by means of sight and touch. (*TFW*, 85-86)

It would be a grave misreading, however, to understand these two types of multiplicity, "the one heterogeneous, that of sensible qualities, the other homogeneous, namely space" (*TFW*, 97), as discrete in experience–and it is from experience, as the title of his dissertation reminds us (*Essay on the Immediate Data of Consciousness*, 1889), that philosophy should begin. In *Matter and Memory* (1896) he notes, not the discrete nature of "pure perception" and "pure memory," but their unceasing fusion in experience, their roles in the heterogeneous nature of a time that unfolds.[16] In *Creative Evolution* (1907) he points out not the mutually exclusive nature of intellect and instinct, but their cohabitation: "There are things that intelligence alone is able to seek, but which by itself, it will never find. These things instinct alone could find; but it will never seek them" (151). Even in *The Two Sources of Morality and Religion* (1932) with his discussion of open/closed societies and static/dynamic religion, he drives not toward a facile categorization of societies or religions, but toward the recognition that these are tendencies, i.e from the static dogma of religion it is possible that there may arise a dynamic religion. Through discussions hinging on such simple oppositions Bergson paradoxically creates a theory that is complex and even *internally* contradictory–this is not merely a the-

---

[16] "That is to say pure perception exists only in theory; in fact it is always mixed with affection" (*MM*, 59). "Pure perception and pure memory constantly intermingle" (*MM*, 71). "We may therefore surmise that time, conceived under the form of a homogeneous medium, is some spurious concept, due to the trespassing of the idea of space upon the field of pure consciousness" (*TFW*, 98).

ory of knowledge, nor only a theory of life, but a theory of both knowledge and life at once: "*theory of knowledge* and *theory of life* seem to us inseparable" (original emphasis, *CE*, xiii).

Bergson offers "intuition," less a concept than a method, as a necessary corrective to the problems of a thought driven by the tendency of a spatializing intellect. Although the philosopher is frequently referenced for his explorations of the concepts of élan vital/vital impetus, durée/duration, l'évolution créatrice/creative evolution, the spatialization of time, and of course memory, it is this method of intuition that enfolds the former ideas in a coherent, if variegated, attempt to restore philosophy to life. Above all else, Bergson's is a philosophy of reconciliation–his goal is to return thought from the abstract categories employed by the tendency of intellect to the flow of living movements as they unfold. This is to move from a static notion of space to an enduring temporality that enfolds space into its duration, its rhythm, its process.

Although, in Spain, Bergson's philosophy was subject to the same controversy and challenges he faced elsewhere, its reception was nothing if not timely. His *Matter and Memory* (1896) was translated into Spanish and published in 1900, and Mary Jo T. Landeira Brisson (1979) asserts that "in 1896 the Spanish were already being informed of Bergson, and those who could read French could begin to know his thinking," even suggesting that this date may be pushed back to 1892 at the earliest (64).[17] The sparks of this early interest caught fire when Bergson paid a visit to Madrid in 1916, giving lectures at the Residencia de Estudiantes on May 1st and the Ateneo on May 2nd and 6th.[18] These Ateneo lectures were heavily attended by notable Spanish intellectuals of the period–including A. Maura, M. Azaña, E. Pardo Bazán, R. Menéndez Pidal, J. Ortega y Gasset, A. Castro, M. de Maeztu, G. Marañón, R. Altamira, and

---

[17] In her masterful dissertation, Landeira Brisson notes that "it was possible for Bergson to have become known in Spain as early as 1892, the year in which he is cited by Clarín in *Ensayos y revistas*. At that time, still untranslated he was nonetheless being read already" (85). Alain Guy (1984) and Sherman Eoff (1961) take the more accepted approach pinpointing 1900 as the year of the earliest engagements with Bergsonism.

[18] The former was published in *Residencia* in the original French, and was later incorporated in Manuel García Morente's study titled *La filosofía de Bergson* (1917/1972: 13-18). The latter two were published in 1916 as *El alma humana* (published in the weekly *España*) and, having been translated from the Spanish, form the appendix of the present volume.

M. García Morente–and Bergson took the opportunity to personally visit M. Cossío of the Institución Libre de Enseñanza.[19] In short, Spain experienced the same flood of interest in Bergson that swept across Europe during the first third of the twentieth century, and Bergson, for his part, had only positive things to say regarding France's southern neighbor.[20]

Largely because of his denunciation of positivism, his name was common currency among many leading Spanish intellectuals, poets, philosophers and novelists who, if not strictly Bergsonians themselves, incorporated his ideas into their own to some degree or another. Over the years, critics have signaled possibilities for the investigation of Bergson's influence on the work of Leopoldo Alas/"Clarín,"[21] Ángel Ganivet,[22] Juan Ramón Jiménez,[23] Rafael Al-

[19] Landeira Brisson (1979) includes these names and others in her exquisite summary of Bergson's visit to Spain (74).

[20] Chevalier (1969) quotes Bergson as saying that "[Spain is] on the same moral plane and at the same moral altitude [as France]" (71). In the latter's address at the Residencia he described France as "la que por su parte ama a España" (16). "A Francia, cuya admiración siempre fue grande por el arte español, por la literatura española, por todas las contribuciones que España ha aportado a la ciencia, a la filosofía, a la civilización. Ninguna nación está mejor dispuesta para comprender la vuestra, para simpatizar con las corrientes de pensamiento y de sentimiento del alma española –alma que siempre estuvo bien viva, pero que está más viva hoy que nunca, y cuya actividad, en todos los campos, va camino de una renovación" (16). He also notes Spain's "elevación moral," its "generosidad," and that it is one of the "naciones nobles" (17). He closes his speech with the words "Dejadme que [...] salude a un tiempo en sus estudiantes y en sus hombres ilustres, a la juventud española" (18).

[21] Regarding Alas, Gonzalo Torrente Ballester (no date) writes: "Estaba al corriente de los grandes movimientos culturales del pasado siglo, y su curiosidad llegó hasta el conocimiento de Bergson y de Nietzsche, cuando el primero de estos pensadores era –entre nosotros– ignorado en absoluto, y el segundo, conocido sólo de segunda o tercera mano, más como nombre escandaloso que otra cosa" (128).

[22] Miguel Olmedo Moreno suggests that Ganivet and Bergson agreed on the question of freedom: "Esta idea de la posibilidad, y aun de la facilidad, de deshacer la civilización técnica sonará hoy a ingenuidad, por la general convicción de que el proceso histórico es irreversible. Sin embargo, en su fe en la libertad humana coincide Ganivet con Bergson, quien muchos años después escribía: 'No creemos en la fatalidad en la historia. No existe obstáculo que no puedan salvar voluntades suficientemente tensas si se lo proponen a tiempo. No hay ley histórica ineluctable'" (201). Olmedo Moreno cites the Spanish translation, *Las dos fuentes de la moral y la religión*, Ed. Sudamérica, 1962, 283.

[23] See Richard Cardwell (1976) for a mention of Bergson's influence. In his study of Machado, Havard (1983) nevertheless notes that many Spaniards had read Bergson in 1900, "with or without French": "Among them was Machado's friend, Juan Ramón Jiménez, who tells us: 'La palabra Modernismo empieza entonces a propagarse a otras disciplinas científicas y artísticas. Cuando yo tenía 19 años

berti,[24] Alejandro Casona,[25] Ramón Pérez de Ayala,[26] "Azorín"/José Martínez Ruiz,[27] Federico García Lorca,[28] Pedro Salinas,[29] and Eugenio D'Ors, who went so far as to call Bergson "la personalitat més eminent del pensament francés" (Roura Roca, 357). Whereas these connections are important–and, it must be added, still relatively unexplored–there are four Spaniards in particular who must be recognized if one is to understand the breadth and depth of Bergson's enduring if underrecognized legacy in Spain–Antonio Machado, Manuel García Morente, José Ortega y Gasset and José Ferrater Mora. While these significant influences do not advance the more strikingly interdisciplinary connections pursued in the present work, they are nevertheless crucial in order to understand how Bergson's influence managed to filter into the history of Spanish ideas indirectly as a generalized legacy.

Antonio Machado, widely considered the greatest Spanish poet of the twentieth century, clearly admired Bergson and was explicit on this matter in his own writings, both poetic and otherwise. In his notes (later published as *Los complementarios*, Ed. Manuel Alvar, 1980), he writes in no uncertain terms that "Henri Bergson es el filósofo definitivo del siglo XIX" (110). Importantly, the poet was also sensitive to how Bergson's philosophy had been simplified by his detractors, writing that "Tampoco faltan los refutadores superficiales que no han comprendido nada ni de Bergson ni de la filosofía

---

(i.e. en 1900), leí la palabra aplicada a Nietzsche, a Ibsen, a Bergson, por ejemplo" (207). Originally from "Juan Ramón Jiménez, *La corriente infinita (crítica y evocación)*, (Madrid, 1980), 33" (Havard 213, n. 23).

24 See Tina Pereda Berona (2002).

25 See H. Kay Moon (1966).

26 Víctor G. de la Concha (1984) writes: "Ayala comparte con Ortega la idea bergsoniana de que lo heroico y lo trágico se degradan por la enfatización de lo corporeal o de su ubicación en lo cotidiano" (84). See also Pelayo H. Fernández (1983, 1987).

27 In Pedraza Jiménez and Milagros Rodríguez Cáceres (1987): "La experiencia del tiempo se concibe como unidad, como totalidad en la que se funden la rememoración del pasado, el presente y la anticipación del futuro. El tiempo deja de ser algo externo y racional para convertirse en vivencia, en algo que pasa por uno mismo. Puede advertirse que Azorín se aproxima, no sabemos si conscientemente, a la concepción bergsoniana." (528). See also Ricardo J. Carlos Sabater Morant (1986).

28 Jacqueline Cockburn (2003) attributes to Lorca "a limited understanding of Bergson" (77), acknowledging a Bergsonian aspect to Lorca's drawing *San Sebastián* (1927) (77-78), and goes so far as to state that: "To what extent Lorca understood Bergson is not the issue here. What is clear is that his name was a buzzword at the time. Bergson was topical, trendy perhaps" (70).

29 See J. M. Aguirre (1978) and Havard (1974).

que esgrimen contra el nuevo filósofo" (118). Given that in some circles the reputation Bergson had as a poet eclipsed his reputation as a philosopher (he did, after all receive the Nobel Prize for *Literature*), it is not surprising that one of Spain's greatest contemporary poets should have been considered Bergsonian. Since for Machado, as for Bergson, poetry and philosophy were similar ways of seeing the world, it is no surprise that the former came to write that "los poetas están todavía bergsonizando, mientras Bergson poetiza" (121).[30]

Perhaps because Antonio Machado was known to have attended Bergson's lectures in Paris during 1910 and 1911, criticism has been relatively quick in developing the connection of Bergson's philosophy with Machado's poems as compared with other poets and writers of the time. Yet, the question as to precisely when Bergson's influence on Machado began has been much debated, even if the influence itself has not. Critics have offered various perspectives on this subject, suggesting that Bergson influenced Machado's poetry directly only after 1910-1911, that the Bergsonian element of Machado's poetry before 1910 can be explained by the latter reaching a Bergsonian intuition of time on his own terms, and even that Machado was influenced by Bergson indirectly through Unamuno as an intermediary.[31] Nevertheless, Havard argues convincingly that Machado had read Bergson, as it appears many in Spain had, *before* attending the philosopher's classes in Paris.

Machado himself most famously called his Bergsonian influence to the attention of future critics when he mentioned both Bergson and his first work by name in his "Poema de un día" (1913, later published in *Campos de Castilla*; 193-99).

---

[30] As Suzanne Guerlac notes, being honored with the Nobel prize had its downside as well. The fact that Bergson was awarded the Nobel Prize in *Literature* may have only solidified Bertrand Russell's critique (and a more widespread opinion) of Bergson as a poet and not a philosopher (13). In this vein, George Boas (1959) notes that "Bergson's weakness was that of most philosophers before his time. Strictly speaking, he ought to have admitted that he was writing lyric poetry" (510). To wit, one of Bergson's earliest works, an essay on Lucretius, has been translated to English as *The Philosophy of Poetry* (Ed. Wade Baskin, 1959).

[31] Interestingly, Machado lends credence to this opinion in a section of his notes where he writes that "Muchos que no habíamos leído a Bergson, bergsonizábamos por cuenta propia hace ya más de veinticinco años" (*Los complementarios*, ed. Manuel Alvar, 110).

> Enrique Bergson: *Los datos*
> *inmediatos*
> *de la conciencia.* ¿Esto es
> otro embeleco francés?
> Este Bergson es un tuno;
> ¿verdad, maestro Unamuno?
> Bergson no da como aquel
> Immanuel
> el volatín inmortal;
> este endiablado judío
> ha hallado el libre albedrío
> dentro de su mechinal. (196)

Even in this brief excerpt Machado intimates a vast debt to the Frenchman, managing to mention the title of Bergson's first dissertation (translated into English as *Time and Free Will: An Essay on the Immediate Data of Consciousness*) as well as his pervasive critique of Kant (strongly present in Bergson's *Creative Evolution*), and his focus on the complex imbrication of the living and the inert. In his introduction to *Campos de Castilla*, the noted critic Geoffrey Ribbans (2003: 37-38) reveals just how conscious this Bergsonian influence was for Machado through discussion of the latter's "Reflexiones sobre la lírica" (1925).[32] As many commendable studies have already explored in depth, Bergson's influence on Machado is one of the most significant and most well-researched connections between Bergson and Spain.[33] The Bergson-Machado connection is in fact so well-established that Robert G. Havard (1983) was able to join in with other noted scholars by concluding that "Discussion of Henri Bergson has long been *de rigueur* in An-

[32] Ribbans, although correct to point out the Bergsonian connection, shys away from noting the influence of Bergson's *Matter and Memory* on the passage he cites from Machado's work of 1925. Through carefully placed italics Ribbans emphasizes the words "*Las cosas están allí donde las veo, los ojos allí donde ven*" (37). This phrase resounds with the sections of *Matter and Memory* where Bergson points out repeatedly that perception is not in the body but rather is located in the thing itself, not the brain (esp. 303-04); thus perception is, for Bergson, our virtual action upon things (57): "The image, then is formed and perceived in the object, not in the brain" (35).

[33] Critical study of this connection, as Landeira Brisson (1979) notes in her excellent dissertation, begins with Carlos Clavería's "Notas sobre la poesía de Antonio Machado" (1945). Mary Jo T. Landeira Brisson (1979), Carl Cobb (1976; 18, 22), Nigel Glendinning (1962), Robert G. Havard (1983), Carolyn Morrow (1961) and Robert S. Piccioto (1964) are some of the most significant.

tonio Machado criticism, it being beyond dispute that the French philosopher influenced the Spanish poet" (204).[34]

The noted philosopher and commentator on relativity Manuel García Morente, who, like Machado, was a former student of Bergson's in Paris, also helped to bolster Bergson's early reception in Spain and was largely responsible for disseminating his ideas to a Spanish reading public. In addition to writing a book on Bergson, titled appropriately enough *La filosofía de Bergson* (1917), and helping to disseminate the insights of his lectures at Madrid's Ateneo during 1916, he also wrote an essay "Sobre la intuición bergsoniana," and frequently alluded to Bergson in essays that did not take on the French philosopher's work directly.[35] Although for the most part García Morente reacted positively towards Bergson's ideas, he took umbrage with his perspective on laughter and the publication of Bergson's last book *The Two Sources of Morality and Religion* brought on his frank disapproval.[36] He writes that "el fracaso de Bergson en este libro era inevitable" (141) and elaborates on the subject saying: "[A]l enfrentarse con la moral y la religión, es decir, con 'cosas', ha olvidado el pequeño detalle de que la moral y la religión son, en efecto, 'cosas', es decir, algo más que estados de conciencia" (142). Ultimately, García Morente seems to prefer a Bergson who sticks to states of consciousness, ignoring that Bergson's very philosophical goal is to bring into question the way in which we distinguish states of consciousness from external things. Nevertheless, García Morente remains one of the most notable advocates of Bergsonism in Spain.

---

[34] Havard's footnote to this statement is instructive: "Typical are the comments, for instance, of López-Morillas, who describes Machado as a 'buen bergsoniano' and 'discípulo declarado de Bergson'", *Intelectuales y espirituales* (Madrid, 1961), 90, 78; Sánchez Barbudo, who says that Bergson "tuvo sobre Machado una influencia indudable y decisiva", *El pensamiento de Antonio Machado* (Madrid, 1974), 57; and J. M. Aguirre, "la presencia de Henri Bergson en la filosofía de Antonio Machado. . . ha sido establecida ya sin dejar lugar a dudas", *Antonio Machado, poeta simbolista* (Madrid, 1973), 111 (212, n. 1).

[35] The essay appears in *Escritos desconocidos e inéditos*, 30-36, and was originally published in *Revista General*, 1918. He also mentions Bergson in the essays "El clasicismo de Santo Tomás," "El 'Curso' de Ortega y Gasset," "La crisis intelectual de nuestro tiempo," and "Sobre la risa."

[36] In "Sobre la risa," he writes: "El error de Bergson consiste, a mi entender, en no haber distinguido convenientemente primero entre la risa y su causa, y luego entre las diversas causas que pueden provocar a risa" (241). See also Pedro Muro Romero's *Filosofía, pedagogía e historia en Manuel García Morente*, "Henri Bergson y Manuel García Morente," 141-46.

José Ortega y Gasset (1883-1955) was not merely one of the greatest Spanish intellectuals of the twentieth century but was also well-known outside of Europe for his philosophical postures and essays. Although Ortega was by no means a strict Bergsonian, he himself articulated the resonance of his own thought with Bergson's explicitly on a number of occasions and situated himself, as did Bergson, as the creator of a "philosophy of life."[37] As Alain Guy (1984) explores in his important essay "Ortega y Bergson," the Spaniard stressed the correspondence of his own razón vital with Bergson's principles ("Esto que Bergson llama *buen sentido* es lo que yo he llamado formalmente *razón vital*"), was fond of a Bergsonian dictum which he cited on a number of occasions (*le desordre, c'est le conflit de deux ordres* / el desorden es el conflicto entre dos órdenes), and likewise saw the static as merely being a remnant of the dynamic. Juana Sánchez Venegas (1985) similarly traces correspondences between the two thinkers in the idea that "la realidad es, por tanto movilidad" (65) while giving reasons to pursue the connection more thoroughly, effectively coming to suggest a correspondence between Bergson's method of intuition and Ortega's discussion of "el pensar que gira sobre sí mismo" (67). Also, despite their more global focus, the works of critic John T. Graham rely on Ortega's own archives to establish Bergson as a formative influence and also to document the ebb and flow of Ortega's praise and denunciation of Bergson's vitalism, as well as the resonance of the French philosopher's ideas with his system as a whole. Significantly, Graham (1994) concludes that "On balance, it seems likely that he derived from Bergson's *élan vital* some initial clues and encouragement for his own vitalism in 1913, and, from that very unhistorical philosopher, some intimations compatible with his reflections on fluid time, becoming, and historicity in human reality as

---

[37] José Ferrater Mora's (1957) opinion is that Ortega y Gasset, although not necessarily Bergsonian, did not completely disregard Bergson either (77). Ortega introduced Bergson for his lectures at the Ateneo in Madrid, 1916, and mentions him sporadically throughout his *Obras completas*: he mentions "los grandes pensadores –Bergson [entre ellos]" (140, I), that Bergson among others should be invited to Spain ["¿Por qué no ha de ocuparse en solicitar a las grandes personalidades europeas para que den conferencias en España?" (140, I)]. References in Ortega's other works abound, including Tomo I 395, 413; Tomo II 84, 180, 220; Tomo V 297, 455, 457; Tomo VI 33, 161, 393, 416; Tomo VII 81, 213, 292, 327, 338, 341, 464, 492; Tomo IX 292, 487; Tomo X 157, 382. See Pelayo H. Fernández (1981), Thomas Mermall (1988).

apt concerns of philosophy" (I. 89-90). These studies suggest that there are still numerous points of comparison to be explicitly analyzed by critics interested solely in the question of direct influence.

Yet the Spanish literary critic who seems to best intuit the complexity of Bergson's work is José Ferrater Mora, who includes a full chapter on the French philosopher in his *Cuestiones disputadas* (1955). In tune with Machado's poetic homage, he similarly describes Bergson as a diabolical figure whose writing leaves the reader "hechiz[ado]" (113), in a spellbound state, in awe, charmed or even bewitched. Like Gilles Deleuze would come to do, Ferrater Mora seems to understand the distance between Bergson's deceptively simple but compelling prose and his complex philosophy, one that borders on paradox: "Lo primero que nos desazona en Bergson es, por lo tanto, lo que constituye su máximo atractivo y su mejor gloria" (114). From the tone of his work, the reader can discern the joy with which Ferrater Mora addresses Bergson's ideas. Given the controversy that has routinely cast a shadow over Bergson's work, Ferrater Mora's enthusiasm stands out for its uncompromising confidence–as when he writes that "el devenir afirmado por Bergson es un devenir radical y aun el más radical que se haya proclamado en toda la historia de la filosofía" (120).[38]

To see this limitless support for Bergson's philosophy in 1955, even before Deleuze had initially drawn attention back to it in his *Bergsonism* (1966) was certainly unexpected, and in Spanish letters it was perhaps even more so.[39] More important than the tone of Ferrater Mora's chapter, however, is his splendid synthesis and articulation of Bergson's ideas. He cites *Time and Free Will*, *Matter and Memory*, *Creative Evolution*, *The Two Sources of Morality and Religion* by name, arguably makes a reference in the text to "The Possible and the Real" (134, Bergson's essay of the same name, later

[38] Also, "Por una parte [la filosofía de Bergson] es una perfecta y cabal continuación [de la tradición de la filosofía del devenir]. Por la otra, es una completa y radical novedad" (122).

[39] Importantly, before publishing *Bergsonism* (1966), Deleuze penned at least two essays on Bergson. These have been re-published in *Desert Islands* (2004): "Bergson (1859-1941)," originally from Maurice Merleau-Ponty, ed. *Les Philosophes célèbres*, Editions d'Art Lucien Mazenbod, 1956, 292-99; and "Bergson's Conception of Difference" originally from *Les Etudes bergsoniennes*, vol. IV, 1956, 77-112. Of course, Ferrater Mora's praise for Bergson in 1955 predates the original publication of both these essays.

published in *The Creative Mind*), and furthermore displays that he has understood that space and time are, for Bergson, two aspects of a variegated whole (137). In the Spain of the 1950s, Ferrater Mora's unconditional acceptance of Bergson is in a class of its own.

Although these four prominent intellectuals–Machado, García Morente, Ortega and Ferrater Mora–are some of the most important voices to speak out in favor of Bergson in Spain, in the following chapters I have chosen to focus on authors and critics whose works allow for a more interdisciplinary conversation. This squares with the aim of the present work not to document Bergson's historical influence in a more traditional manner, but instead to approach his influence in Spain through the eclectic method Bergson himself followed throughout his work.

This book's first two chapters on Pío Baroja and Miguel de Unamuno, respectively, attempt to correct the blind-spot of an otherwise impeccable critical work that documents the philosophical stance of Spanish novelists of the first part of the twentieth century (Johnson, 1993). They explore not only the explicit mention of Bergson by both of the aforementioned turn-of-the-century Spanish philosophical writers but also the relatively unexplored connections between their literary output, philosophical ideas and the French philosopher's methodology. Given that Bergson's philosophy was "compulsory reading" (Havard 1983: 207), for Spanish intellectuals and artists at the turn of the century, that *Matter and Memory* had been translated into the Spanish as early as 1900 (Havard 1983: 206), and that Bergson's works had been read in the original French as early as 1896 and even 1892 (Landeira Brisson 1979: 64, 85), it is not surprising to see Bergsonism manifested in the work of Baroja and Unamuno, two of the period's most important novelists. The wide scope of Bergson's philosophy–its importance not only for rethinking traditional metaphysical distinctions but also key questions of memory, biology and religion–made it accessible to different contemporary thinkers each in their own way. It was, in fact, difficult to be an intellectual in Europe at the turn of the century and not to have been affected by his intuitions in one way or another.

The connection between Baroja and Bergson gives cause to reformulate questions of science and religion. The former was certainly exposed to Bergson's ideas and even acknowledged them on many an occasion. Although the precise date of his exposure to Bergson, not to mention the extent and frequency of this contact, may never be known, he wrote positive comments regarding the latter in writings such as *Las horas solitarias* (1918). Starting from this connection I argue that Baroja's critique of traditional medicine in *El árbol de la ciencia* (1911) squares with Bergson's rejection of positivist science and moreover anticipates recent developments in nursing theory that have an indirect Bergsonian legacy. The later part of the first chapter turns to *Camino de perfección: (Pasión mística)* (1902) where his exploration and inversion of mysticism resonates with Bergson's ideas on the self, anticipating aspects of the latter's last work, *The Two Sources of Morality and Religion* (1932).

Through the articulation of Unamuno with Bergson, the second chapter explores the intense (and intensive) reaction against an externally-conceived positivism and the traditional ontological distinctions of the time period. The Spaniard's personal library contained copies of several of Bergson's books, and Unamuno mentioned him explicitly in his own philosophical works. Unamuno was even personally disappointed not to have met Bergson during his trip to Spain in 1916.[40] His implicit philosophical debt to Bergson, in fact, far overshadows his explicit incorporation of Bergsonian ideas in his key texts, *Del sentimiento trágico de la vida* and *En torno al casticismo*. As this chapter will explore, in these works Bergson is present to such an extent that, at times, even the language used by Unamuno in expounding his own ideas recalls specific passages of Bergson's works–a connection that perhaps was so evident to his readers in during the time period as to render direct acknowledgment unnecessary. Study of this connection has often been hindered by a traditional metaphysical legacy that bifurcates experience into a standard dualism and sees either Unamuno, Bergson, or even both as dualists. Dispensing with this erroneous conception of both thinkers allows a more accurate assessment of their common philosophical premise. Furthermore, in his novels *Amor y pedagogía* (1902) and later *Niebla* (1914), Unamuno's presentation of conflicting and entwined opposing forces breathes life into the Bergsonian struggle between quantitative/qualitative multiplicities and intellect/intuition.

The third and fourth chapters on Juan Benet and Belén Gopegui explore the Bergsonian ideas that underlie the works by two key

[40] After visiting Madrid and Toledo, Bergson unexpectedly went back to France directly from Sevilla (García Blanco 1965: 38).

novelists of the mid-to-late twentieth century. First, an engineer-turned-writer named Juan Benet returned to the stream-of-consciousness style popular among the turn-of-the-century European avant-garde. Apart from being one of the most compelling authors of this period, Benet is of great interest as he explicitly signalled the influence of Bergson's philosophy on his novels in an interview with Nelson R. Orringer (1980). His first and second novels *Volverás a Región* (1967) and *Una meditación* (1969) are Bergsonian both in form and in content. When read along with the Bergsonian content of Benet's significant essays, the style and images Benet employs in these novels resonate profoundly with Bergson's theories regarding the movement of life, the relationship of the past to the present, memory, duration vs. clock time and ultimately the recalibration of space as part of an enduring temporality.

Where Benet's works provide a remarkable, if heretofore unexplored, opportunity to expose the direct influence of Bergson on Spanish letters, the first novel of Belén Gopegui, who has been favorably compared to Benet, presents a remarkable indirect connection with Bergsonism. The fourth chapter thus takes on her prize-winning text, *La escala de los mapas* (1993), in order to suggest what a modern-day Bergson might have had to say on the question of the production of city-space. A close analysis of Gopegui's undeniably philosophical novel about the struggles of an urban geographer living in Madrid highlights the work's resonance with Bergsonian ideas. Discussion of this work closes the more historical and literary first part of the book on "The Spanish Novel" while at the same time it introduces the key theoretical questions to be addressed in the book's second and third parts. Specifically, an analysis of the novel's reliance on the cinema as content as well as novelistic structure will prepare the reader for the application of Bergson's methodology undertaken in part two on "Film Studies." Additionally, the novel's theme of urban geography and Gopegui's philosophical take on spatial processes will lead into the discussion of cultural geography to follow in part three on "Urban Theory." Ultimately, the novel suggests an important corrective to theories of the urban which might imagine mental space and cartographic space to be distinct from one another at the same time that it calls for the return of an isolated thought to the realm of action. In so doing, *La escala*, like Bergson's philosophy, argues against the traditional intellectual and metaphysical displacement of space from time in favor of their intimate union. Fusing the two categories together, Gopegui continues Bergson's reconciliatory project arguing compellingly that urban space is at once both material and mental.

Marking a shift from the historical focus on the direct and indirect influence of Bergson in the first part of the book, "Part II. Film Studies" uses Bergsonian methodology to explore undervalued theoretical advances in the fields of film studies and geography. Although cinema is widely regarded a privileged artistic representation of time and geography is taken to emphasize the study of spatial phenomena, there are recent theoretical movements which have emphasized the importance of spatial concerns to cinema (Aitken & Zonn 1994), and the relevance of temporal movements and mobility to geography (Latham & McCormack 2004). Detailing these important theoretical shifts, and building on the questions raised by the earlier analysis of Gopegui's novel, chapter five traces the importance of Bergson's conception of the cinema from its key role in *Creative Evolution* (1907) through its development by Gilles Deleuze in his works on the subject (*Cinema 1: The Movement-Image* & *Cinema 2: The Time-Image*). This chapter then explores two Bergsonian approaches to film, taking on the notions of duration and multiplicity with reference to Víctor Erice's *El sol del membrillo* and Alejandro Amenábar's *Abre los ojos*. Chapter six stresses the Bergsonian spirit of film theories that assert the redemption of reality (Balázs 1945 and Kracauer 1960) and ultimately recovers the importance of reconciling indexical/iconic approaches to film (Prince 1993, Pasolini 1988, Wollen 1972) with more formalist approaches in order to perform a Bergsonian analysis of the intimate connection between city-space and filmspace. The seventh chapter builds upon the theoretical discussions in chapter six to explore how Bergson's reconciliatory project suggests interrogating Madrid's Retiro Park on-screen in Carlos Saura's film *Taxi* (1996) with its off-screen double. This approach assesses the disconnect between traditional auteur and structural approaches to film and the interpretations of cinema that emphasize theories of urban geography and privilege the lived realities of city-life.

Beginning the book's "Part III. Urban Theory," the eighth chapter argues that Bergson's philosophical work functions as a revitalizing force and even an implicit point of departure for the more urban-oriented criticism of one of the most important names in contemporary spatial theory: Henri Lefebvre (1901-1991). Echoing

Bergson's philosophical works, Lefebvre's key texts (*La production de l'espace/The Production of Space*, *The Critique of Everyday Life*, *Urban Revolution*) seek to understand space as a process, simultaneously ideal and real. Although he only mentions Bergson in passing, Lefebvre is similarly concerned with the complex interaction between mental space and physical space, what Bergson calls temporal and spatial multiplicities, in that complex compound termed social space. Even though Lefebvre notes the philosophical basis of this division and is critical of traditional metaphysical distinctions, lamentably, he refuses to solve the very philosophical problem he poses through a critical philosophy such as Bergson's. Through a close look at Lefebvre's work and its continuation through the key arguments of urban geographers, this chapter argues that Bergson is in fact an unacknowledged precursor of Lefebvre's urban theory.

The ninth chapter turns explicitly to the Spanish context in order to trace the explicitly Bergsonian/Lefebvrian roots of urban anthropologist and Spanish critic/anti-urbanist Manuel Delgado Ruiz. While present in his earlier works *El animal público* (1999) and *Memoria y lugar* (2001), ultimately these roots manifest themselves most clearly in his recent work *Sociedades movedizas: Pasos hacia una antropología de las calles* (2007) in the priority Delgado gives to the enigma of the urban, in his critique of spatializing approaches to urban planning and in the way he addresses the question of method. Building on the critique of intellectual or analytical approaches advanced by the combined works of both French philosophers, Delgado Ruiz echoes the Bergsonian/Lefebvrian call for a return to concrete experience, everyday life and a more intuitive approach to understanding urban process.

As evidence of Bergson's interest in Spain and support for the present work's historical contribution, the appendix of this work presents an English translation of Bergson's two addresses in Madrid at the Ateneo on May 2 and 6, 1916. These lectures were published in Spain–the same year they were delivered–in the journal 'España': (*El alma humana. Precedido de un estudio de Manuel García Morente*. Trans. Manuel García Morente. Madrid: Biblioteca 'España', 1916). In this way, "Encounters with Bergson(ism) in Spain" attests to not only the philosopher's historical and methodological legacy in Spain, but his physical presence there as well.

I want to close this introduction by returning to the epigraph with which I began and insist–as I believe Bergson himself would–

that the following chapters and their eclectic interdisciplinary approach be judged “by the variety of ideas which they unfold.” From this perspective, the present work’s reconciliations across philosophy, literature, film studies and urban theory may raise more problems than they are able to solve–but in this, too, there is a Bergsonian conceit. As the philosopher himself asserted: “The truth is that in philosophy and even elsewhere it is a question of finding the problem and consequently of positing it, even more than of solving it” (*CM*, 51). In this spirit, the central problem addressed by this book is one of reconciliation. The solution to this problem, of course, continues to unfold.

PART I. THE SPANISH NOVEL

PÍO BAROJA:
MEDICINE AND MYSTICISM

THE traditional paradigm of medical practice is wholly spatial. It proceeds by division–spatially isolating and extracting illness from its surroundings. In so doing it severs the physical body from the social body and methodologically cleaves the concept of disease from the concept of health which it takes as its necessary, if idealized counterpart. Yet in opposition to this traditional medical paradigm of spatialized difference there is a growing body of nursing theory and practice which acknowledges the interdependent relationship between the illness and its environment, the immanence of the physical in the social body, and the porous, if not friable, boundary between the concepts of health and disease themselves. This paradigm shift in healthcare and its implicitly Bergsonian approach to disease permit a new reading of a now classic twentieth-century Spanish text–Pío Baroja's *El árbol de la ciencia* (1911).

In its depiction of the plight of the disillusioned medical student and protagonist of the novel, the 'precursor' Andrés Hurtado, Baroja's work prefigures nursing theorist Margaret Newman's explicitly philosophical method of internal differentiation–one grounded implicitly in the works of Bergson, Baroja's near-contemporary–in an effort to widen our prevailing ideas of health and disease and in renunciation of a traditional, stagnant, even spatialized medical paradigm of illness. The first section of this chapter will first explore the unacknowledged Bergsonian philosophical roots and consequences of Newman's theory of health and disease before then investigating Baroja's own philosophical trajectory as well as his take on pain. Finally, it will explore the application of Newman's Bergsonian ideas, and those of Baroja himself, to *El árbol de la ciencia* in order to assess the novel's relevance to the recent paradigm shift in nursing research. This is not to suggest in any way a direct connection between Baroja and Newman–a complete chronological impossibility–nor even between Baroja (1872-1956) and Bergson (1859-1941)–although there is good reason to speculate on the possibility of such an influence. It is certain, for example, that Baroja had read Bergson by the time he wrote *Las horas solitarias* (1918), a chapter of which is devoted to a discussion of the *Ensayo sobre los datos inmediatos de la conciencia.*[1] Nevertheless, this section merely proposes that all three have taken to a certain set of philosophical principles and have used them to denounce the all-too-rigid scientific paradigms of their day. In each case, the effect has been to attempt to find life where there was only disease, to embrace meaning where there was only measurement, and to holistically envision a human being where the medical paradigm sees a mere assemblage of separate parts.

Although the effect may be to reverse chronology, an introduction to the theories of Margaret Newman and their implicitly Bergsonian framework will pave the way for an exploration of the writings of Pío Baroja himself. As the argument is that Andrés Hurtado is a precursor of modern nursing theories and their rejection of an instrumentalist medical paradigm, it is important to explore this theoretical understanding of health and disease before inserting Baroja's novel in such a framework. This approach has the additional benefit of directly confronting the way in which an understanding of the past is necessarily rooted in present concerns. Along the way, the implicit resonance between Newman's work and Henri Bergson's philosophy of difference will be emphasized. Just as the French philosopher avoided a simplistic articulation of time and space, Newman avoids a crude oppositional understanding of health and disease. In both cases, the outcome is a more nuanced

---

[1] See Baroja's *Las horas solitarias* (1918), alternatively in *Obras Completas* V, 299-303. Baroja also refers to Bergson's concept of *élan vital* (from *L'Évolution créatrice*) in *Momentum catastrophicum* (1919), alternatively in *Obras Completas* V, "La mutación brusca ha constituído el neodarwinismo, y Bergson ha sacado de ella un argumento para defender su teoría del impulso vital que crea constantemente; *l'élan vital*, que dice el filósofo francés" (370). Sherman Eoff (1961) in his *The Modern Spanish Novel. Comparative Essays Examining the Philosophical Impact of Science on Fiction*, places the possible point of contact even before the 1911 publication of *El árbol de la ciencia*. It is also interesting that, as an evolutionist, Baroja does not discuss the Lamarckism of Bergson's idea of *élan vital.*

understanding of the tendencies involved in a unitary, if variegated, human experience. More importantly, this nuanced approach argues against a monolithic concept of meaning and instead allows for the participation of the individual in determining the meaning of their life events–particularly those involving pain, illness and disease.

Newman is a nursing theorist who has produced a theory of nursing, of illness, that departs radically from the traditional instrumentalist medical paradigm in its divergent philosophy and interdisciplinary relevance. As Abby Fuoto notes in her engaging critique of Newman's work, "Outside of nursing, Margaret Newman drew from many fields, including physics, philosophy, quantum theory and chemistry" (5). Indeed, in the introduction to her most important work *Health as Expanding Consciousness* (1999), Newman allies herself with the works of Itzhak Bentov (1978), Pierre Teilhard de Chardin (1955),[2] David Bohm (1980), Arthur Young (1976a, 1976b), Richard Moss (1981), and perhaps most importantly Martha Rogers (1970) in what is a holistic approach to disease. Rogers, herself a teacher of Newman, is largely heralded as the progenitor of a push for a nursing theory that resolves to avoid the problematics of traditional medicine. Newman (1999) sees Rogers as introducing a revolutionary critique to the spatializing character of medicine's conceptual framework:

> When Rogers introduced her conceptual framework, which called for a distinctly different science–nursing science–based on assumptions of wholeness, pattern and unidirectionality, most nursing scientists could not envision such a science. The prevailing paradigm said that it was valid to analyze human beings into parts, reduce those elements to measurable entities, control and manipulate the parts, and try to extrapolate the whole based on knowledge of the parts. (81)

The prevailing paradigm, that of instrumentalist medicine as Newman describes it here, indeed works in a spatial manner. The intellect as a spatializing tendency partitions and stitches together again. It works from the parts to the whole, it measures, controls and manipulates a perceived divisible homogeneity and in so doing imag-

---

[2] Teilhard de Chardin was himself a follower of Bergson.

ines that homogeneity as distinct from heterogeneous qualities.[3] The instrumentalist medical tradition thus operates unceasingly from a position that identifies disease as an error in the otherwise flat planar surface of a fundamental and inherently stable idea of health. Health is taken to be normality and disease an unnatural rupture of that normality. As a reaction to this paradigm, the nursing theory proposed by Newman refuses to follow this over-rational procedure, as she documents succinctly in "The Pattern that Connects" (2002):

> Integration is a step in the overall cyclic scheme of things, *but not enough*. Just as one cannot understand the whole of a person by integration of the parts, we cannot understand the unity of nursing knowledge by an integration of the parts. In a hologram, each part contains the whole; each part is reflective of the whole. Mind and matter are not separate, interactive parts; they are different dimensions of the whole and unbroken movement of reality. (5, original emphasis)

This position, as Newman (1999: 82) herself notes, suggests two revolutions of thought each representing different ontological positions.

The first revolution of thought, more easily reappropriated back into the traditional paradigm, would hold that instead of a positivist or objectivist scientific "single" paradigm of health there should be an interactive paradigm that embraces both objectivism and subjectivism. Yet such an approach merely begs the question of the ontological status of the categories "objective" and "subjective" themselves. The second revolution Newman offers finds the aforementioned shift to a consideration of "mind-body-environment factors in health" a mere extension of the "control and predictability" present in the first paradigm, and states that instead what is necessary is a "view of the human being as a unitary phenomenon unfolding in an undivided universe" (1999: 82).[4] This of

---

[3] This is also Bergson's understanding of intellect. Bergson sees the intellect as that part of thought most attuned to space and thus most suited to measure and divide–to understand quality only through quantity. The reader is directed to three key Bergsonian texts: *Time and Free Will. An Essay on the Immediate Data of Consciousness* (1889), *Matter and Memory* (1896) and *Creative Evolution* (1907).

[4] See also Newman's "Prevailing Paradigms in Nursing" (1992).

course can be read in philosophical terms as a familiar two-stage revolution–first, the dualistic limited Cartesian system wrought of the transition from medieval to Renaissance thought and defined by a broadening of epistemology without a severe questioning of ontology, and second, by the Bergsonian non-dual system which rejects the ontological distinctness of what are, rather, cohabiting tendencies. This second revolution actualizes what was only virtual in the first revolution and thus posits a more sophisticated model of disease.

Newman avoids approaches that imagine disease and health as two ends of a continuum as well as those that figure them as opposite sides of a coin. Both of these are insufficient to explain the cohabitation of each tendency with the other. Instead, she argues, disease is a tendency which always exists with health, and conversely, health is a tendency which always cohabits with disease. It is the implicit assumption of the instrumentalist medical paradigm that health and disease are simple opposites–that is, where one ends, the other begins. Yet what Newman proposes is altogether different–"In this case, DISEASE fuses with its opposite, absence of disease, NON-DISEASE, and brings forth a new concept of HEALTH" (1999, 6). In effect, she is performing not an intellectual or spatializing analysis of health, but an intuitive, holistic one. Health is thus produced as a composite instead of as a mere reflection of disease. Just as Bergson argued that space and time were cohabitating tendencies of a larger time (*TFW*), instinct and intelligence of a larger idea of thought (*CE*), matter and memory of a larger idea of perception (*MM*), Newman argues that health and disease are both tendencies posited in a larger idea of health.[5] Under the traditional instrumentalist medical paradigm disease is thus cleaved from health as aberrant in order to be excised, often at great consequence to the person from whom the aberration is extracted. In contrast, the idea of health as expanding consciousness enfolds disease back into a larger idea of health where disease is no longer an ontologically distinct object, but rather is illustrative of a larger pattern present in the whole. She states most succinctly that "This would mean that health includes disease, *and* disease includes health" (1999: 6). It is this method of division that points toward a Bergsonian under-

[5] Bergson is arguably present in her analysis indirectly through the work of David Bohm.

standing of internal difference as the implicit methodology which obtains in Newman's analysis. The division of the composite "health" reveals two cohabitating tendencies that differ in nature, and also a difference in nature itself as one of the two tendencies. Thus there is 1) disease, which differs from itself by degree, that is, by its location in space; and 2) non-disease, which differs from itself by nature, that is, by changing qualitatively from non-disease to disease.

From the perspective of the traditional paradigm of medicine, disease divides by spreading to this or that location–it is divisible in space–yet the relationship of disease to non-disease goes unacknowledged and unexplored. This spatializing approach is suited to analyze and measure disease quantitatively, that is, it defines the location of disease, extracts it, and believes it has re-established a whole. Metastasis of cancer of the colon to the liver differs in location but not in nature. It is in this sense that disease differs from itself in degree. And yet framing the question of health myopically in terms of disease allows neither an awareness of the relationship of disease to non-disease nor the relevance of qualitatively-conceived meaning that grounds disease in an individual's life experience. Newman writes: "Disease and non-disease are not separate entities but *are each reflections of the larger whole*, a phenomenon of greater dimensions" (1999: 9, original emphasis). Newman's approach takes great care in assessing the question of health from the outset and avoids the false problems of health just as Bergson avoided the false problems of philosophy (see Deleuze 1966). She avoids limiting the problem to disease itself as a thing, as does the instrumentalist paradigm, but takes a broader view which in a sense exists prior to disease. Her concern is rather the capacity or the potentiality of disease to manifest itself as such. This philosophical move returns disease from the objectively delineated physical body to the properly physical-social body. But even more importantly, this approach accounts for the way in which life is experienced as a whole and therefore allows meaning to be assessed by the patient him or herself instead of it being handed down from above by the supposedly all-powerful physician.

Newman's methodology thus resonates with the works of philosophers who have criticized overly rational approaches to experience, not only Bergson (1859-1941), but also Maurice Merleau-Ponty (1908-1961) and Gilles Deleuze (1925-1995). This resonance is worthy of brief attention here as it allows further evaluation of Newman's holistic approach and her emphasis on intuitive rather than intellectual assessment of health. Just as Deleuze pointed out that the more powerful Bergsonian statement that "all consciousness *is* something" trumps Husserl's "all consciousness is consciousness *of* something" (1983: 56), there is a strange and close parallel in Newman's assertion that "The person does not *possess* consciousness–the person *is* consciousness" (1999: 33, original emphasis). Her statement that "Mind and matter are made of the same basic stuff. The difference is in the speed and intensity of the energy waves: Mind represents faster, higher energy waves, and matter represents slower, lower energy waves" (1999: 36), echoes the whole of Bergson's *Matter and Memory* with its insistence on a unitary consciousness of matter/consciousness of mind which articulates a composite movement of tension and relaxation. Bergson spent quite a few pages of his works relating the Eleatic philosopher Zeno's paradoxes of movement, which, he explained, showed the errors of confusing an indivisible movement with the divisible space covered by the movement.[6] Newman, for her part, also argues the indivisibility of movement most successfully, even if seemingly unaware of her philosophical precursor. She writes that "In this sense, movement is not thought of as a succession of bodily locations but as a pattern of the total dance present in each movement, like a holographic view of the universe in which all of space-time is captured in any one place-movement" (1999: 57).[7] Her take on language embraces Merleau-Ponty's idea of communication as immanent: "When two people are relating well, the rhythm of the speaker is shared by the listener in a kind of mutual dance or empathy. The listener is not reacting or responding to the speaker but is *one with* the speaker" (1999: 58, original emphasis). Like many turn-of-the-century vitalists she valorizes the heterogeneous and qualitative succession of musical notes: "In music, for instance, the notes are incomplete without the rhythm of relationship between them" (1999: 73; see al-

[6] One of the most famous of these is Zeno's insistence that if Achilles moves ten times faster than the tortoise, but the tortoise has a ten-meter head start, then Achilles will never surpass the tortoise. Zeno's explanation is that by the time Achilles has moved the ten meters, the tortoise has already moved one meter more, and so on.

[7] See also one of Bergson's most notable passages–that on the cinematograph of the mind in *Creative Evolution*, 306 ("We take snapshots [...]").

so Bergson *TFW*). In the spirit of Deleuze she dismantles the objectivist opposition of seer and seen: "The observer and the observed are interpenetrating aspects of one whole" (1999: 106).

The method of intuition she advances is not that of a disembodied and objective rationality, but that of an embodied subjectivity which shares a common world with others: "Pattern recognition occurs, as the holographic model suggests, by going into ourselves and getting in touch with our own pattern and through it in touch with the pattern of the person or persons with whom we are interacting" (1999: 107). The connection between the observer and the observed, which obtains in a shared common world of experience does not cloud meaning, as it might in a supposedly objective and rational understanding, but rather makes meaning possible.

> The crux of action is *meaning* and precludes a paradigm of reason that detaches the observer from the observed. In situations where decisions and action are required, the person involved finds himself/herself in a situation of not knowing exactly what one wants to achieve or what means there are to achieve it. Action involves extemporization and is not for those who enjoy the mechanistic, hypothetico-deductive logic of the old paradigm. The old paradigm is about the general case. The new paradigm of action and being is about specific persons in specific situations. (1999: 77)

Newman's grandest critique of the traditional spatial paradigm of medicine seems to be that in sacrificing subjectivity to an objective rationality capable of measuring disease quantitatively, making incisions and sewing parts of an organism back together, meaning has lost its indispensably qualitative aspect. Struggles over disease are necessarily bound up with an individual's qualitative struggle for finding meaning in his or her life experience–that very meaning from which the medical paradigm distances the patient. The struggle for meaning that Baroja develops as the plot of his novel *El árbol de la ciencia*, incarnated in the protagonist Andrés Hurtado, questions the easy solutions of traditional medicine in much the same way that Newman has done, albeit in literary narrative and a good part of a century earlier. A discussion of the Spanish novelist's philosophical trajectory as well as his work on pain will better contextualize the subsequent exploration of the novelistic space inhabited by Baroja's medically-trained protagonist.

Before exploring the novel itself, it is important to briefly consider 1) the connections of Baroja with philosophy, and with Bergsonian philosophy in particular; and 2) Baroja's conception of pain as intimately connected with perception. As readers of *El árbol de la ciencia* (1911) will doubtless know, Pío Baroja was a medically trained doctor who studied, practiced and became disenchanted with medicine in its capacity as science. With this in mind, it is more than relevant to pursue his doctoral thesis, submitted in 1893 and later published in 1896 under the title: *El dolor: estudio de psico-física*,[8] in articulation with Newman's theory. As such, I am undertaking an implicit articulation of Baroja's work and ideas with Bergsonism. It cannot be overstated that the connection of Baroja to Bergson has not been sufficiently explored. There is no precise recognition of the moment when Baroja read Bergson, although he did indeed do so. Nevertheless, there are points of contact between Bergson and Baroja just as there are between Baroja's work and Newman's theory of health. This is not to suggest any causal explanation between any of the three, but to emphasize their common critique–even if from within different disciplines: philosophy, literature and nursing theory–of a common intellectual paradigm that has obtained in the traditional medical approach to health.

In the main, philosophical connections to Baroja are limited to Nietzsche, Schopenhauer and Kant, with a noticeable preference for Schopenhauer above all.[9] Nevertheless it is important to acknowledge the indirect connection between Baroja and Bergson –both of whose philosophical musings developed during the same time period–if not to recognize a more direct connection between the two contemporaries. Drawing on Baroja's *Memorias*, Carmen Iglesias (1963) reminds us that "le interesa [a Baroja] poco el relativismo pragmatista de William James y de Bergson, con su tendencia deliberada, reaccionaria y conservadora y sus premisas preparadas de antemano" (42), but then a page later reflects on the Bergsonian dimensions of his acceptance of "la teoría heraclitiana" (43). Baroja himself makes the connection between Bergson and

---

[8] A later article "Sufrir y pensar," is a continuation of the ideas of his thesis, and is included in *Obras completas*, VIII, 865-66.

[9] See César Barja (1935), Félix Bello Vázquez (1993), E. Inman Fox (1963), C. Alex Longhurst (2005), Roberta Johnson (1993).

Heraclitus in his later *Memorias*,[10] and even praises Bergson in *La intuición y el estilo* (1948).[11] Yet, besides the mention of Bergson by Baroja himself, who certainly does not wholeheartedly embrace Bergson's writings,[12] there are many connections between the two.

Baroja's understanding of pain, as developed in his thesis *El dolor: estudio de psico-física* and a later article "Sufrir y pensar" (1899),[13] was neither an important contribution to the science nor to the philosophy of his day. His project is largely impressionistic and his emphasis is strongly literary, as can be seen elsewhere in his use of disease as metaphor.[14] Yet what his approach does properly accentuate is the foundational importance of perception to the identification of pain. Just as the idea of health as expanding consciousness frames health as a composite in which disease is only a tendency which adheres to the tendency of intellect in thought, Baroja in fact produces the idea of a pain which is attached to intellection as a similar (if not identical) tendency.

In contrast to others of his day, he posits neither happiness nor pain as the natural state of human affairs, but rather argues that the human being traces the articulations of pain or happiness in the world in direct complementarity to his or her tendencies. Not car-

---

[10] Pío Baroja, *Obras completas*, VII, 926. Baroja mentions Zeno of Elea on the same page, perhaps evoking Bergson's understanding of the Eleatic paradoxes of movement. His *Galería de tipos de la época* (1947), from the same volume of the *Memorias* in the *Obras completas*, mentions Bergson along with other thinkers of the turn of the century, although with no precise mention of when Baroja might have read the latter.

[11] Baroja notes in *La intuición y el estilo* that "El más inteligente de todos esos filosóficos modernos, que ha sido, probablemente, Bergson, ha ido armado con hechos deducidos de la teoría de Einstein a ver si podía desmoronar las bases kantianas" (*Obras completas*, VII, 994). Baroja here perhaps falls into the trap of a common conservative Catholic notion–one common at the time–that supporting relativity was necessarily to oppose Kantian modernism. Although Bergson himself was critical of Kant in many of his works, particularly in *L'Évolution créatrice* (1907), it is important to note that most of Bergson's work up to and including *L'Évolution créatrice* was written with no knowledge of Einstein's special theory. It was not until 1922 with the original publication of Bergson's *Duration and Simultaneity* that the real confrontation between the two began. See also Timothy S. Murphy (1999).

[12] See for example Baroja's *La intuición y el estilo*, *Obras completas*, VII, 1001-02.

[13] Baroja, *Obras completas*, VIII, 865-66.

[14] To cite just one example, his essay "Patología del golfo," which appears in *El tablado de Arlequín* (1904), purports to be a medical study of a social pathology, moving through sections titled "concepto del golfo," "etiología," "síntomas," "variedades," "pronóstico," and "tratamiento" (Baroja, *Obras* completas, V, 55-59).

ing to discuss whether these are evolutionarily or vitally engendered, he admits that there are cosmic, organic and psychic factors involved in the experience of pain (*El dolor*, 50). He clearly details that intelligence rests on and organizes sensation from a protoplasmic confusion, and that this organized sensation either contradicts or supports the tendencies of the individual.[15] Pain in this psychophysical sense is not merely possessed by an individual but is rather an interaction, then, between intentionality and world just as in Newman disease is nothing apart from its articulation in the life pattern of disease and non-disease.

Pain is not just a crude sensation, but rather relies on its perception by the organism itself for identification. Baroja explains that "Los que consideran el dolor sólo como un trastorno del sistema nervioso no están en lo cierto, porque la impresión de un tejido irritable sin ser sentida y sin ser percibida no es un dolor. Excitación, impresión, sensación y percepción, son los actos necesarios para que se produzca el dolor" (*El dolor*, 9). Rather than restricting Newman's analysis, Baroja's treatise on pain allows us to open it further. Whereas for the instrumentalist medical paradigm pain is always considered in terms of its relation to a mechanical understanding of the objective body–conceived as a relation of separable parts–for both Baroja and Newman, the notion of pain is not merely physical but inherently mental. The very idea of mental pain underscores the intimate relationship of the individual with his or her environment, and moreover encourages a conception of meaning that is tied to an individual's perception, and not merely to the gridded space of the medical model of the body.

Following Schopenhauer, pain for Baroja is intimately tied to intellect (Johnson 55). One of the many statements that conclude his study of pain recognizes that "La capacidad para sentir el dolor físico en las especies y en las razas está en razón directa de la inteligencia" (Johnson 48). It is the process of intellection that causes pain when intellect-motivated action fails to achieve the desired result. If, as Bergson argues in *Creative Evolution*, intellect is that part of

---

[15] Baroja writes: "Ese *summum* de sensaciones llamado *cenestesia*, es el protoplasma ó materia prima de la sensibilidad, como todo lo que viene de los sentidos externos, es la materia prima de la inteligencia. Esta cenestesia, ó sensación confusa del estado actual del organismo, se manifiesta por necesidades ó tendencias permanentes ó transitorias que cuando se satisfacen van seguidas de placer y de dolor cuando se contrarían" (*El dolor,* 6).

mind that has molded itself to matter, to space, to extension, to divisibility, acting in the world on behalf of this intellect will doubtless create the sensation of pain. Just as does Baroja's thesis, Newman's assertion that action needs to be guided by a non-intellectual notion of meaning, one that does not detach the observer from the observed in order to achieve the goals of a directed intellect, but rather which acknowledges its position as already in the world, pointing toward the way in which simplified "common sense" notions of pain and disease prevent a better understanding of both one and the other. Whether pain is understood as either the natural state of affairs, a position which Baroja labels pessimism, or on the other hand as a rupture in the normal fabric of happiness, which he calls optimism, the end is the same. Neither one is the ground of experience. Instead, pain is best understood as a relation. To reify pain as somehow outside the intentions or tendencies of the individual, to posit that it, like disease, can be avoided–that is, to ontically limit the very notion of pain–is to give up the chance of seeing how it comes into being, just as a narrow definition of disease prevents seeing a larger pattern of disease. Next, I will emphasize Baroja's rejection of the medical paradigm in its error to separate the whole human being into discrete parts and thus to displace the search for meaning in favor of a seemingly objective presentation of disease. The novel works with Newman's nursing theory in that it shows the frustrating consequences both of separating the physical body from the social body and of imagining disease and health to be mutually exclusive categories.

From its opening disenchantment to its enigmatic closing words, *El árbol de la ciencia* documents the categorical rejection of the traditional instrumentalist medical model of health. This disenchantment with the medical model of health is first apparent in Andrés Hurtado's arrival at the School of Architecture to begin his classes. Baroja writes: "*Por una de estas anomalías clásicas de España*, aquellos estudiantes que esperaban en el patio de la Escuela de Arquitectura no eran arquitectos del porvenir, sino futuros médicos y farmacéuticos" (7, emphasis added). This disciplinary dislocation certainly testifies to the backward nature of the sciences in Spain at the turn of the century–but merely contextualizing this detail within the historical discourse of the general and scientific *atraso* of Spain, rewritten extensively by figures associated with the Generation of 1898, discourages an understanding of how the text's aim is not solely historical in the traditional sense, but also of intimate interest to the idea of health as expanding consciousness.[16]

When the young student lines up with his cohorts to begin his medical classes, the description of the event maligns not only a superficial bourgeois class and a stagnant institutionalized educational paradigm, but also a methodological approach to illness. It is in this sense that frequent references to the *theatricality* of the event must be understood.[17] It is for this reason that Andrés proclaims "Esto es una ridiculez" (11). Iturrioz notes the rote memorization requisite of this intellectual approach to health–"Es que hay que saber estudiar. Salir bien de los exámenes es una cuestión mnemotécnica, que consiste en aprender y repetir el mínimo de datos hasta dominarlos" (36). The disrespect shown by the medical students toward the corpses, which are modeled into poses of waving, or upon which

[16] It may be relevant to recall the case of Nietzsche here. The Nietzschean inheritance in Baroja's works has been overly noted (see esp. Sobejano (1967)–but this case allows a brief discussion of Nietzsche's own struggle with illness. Deleuze's essay on Nietzsche republished in *Pure Immanence: Essays on a Life* (53-102) provides a look at how Nietzsche struggled not only with disease as content but as a formal element, itself an implicit reminder of Newman's own theory of health as expanding consciousness. Deleuze writes: "In what sense is illness–or even madness–present in Nietzsche's work? It is never a source of inspiration. Never did Nietzsche think of philosophy as proceeding from suffering or anguish, even if the philosopher, according to him, suffers in excess. Nor did he think of illness as an event that affects a body-object or a brain-object from the outside. Rather, he saw in illness a *point of view* on health; and in health, a *point of view* on illness. 'To observe, as a sick person, healthier concepts, healthier values, then, conversely, from the height of a rich, abundant, and confident life, to delve into the secret work of decadent instincts–such is the practice in which I most frequently engaged...' Illness is not a motive for a thinking subject, nor is it an object for thought: it constitutes, rather a secret intersubjectivity at the heart of a single individual. Illness as an evaluation of health, health as an evaluation of illness: such is the 'reversal', the '*shift in perspective*' that Nietzsche saw as the crux of his method and his calling for a transmutation of values. Despite appearances, however, there is not reciprocity between the two points of view, the two evaluations. Thus movement from health to sickness, from sickness to health, if only as an idea, this very mobility is the sign of superior health; this mobility, this lightness in movement, is the sign of 'great health'" (Deleuze, 57-58, original emphasis).

[17] Four examples early in the narrative are as follows (emphasis added): "Los chicos se agrupaban delante de aquella puerta como el público *a la entrada de un teatro*" (8); "Abrieron la clase, y los estudiantes, apresurándose y apretándose *como si fueran a ver un espectáculo entretenido*, comenzaron a pasar" (9); "Desde el suelo hasta cerca del techo se levantaba una gradería de madera muy empinada con una escalera central, lo que daba a la clase *el aspecto del gallinero de un teatro*" (10); and "*Aquella aparición teatral del profesor y de los ayudantes* provocó grandes murmullos" (10-11).

hats are placed (38), is indicative of a more fundamental disrespect towards the humanity of a person who is misidentified with his/her illness: "En todos ellos se producía un alarde de indiferencia y de jovialidad al encontrarse frente a la muerte, como si fuera una cosa divertida y alegre destripar y cortar en pedazos los cuerpos de los infelices que llegaban allá" (38). This medical paradigm reveals itself, just as do the students themselves, "en cierto entusiasmo por la brutalidad quirúrgica, y en un gran desprecio por la sensibilidad" (39). The course he takes in Physiology at first promises a glimpse of the mysteries of life, but soon merely confirms a bifurcative model of health and illness.

> Tenía Andrés cierta ilusión por el nuevo curso; iba a estudiar Fisiología, y creía que el estudio de las funciones de la vida le interesaría tanto o más que una novela; pero se engañó: no fué así. Primeramente, el libro de texto era un libro estúpido, hecho con recortes de obras francesas y escrito sin claridad y sin entusiasmo; leyéndolo no se podía formar una idea clara del mecanismo de la vida; el hombre parecía, según el autor, como un armario con una serie de aparatos dentro, completamente separados los unos de los otros, como los negociados de un ministerio. (51)[18]

Andrés's disgust for the textbook may seem at first to be grounded in questions of pedagogy–it lacks clarity, it lacks passion. Yet the form of the book mimics the methodological assumptions of traditional medicine. The textbook, just as the medical model itself, is predicated upon the spatializing–intellectual, in the Bergsonian sense–partitioning of the body. The complaint that Andrés makes has clear connections with that critique of instrumentalist medicine made first by Martha Rogers and subsequently by Margaret Newman. What he finds objectionable is not merely the lack of clarity or the unenthusiastic style of the material's presentation but rather the depiction of the human being as a series of apparatuses that are completely separated from one another. He resists the temptation of the prevailing paradigm "to analyze human beings into parts, reduce those elements to measurable entities, control and manipulate the parts, and try to extrapolate the whole based on knowledge of

[18] Consider Merleau-Ponty: "It is science which has accustomed us to regard the body as a collection of parts, and also the experience of its disintegration at death" (*Phenomenology of Perception*, 501).

the parts" (Newman 1999: 81). Yet with no theories such as those of Rogers and Newman at his disposal, he is forced to look elsewhere for a holistic view of human life and disease.

Faced with the fragmented instrumentalist view of the human body, his search leads him quite far from traditional medicine indeed: "Andrés iba formando su espíritu con el aporte de conocimientos y de datos un poco heterogéneos" (43). Following this tendency he spends much time reading novels (34), and briefly ventures into the decidedly musical subculture of Sañudo and his childhood friends who listen to Wagner and frequent cafés (45). Even so, he in effect finds that this musical subculture contains just as much dogma as the medical paradigm from which he is escaping.

> Empezó a creer que esa idea general y vulgar de que el gusto por la música significaba espiritualidad, era inexacta. Por lo menos, en los casos que él veía, la espiritualidad no se confirmaba. Entre aquellos estudiantes amigos de Sañudo, muy filarmónicos, había muchos, casi todos, mezquinos, mal intencionados, envidiosos. (46)

In this early stage of searching he is in fact quite far from acknowledging the cohabitation characteristic of the Bergsonian composite and reformulated later in Newman's work. Yet he continuously looks for ways to complement what he sees as a pervasive and rigid (homogeneous) dogma. Through his dissatisfaction with Letamendi (63), whom he initially admired, he is able to reject mathematical theories of experience and take on his professor's literary and philosophical style–the narrator reports of the professor that "Su único mérito era tener condiciones de literato, de hombre de talento verbal" (63) and "escribía con gran empaque un lenguaje medio filosófico, medio literario" (60)–interestingly, a description that could just have easily been applied to Bergson. It is this encounter that leads him down a more philosophical path: "La palabrería de Letamendi produjo en Andrés un deseo de asomarse al mundo filosófico, y con este objeto compró en unas ediciones económicas los libros de Kant, de Fichte y de Schopenhauer" (63-64). He moves away from more determinist models of experience, like that of Lombroso (65-66)–widely regarded as the father of criminology–with the idea that "lo que quería encontrar era una orientación, una verdad espiritual y práctica al mismo tiempo" (65).

At this point, Andrés, half-aware, begins to accept illness into his life. Soon after his friendship with the arthritic Fermín (48), who walks with a thick cane, Andrés is forced to accept that his brother Luisito has fallen ill of typhoid fever (67). The medical model is particularly ill-equipped in this case to articulate an inclusive model of health, instead identifying Luisito with the disease and encouraging Baroja's protagonist to see illness as meaningless. The doctor tells Andrés that: "Es una enfermedad que no tiene tratamiento específico –aseguraba–; bañarle, alimentarle y esperar, nada más" (67). The result of this narrow view of health/illness leaves Andrés pondering the failure of the medical paradigm without providing a wider notion of health itself. Thus,

> Andrés adquirió con este primer ensayo de médico un gran escepticismo. Empezó a pensar si la Medicina no servía para nada. Un buen puntal para este escepticismo le proporcionaba las explicaciones del profesor de Terapéutica, que consideraba inútiles, cuando no perjudiciales, casi todos los preparados de la farmacopea. (68)

From this close experience with the narrowly defined medical illness diagnosed in his brother, Andrés moves towards a more widely-defined notion of illness in himself that, with quite a few ups and downs, will eventually lead to his suicide.

The fact that the protagonist is poised precipitously between fully accepting the deterministic medical idea of illness and definitively releasing it is brilliantly captured in his perception of "el hermano Juan," a mystic and social pariah (90). As the text reads, "Había en él algo anormal, indudablemente. ¡Es tan lógico, tan natural en el hombre huir del dolor, de la enfermedad, de la tristeza! Y, sin embargo, para él, el sufrimiento, la pena, la suciedad, debían ser cosas atrayentes" (92). Partly because of his experience with Luisito, and partly because of his own frustrated vital instinct, Andrés is fascinated with this man who seems bent on surrounding himself with pain and suffering. "Andrés comprendía el otro extremo, que el hombre huyese del dolor ajeno, como de una cosa horrible y repugnante, hasta llegar a la indignidad, la inhumanidad; comprendía que se evitara hasta la idea de que hubiese sufrimiento alrededor de uno; pero ir a buscar lo sucio, lo triste, deliberadamente, para convivir con ello, le parecía una monstruosidad" (92-93). Though he never reaches the state of seemingly craving the unfortunate as we are led to believe el hermano Juan does, Andrés does in fact move towards accepting illness. He is attracted to Lulú, represented in the text herself as somewhat of a monstrous personality, "un producto marchito por el trabajo, por la miseria y por la inteligencia," (99) because of her marginality. This movement towards illness, of course, is better understood as the lack of a movement away from illness. Near the end of the work, Andrés even suggests that rather than be married, he would rather be sick ("No; preferiría estar enfermo," 293).

Andrés is still holding illness at bay, however. As his statement makes clear, he is following the ontology and methodology requisite of a traditional instrumentalist paradigm which defines illness as other, isolates it conceptually and attempts to extract it physically from a presumably naturally-occurring stable state of health that exists before and underneath all illness. According to Newman, the alternative is to conceive of illness as a health-illness composite, with health and illness each representing a discernible tendency, but one which may never be ontologically separable from the other tendency which inhabits it and which it also inhabits. The opportunity for a conceptual reworking of health-illness notwithstanding, Andrés's experience of the built environment of medical illness confirms his distrust of the medical paradigm, and yet he is reluctant to provide evidence for this very reworking. His visit to San Juan de Dios hospital to see venereal diseases confirms his Schopenhauerian beliefs (76). The building itself has an architectural design that conforms to the tendency of intellection to separate and reify where there can be only the flow of movement, thus providing a stultifying and rightly dirty view of traditional medicine. "El hospital aquel, ya derruido por fortuna, era un edificio inmundo, sucio, maloliente; las ventanas de las salas daban a la calle de Atocha, y tenían además de las rajas, unas alambreras, para que las mujeres recluidas no se asomaran y escandalizaran. De este modo no entraba allí ni el sol ni el aire" (77). Worse still, a doctor of the hospital is described as treating patients much in the manner of prisoners, further developing this sad view of instrumentalism (78).

In Baroja's novel, the posture toward human illness is intimately connected to attitudes of class, race and nation. This is to say that the flaws present in the medical paradigm are not institutional, or rather that they are not only institutional, but are ultimately wrought of a human cultural practice that finds expression in various historical forms of knowledge, themselves separated from each other by this very process of severing immobile sections out of indivisible flows. As Bergson says, "Just as we separate in space, we fix in time" (*CE*, 163). In this manner, this freezing movement of thought creates identity divisions and the stagnancies of self and other where there is only internal and not external contradiction. The three young students, natives of Madrid, thus hate the provincial outsiders (42-43). The professors are typically nationalist, recalling a fixed myth of the past that is already molded and reified by a present interest and projection of unity that suppresses marginalities as do all attempts at homogeneous history: "Luego, el catedrático era un hombre sin ninguna afición a lo que explicaba, un señor senador, de esos latosos, que se pasaba las tardes en el Senado discutiendo tonterías y provocando el sueño de los abuelos de la patria" (51). During Andrés's year in a rural town, there is no sense of solidarity in the region: "No había solidaridad; nadie sabía ni podía utilizar la fuerza de la asociación" (266), and "Por falta de instinto colectivo, el pueblo se había arruinado" (267). The inhabitants are so separated from each other in thought that the connections they do have in life tend to take place along the lines of routines that freeze interactions into manageable divisions. "Era natural que así fuese; cada ciudadano de Alcolea se sentía tan separado del vecino como de un extranjero. No tenían una cultura común (no la tenían de ninguna clase); no participaban de admiraciones comunes: sólo el hábito, la rutina, les unía; en el fondo, todos eran extraños a todos" (268). This fragmentary understanding has the effect of rationalizing away very real disparities of wealth, as Andrés finds in talking to la señora Venancia (139).[19]

Andrés's philosophical searching also parallels his growing disgust with traditional medical paradigms of health. As he puts it simply, his search is for "una filosofía que sea primeramente una cosmogonía, una hipótesis racional de la formación del mundo; después, una explicación biológica del origen de la vida y del hombre" (200). This leads him to Kant and Schopenhauer. In Kant he

---

[19] The quotation reads: "Algunas veces Andrés trató de convencer a la planchadora de que el dinero de la gente rica procedía del trabajo y del sudor de pobres miserables que labraban el campo, en las dehesas y en los cortijos. Andrés afirmaba que tal estado de injusticia podía cambiar: Pero esto para la señora Venancia era una fantasía" (139).

finds a rejection of traditional philosophy ("él vió que todas esas maravillas descritas por los filósofos eran fantasías, espejismos," 202) that escapes from the standard philosophical postulates of God and freedom in a concomitant rejection of traditional intellection: "pero la vida es estúpida, y creo que en todas partes, y el pensamiento se llena de terrores como compensación a la esterilidad emocional de la vida" (202). His posture accentuates the philosophical legacy of Descartes's radical method of doubt ("Claro que [la duda] lo destruye todo," 206) and takes up the phenomenological precept found in Kant in spite of himself that space, time and causality cannot exist outside of a thinking subject.[20]

> La inteligencia lleva, como necesidades inherentes a ella, las nociones de causa, de espacio, y de tiempo, como un cuerpo lleva tres dimensiones. Estas nociones de causa, de espacio y de tiempo son inseparables de la inteligencia, y cuando ésta afirma sus verdades y sus axiomas *a priori*, no hace más que señalar su propio mecanismo. (206-07)

His philosophy approaches the Bergsonian method of division as seen in his description of *voluntad* and *inteligencia*–which in this sense may be taken as correlates of Bergson's composite of instinct and intelligence as developed in *Creative Evolution*. "Yo no digo inteligencia a un lado y voluntad a otro –replicó Andrés–, sino predominio de la inteligencia o predominio de la voluntad. Una lombriz tiene voluntad e inteligencia, voluntad de vivir tanta como el hombre, resiste a la muerte como puede: el hombre tiene también voluntad e inteligencia, pero en otras proporciones" (218). The language he uses clearly avoids falling into the pitfall of reifying either instinct or intelligence, and yet nevertheless Andrés is unable to achieve a larger grasp of the Bergsonian intuition whose method he implicitly undertakes in the former passage. For although the instinct and intelligence he points to are clearly cohabitants, tendencies in both the species he mentions, he does not see how intelligence may be led to question itself and surrender its normal function to that of a truly Bergsonian intuition.

Part of this failure perhaps lies with the way in which he conceptualizes the opposition between this instinct and intelligence.

---

20 This is Bergson's understanding of Kant. See *Creative Evolution* for a fuller exploration of Bergson's reading.

The concept of *voluntad* he outlines is driven by the concept of desire. "La voluntad, el deseo de vivir, es tan fuerte en el animal como en el hombre. En el hombre es mayor la comprensión. A más comprender, corresponde menos desear" (211). He does not see that intelligence is a desire of its own, that both instinct and intelligence are methods of living. This is, in short, an error which prevents him from a deep understanding of the composite. In instinct there is an amount of intellection, just as in intellect there is an amount of instinct.[21] Thought as motor activity has a component which desires in an unmediated fashion and one which desires by partitioning a perceived homogeneous space. These two desires are present in any action and are inseparable from it. And yet intuition is neither this nor that, neither desire nor the lack of desire, neither utilizing intelligence over instinct nor utilizing instinct over intelligence, for in either case intellection is present more or less explicitly as a tendency. Intuition may be present only when intellection is conscious of itself, only when desire is conscious of itself, only when thought is conscious of itself. This is the point when thought turns back upon itself, the point that Andrés is unable to reach even though he feels it and tries through his rejection of medicine and through his philosophical search to locate it. He fails in seeking to separate himself from the world, albeit under the direction of a supposedly mystic formula. He intermittently seeks an ascetic lifestyle, following the first of two options that Iturrioz presents to him: "ante la vida no hay más que dos soluciones prácticas para el hombre sereno: o la abstención y la contemplación indiferente de todo, o la acción limitándose a un círculo pequeño" (154). Soon after this conversation he backs away from life to ponder, "–¿Qué hacer? ¿Qué dirección daré a la vida? –se preguntaba con angustia. Y la gente, las cosas, el sol, le parecían sin realidad ante el problema planteado en su cerebro" (159), and it is thus later that "Andrés decidió limitar la alimentación, tomar sólo vegetales y no probar la carne, ni el vino, ni el café" (293). Through this asceticism he arrives at a powerful feeling of serenity, yet one that is nevertheless false.

> Ahora se sentía como divinizado por su ascetismo, libre; comenzaba a vislumbrar ese estado de 'ataraxia' cantado por los epicúreos y los pirronianos.

[21] This is Bergson's assessment of instinct and intelligence. A thorough exploration of the theme occurs in *Creative Evolution*.

> Ya no experimentaba cólera por las cosas ni por las personas. (294)

Under the guise of an enlightened knowledge of self by self, of thought by thought, of intellect by intellect, he detaches himself from the world in what is falsely taken to be a mystical state. For a true feeling of serenity comes from being in the world, and asceticism, if we are to believe in its relation to mysticism at all, is a mere path to knowledge, whereas Andrés takes it to be the end of the road. If Andrés's suicide is to come as a surprise to us at all in fact, it must come as such because we have believed in this project–his project–of purposefully distancing oneself from the world. This distance is not, however, achieved by intuition, but is in fact the ontological condition of intellection itself–for intuition is a return to the world from intellection. Baroja is in the right in his thesis when he affirms the connection between intellection and pain, an affirmation which certainly sheds light on Andrés's downward struggle.

Despite his failed search for intuition, Andrés is indeed a precursor as the last line of the work asserts (398). Andrés is a precursor because he is close to finding intuition in the Bergsonian sense, because he strives for an understanding of the whole of experience and not merely a piece-meal approach to life, even though he stops short of acknowledging anything other than intellection as a process of thought.

> Para mí es un consuelo pensar que, así como nuestra retina produce los colores, nuestro cerebro produce las ideas de tiempo, de espacio y de causalidad. Acabado nuestro cerebro, se acabó el mundo. Ya no sigue el tiempo, ya no sigue el espacio, ya no hay encadenamiento de causas. Se acabó la comedia, pero definitivamente. Podemos suponer que un tiempo y un espacio sigan para los demás. Pero ¿eso qué importa, si no es nuestro, que es el único real? (204)

This approach is insufficiently phenomenological. It begins with the irrefutable reality of the body, and yet what Andrés has here explained is just short of the errors of the thought that Bergson labels idealism or what for Merleau-Ponty is a false intellectualism. He supposes only a world of privileged consciousness which thinks space, time and causality without a world of immanent things in which not only is the thinking consciousness simultaneously in space and in time but is itself wrought of space and time. We are not in space. Rather space is in things (Bergson 1889, Harvey 1996, Hewitt 1974). We do not look upon time but instead live it. In Andrés's conclusion that it is unimportant whether space and time exist for others there is an idealistic pessimism that produces the failure to see his own cohabitation in a world of fused opposites. He believes himself able to mentally separate himself from the world he perceives, an error which is the sole fruit of the intellect. It is this attempt to rise above experience, rather than dissolve into it that elicits caution from Iturrioz: "No creo en esa indiferencia automática que atribuyes a la inteligencia. No somos un intelecto puro, ni una máquina de desear; somos hombres que al mismo tiempo piensan, trabajan, desean, ejecutan" (219). Andrés struggles to turn the intellect back upon itself, but is ultimately unable to do so. Nevertheless this struggle, implicit in his philosophical search and his rejection of a traditional model of health, allows the expression of a certain contradiction between the insufficiency of determinism and the longing for a freedom that exists outside of determinism. The two are understood by Andrés to be different paths–that is, he looks not for the difference *in* determinism or *in* freedom, but for the difference *between* the two. He is unable to locate disease *within* health nor the health *within* disease. He can neither accept pessimism in optimism, nor optimism in pessimism. Faced with the opportunity of a contradiction he follows the line of the intellect which goads him into resolving it decisively. Faced with the loss of Luisito, his unborn child and finally Lulú, and against the background of his ventures into suffering and disease, this necessity for resolution ends in his suicide.

And yet the investigation of this contradiction throughout the novel reveals, as we have been suggesting, the expression of an optimism. To one of Iturrioz's more naturalistic moments Andrés responds with the conviction of possible social change.

> –¿Y para qué descomponer la sociedad? ¿Es que se va a construir un mundo nuevo mejor que el actual?
> –Sí, yo creo que sí. (223)

Whereas the narrative emphasizes the narrow view of life taken by many doctors who, following a traditionally rigid and rationalistic scientific outlook, have isolated themselves from the world as a whole (84),[22] Andrés leaves the confining space of traditional medicine for things literary, political and philosophical. Although faced with Luisito's condition he initially installs a "dictadura científica" (184) in the house in an attempt to keep suffering and disease at bay, his concern for patients is decidedly holistic and, even if he is incapable of formulating his approach in such terms, prepares the road for an acceptance of disease in health: "A Andrés le preocupaban más las ideas y los sentimientos de los enfermos que los síntomas de las enfermedades" (85). But this path away from traditional medicine leads him equally away from an awareness of intuition and into an unmitigated despondency. He rejects contradiction explicitly,[23] believes optimism and pessimism to be expressions of a determinism of inalterable organic origin,[24] becomes trapped in an unfruitful intellectual mode,[25] opts for a theory of life that blocks him off from action[26] and even cautions youth away from enacting social change.[27] Because he never quite arrives at a Bergsonian conception of difference, the elements of the contradiction which he feels remain external to each other, an error which is conceptually and quite visually manifest in the overriding image of the novel–that of the Biblical tree of knowledge and the tree of life (212). The very image of two distinct trees posits a false ontological separation between a theory of knowledge and a theory of life.[28] Yet what Baroja's novel, Bergson's philosophy, and even Newman's the-

---

[22] The following description seems typical of this attitude: "El médico, hombre estudioso, había llegado a dominar el diagnóstico como pocos. Fuera de su profesión, no le interesaba nada: política, literatura, arte, filosofía o astronomía; todo lo que no fuera auscultar o percutir, analizar orinas o esputos, era letra muerta para él" (84).

[23] He is fond of a phrase of Democritus found in Lange's *Historia del materialismo* that reads "El que ama la contradicción y la verbosidad, es incapaz de aprender nada que sea serio" (286).

[24] "Andrés pudo comprobar que el pesimismo y el optimismo son resultados orgánicos como las buenas o malas digestiones" (192).

[25] "Estos vaivenes en las ideas, esta falta de plan y de freno, le llevaban a Andrés al mayor desconcierto, a una sobreexcitación cerebral continua e inútil" (83).

[26] "Se iba inclinando a un anarquismo espiritual, basado en la simpatía y en la piedad, sin solución práctica ninguna" (82).

[27] "¡Qué van ustedes a hacer! Lo único que pueden ustedes hacer es marcharse de aquí" (273).

[28] Bergson writes that "*a theory of knowledge* and *theory of life* seem to us inseparable. [...] It is necessary that these two inquiries, theory of knowledge and a theory of life, should join each other, and, by a circular process, push each other on unceasingly" (*CE*, xiii, original emphasis).

ory of health all suggest is the interconnectedness of these theories. In distancing one from the other we lose the ability to find meaning in the experience of illness.

El árbol de la ciencia thus provides a relatively straightforward rejection of the traditional instrumentalist medical paradigm of disease while pointing towards a model of health in which contradiction is present and unresolved, even if the protagonist himself never reaches a conscious awareness of this possibility. It is in this sense that Andrés is a precursor and that Baroja's work even prefigures Newman's implicitly Bergsonian method of differentiation–he prefigures the contemporary effort to deepen our prevailing ideas of health and disease. Disease is not the simple opposite of health, but is a necessary and moreover important tendency within life itself. As Baroja and Newman are both aware, this understanding is indispensable if we are to search for meaning in our lives. While the direct ties between Baroja and Bergson may remain somewhat unclear, what is certain is that the Spaniard indirectly made use of Bergsonian method to challenge what he saw as the stagnant medical paradigm of his day, even anticipating more recent and developing models of health and illness that are rooted in Bergsonian methodology.

In *Camino de perfección* (1902), Baroja's challenge to closed forms of religion was just as innovative as his critique of traditional medicine was in *El árbol*. Like Unamuno's *Amor y pedagogía* (to be discussed in chapter two), Baroja's novel was one of many that in 1902 signaled a shift in the direction of the contemporary Spanish novel (along with Valle-Inclán's *Sonata de Otoño* and Azorín's *La voluntad*). It chronicles, just as *El árbol de la ciencia* did, the philosophical struggles of a young medical student. Here Fernando Ossorio travels through Madrid, Toledo and Yécora experiencing suffering and contemplating life, art and religion. Given the explicit mention of Nietzsche's philosophy in the novel through the character Schultze (a character based on Pablo Schmitz, whom Baroja came to know in Madrid), not to mention its monstrous fusion of life and death, certainly the novel owes much more to Nietzsche than to Bergson. It is important to point out, however, that both Nietzsche and Bergson exerted a significant influence on writers of the time. Not surprisingly, José Alberich (1966) reports that Bergson was found among the works of philosophy in Baroja's library

(51).[29] In this context, I believe that developing the novel's connection with Bergsonism sheds light on the significance of its incorporation of mysticism in a way that the Nietzschean-inspired criticism has not.

Mysticism itself is of problematic nature, and its meaning to both Bergson and Baroja must be carefully explored due to the prejudices it may arouse. In many circles it is regarded as philosophically suspect, perhaps, due to common use of the term as a short-hand for idealism. By the secular it is lumped in with organized religion, by the doctrinally religious it is heterodox and thus condemned. Many have used Bergson's praise of mysticism as cause to discredit his philosophy. Even those sympathetic to his ideas have referred to him as a mystic in a derogative fashion. This is the case even with Ortega y Gasset, who although clearly sympathetic to many aspects of Bergsonism (see introduction of the present work), nevertheless takes care to distinguish Bergson from, as Landeira Brisson (1979) puts it, "the pure mystics who do not produce anything intellectual" (89). That the relationship between mysticism and religion is difficult to articulate is only compounded by the ambiguous or contentious position occupied by Bergson himself regarding mysticism. Despite the latter's resounding respect for the mystic traditions of the west as articulated in *The Two Sources of Morality and Religion* (1932), Joaquín Iriarte (1959) hestitates to label him a mystic, stating that "Bergson, él, no es místico, pero se considera emparentado con quienes lo son" (28). Overall, the connection has proved difficult to confront for critics both sympathetic to and fearful of mysticism.

To approach Bergson's understanding of mysticism is to uncover a complement to his influence on Spanish letters in that the Frenchman proclaims great enthusiasm for Spain's notable Christian mystics. In his "Bergson y la mística española" (1991), Jorge Uscatescu develops the assertion that "España y la espiritualidad hispana han ejercido un singular influjo sobre la formación y el espíritu de Henri Bergson" (465). Bergson himself acknowledged

---

[29] After listing Bergson's name along with others, he continues: "Me llamó la atención un ejemplar anotado de *Le rire*, de H. Bergson, en traducción española de la editorial valenciana Prometeo, con anotaciones marginales que modifican de un modo muy típicamente barojiano las teorías del filósofo francés" (51). In *La caverna del humorismo*, Baroja comments at length on this work of Bergson's (*Obras completas* V, 404; Bergson is also mentioned on 425-26).

the influence of the Spanish mystics, and wrote at length on mysticism in *The Two Sources of Morality and Religion*, mentioning Santa Teresa by name (84). For him, Santa Teresa and others are not idealists uprooted from the concerns of daily life but rather socially engaged actors. Uscatescu quotes Bergson thusly: "A San Juan de la Cruz y a Santa Teresa [...] se les debe colocar por encima de todos los místicos. Su lectura me ha iluminado mucho" (466).[30] In the philosopher's book on the topic, this respect for mystical traditions is explicitly opposed to what Bergson considers to be the intransigent character of religious dogma.

Whereas many critics have assumed that Baroja's hatred of religion must apply also to mysticism, his position is closer to Bergson's than has been acknowledged. Daniel Testa (1984) recognizes that Baroja was sympathetic to a certain unpopular view of mysticism, declaring that "[N]o creo que Baroja sea anti-místico" (803). In this vein, Baroja even proved himself to be supportive of what he called a "misticismo realista" in using this phrase to praise Galdós.[31] This is also the source of his fondness for El Greco, a trait shared by many members of the generation of '98, whose art figures prominently in *Camino de perfección*.[32] In this work, Baroja prefers to treat mysticism as a social phenomenon rightly outside the context of traditional Catholicism, thus approximating Bergson's subtle position that opposed the mystical tradition to dogma. Bergson, too, it must be noted, though he was frequently derided and labeled a mystic by such people as, for example, George Santayana in *Winds of Doctrine* (13), earlier in his career even worked to distance himself from the popular understanding of mysticism.

> Bergson was asked if he was a mystic. He replied: 'If one understands by mysticism (as one almost always does today) a reaction

[30] Originally from *Conversaciones con Bergson*, Jacques Chevalier (no pub.: no date, no pag.). Although Uscatescu gives no further publication information he continues to cite the Chevalier text throughout his intriguing essay.

[31] The quotation is originally from "Literatura y bellas artes" (1899), reproduced in *El modernismo visto por los modernistas*, ed. Ricardo Gullón (1980). The phrase is also mentioned by Alex Longhurst in his compelling "The Turn of the Novel in Spain: From Realism to Modernism in Spanish Fiction" (1999).

[32] In *La caverna del humorismo*, Baroja writes that "*El Greco* pintó de una manera realista los asuntos místicos. Es posible que en él no había nada de creyente. Es muy posible que no fuera un espíritu religioso y que las cuestiones de fe le tuvieran sin cuidado" (*Obras completas* V, 469, original emphasis). El Greco, of course, was an important artist for the most all of the *noventayochistas*.

> against science, the doctrine I uphold is nothing from one end to another but a protest against mysticism, for it proposes to reestablish the bridge (broken since Kant) between metaphysics and science. This divorce between science and metaphysics is the great evil from which our philosophy suffers. . . . But now, if one understands by mysticism a certain appeal to internal and profound life, then all philosophy is mysticism" (Scharfstein, *Roots of Bergson's Philosophy*, 134).[33]

Further, he even later on seems to have found mysticism of interest more for its philosophical significance–for what it reveals regarding the possibilities of intuition within the closed-system of intellect– than for the position it occupies within any one cultural or historical tradition. In this way he is given to statements such as "Let us leave aside, for the moment, their Christianity" when speaking of the mystics (*MR*, 227). He takes every effort to avoid equating mysticism with the dogmatic closed-belief system of any one specific religious creed. It would take a great misreading of Bergson, who advocated, even in his last work, the notion of a global humanity which overflowed national boundaries, to think otherwise.[34]

In *Camino de perfección*, Baroja draws indirectly from Bergsonism, even anticipating Bergson's own later development of his method to include social and religious systems in *The Two Sources of Morality and Religion*. As he would in *El árbol de la ciencia*, in this earlier novel Baroja, like Bergson, denounces the pre-formed concepts and dogma that mediate, structure and limit our experience of life. Here, Baroja anticipates Bergson's fashioning of the mystic as a freethinker attentive to life and preserves both the Frenchman's and his own vitalistic approach to living realities. The novel's connection with Bergsonism lies in Baroja's rejection of the dogma of the Catholic Church and Bergson's more general and philosophical critique of "static" religion. In *The Two Sources of Morality and Religion*, following the method articulated throughout his earlier writ-

---

[33] The quotation is originally from "Le parallélisme psycho-physique et la métaphysique pure," *Bulletin*, I (1901), 63-64; the translation is Scharfstein's.

[34] In *The Two Sources of Morality and Religion* Bergson writes "For between the nation, however big, and humanity therelies the whole distance from the finite to the indefinite, from the closed to the open" (32). See also the appendix to the present work–a translation of speeches delivered by Bergson in Madrid in 1916.

ings, Bergson documents a difference in kind between mystical experience ("dynamic religion") and the dogmatic intransigence of organized religion ("static religion"), just as he had earlier pointed out differences in kind between the nevertheless coexisting and interdependent notions of time and space (*TFW*), memory and matter (*MM*), intellect and intuition (*CE*), and even science and philosophy (*CM*).[35] On this topic he writes:

> Static religion, such as we find it when it stands alone, attaches man to life, and consequently the individual to society, by telling him tales on a par with those with which we lull children to sleep. Of course they are not like other stories. Being produced by the myth-making function in response to an actual need and not for mere pleasure, they counterfeit reality as actually perceived, to the point of making us act accordingly: other creations of the imagination have this same tendency, but they do not demand our compliance; they can remain just ideas; whereas the former are ideo-motory. They are none the less myths, which critical minds, as we have seen, often accept in fact, but which they should by rights, reject. (211)

Bergson's critique of religious dogma as "tales with which we lull children to sleep" and which we "should by rights, reject" resonates with Baroja's more voracious denunciation of the priesthood in his novels and stories, as can be seen concisely in the exquisite story "La sima," where a boy who falls into a cavern is left to die as the superstitious priest and ignorant townspeople believe the devil himself is lurking in the depths of the hole below. When read in the context of his work as a whole, Bergson's similar denunciation of static religion, then, is the necessarily social product of the path of what he earlier termed intellect (see particularly in *Creative Evolution*). Bergson's theory of society and religion as presented in *The*

---

[35] Some critics have seen Bergson's last work as a departure from his earlier writings, although this view is contradicted by Bergson's text itself, which refers repeatedly to ideas he put forth in earlier works. Cognizant of this fact, and implicitly responding to this trend of criticism, G. William Barnard (2002) writes that "However, while much of the material explored in *The Two Sources* was new territory for Bergson, the striking originality of this work did not signal an abrupt change of position. Instead, *The Two Sources* emerged organically from the richness of his prior philosophical investigations, acting, in essence, as the final fruit of years of concerted, diligent inquiry into the nature of consciousness, the relationship between mind and matter, and the evolution of life" (309).

Two Sources of Morality and Religion is thus developed on the basis of his arguments surrounding the intellect of the individual in *Time and Free Will.*

In this first work of Bergson's, foreshadowing his later distinction between static (as quantitative/intellectual) and dynamic religion (as qualitative/intuitive), he relates the uncomfortable relationship between qualitative and quantitative multiplicities in philosophy to their corresponding manifestation in the individual. Just as psychic states, which are qualitative, are mistakenly taken by the intellect as quantitative and divisible, so follows the intellectual division of the self. He returns again and again to stress this idea:

> As the self thus refracted, and thereby broken to pieces, is much better adapted to the requirements of social life in general and language in particular, consciousness prefers it, and gradually loses sight of the fundamental self. (128)
>
> An inner life with well distinguished moments and with clearly characterized states will answer better the requirements of social life. (139)
>
> Hence two different selves: (1) the fundamental self: (2) its spatial and social representation: only the former is free. (231)

In noting the correspondence between processes of differentiation occurring at both the individual scale and the social scale, Bergson's path between his first major work *Time and Free Will* and his last *The Two Sources of Morality and Religion* remains true to his original philosophical premise.[36] The individual tendency of intellect, which of course has molded itself to matter over the course of evolution as a tendency of species (*CE*), thus obtains in the social tendency toward obligation. In every case, the result of Bergson's philosophical corrective to simplistic dualisms is to emphasize the constraints placed on what he calls a living *élan vital*/vital impetus through its imbrication with matter.[37] In this sense, Bergson's phi-

[36] This aspect of Bergson's work, in effect, anticipates more recent work in cultural geography such as Sallie Marston's assertion regarding "The Social Construction of Scale" (2000). In *The Two Sources of Morality and Religion*: "As a matter of fact, the individual and society are implied in each other: individuals make up society by their grouping together; society shapes an entire side of individuals by being prefigured in each one of them. The individual and society thus condition each other, circle-wise" (199).

[37] The élan vital, although taken up by Bergson as a part of his original philosophical approach, was a Lamarckian idea and was very current among French biologists and their philosophical commentators.

losophy is profoundly vitalist, and his philosophical problems are the problems of the movement of life itself.

In Baroja's novel, Fernando Ossorio's vitalism is undoubtedly expressed directly and highlighted contextually through notable references to Nietzsche.[38] Yet more generally speaking, this vitalism may also be considered Bergsonian, a connection that provides an explanation of the novel's mystical dimensions at one and the same time. In the interests of most concisely presenting the vitalist aspect of the novel, one captivating scene in particular seems to typify the novel's rejection of rational intellectual concepts in favor of a return to the vital path of life. This scene is of great relevance to Bergsonism, and is important also in light of more recent comments by Roland Barthes (and Michel de Certeau). The scene is this: In Yécora, Fernando visits the Castle and ventures to the top of a high cliff overlooking the city. On the way, he passes a grotesque landscape of "extraños peñascales laberínticos de fantásticas formas, unos de aspecto humano, tétricos sombríos, con agujeros negros que parecían ojos, [...] otros afilados como cuchillos agudos, como botareles de iglesia gótica" (266). Once at the top, he sits down to contemplate

> el lugarón [...] con los tejados blanquecinos y grises, húmedos por el rocío, que se extendían y se alargaban como si no tuvieran fin, simétricos, como si todo el pueblo fuera un gran tablero de ajedrez. Cerca se destacaban con una crudeza fotográfica las piedras y los peñascos del monte. (266-67)[39]

The allusion to the photographic eye works with the symmetry of the town's rigid lines to critique rationality itself, summoning the

---

[38] Consider the following passage: "¡Cuánta vida y cuánta vida en germen se ocultará en estas noches! –se me ocurre pensar [...] Y al mismo tiempo de esta germinación eterna, ¡qué terrible mortandad! ¡Qué bárbara lucha por la vida! ¿Pero para qué pensar en ella? Si la muerte es depósito, fuente, manantial de la vida, ¿a qué lamentar la existencia de la muerte? No, no hay que lamentar nada. Vivir y vivir... ésa es la cuestión" (281).

[39] Baroja, here, clearly anticipates other key narrations in Spanish letters. Notable in this regard is Juan Goytisolo's protagonist in *Señas de identidad* (1966), who looks down on Barcelona from Montjuïc and, although in another time and place, captures the disorientation of the rapidly urbanizing Spanish landscape and the concomitant cultural economy of tourism. See Fraser (2008a), "A Snapshot of Barcelona from Montjuïc: Juan Goytisolo's *Señas de identidad*, Tourist Landscapes as Process and the Photographic Mechanism of Thought."

anti-dogmatic, irrationalist and vitalist stance of both Nietzsche and Bergson and prefiguring the twentieth-century critique of detached rational city-planning (see chapter nine of the present work).

This bird's eye perspective of the city that Ossorio contemplates as he stares down on Yécora (Yecla), "permits us […] to see things *in their structure*" through "an intellectualist mode" (9), as Roland Barthes (1979) has written.[40] I consider the key word here, because of its importance for Bergsonism, to be "intellectualist." This critique of the birds-eye view (coming from Barthes and later de Certeau 1984) was to be explicitly incorporated into scholarship of the city (via Harvey 1989), but was also interestingly put forth in a similar manner by Bergson. In *The Creative Mind* he writes: "Though all the photographs of a city taken from all possible points of view indefinitely complete one another, they will never equal in value that dimensional object, the city along whose streets one walks" (160-61). The latter observation, like that of his predecessor Barthes, makes reference to the manner in which intellect metaphorically distances itself from experience, only to return to it in the strict terms of structure through the partitioning of fluid experience. Barthes mentions an "intellectualist mode" explicitly, whereas Bergson's critique of the intellect is present through his derision of photography, an illustration of the critique of the "cinematographic" quality of thought he denounces in *Creative Evolution* (306-07). In any case, Baroja's description of the scene in Yécora functions as a powerful critique of intellectual modes of approaching fluid experience, and as such, highlights and even represents the novel's significant and pervasive commitment to the irrational or anti-rational component of vitalist philosophy.

Significantly, Baroja's philosophical vitalism is not merely relegated to the position of content in the novel, as in the description of the above scene, but is also innovatively paralleled in its narration

---

[40] In this vein, Michel de Certeau (1984) has echoed Barthes: "To be lifted to the summit of the World Trade Center is to be lifted out of the city's grasp. One's body is no longer clasped by the streets that turn and return it according to anonymous law; […] His elevation transfigures him into a voyeur. It puts him at a distance. It transforms the bewitching world by which one was 'possessed' into a text that lie before one's eyes. It allows one to read it, to be a solar Eye, looking down like a god. The exaltation of a scopic and gnostic drive: the fiction of knowledge is related to this lust to be a viewpoint and nothing more" (92). David Harvey begins his *The Urban Experience* (1989) with a similar passage.

and style. The idea of "un río interior" (279), itself an allusion to mysticism as well as an inner and enduring consciousness in general if not the fluid movement of Bergson's non-intellectual thought, finds its external complement in the *paisajismo* characteristic of the literary production of the so-called Generación del '98. Baroja takes pause repeatedly in the novel to develop ecstatic and sensual (mystical) descriptions of Fernando's surroundings. In this vein, Jesús Torrecilla (1996) notes the synthesis between the cities Fernando visits and his personality (339). What we see in *Camino de perfección* is in fact a return from the intellectual category of refuge to the vital flux of real life that overflows its conceptualization. For Baroja, profoundly affected as he was by the demolition of the traditional metaphysical distinction between subject and object (professed, of course, by Bergson himself and characteristic of the broader turn-of-the-century philosophical revolution against positivism), this return involved the de facto recovery of a pre-Christian pantheism (Iglesias 77) or even Pythagorean animism (see Baroja 259). Accordingly, the novel's closing pages highlight "la reintegración vigorosa de todos los instintos, naturales, salvajes" (334) as well as Fernando's desire to return to life. He yearns to have his child embrace life over all else, with all his instinct and passion intact.[41]

While critics of Baroja's novel have been quick to underscore its vitalist presence, once again perhaps due to the explicit Nietzschean connections, a Bergsonian perspective allows a discussion of the novel's fusion of mysticism and vitalism as a totality. Much previous criticism of the novel has been rooted in an unacceptable bifurcation of the spiritual and the vital. Roberta Johnson (1993), for one, sees the novel as a passage from spiritualism to vitalism (69). From a perspective that sees spirit as pertaining to the realm of organized religion–where the notion of vitalism entails a simple dualism opposing spirit (as transcendence) to life (as immanence)–

[41] He explains this vital desire thus: "El le dejaría vivir en el seno de la Naturaleza; él le dejaría saborear el jugo del placer y de la fuerza en la urbe repleta de la vida, la vida que para su hijo no tendría misterios dolorosos, sino serenidades inefables" (334-35). And then "El dejaría a su hijo libre con sus instintos: si era león, no le arrancaría las uñas: si era águila, no le cortaría las alas. Que fueran sus pasiones impetuosas como el huracán que levanta montañas de arena en el desierto, libres como los leones y las panteras en las selvas vírgenes, y si la naturaleza había creado en su hijo un monstruo, si aquella masa aún informe era una fiera humana, que lo fuese abiertamente, francamente, y por encima de la ley entrase a saco en la vida, con el gesto gallardo del antiguo jefe de una devastadora horda" (335).

this comment is indeed warranted. Nevertheless, in the context of a vitalism where spirit is linked with life itself in opposition to matter (particularly but not exclusively Bergsonian vitalism as expressed in *Creative Evolution*) it is not. In tune with Bergson's later vitalist formulation of mysticism, Baroja's turn-of-the-century vitalism seeks to recapture spirit from the clutches of organized religion, thus portraying the former as tainted by the institutional power of the latter. This is certainly the effect created by the *paisajismo* in the novels and the poetry and lyrical stance of members of the so-called Generation of '98 in general–to awaken the senses to the spirit imbricated in ordinary matter (see also Bergson, *MM*). In this way Fernando's powerful, arguably even mystical, experiences of music and the rural landscape in Baroja's novel represent a complex fusion of mysticism and vitalism that deserves more attention.

Significantly, Bergson's *The Two Sources of Morality and Religion*, as a follow-up to his vitalist *Creative Evolution*, synthesizes the common thread of both vitalism and mysticism in a rejection of institutional Church dogma. Since Baroja was widely-known as a critic of organized religion it is no surprise to read Carmen Iglesias's (1963) assertion that "el misticismo barojiano no aspira a lo divino, no encierra un verdadero sentimiento religioso" (75). Instead, Baroja's mysticism is "más bien, un estado de hiperestesia que se produce por el estímulo de la música sacra o por el recogimiento de una iglesia del campo" (Iglesias 75)–a mysticism that has broken *completely* with the Church. Nevertheless, because of the powerful incorporation of mysticism in Baroja's novel, it is with great difficulty that one reads Iglesias's statement that "Baroja escribió cuatro obras de inspiración religiosa" (74) of which one was *Camino de perfección*. This statement is difficult because the mysticism in Baroja's novel is clearly opposed to the Church as institution and also, given the present reconciliation, on account of the distinction Bergson makes between mysticism and religion. The novel presents mysticism as, in fact, intimately connected with philosophical vitalism, revealing itself as a profoundly anti-religious book, spurning "static" religion in the Bergsonian sense of a dogmatic and closed system of belief.

Based on the full title of Baroja's book, *Camino de perfección: (Pasión mística)* (1902), which unabashedly makes reference to mysticism directly (and indirectly through reference to the classic work of the same name by Santa Teresa de Jesús), critics have perceptively read the work as an allegory of the path to mystic union with the divine. In this way, Weston and Norma Flint (1983) thus discuss the relevance of the three stages on the path to mystical union: the *vía purgativa*, the *vía iluminativa* and the *vía unitiva* (14-15), after which the soul is ready to unite with God through the *vía simple o activa* or the *vía unitiva pasiva o mística* (15).[42] The authors assert that Baroja "bases his book structure on the classic mystic formula" (13), and, while noting initially that "the novel seems to reject St. Theresa's mysticism" (14), they conclude that "the novel is mystical in a much more general way" (14). While I agree with the prevailing opinion on the novel that it is not mystical in this strict historical sense, that is, it does not conform exactly to expectations set by the classic mystic formula, I propose that it is best understood as a problematic inversion of the mystical that frees the latter of transcendental notions and restores it to life.

The problem with understanding the work according to the classic mystic formula is that this approach is grounded in a problematic conception of a mysticism that itself borders on doctrine. In *The Two Sources of Morality and Religion*, Bergson clearly opposes mysticism to the dogma of the Church. It follows that if Christian mysticism broke away from the Church during the Renaissance, its initial dynamic and revolutionary push was, over the course of the three centuries hence, able to coalesce into static dogma again. This is, in fact, the nature of the revolutionary for Bergson, a spark that may be at any time fanned into a flame, or that may be covered over by requirements more useful to social life. When this revolutionary spark is covered-over by dogma, as has been the case, Bergson argues, with mysticism, the closed tendency of dogma eclipses the open tendency of real movement. It follows that mysticism, in its necessary manifestation as a social phenomenon like any other, is thus constantly at risk of becoming systematized. This issue, of course has been the perennial problem of mysticism in both the West and the East where it has flirted with formula and dogma while at the same time striving to reject them.[43] For Bergson, then, organized religion is the hard-shell that forms around mystical intuition.

---

[42] See also José Ares Montes (1972) and Daniel P. Testa (1984).

[43] For some critics, Bergson provides a bridge between Eastern and Western mysticism; see Bhattacharya (1972).

The thrust of Bergson's differentiating method in his presentation of mysticism and organized religion provides the opportunity to see mysticism as a tendency and not as a thing. Its conception as a thing is wrought of intellectual process, and yet just as life is imbricated with matter, mysticism arises in connection with static organized religion. Differentiation between the two, while possible, is difficult given their coexistence and interdependence in social life.

> Whether or not we subscribe to religion, it is always possible to assimilate it intellectually, even if we must admit its mysteries to be mysterious. On the contrary, mysticism means nothing, absolutely nothing, to the man who has no experience of it, however slight. Therefore everyone will appreciate that mysticism may assert itself, original and ineffable, now and then, in a pre-existing religion which is formulated in terms of intelligence, whereas it is difficult to obtain acceptance for the idea of a religion which exists only through mysticism, and which is a mere extract of it–an extract capable of being formulated by the intellect and therefore grasped by all. (*MR*, 237-38)

Although mysticism is often given imagined as yet another religious dogma, it is not a thing in and of itself, but a tendency that co-exists with and even despite religious dogma. The most common appearance of mysticism as a thing is in the form of a model divisible by the intellect into stages. The settling of the mystical path into a three-stage model, such as that embraced by Flint and Flint (1983) in their reading of the work (above), accordingly conforms to that spatialized treatment of time denounced by Bergson in *Time and Free Will*. This quantitative treatment of mysticism is, of course, advocated by some mystics themselves, perhaps in order to acculturate to the way the tendency of intellect processes information. Yet as Bergson notes, underscoring the socially-constituted nature of so-called mystic practices, the progression of mystic states varies from mystic to mystic. Consequently, while certain practices may be advocated by mysticism, mysticism itself is not merely that set of programmatic practices.[44]

If Baroja does structure the novel based on mystical formula, it

[44] Baroja's mockery of a "static" or dogmatic mysticism finds complement in Bergson's derision, in *The Two Sources of Morality and Religion*, of detachment (thus asceticism) as a "half-virtue" (65).

is not only to mock this classic three-stage approach to mysticism but to shift attention from the static closed forms of mysticism back to the vital movement of life itself. This vital movement of life was arguably the original intention of the Christian mystics–who, it should be noted, were understood as advocates not of escape from life but of action and presence in life. This was also, notably, Bergson's understanding of them as "men and women of action" and the motivation for his constant praise.[45] Bergson goes so far as to actually define mysticism explicitly in relation to the vital impulse (*MR*, 213). It is perhaps paradoxical that Baroja, an ardent critic of religion, should write such a mystical work. But, in a sense, this is not at all surprising. If *Camino de perfección* is seen as an endorsement of mysticism, it is not a transcendental mysticism corrupted by doctrine, dogma and creed, but one which roots the mystical in this world, and not in any other–thus recovering the vital impulse of mystical thought throughout the ages. If the novel is, at least in part, a critique of mysticism, it successfully articulates what mysticism should be, although this may be in spite of Baroja's intentions. It should thus be seen not a set of imitable practices, but a process of reaction against the rationalism that obtains most fervently in dogma. As either ridicule or reformulation, Baroja has in either case proposed that definition of the mystical is an essentially social problem, in effect recovering Bergson's essential assertion regarding the interpenetration of life/spirit and matter and even anticipating his stance on static and dynamic religions. Both thinkers eschew dualist or transcendental models of experience and take it upon themselves to restore an attention to *life* itself, irrespective of the intellectual models and conventional systems that have sought to represent it.

Ultimately, Baroja's ridicule of, or inversion of, the mystic path is based upon a critique that squares quite well with Bergsonian philosophy. In the classic mystic formula, going against the very grain of Bergson's philosophy, time has been spatialized, quality has been reduced to quantity. The illustration of the flaws in the Eleatic interpretation of the story of Achilles and the tortoise (*TFW*) shows

[45] Joaquín Iriarte (1959) explains Bergson's admiration of the mystics thusly: "¿No serán [los místicos] unos enfermos mentales, como dice Janet? No, replica Bergson, con un análisis tan pulcro como perspicaz de las varias místicas que conoce la historia. Los místicos cristianos, al revés de lo que ocurre con los orientales, son activistas, dinámicos, viven entre las gentes, no pierden el gusto de la acción, no se encierran en morbosos solipsismos" (36).

the dangers of equating movement with the space covered. Mysticism is a real movement in the Bergsonian sense, whereas the three stage model of it is a product of intellectual conceptualization. This intellectualized model of fluid experience, which obtains also in structuralist models of the three-stage rite of passage in Anthropology,[46] is the force or the tendency of thought behind social "obligation" as Bergson expresses it (1932). This idea resonates powerfully with Baroja's novel where the author takes it upon himself to stridently reject the traditional conservatism of Spanish Catholicism and its formulaic reception by Spaniards.

Baroja's rejection of organized religion is total, after all. As he puts it concisely in a short essay in *Juventud, egolatría*, "La gran defensa de la religión está en la mentira."[47] In another essay titled "El monoteísmo" (1933) he writes that "Los religiosos dogmáticos creen en la revelación y en que las verdades religiosas son demostrables como si fueran axiomas matemáticos" (*Obras completas* V, 1144). To the cleansed orthodox view of a heavenly life, Baroja's novel thus opposes the reality of an earthly death, necessarily shocking in all its grisly details. The opening page of the novel initially positions the reader as witness to Fernando's interaction, not with a living person, but with the dead by way of the cadaver of a nameless woman.[48] Baroja later describes a rotting corpse in shocking clarity, noting pus and all.[49] In the description of the corpse of the dead bishop, Baroja's retreat from orthodox religious postures is evident in an extensive passage that describes death in physical terms while the language and tone of the narration allude to the spiritual component of material lived realities through the transference of atoms–themselves a large part of animistic and mystical world-views.

---

46 This model is expounded by Van Gennep (1909).

47 "La defensa de la religión," in *Juventud, egolatría* (1920: 30).

48 "Un día vi a Ossorio en la sala de disección, que quitaba cuidadosamente un escapulario al cadáver de una vieja, que después envolvía el trapo en un papel y lo guardaba en la caja de los bisturís" (7).

49 "[...] mientras tanto, el tío abuelo, solo, bien solo, sin que nadie le molestara con gritos, ni lamentos, ni otras tonterías por el estilo, se pudría tranquilamente en su ataúd, y de su cara gruesa, carnosa, abultada, no se veía a través del cristal más que una mezcla de sangre rojiza y negra, y en las narices y en la boca algunos puntos blancos de pus" (34).

> ¡Qué hermoso poema el del cadáver del obispo en aquel campo tranquilo! Estaría allá abajo con su mitra y sus ornamentos y su báculo, arrullado por el murmullo de la fuente. Primero, cuando lo enterraran, empezaría a pudrirse poco a poco: hoy se le nublaría un ojo, y empezarían a nadar los gusanos por los jugos vítreos; luego el cerebro se le iría reblandeciendo, los humores correrían de una parte del cuerpo a otra y los gases harían reventar en llagas la piel: y en aquellas carnes podridas y deshechas correrían las larvas alegremente…
>
> Un día comenzaría a filtrarse la lluvia y a llevar con ella substancia orgánica, y al pasar por la tierra aquella substancia se limpiaría, se purificaría, nacerían junto a la tumba hierbas verdes, frescas y el pus de las úlceras brillaría en las blancas corolas de las flores.
>
> Otro día esas hierbas frescas, esas corolas blancas darían su substancia al aire y se evaporaría ésta para depositarse en una nube.
>
> ¡Qué hermoso poema el del cadáver del obispo en el campo tranquilo! ¡Qué alegría la de los átomos al romper la forma que les aprisionaba, al fundirse con júbilo en la nebulosa del infinito, en la senda del misterio donde todo se pierde! (91)

The shocking realist description of the process of death is narrated through the ecstatic style of mystic revelation, thus shifting attention away from a transcendent after-life to the fusion of life and matter that forms and deforms in this world only.

Decay is prevalent throughout the novel, not merely in its effects on human beings, but also on all substances (to give an example, crosses are made of "madera carcomida," 90; even the paintings inside a café are "carcomidas," 192). At the end of the novel, the significance of the novel's consistent focus on decay is clearly linked with organized religion. This organized religion is in clear opposition to the almost animistic union of body and soul propounded by Bergson and explored novelistically in the mystic evocation of landscape throughout Baroja's novel. Organized religion, in fact, is consistently opposed to interior experience throughout *Camino de perfección*. Fernando's beliefs are denounced by a priest as "misticismo puro" (256), and the former likewise criticizes "la petulancia de aquel clérigo imbécil que creía encerrada en su cerebro toda la sabiduría divina" (257). He rejects the idea that the material or the spiritual have an end and uses spirit and matter interchangeably in describing the essence common to all things (259). The Nietzschean vital impulse present in some of the work's descriptions might just as well relate to a Bergsonian articulation of becoming.[50] In this way, Baroja's critique of organized religion is not an end in itself, but rather is, more generally speaking, a philosophical argument whose end result is to fuse mysticism and vitalism in dynamic contrast to the restrictions that static religion places on life.

In summary, from the Bergsonian perspective of mysticism as expressed in *The Two Sources of Morality and Religion*, there must be necessarily a difference of kind between, on the one hand, that mystical state envisioned as the end-product of the application of a three-stage model, and, on the other, the mystical process that is never completely attained. If his philosophy as a whole enlightens our reading of *The Two Sources of Morality and Religion* at all, it is to denounce the mystical as a state to be attained once and for all, and recategorize it as a process. This reading highlights Bergson's commitment to intuition itself as a process, a practice that must always work against the intellectual path with which it is fused. This is to encourage a lack of confidence in teleological visions of process just as in *Creative Evolution* Bergson rejects both mechanism and finalism explicitly in favor of the indeterminate nature of life. If his method of intuition is understood correctly as a process, there can be no final union with spirit that fully escapes the tendency of matter to pull life down to its level. These two tendencies interpenetrate each other, yet are never fully reconciled (recalling Unamuno's "tragic sense of life," see chapter two of the present work). The result of this Bergsonian perspective is to leave us eternally "betwixt and between," as anthropologist Victor Turner (1969) famously wrote of liminal states, to realize the contradictory nature of the combination of life and matter to which our experiences are tethered. There is, in this realization, the Bergsonian contrast between the closed and the open. The open is always threatened by the closed system, real life and movement is perennially threatened by dogmaticly religious and supposedly transcendent values.

It is this realization that Baroja underscores at the end of *Ca-*

---

[50] "A veces la luna vertía por debajo de una nube una luz que dejaba al mar plateado, y entonces se veían sus olas redondas, sombreadas de negro, agitadas en continuo movimiento, en eternal violencia de ir y venir, en un perpetuo cambio de forma" (326).

mino de perfección, where he writes "Y mientras Fernando pensaba, la madre de Dolores cosía en la faja que habían de poner al niño una hoja doblada del Evangelio" (335). Far from the halcyon finale envisioned by critic Roberta Johnson ("Ossorio [...] marries, has a child and seems to achieve a kind of happiness and stability," 52), we are left with the vision of the contrast between Fernando's open-ended hesitation and the dogma of a stolid Catholicism as an ongoing struggle. The irreconcilable nature of this struggle is not only a hallmark of Baroja, Nietzsche, and Unamuno, but also of none other than Bergson himself. For the latter, this vital struggle is borne of the conflictive union of intellect with intuition in our experience of a constantly evolving spatio-temporal whole. As Baroja sought to express with the phrase "misticismo realismo" (above), and as the philosophy of Bergson sought to do in its reconciliation of traditional metaphysical dualism, vitalism in fact embraces the notion of spirit, now reformulated as an aspect of this world and not of any other. This spirit is more properly understood as the vital impetus of life itself. While Baroja found a more explicit model for this philosophy in Nietzsche, discussing him in *Camino de perfección* through Fernando's encounters with Schultze, Bergson's élan vital as the basis for his study of dynamic religion makes possible a more intricate fusion of the novel's twin incorporation of mysticism and vitalism.

MIGUEL DE UNAMUNO: AGAINST ABSTRACT PHILOSOPHY

MIGUEL de Unamuno y Jugo (1864-1936) and Henri Bergson (1859-1941) were more than merely contemporary thinkers –they shared not only a historical period but moreover a philosophical language, a methodology based in contradiction, and the goal of returning philosophy from abstract categories to the concrete movement of life itself. A close reading of a selection of Unamuno's philosophical writings, essays and novels inspired by previous critical studies linking Bergson and Unamuno reveals that there can be no doubt that the French philosopher influenced the Spaniard directly.[1] A further goal of this comparison, given the relatively recent resurgence in studies of Bergson, is to propose a complementary renewed interest in Unamuno's philosophy. It is in the context of the significant historical connections between Bergson and Unamuno that this chapter explores the appearance of Bergsonian ideas both explicitly and implicitly in the Spaniard's philosophical treatise *Del sentimiento trágico de la vida* (1912) with reference to his earlier essays as published in *En torno al casticismo* (1895). Their shared philosophy "of life"–their philosophical attempt to return from the abstract categories of thought which are incapable of capturing experience as it is lived–is bolstered by a methodology that emphasizes contradiction, heterogeneity and paradox over the simplified designs of intellect and rationality. Moreover, this congruence can be traced through Unamuno's novels–particularly *Amor y pedagogía*

[1] These previous studies include Ferrater Mora (1955, 1985), Eoff (1961), Meyer (1962), Marías (1968), Turiel (1970), Nozick (1971), Batchelor (1972), Ouimette (1974) and Sinclair (2001), among others.

(1902) and *Niebla* (1914)–which are one of the main vehicles for his philosophical ideas if not philosophical works in their own right.

The connections each philosopher had with key literary and philosophical figures such as Antonio Machado and William James are certainly well known, as are their relative positions in the post-Kantian history of philosophy. Characterizing the work of both Unamuno and Bergson in the broadest of strokes, one is led to the following result: each eschewed the mechanistic view of life popular in the positivist thought of the late nineteenth century, each conceived of philosophy as distinct from science, and each, in his own way, sought a reconciliation between the isolated worlds of philosophy and science.[2] These commonalities are of course demonstrated by a shared antagonistic attitude toward Herbert Spencer as well as the praise each directed toward the experimental method of Claude Bernard.[3] It is known that Bergson's work *Matière et mémoire* (1896) was published in Spain by 1900, and furthermore that Unamuno's personal library held the following works by Bergson: *Essai sur les données immédiates de la conscience* (1889), *Matière et mémoire* (1903), *L'Évolution créatrice* (1907) and *L'Énergie spirituelle; essais et conférences* (1919).[4]

Establishing similarities between the two philosophers is in fact no difficult task. Both Unamuno's and Bergson's methodologies emphasize contradictions that similarly escape facile resolution in pursuit of a common philosophical goal. In the case of Unamuno, these differences play out in the terms of an eternal struggle that defies characterization as a base dualism due to its undermining of traditional reason. In Bergson's work, the contradiction is one between spatial and temporal multiplicities whose relationship is ar-

---

[2] In *Del sentimiento trágico de la vida*, Unamuno writes "Cúmplenos decir, ante todo, que la filosofía se acuesta más a la poesía que no a la ciencia" (8). See Bergson's *The Creative Mind* for a lengthy exploration of the relationship of philosophy to science. As has been mentioned, his *Duration and Simultaneity* famously takes on Einstein's theories of relativity. Einstein, of course, refused to entertain Bergson's work at length, perhaps because in his view physical space and philosophical space are two very different concepts (see Gunter 1969).

[3] On Spencer, see Unamuno's *En torno al casticismo*, Bergson's *Creative Evolution*, and Valdés and Valdés (1973, xix). On Bernard, see Unamuno's "Cientificismo" in *Mi religión y otros ensayos breves* and Bergson's "The Philosophy of Claude Bernard" in *The Creative Mind*.

[4] Eoff (1961) notes that evidence of the translation appears in "(Palau y Dulcet, *Manual del librero hispanoamericano* [Barcelona: A. Palau, 1949])", 183, n. 43. On the latter, see Valdés and Valdés (1973, 27).

guably neither wholly monistic nor dualistic. Thus although both philosophers are forced by the language of reason to explain their positions through simplistic dualisms, each, in turn, explodes these dualisms, positing the irreconcilable nature of such simple opposites and thus underscoring the limits of rationality (Unamuno) and the dangers of the spatialization of time (Bergson). Whether regarding Unamuno's faith or Bergson's temporality, each philosopher's focus on methodological contradiction draws attention to the insufficiency of a spatialising tendency of reason when faced with a qualitative multiplicity.

The central role of contradiction in the work of Bergson has proved difficult for many critics who have relied on a mere cursory review of his texts. Some have sustained, for example, that he espouses a metaphysical idealism (for just one example see Elliot 1912), apparently unaware that Bergson directly attacks both idealism and realism repeatedly throughout his oeuvre (see *MM* 14-15; 307-09). In characterizing this mistaken attitude, Daniel Herman (1980) reports that "Other criticisms and interpretations [...] have turned Bergsonism into an irrationalism, pantheism and monism. [...] And finally the lack of distinction between mind and matter, with a strong preference for mind, has convinced some commentators that the philosophy of Bergson is an idealistic monism" (xi).[5] Interesting in this regard is the fact that while studying at the École Normale, he was "considered by his classmates to be a positivist, or even a materialist" (Gunter 1969b: 6). Bergson's philosophy is thus best understood neither as mentalist or materialist, nor as dualist or monist, but as nondualism. Bergson eschewed doctrine itself, the closed system that categorizes, that apprehends movement only through static, bounded categories. It is thus not enough, to see Bergson as "establishing a series of binaries" (Rob Shields 2003; 28, actual/virtual, matter/memory, spatial/temporal, complete/in-process) and then to go no further. Rather, his works provide a dissection of the very methods through

[5] This attitude is prevalent also in Hispanism. Fiddian's (1974) study of Bergson and Unamuno, for example, ends up reducing Bergson's complex and variegated ontology to a monism that "may ultimately be distinguished from Unamunian dualism" (790). The erroneous appraisal of Bergson as a "mentalist" likewise obtains in the assertions that he is not a phenomenologist because he insists on the "primacy of memory" instead of that "primacy of perception" proclaimed by Merleau-Ponty (Lawlor 2003).

which space and time *are perceived as* separate by the intellect. If Bergson establishes such binary oppositions, it is only provisionally in order to reject them and subsequently recover the real movement of experience. His is not a dualism in the strict sense, but as Ignacio Izuzquiza Otero (1986) notes, "Un dualismo peculiar" (118).

Nevertheless, the recent resurgence of interest in Bergson's work has led to a number of more sophisticated views of his philosophy. Elizabeth Grosz (2004), for one, a feminist scholar with a notable Bergsonian influence, has properly understood the nondual complexity of Bergsonism. She writes that "Although Bergson is commonly understood as an irredeemable dualist, for whom binary oppositions, such as mind and matter, are given, his position is more complex and less easy to decipher than oppositional models allow" (163). His method does not advance a dualism, but a *non*dualism, and as such, has "an unrecognized relevance to feminists and cultural theorists" (Grosz 2004: 13; see also Grosz 1994, 1995, 2001, 2005).[6] This recognition of Bergson's nondualism has not just appeared suddenly with the works of Elizabeth Grosz, Gilles Deleuze (1966) and others. William James, among other contemporaries of Bergson's, acknowledged that the latter had reached "a conclusive demolition of the dualism of object and subject in perception" (R. Richardson 2006: 428), Arthur Mitchell noted "the central idea of his epistemology, the identification of subject and object" (102) and Bergson himself, of course, addresses "The problem of dualism" (*MM*, 233-38) without sacrificing complexity.

In his most significant works, Bergson avoided such simplistic dualisms and stressed the complex, even contradictory relation of quantitative and qualitative opposites. In *Time and Free Will* (1889), *Matter and Memory* (1896), and yet again in *Creative Evolution* (1907), Bergson dissolves from provisional dualisms–of space and time, matter and memory, intellect and instinct–in order to emphasize their union as composites. The composite is wrought of two tendencies which cannot be isolated from each other. Put most suc-

[6] Grosz (2004) goes on to note of Bergson that "his notion of the virtual, embedded in his understanding of duration, is a crucial if commonly unrecognized concept for reconceptualizing the dynamics of political change and social and cultural upheaval. This is a concept that will develop increasing relevance as feminist theorists come to consider how change is developed and the new brought into existence" (13).

cinctly, the opposition is one between "[...] two different kinds of reality, the one heterogeneous, that of sensible qualities, the other homogeneous, namely space" (*TFW*, 97). Although language invites us to consider time and space as distinct or opposed facets of reality (see *Creative Evolution*, 298-304), it does not encourage us to think about how it is that we ourselves separate one from the other, nor does it clarify how each is implicated at every moment of our perception. For Bergson, time and space are not two independent things but two ways of thinking about experience; equally, for Unamuno, "El tiempo, el espacio y la lógica son nuestros tres más crueles tiranos."[7] Put a different way, there are "[...] two kinds of multiplicity, two possible senses of the word 'distinguish,' two conceptions, the one qualitative and the other quantitative, of the difference between *same* and *other*" (*TFW*, 121, original emphasis).

More important than this first manoeuvre in which Bergson references the two multiplicities, the two tendencies that are themselves abstracted from a unitary if variegated space-time, is the way he brings up their interdependence (see also *MM*, 72):

> And yet we cannot even form the idea of discrete multiplicity without considering at the same time a qualitative multiplicity. When we explicitly count units by stringing them along a spatial line, is it not the case that, alongside this addition of identical terms standing out from a homogenous background, an organization of these units is going on in the depths of the soul, a wholly dynamic process, not unlike the purely qualitative way in which an anvil, if it could feel, would realize a series of blows from a hammer? [...] In a word, the process by which we count units and make them into a discrete multiplicity has two sides; on the one hand we assume that they are identical, which is conceivable only on condition that these units are ranged alongside each other in a homogeneous medium; but on the other hand, the third unit, for example, when added to the other two, alters the nature, the appearance and, as it were, the rhythm of the whole; without this interpenetration and this, so to speak, qualitative progress, no addition would be possible. Hence it is through the quality of quantity that we form the idea of quantity without quality. (*TFW*, 122-23)

7 Quoted in Frank Sedwick (1955, 463).

Here it can already be seen how quality plays a role in quantity, intensivity in extensivity, inclusive succession in simultaneity, duration in matter, time in space. For Bergson, perception is thus the composite of two cohabitating, interpenetrating tendencies. It is important to understand, as he does that "Memory is something other than a function of the brain, and there is not merely a difference of degree, but of kind, between perception and recollection" (*MM*, 315). The first, memory, is an amalgam of heterogeneous qualitative moments contracted and each fusing with the other so that none can be isolated from the rest without causing a change in the whole. The second, matter, is that through which we place ourselves in things, which allows, and necessitates the acknowledgement that it is not that we are in space, but rather that space is *in* us, that our senses are an opening outward onto a homogeneous plane whose division by the intellect involves only a change in degree rather than one in nature. Perception is thus inextricable from memory, while memory is mingled with perception. The whole of *Matter and Memory* departs from a discussion of "pure perception" and "pure memory" only to end by discarding these insufficient terms in favour of a variegated fusion of both perception and memory.

Bergson accomplishes the same thing in *Creative Evolution* with the composite of instinct and intelligence. There is one form of movement motivated by intellect, and another by instinct. "When the little chick is breaking its shell with a peck of its beak, it is acting on instinct, and yet it does but carry on the movement which has borne it through embryonic life" (*CE*, 165). Instinct does but move, whereas intellect on the other hand–"Of the discontinuous alone does the intellect form a clear idea" (*CE*, 154), "Of immobility alone does the intellect form a clear idea" (*CE*, 155). There is, then, "instinct," a mode of thought which possesses the body itself indivisibly, immediately, that is with *no mediation*; and there is "intellect," the movement of thought which decomposes and recomposes, a mechanism whose first move is always to divide, to separate, to classify, to delineate, to displace, to categorize, to spatialize in order to accomplish a given goal. It is intellect Bergson refers to when he undertakes the renowned description of the "cinematograph of the mind" (*CE*, 306-07; discussed further below). Instinct moves without knowing in this sense, without partitioning, without dividing and recomposing a homogenous medium, and yet everything happens *as if* it did so. In this way, true to the idea of the

Bergsonian composite and recalling Unamuno's eternal struggle, there is no instinct without intelligence and no intelligence without instinct. Furthermore, these tendencies coexist in all animal life to one degree or another (*CE*). Human thought is a composite that divides into two tendencies: the divisible predominates in intellect, which is a method of division by degree, presuming the fragmentation of an imagined homogenous space; the indivisible predominates in instinct, which is a difference of nature or kind. Said another way, "There are things that intelligence alone is able to seek, but which by itself, it will never find. These things instinct alone could find; but it will never seek them" (*CE*, 151). Although at first Bergson takes care to define intellect and instinct in opposition, he then moves to argue for their cohabitation. Neither, in fact, exists without the other.

The contradictory nature of Unamuno's philosophy, of course, has long been well established in critical studies, if it is not self-evident. His work is undoubtedly a constant production of crisis and conflict. Any reader who may have glanced at his biography will be familiar with the "crisis of 1897" and what is described as a struggle between reason and faith which was to envelop his writing and thought for the rest of his life–a struggle that takes on a life of its own in the short narrative *San Manuel Bueno, mártir* (1930).[8] Julián Marías (1968) provides concise recognition of this character of Unamuno's work: "Se está acostumbrado a pensar, apoyándose en palabras del propio Unamuno, que su obra es paradójica y agónica, llena de contradicción" (2). Likewise, Frances Wyers (1976) states that "[Unamuno's] writings constitute an extensive and almost lucid record of internal cleavage" (ix). Not surprisingly, contradiction has been not only a pervasive thematic concern of his works, but has also appeared in the plot elements of his narrative works themselves.[9] It is this high priority given to contradiction that leads Carlos Blanco Aguinaga (1975) to label the epilogue of his study "Los dos Unamunos" and Luis A. Arocena to title his book *Unamuno, sentidor paradojal* (1981).

Significantly, the challenge criticism has faced when approach-

[8] On the subject of the crisis of 1897 see Allen Lacy (1967: 77-92) and Antonio Sánchez Barbudo (1974).

[9] Regarding the former, see Julián Marías (1968). Regarding the latter, see David G. Turner (1974: 2).

ing the complexity of the works of both philosophers has been the same–to accept the idea of a struggle between opposing tendencies without forcing this struggle toward resolution. This challenge for critics of Unamuno thus approximates the challenge that Bergson's critics have faced and, in many cases, failed, through the facile solution of labelling him a dualist. Paul Ilie (1967), for one, does well in noting that "in general, [Unamuno's] ideas and feelings spilled over onto the pages of an essay as they were conceived and lived, *without ever resolving* the question that the essay had originally proposed at the beginning" (5, emphasis added). Nevertheless, other critics have proven themselves uncomfortable with the idea of unresolved conflict. Instead of remaining "betwixt and between," to use anthropologist Victor Turner's assessment of liminal states, criticism pushes toward one side or other of a simple dualism.[10] Reflecting the tendency that has likewise simplified Bergson's philosophy, this has resulted in statements such as David G. Turner's (1974) that "Unamuno's most agonizing problem was his *failure to attain* faith" (167, emphasis added). Faith, for Unamuno, was not a static state of acceptance, but an evolving struggle. Consistantly avoiding any such resolution, Unamuno himself took great care to emphasize the perennial nature of the struggle between reason and faith, with neither ultimately trumping the other. This is expressed by Unamuno's dictum that "el creyente que se resiste a examinar los fundamentos de su creencia es un hombre que vive en insinceridad y en mentira"–even the believer must question his beliefs.[11] When seen dynamically, what might be perceived in static terms as a simple dualism is but a provisional starting point for understanding a more complex enfolding of opposites.

Although demonstrating the importance of contradiction to both philosophers is a relatively straight-forward task, what is important is to see how each thinker used complexity in their reformulation of traditional abstract philosophical postures. Through the use of contradiction, paradox and the emphasis on interdependent tendencies over ontologically self-sufficient things, both Bergson and Unamuno signal the inadequacy of intellectual or rational methods of perceiving the world, of using abstract thought to introduce clean divisions between concepts that, in practice, cohabit

---

[10] See V. Turner (1995: 95).

[11] Unamuno, "Verdad y vida" (22).

with one another. In either case, this criticism of intellectuality/rationality is not used merely as a simple escape to an extra-rational world, but rather to problematize the easy solutions presented by the intellect and to return, through intuition, to that immediate world from which intellection distinguishes itself. Bergson's desire to return philosophy to the real movement of experience is complemented by Unamuno's need to return to the being of "flesh and bone." A close-reading of the Spaniard's philosophical writings reveals that he shared, with Bergson, not merely an era but moreover a *philosophy of life* that underscored the insufficiency of the abstract categories of purely intellectual thought.

Although Unamuno may never have met Bergson personally,[12] it is clear that he was familiar with the latter's philosophical works. Significantly, Bergson is mentioned explicitly twice in the Spaniard's most significant philosophical text *Del sentimiento trágico de la vida* (1912). The first instance reveals that Unamuno had read *L'Évolution créatrice* (1907) before he finished the work: "¿Qué son los esfuerzos de un Bergson, verbigracia, sobre todo *en su obra sobre la evolución creadora*, sino forcejeos por restaurar al Dios personal y la conciencia eterna? Y es que la vida no se rinde" (131, emphasis added). The second, reserved a spot on the penultimate page no less, demonstrates Unamuno's fondness for Bergson's philosophy of life: "A la filosofía de Bergson, que es una restauración espiritualista en el fondo mística, medieval, quijotesca, se la ha llamado filosofía *demi-mondaine*. Quitadle el *demi*; *mondaine*, mundana. Mundana, sí para el mundo y no para los filósofos, como no debe ser la química para los químicos solos" (279). Unamuno seems to recognize that Bergson's philosophy is an anti-philosophy–that is, one that challenges the traditional metaphysical, transcendent abstractions of philosophy in order to recover the *mundane* complexity of life. Of course, Unamuno's praise for Bergson's mundane approach comes decidedly from its coincidence with his articulation of his own philosophical aims. Accordingly, he starts *Del sentimiento trágico de la vida* with a call for the study, not of

---

12 "En la primavera de 1916 visitó España una misión del Instituto de Francia [...] Uno de los frutos de esta misión fue la fundación de la Casa Velásquez, en Madrid, y uno de los puntos de su itinerario la visita a Salamanca y a Unamuno. Este salió a su encuentro deseoso, sobre todo, de conocer personalmente al filósofo Bergson, lo que no fue posible por haber tenido que regresar éste a Francia desde Madrid" (Manuel García Blanco 1965: 38).

some abstract category, but of the person of "carne y hueso, el que nace, sufre y muere –sobre todo muere–, el que come y bebe y juega y duerme y piensa y quiere, el hombre que se ve y a quien se oye" (7). These explicit references, however crucial in and of themselves, are better understood as an invitation to seek out the more pervasive influence of Bergsonian philosophy on Unamuno's work. In effect, Unamuno's explicit mention of Bergson leads the reader to an assessment of his implicit mention of Bergson, then to a discussion of their common stance on the relation between the past and present and finally to their similar beliefs on mysticism and religious orthodoxy. This discussion grows out of the way each thinker, in his own manner, approaches his subject through simple oppositions that he later discards or problematizes, and ultimately paves the way for a consideration of each as an investigator seeking to reconcile a brute realism with a simplistic idealism.

Recognizing the deep methodological similarities between the two means that the infrequent yet significant explicit references to Bergson in Unamuno's text are perhaps less interesting than the many implicit references therein. For example, in *Del sentimiento trágico de la vida*, Unamuno provides an insight into how powerfully his philosophy implicitly resonates with Bergson's by neglecting to cite a crucial work of the Frenchman that no doubt has influenced him–a revealing omission to say the least. A vital idea of Bergson's (one that has proved quite lasting if its role in the works of Gilles Deleuze is fully acknowledged), was the metaphor of the so-called "cinematograph of the mind." For Bergson, one of the powerful aspects of consciousness, or at least of the imbrication of intellect in consciousness, was the capacity it had to mould itself to matter. This was that tendency of consciousness that Bergson considers to be "spatialized," that perceives quality only through quantity, partitioning and measuring space in the name of the speculative interests of future action. In the contemporaneous developments of cinema, which of course accelerated in the last decade of the nineteenth century, he found a compelling metaphor for this process of intellection.

> We take snapshots, as it were, of the passing reality, and, as these are characteristic of the reality, we have only to string them on a becoming, abstract, uniform and invisible, situated at the back of the apparatus of knowledge, in order to imitate what there is that

> is characteristic in this becoming itself. Perception, intellection, language so proceed in general. Whether we would think becoming, or express it, or even perceive it, we hardly do anything else than set going a kind of cinematograph inside us. We may therefore sum up what we have been saying in the conclusion that the *mechanism of our ordinary knowledge is of a cinematographical kind.* (306, original emphasis)

Given that Unamuno's library held a copy of Bergson's *Creative Evolution*, and that additionally he referred to "su obra sobre la evolución creadora" in this very work (*DST*, above), it is not surprising to see the content and language of this key passage of Bergsonism replicated in *Del sentimiento trágico de la vida*:

> Nada se pierde, nada pasa del todo, pues que todo se perpetúa de una manera o de otra, y todo, luego de pasar por el tiempo, vuelve a la eternidad. Tiene el mundo temporal raíces en la eternidad, y allí está junto el ayer con el hoy y el mañana. *Ante nosotros pasan las escenas como en un cinematógrafo, pero la cinta permanece una y entera más allá del tiempo.* (177, emphasis added)

Both the metaphor of intellectual consciousness as cinema and the wording of Unamuno's passage are reminiscent of Bergson's famous passage from *Creative Evolution*, published a good five years prior. Unamuno's use of this metaphor becomes more significant as greater similarities between the two philosophers are explored–similarities regarding the characterization of psychic states, the relationship between the past and the present, and the conflict between static religion and dynamic religion.

For Bergson, the "cinematograph of the mind" was a metaphor not only for the activity of one tendency of consciousness (intellection, perception, language, spatialized thought) but simultaneously for the spatialized psychological models of thought that divided the individual's psychic activity into distinct states, thus imposing a quantitative and spatial organization on what should only be understood as a qualitative inclusive flow. Unamuno himself points out the errors of this spatializing thought in *Del sentimiento trágico de la vida* in a discussion that recalls the main thrust of Bergson's *Matter and Memory*. He writes:

> Los más de los que el positivismo llamaba hechos, no eran sino fragmentos de hechos. En psicología, su acción fue deletérea. Hasta hubo escolásticos metidos a literatos –no digo filósofos metidos a poetas, porque poeta y filósofo son hermanos gemelos, si es que no la misma cosa– que llevaron el análisis psicológico positivista a la novela y al drama, donde hay que poner en pie hombres concretos, de carne y hueso, *y en fuerza de estados de conciencia, las conciencias desaparecieron*. (12, emphasis added)

In a rejection of the positivist proclivity for quantification, both philosophers emphasize that a consciousness understood qualitatively cannot be cleanly divided into separate states. This is, of course, one of many particular applications of a common methodology that seeks to explore the faults of analysis grounded in a spatializing rationality (Unamuno) or intellection (Bergson). Contradiction thus becomes a key tool for both philosophers in approaching the nature of consciousness since it turns the spatializing tendency of intellectual analysis back upon itself in order to reveal the inadequacy of reason.

From the idea of consciousness, one may pass easily to the question of the relation of the past to the present in social terms. Although the experience of the individual was perhaps a convenient starting point for their philosophies, neither thinker was content to sever the individual off from an enveloping notion of society, and each extended their differential methodology into the realm of the social phenomenon of religion. For Bergson, the past is enduring, it is all around us, not decided once and for all but a virtuality activated by the actual needs of the present–not as what once *was*, but as what *is*. This idea of a past not severed from the present but contained within the present is of course the basis of many of Unamuno's early writings themselves. Interesting in this regard is the fact that Unamuno maintains Bergson's notion of past as enduring, even as virtual, while not following his warning against conceptualizing memories/past as stored in the brain (see *MM*). Unamuno writes:

> Toda impresión que me llegue *queda en mi cerebro almacenada*, aunque sea tan hondo o con tan poca fuerza que se hunda en lo profundo de mi subconciencia: pero desde allí anima mi vida, y si mi espíritu todo, si el contenido total de mi alma se me hiciera conciente, resurgirían todas las fugitivas impresiones olvidadas

> no bien percibidas, y aun las que se me pasaron inadvertidas. (*DST*, 178, emphasis added)

It is this path that, as early as 1895, led Unamuno to take up the Galdosian project of the "Episodios nacionales" in the invigorated idea of intra-historia that appears in *En torno al casticismo*: "Esa vida intra-histórica, silenciosa y continua como el fondo mismo del mar, es la sustancia del progreso, la verdadera tradición, la tradición eterna, no la tradición mentida que se suele ir a buscar en el pasado enterrado en libros y papeles, y monumentos y piedras" (42). The secular reader of Unamuno's text may too easily be led astray by talk of eternity in *Del sentimiento trágico de la vida* just as in *En torno al casticismo*. And yet Unamuno's project is not geared toward an acceptance of static religious dogma, but rather to reconfigure the very notions of a stolid Catholicism by wrenching terms such as *castizo* and *tradición* away from it in order to show how the eternity of which he writes is not that of which the institution of the Church speaks. As the essay "Mi religión" (1907) (and "Verdad y vida" in 1908 for that matter) makes clear, his 'religion' is not Catholicism proper but rather to "buscar la verdad en la vida y la vida en la verdad" (10). Like Bergson, who was also moved by the Spanish mystics Santa Teresa de Jesús and San Juan de la Cruz (see chapter one of the present work), Unamuno, too, wrote at length of the opposition between Catholic mysticism and the institution of the Catholic Church:

> Y es que el catolicismo oscila entre la mística, que es experiencia íntima del Dios vivo en Cristo, experiencia intrasmisible, y cuyo peligro es, por otra parte, absorber en Dios la propia personalidad, lo cual no salva nuestro anhelo vital, y entre el racionalismo a que combate [...]; oscila entre ciencia religionizada y religión cientificada. (*DST*, 72)

This opposition resonates quite powerfully with the conflict that Bergson explores extensively in his last work, *The Two Sources of Morality and Religion* (1932) in which he contrasts "dynamic religion" and "static religion," the mystical flame of religion and the hard dogmatic orthodox shell which forms around it. Of course, familiarity with Bergson's writings as a whole reveals that this book is no isolated case but rather squares with the contrast between spatial quantities and temporal qualities that obtains throughout his works.

In their philosophical approaches to the complexity of life, both thinkers necessarily wrestle with contradiction as a way of questioning the overly simplistic views of extreme realism and extreme idealism. Bergson wrote at length on the fallacies of both (see *MM*). Unamuno, for his part, denounced "un realismo vulgar y tosco y un idealismo seco y formulario" (*ETAC*, 75) in favour of a more subtle articulation of opposites. To think that the friction between these opposites may be resolved is, in either case, to state the problem at hand poorly. From Unamuno's perspective, this ignores the perennial nature of the struggle between reason and faith. As Martin Nozick (1971) writes, "[Unamuno] could accept no given conclusions and labored against stiff-necked righteousness in pedagogy, science, politics, and above all, religion" (204). From Bergson's perspective, attempting to resolve these opposites ignores that it is necessary to pose the question in terms of time rather than space. In either case, the opportunity is to see how the problem of conflict, of contradiction, of *differentiation* undergoes an ontological change once conceived in terms of its divergent and convergent expression as *tendencies* within a folded immanency rather than as the discrete objects that form part of a strict dualism. This is neither monism, nor dualism, but the initial simple bifurcation and subsequent complex reconciliation of two cohabiting tendencies in what amounts to a nondualism. For both Unamuno and Bergson, there are two opposing tendencies or directions of consciousness, one that differentiates itself from the other tendency spatially through the tidy incisions of rational thought and another that envelops and makes possible this very differentiation.

In *Del sentimiento trágico de la vida*, Unamuno implicitly acknowledges Bergsonian method by in effect rejecting a false problem of philosophy and asking the reader to step back from the way questions of materiality or ideality are posed.[13]

> En otro sentido cabe decir que como no sabemos más lo que sea la materia que el espíritu, y como eso de la materia no es para

[13] Bergson stressed that the most important thing is not to solve problems, but to pay attention to how they are posed. A concise presentation of this aspect of his work is to be found in Deleuze's *Bergsonsim*. This is also an emphasis of the first chapter of Bergson's *Matter and Memory* where he argues against both materialism and idealism (also 314-15).

> nosotros más que una idea, el materialismo es idealismo. De hecho y para nuestro problema –el más vital, el único de veras vital–, lo mismo da decir que todo es materia como que es todo idea, o todo fuerza, o lo que se quiera. (76)

Later, he performs the same critique on Descartes's flawed dualism (which is, of course, also critiqued by Bergson) already setting his sights on a nonduality. "Descartes dividió el mundo entre el pensamiento y la extensión, dualismo que le impuso el dogma cristiano de la inmortalidad del alma. Pero ¿es la extensión, la materia, la que piensa o se espiritualiza, o es el pensamiento el que se entiende y materializa?" (*DST*, 195). This citation is merely one among many that present an obstacle to characterizations of Unamuno's thought as dualist in the simple sense. Rather than embrace a traditional dualism whose terms are mutually exclusive and whose relationship to each other is external, Unamuno describes a nondualism whose terms are internal to one another, as is also the case in Bergson's nondual explication of composites that are defined by *internal difference* (see also Deleuze 1966). Each term in the composite contains the other just as Bergsonian instinct and intelligence contain each other (*CE*), just as matter and memory contain each other (*MM*) and are indivisible, just as space and time are only separable from a spatio-temporal whole by the act of intellection. In fact, the very cohabitating multiplicities (spatial and temporal) analysed by Bergson (*TFW*) are present in Unamuno's work as well. In *En torno al casticismo* he comes quite close to a parallel articulation of the Bergsonian nondual consciousness:

> Pero tal distinción [entre una cosa y las demás por la percepción] no podría darse sin una analogía profunda sobre que reposara; la diferencia sólo se reconoce sobre un fondo de semejanza. En la sucesión de impresiones discretas hay un fondo de continuidad, un *nimbo* que envuelve a lo precedente con lo subsiguiente; la vida de la mente es como un mar eterno sobre que ruedan y se suceden las olas, un eterno crepúsculo que envuelve días y noches, en que se funden las puestas y las auroras de las ideas. Hay un verdadero tejido conjuntivo intelectual, un fondo intra-conciente, en fin. (72, original emphasis)

Here, Unamuno's comment that "la diferencia sólo se reconoce sobre un fondo de semejanza" recalls Bergson's effort to reveal the qualitative basis for quantitative multiplicities (*TFW*, 122-23 above).

In this shared rejection of both realism and idealism, both thinkers are suggesting a self-conscious methodology in which knowledge itself is problematized. Paul Ilie writes: "[In Unamuno's case] an individual self sets about to explore its own structure, its feelings, and its position with regard to everything that is not itself. Fundamentally this is a phenomenology of consciousness" (7). In sheer opposition to the realist, or the idealist–for in this sense they are the same, Unamuno starts his investigation not from ideas themselves, but from the vital direction from which the idea is born.[14] "No suelen ser nuestras ideas las que nos hacen optimistas o pesimistas, sino que es nuestro optimismo o nuestro pesimismo, de origen fisiológico o patológico quizá, tanto el uno como el otro, el que hace nuestras ideas" (8-9). In doing so, he embraces the pre-eminence of the Nietzschean emotion over the rational, or of course the Bergsonian affect-interval. "Porque vivir es una cosa, y conocer otra, y como veremos, acaso hay entre ellas una tal oposición, que podamos decir que todo lo vital es antirracional, no ya sólo irracional, y todo lo racional, antivital. Y ésta es la base del sentimiento trágico de la vida" (*DST*, 35). Emotion is opposed to reason, life is opposed to intellection just as in Bergson heterogeneous succession was *initially* dualistically contrasted with homogeneous extension (*TFW*) and then later shown to envelop it as time envelops space (*MM*).

In the philosophies of both Bergson and Unamuno there is a clear distinction between two ways of knowing–there is one path to knowledge, intellection, which differentiates itself from a second path, intuition. Regarding this first kind of 'intellectual' knowledge, Unamuno writes of its tendency to understand the fluid only through staticity: "Para comprender algo, hay que matarlo, enrigidecerlo en la mente" and "La mente busca lo muerto, pues lo vivo se le escapa; quiere cuajar en témpanos la corriente fugitiva, quiere fijarla" (*DST*, 84). His critique of the intellect is thus remarkably similar to that of Bergson, who frequently writes of its spatializing tendency to freeze, to partition fluid experience into immobile units, as in his memorable quotation on the 'cinematograph of the mind.' Yet just as in Bergson each multiplicity is pregnant with its opposite, here too Unamuno notes that reason is imbued with life, once again recalling the complex internal differentiation of the Bergsonian composite:

---

[14] Consider Bergson's rejection of concepts, esp. as in *The Creative Mind*.

> La ciencia es un cementerio de ideas muertas, *aunque de ellas salga vida*. También los gusanos se alimentan de cadáveres. Mis propios pensamientos, tumultuosos y agitados en los senos de mi mente, desgajados de su raíz cordial, vertidos a este papel y fijados en él en formas inalterables, son ya cadáveres de pensamientos. ¿Cómo, pues, va a abrirse la razón a la revelación de la vida? Es un trágico combate, es el fondo de la tragedia, el combate de la vida con la razón. ¿Y la verdad? ¿Se vive o se comprende? (*DST*, 84, emphasis added)

The implicit answer to Unamuno's rhetorical question is undeniably that there is indeed no reason without emotion. For the Spaniard, reason stems from emotion, intellect from sensation, and the dead idea freezes life, just as for Bergson "The word turns against the idea" and "The letter kills the spirit" (*CE*, 127). Just as Unamuno comments that from dead ideas life may come, Bergson explains in *The Two Sources of Morality and Religion* that dynamic religion may spring from within static religion. Intellect thus distinguishes itself from flux through repeated staticity, maintained fixity. There are in Unamuno two traditions, one eternal the other fleeting, just as in Bergson there is a philosophy and a philosophy of philosophy, a science coexisting with a science of science (see *The Creative Mind*). It is with this in mind that the Spaniard writes "Hay una tradición eterna, legado de los siglos, la de la ciencia y el arte universales y eternos; he aquí una verdad que hemos dejado morir en nosotros repitiéndola como el Padre-nuestro" (*ETAC*, 41). In this phrase the attentive reader finds an echo of Bergson's previous statement that "The most living thought becomes frigid in the formula that expresses it" (*CE*, 127).

Thus for both thinkers there are thus two consciousnesses, two ways of knowing: a spatializing intellect and intuition for Bergson, reason and life for Unamuno. The result of this distinguished and differentiated (and differentiating) intellect is given from the outset, predetermined. When Unamuno writes that "Todo conocimiento tiene una finalidad" (*DST*, 19) he is in effect affirming the Bergsonian dictum that the intellect is the part of consciousness that is turned towards matter, perception in this capacity being the virtual action of the body on things (*MM*). Rejecting the confines of a limiting rationality, Unamuno embraces the qualitative nature of consciousness, "Un principio de unidad primero en el espacio, merced al cuerpo, y luego en la acción y en el propósito" (*DST*, 13). Nevertheless, intellect cannot ultimately be severed from the vital force that literally embodies the former:

> Lo de saber para saber, no es, dígase lo que se quiera, sino una tétrica petición de principio. Se aprende algo, o para un fin práctico inmediato, o para completar nuestros demás conocimientos. Hasta la doctrina que nos aparezca más teórica, es decir, de menor aplicación inmediata a las necesidades no intelectuales de la vida, responde a una necesidad –que también lo es– intelectual, a una razón de economía en el pensar, a un principio de unidad y continuidad de la conciencia. (*DST*, 19)

The irreconcilable nature of life and reason, sensation and intellect, in Unamuno is parallel to the Bergsonian composite which divides only into tendencies, one bent toward divisible and spatialized homogeneity and the other towards an indivisible and concatenating succession of heterogeneity. That these tendencies are ultimately irreconcilable when subject to traditional intellection or rationality means that both extreme realism and extreme idealism are insufficient paths into experience. For Unamuno, this conundrum is the most tragic problem of philosophy:

> Y el más trágico problema de la filosofía es el de conciliar las necesidades intelectuales con las necesidades afectivas y con las volitivas. Como que ahí fracasa toda filosofía que pretende deshacer la eterna y trágica contradicción, base de nuestra experiencia. (*DST*, 19)

This contradiction, of the heart and the head (*DST*, 17), of sensation and reason, of qualities and quantities, of time and space, of memory and matter, of idealism and realism, is for both philosophers the very struggle of consciousness, of life. Both Bergson and Unamuno acknowledge this struggle by seeking not to clarify experience but rather to problematize it, not to establish a simple answer to life but rather to pose a more complex question.

Up until now, this chapter has demonstrated not only that Unamuno and Bergson shared a contemporary historical moment, but also that they shared a philosophical language and methodology in which contradiction played an important role. It is not the case that one of the philosopher's writings can be reduced to a mere copy of the other's. Instead, Unamuno's philosophy explicitly incorporated Bergson's ideas and continued to implicitly build upon those ideas. In some respects he may have even anticipated Bergson's writings. What both philosophers shared was not an identical philosophical perspective, but a similar methodological premise. In each case, the use of contradiction in their methodologies was intended to do much more than merely establish a simple dualism. Through contradiction, both thinkers sought to challenge the rational (Unamuno) or intellectual (Bergson) thought process itself and to return from the simplistic realm of philosophical abstraction to the complex vitality of life. The next section of this chapter will delve into the Spaniard's novels as an illustration of his (Bergsonian) philosophical thought.

Unamuno's novels *Amor y pedagogía* (1902) and *Niebla* (1914) are best understood as illustrations of the Bergsonian philosophical struggle he explored in his writings, particularly in *Del sentimiento trágico de la vida.* Each shows how Unamuno's philosophical methodology closely approximated Bergson's own method in its emphasis on contradiction and process over the mere application of static intellectual categories.[15] This methodological similarity plays out in *Amor y pedagogía* in the areas of science, intellect and pedagogy, and is significantly accompanied by a kind of humor that is enriched by articulation with what Bergson, in *Laughter* (1900), describes as the contrast between the mechanical and the living.[16] In *Niebla*, Unamuno approaches the Bergsonian method of intuition through a consistent critique of intellect and the use of metafictive device that highlights the inadequacy of his agonist's use of intellect. Neither of these two Bergsonian correspondences should be surprising given Unamuno's own conception of the novel as a tool in the critique of rational systems: "[E]l sentimiento, no la concepción racional del universo y de la vida, se refleja mejor que en un

[15] Batchelor (1972) notes that "In keeping with his contemporary Bergson and his predecessor Dostoievsky, Unamuno contributed largely to the dissolution of the rational categories extolled by Comte's positivism which attempted to present life as immutable and intellectually satisfying" (35). Nevertheless, he mentions Bergson only in passing (also 43, 214).

[16] Interestingly, Bergson referenced Don Quijote and Sancho repeatedly in his work on *Laughter*. Also, in a discussion of Unamuno's *Vida de don Quijote y Sancho* (1905), Martin Nozick (1971) notes that Unamuno's theory of why we laugh at Don Quijote is "surprisingly close to Bergson's *Le Rire*" (99). Nevertheless, Bergson is mentioned in Nozick's work only in passing (26, 77, 99).

sistema filosófico o que en una novela realista, en un poema, en prosa o en verso, en una leyenda, en una novela" ("Prólogo-epílogo a la segunda edición," *Amor y pedagogía*, 33). The novel of sentiment is thus conceived as a counterbalance to, if not an attack on, the methodology of rationalist science. In seeking to restore balance to the perennial struggle between rationality and faith, these novels of sentiment square with Bergson's critique of an intellectual thought that fragments fluid experience and that reduces interior life, emotions and sentiments to self-enclosed successive states (*TFW*, *MM*, *CE*).

Although Roberta Johnson's (1993) important study of philosophy in the Spanish novel from 1900-1934 mentions Bergson only in passing, her analysis is an excellent starting point for exploring and developing, not only the sympathy between Unamuno and Bergson's work, but the very plausible direct influence of the latter on the former. Certainly, as Johnson warns, it is difficult to look for sources in Unamuno's work–he was, after all, "a voracious reader with an amazing memory" who "drew on his vast store of received knowledge to forge his own highly original works" (n. 24, 197-98). But this is also precisely why pursuing the Bergson-Unamuno connection is so worthwhile. What the study does well is make possible a methodological comparison through a discussion of Unamuno's early, and unpublished, philosophical work titled "Filosofía lógica" (1886)[17] with the ideas Bergson was to publish in his own dissertation *Time and Free Will* (1889). Therein, he proposed "*la percepción directa de las cosas*" (Johnson 37, the emphasis is Unamuno's), anticipating Bergson's original French title "*Essai sur les données immédiates de la conscience.*"[18] During the same *lustro* (a five-year pe-

[17] For a description of this unpublished work, see Armando F. Zubizarreta (1960), 15-32. Neither, of course, does Zubizarreta mention Bergson's name, sticking instead to Ortega, Heidegger (himself influenced by Bergson), and Husserl.

[18] Interestingly, in noting how this work anticipated later philosophical positions of Edmund Husserl and Maurice Merleau Ponty (who was Bergson's student), she does not mention Bergson at all. This omission may be attributed to the powerful suspicion aroused in Bergsonism as a testament to its lingering effects. This entrenched suspicion rears its head in the thesis of Johnson's book itself. Of the four traits she lists concerning the philosophical context of the time preceding the period in question (1900-1934) (they are 1. the place of the will and the intellect, 2. the role of the environment, 3. the nature of time and history, and 4. the importance of art and science; 16), Bergson is linked only with number 3, reflecting the widespread misunderstanding of Bergson as merely a "philosopher of time" and negating the very significant other aspects of his philosophy which comprise all four of these areas.

riod), both thinkers were attempting to resolve the key error of positivism's intellectual bias by returning from the notion of a disembodied mind to the fluid if contradictory experience of real life. Both *Amor y pedagogía* and *Niebla* show this concordance of Unamuno's thought with Bergsonism, even if each does so in its own way.

Amor y pedagogía narrates the story of Don Avito Carrascal, who attempts to produce a genius child relying on pedagogical and overly rational beliefs. To achieve this end, he (quite unsuccessfully) applies his faith in rationality to the entire process of child-rearing, from the selection of his wife to the education of his son. The novel is Bergsonian in its non-dualistic premise, its strong denunciation of overly-rigid approach to scientific knowledge, and even its humor. The work is clearly an attack on the positivism of Comte and the pedagogical theories of Spencer, two figures of whom Bergson was also critical. Unamuno even mentions the latter's name specifically in a scene in which, lampooning these ideologues of rationality, his protagonist, or perhaps more appropriately *agonist*, Avito Carrascal, wants his son to "hear this name well:" "[…] fíjate bien en este nombre, hijo mío, Spencer. ¿Lo oyes? Spencer, no importa que no sepas aún quién es, con tal que te quede el nombre, Spencer, repítelo, Spencer" (90). Ultimately, despite his attempts to apply his rational beliefs to the production of his genius child, once grown his son Apolodoro hangs himself.

The novel boasts remarkable philosophical similarities with Bergson's philosophy in its consistent formulation of two opposing abstract philosophical postures which it subsequently undermines –abstract philosophical postures as they are embodied in two different living beings.[19] While Johnson (1993) counterposes Avito Carrascal "the arch-positivist" to Don Fulgencio Entreambosmares as "a German idealist" (19), I propose that the great contrast of the novel is not between Don Fulgencio and Avito, but between Avito and his projected image of Mariana, that is, a dichotomy endemic

---

[19] In the prologue to the second edition (1934), another similarity is apparent regarding the notion of time, although in the novel as a whole this connection is not wholly evident. We have seen, above, that Unamuno's notion of *intrahistoria* was compatible with Bergson's *durée* in its rejection of spatialized time periodization in favor of an accumulating totality of passing time. He writes of the thirty years that have gone by: "Más de treinta años han pasado por mí. No, no han pasado, sino que se me han quedado" (31).

to Avito's own thought. Avito Carrascal is thus the quantitative, rational, scientific force while Marina, his wife and the mother of his child, is the qualitative force of emotion, love. Don Fulgencio is best understood, as his surname "Entreambosmares" suggests, as not simply an idealist, but a fusion–Johnson importantly notes that Unamuno was fond of fusing and not mixing two things (1993, 41)–of idealism and realism. Thus he is more accurately compared to Unamuno and even Bergson himself.[20]

While there is certainly a very traditional and conservative gender distinction at work in Unamuno's embodiment of such philosophical tendencies in Avito and Marina, tendencies that are after all present in all human beings, this problematic embodiment does not preclude a philosophical interpretation. Avito's conception of their relationship mirrors the Bergsonian intellect's active production of the notion of a reality it takes to be in inert "El arte, la reflexión, la conciencia, la forma lo seré yo, y ella, Marina será la naturaleza, el instinto, la inconciencia, la material" (49). Imagined as a superior rational ordering force, Avito, as the embodiment of intellect, distinguishes himself from life itself, in order to better control the latter, which he places in a subordinate position. This motivation is reflected in Avito's choice of name for his son, Apolodoro: "don de Apolo, de la luz del sol, padre de la verdad, y de la vida" (64). Avito is brought to this name by his supposedly intellectual admiration of rational order, but as the text suggests, there is another motivation for this choice, as the initials A. C. are also his own.

In Bergsonian terms, of course, Avito's self-identification with rationality reflects the outcome of an evolutionary path which has modeled the intellect of all human beings closely on the properties of matter (*CE*), sacrificing the real flux of life to achieve practical ends through the detached power of intellect. The problem is, nevertheless, that the intellect takes this practical view to be ontologically unquestionable, and places all too much faith in its own production of clear spatial distinctions and the spatialization of time. Bergson's critique of this process and acknowledgment of two cohabiting multiplicities (*TFW*) is most clearly associated with the character of Don Fulgencio Entreambosmares, who, for his part, represents a reconciliation between the rational order of the intellect (thus the legacy of positivism) and the vital stream of life. This

[20] See Johnson 44-where this take on Don Fulgencio is more apparent.

is true to such an extent that he may be read allegorically as embodying not only Unamuno's "tragic sense of life" but also Bergson's fusion of intellect and intuition. Just as for Bergson quality underlies quantity, in fact making quantity possible (see *TFW*, 122-23), for Don Fulgencio, the purpose of science is not only to catalogue the universe, as he tells Avito, but also to hand it over to God, to impose quantity upon quality only to turn this quantity back over to quality (75). In this way, Don Fulgencio's stance differs greatly from Avito's, even though the latter finds support for his ideas in a certain aspect of the former's ideas, through discarding that which does not interest him.

In Unamuno's novel, the physical embodiment of these tendencies (intellect and instinct) in two different characters also effects a more profound questioning of the traditional ontological position that stresses internal consistency of the object. In *Matter and Memory*, which was translated into Spanish by 1900 and thus most certainly read by Unamuno either in Spanish if not the original French (as above, Unamuno's personal library held a copy of the book in the original French), Bergson introduced the idea of a pure perception and a pure memory only to undermine that distinction by the end of the work. This process, which in itself underscores the philosopher's emphasis on dialectical movement over the purported precision of static intellectual categories, is consistent with his ontological posture that eschews the popular idea of the thing as a pure internally homogeneous spatial entity. Instead, Bergson argues, this view of the thing is the product of a certain kind of thinking he terms spatial. What we commonly call the thing is, for Bergson is wrought of two tendencies, both spatial and temporal multiplicities which are coexistent and interpenetrating. In fact, our notion of the object is neither the object itself (a position he terms realism) nor is it our idea of the object (which he calls idealism), but a point half-way between these two: the object is the thing itself minus that which does not interest us. In this way, as part of phenomenological thought understood in a general sense, he implicates perception as already infused with thought in order to effectively critique the ontological relationships produced by intellectual thought. The product of this intellectual thought, which, he reminds us, is only a tendency that may be countered by the possibility of intuition, has thus no traditionally ontological status. It is, instead, produced as such by our intellect, which is insufficient in itself to grasp the nature of things.

Unamuno, like Bergson (1934), distances himself from an overly-rigid scientific approach to knowledge. In the prologue to the first edition of *Amor y pedagogía* he writes:

> A muchos parecerá esta novela un ataque, no a las ridiculeces a que lleva la ciencia *mal entendida* y la manía pedagógica *sacada de su justo punto*, sino un ataque a la ciencia y a la pedagogía mismas, y preciso es confesar que si no ha sido tal la intención del autor –pues nos resistimos a creerlo en un hombre de ciencia y pedagogo–, nada ha hecho, por lo menos, para mostrárnoslo. (25-26, emphasis added)

This statement conveys that while science and pedagogy carried to rational extremes are clearly suspect, they nevertheless have a role to play. This is quite in tune with the balanced presentation of rationality and faith that obtains in his "tragic sense of life"–each side nurtures the other to prevent its reduction to a rigid formulaic dogma. Equally, Bergson's view is not entirely dismissive of science, however much this view might have been pervasive among those who saw him as a mystic, but is rather an attempt to bring science and metaphysics together. In *The Creative Mind*, Bergson states that:

> To metaphysics, then, we assign a limited object, principally spirit, and a special method, mainly intuition. In doing this we make a clear distinction between metaphysics and science. But at the same time we attribute an equal value to both. I believe that they can both touch the bottom of reality. I reject the arguments advanced by philosophers, and accepted by scholars, on the relativity of knowledge and the impossibility of attaining the absolute. (37)[21]

---

[21] Bergson continues to elaborate upon this idea: "Quite different is the metaphysics that we place side by side with science. Granting to science the power of explaining matter by the mere force of intelligence, it reserves mind for itself. In this realm, proper to itself, it seeks to develop new functions of thought. Everyone can have noticed that it is more difficult to make progress in the knowledge of oneself than in the knowledge of the external world. Outside oneself, the effort to learn is natural; one makes it with increasing facility; one applies rules. Within, attention must remain tense and progress become more and more painful; it is as though one were going against the natural bent. Is there not something surprising in this? We are internal to ourselves, and our personality is what we should know best.

Yet such is not the case; our mind is as if it were in a strange land, whereas matter is familiar to it and in it the mind is home. But that is because a certain ignorance of self is perhaps useful to a being which must exteriorize itself in order to act; it answers a necessity of life" (41).

In this way, from the very first word of Unamuno's novel, it is not all of science, but only that overly-rational science that is mocked: "Hipótesis más o menos plausibles, pero nada más que hipótesis al cabo, es todo lo que se nos ofrece respecto al cómo, cuándo, dónde, por qué y para qué ha nacido Avito Carrascal" (41). So focused is Avito on science that when asked "¿Le gustan a usted las flores? He responds "¿Cómo estudiar botánica sin ellas?" (47). For him, the world of sensation is irrefutably subordinate to the world of scientific study, and it is this hierarchy that Unamuno lampoons, for example, in Avito's insistence that Mariana not kiss their son–fearing an exposure to microbes (67).

This critique of the extreme positions of rational science is also manifested in a critique of rational pedagogy. Unamuno, of course, had been profoundly affected by his experiences at the Institución Libre de Enseñanza, and by Don Francisco Giner in particular. In the essay "Recuerdo de don Francisco Giner" Unamuno comments thusly on the qualitative nature of education: "no es posible reducirla a fórmulas trasmisibles y menos a recetas. Era el hombre y el hombre se da en espíritu, pero no es posible traducirlo en letra" (3). Avito's worry regarding the education of his son stems from his idea that the child is irrevocably programmed by the most minute details. Due to his excessive rationality, the early babbeling/protospeech of his child is taken as a mystery to be solved and he decides that the words he produces in his first attempts ("puchulili, pachulila, titamimi, tatapupa, pachulili," 82) simply must have their own meanings.

A look at the humor of the novel informed by Bergson's treatise *Laugher* (1900) continues the philosophical critique of mechanism advanced by Unamuno in the realm of science and pedagogy. Bergson argued that we find things funny to the extent that they make us aware of the imbrication of the mechanical in life. Bergson gives the illustration of the classic gag of someone slipping on a banana peel. This produces laughter, he argues, because the person has been acting in a mechanical fashion, out of tune with their environment–humor results from our realization that this person is inattentive to life. It is the strong contrast between organic life and the mechanical nature of matter, always fused, as Bergson discussed at length in *Creative Evolution*, which makes us laugh. That Unamuno's novel explicitly takes on the contrast of these two tendencies makes it ripe for this type of humor that has as its base the juxtaposition of abstract categories.

Repetition becomes the key vehicle of this juxtapositional humor and simultaneously Unamuno's advocation of vitalism in the face the mechanism characteristic of intellectual/rational systems. There is the word-for-word repetition of the description of Leoncia as "muchacha dólico-rubia, de color sano, amplias caderas, turgente y levantado pecho, mirar tranquilo, buen apetito" on two different pages (45, 48), serving to highlight the mechanical nature of his thought and make fun of the process whereby the intellect grasps the mobile only through a static conception of it.[22] Humor also results from the narrator's first substitution of "Forma" and "Materia" for the names Avito and Marina (52-54, also "la Ciencia y la Conciencia," 53) and its establishment as pattern throughout the novel ("la pobre Materia," 58), mechanically copying and thus mocking Avito's simplistic dualist conception of the world. In resonance with Bergson's crtique of intellect as envisioning a homogeneous spatial field that may be infinitely divided by the intellect, Marina is even, for Avito, that homogeneous notion of space. As he says in the novel "–Y tú, Marina, eres muy homogénea" (59). These embodied concepts continually produce humor when their substitution for the names leads to scenes in which it appears that the concepts themselves are found accomplishing quotidian human tasks. This is matter imitating life–the mechanical, as Bergson notes, is not living, although it is imbricated with organic life. The novel's humorous reduction of life to pure mechanism obtains, perhaps most memorably, in a memorable description of the heart itself–that highest symbol of sensation, feeling and emotion. Humorously, from the reader's perspective, at a moment of passion Avito's interior monologue reduces quality to quantity and recurs to scientific data to give meaning to emotion: "Y la vox interior le dice a Carrascal: 'El corazón humano, esta bomba impelente y absorbente, batiendo normalmente, suministra en un día un trabajo de cerca de 20.000 kilográmetros, capaz de elevar 20.000 kilos a un metro…'" (53).

Simple repetitions, inversions and the propagation of finite rational series to infinite irrational ends also become humorous aspects of the narration. The contents of Avito's house are described in a way that takes advantage of the metonymic properties of lan-

[22] The narration also repeats Avito's thought that ontogeny recapitulates phylogeny to humorous effect (69, 84).

guage (see Jakobson and Waugh 1979): "Por todas partes barómetros, termómetros, pluviómetro, aerómetro, dinamómetro, mapas, diagramas, telescopio, microscopio, espectroscopio, que a donde quiera que vuelva los ojos se empape en ciencia; la casa es un microcosmo racional" (61). Later, the narration again plays with language for humorous effect in a similar way: "Ese enjambre de ideas, ideotas, ideítas, idezuelas, pseudoideas e ideoides con que su padre le tiene asaeteado" (113). Don Fulgencio's exposition of his philosophical ideas leads from "las cuatro ideas madres" (73, see also Johnson 43-44) to an illogical and infinite regression of comparisons and comparisons of comparisons ("la muerte de la muerte de la muerte," 73). This philosophical method, which Don Fulgencio terms "el método coordinatorio" (74), produces much humor from the simple reordering of terms within a system: "¿te proponen la cuadratura del círculo?, medita en la circulación del cuadrado" (74).

All of the humor that results from this contrast between mechanism and life is the direct result either of Avito's overly rationalistic worldview or its parody by the narrative voice. The whole of Avito's scientific thought will not relinquish its abstract conceptual framework to return to the changing movement of life. Instead, he applies mechanical thought explicitly and consciously to living beings. At first, carefully overseeing his child's food intake, his mechanical quantitative approach merely involves scheduling meals at the same time every day. As time passes, however, weighing the food soon turns into weighing the child, a development that results in humor due to the application of the same quantitative method to both matter and life–the food and the child–through the use of the scale (81). Although this confusion is humorous at the outset, with each iteration, as Avito clings more and more to his rationality, the humor begins to take on a tragic tone as Unamuno's agonist becomes more and more distanced from life, leading, of course, to the novel's tragic end. What has been used to humorous effect–the importance of Avito's scientific world view–becomes undermined, quite predictably in fact if we heed Bergson's view on laughter, as Avito's mania leads to tragedy and his child kills himself. Humor, as Bergson writes (1900) is stopped short by feeling. The reader is brought more and more to sympathize with Avito as the narration is infused more and more with Apolodoro's emotional development –with life itself–and we are ultimately brought tragically from the detached world of static abstract concepts to the real and dynamic movement of life, from excessive rationality to unmediated sensation and the reality of death.

As a continuation of *Amor y pedagogía*,[23] *Niebla* is a natural choice to pursue the Unamuno-Bergson connection further (see Johnson 93). The former's agonist, Don Avito Carrascal even makes an explicit appearance in the novel (chapter XIII), where Unamuno takes the opportunity to refer the reader to his earlier text through a footnote (73). Similarly, *Niebla*'s prologue, written by the character Víctor Goti, explicitly mentions the earlier work and its character Don Fulgencio (13). Moreover, the composition of the latter, dating from 1907 through its publication in 1914 (see Johnson, chapter five), takes place after the publication of Bergson's *Creative Evolution*, from which Unamuno was to draw significantly for his *Del sentimiento trágico de la vida* (1912, above). The novel begins as Don Augusto Pérez steps out into the streets where he wanders somewhat aimlessly until he ends up fixated on a woman named Eugenia, whom he follows to her home. Although she is promised to another man (Mauricio), her aunt and uncle Ermelinda and Don Fermín become interested in Augusto for his money. Over the course of the novel Augusto hears stories of many marriages, develops feelings for the servant Rosario, spends time with his newfound dog Orfeo, plays chess with Víctor, and ultimately brokenhearted, he thinks of committing suicide. *Niebla* is most memorable on account of its attempt at metafiction as explored in Augusto's subsequent visit to Salamanca to speak with Unamuno, the author of the very book we are reading (in chapter XXXI), who tells him that he is a mere fictional character.

From a Bergsonian perspective there is much of interest in the novel. As in *Amor y pedagogía*, the protagonist of *Niebla* is likewise fond of a cerebral mode of abstract thinking. If "Augusto's knowing is purely cerebral" (Johnson 98), it is cerebral in the sense of being akin to the Bergsonian intellect. Just as intellect, for Bergson, manifested itself in the static character of language–its division into adjectives (qualities), nouns (things) and verbs (actions) (*CE*, 298-304)–Augusto is similarly preoccupied by the grammar of language. This preoccupation takes precedence over and even interferes in

[23] In the subsection titled "Historia de niebla," Unamuno refers to his previous novel explicitly (19, 22).

life itself, as when Augusto argues with Margarita over the concordance of Eugenia's surname "Domingo" (27) saying it should be "Dominga" since she is a woman, and later when he ponders the meaning of the diminutive form (35, "Por qué el diminutivo es señal de cariño [...]"). In a moment of doubt, the character comes even to intuit Bergson's view of grammar when his own faith in language is questioned, stating that: "La palabra, este producto social, se ha hecho para mentir" (97).[24]

Recalling the character of Avito in Unamuno's earlier *Amor y Pedagogía*, Augusto's conception of himself as pure intellect is so total that he is content to imagine himself entirely separated from his body, as when he talks to the dog Orfeo of his feeling of being invisible in the streets, a fully-disembodied objective observer (49). Over the course of the nivola, the pair Augusto-Orfeo undergoes a process that mirrors Cervantes's quijotización of Sancho Panza and the sanchopancificación of Don Quijote. Augusto kills himself through bodily excess, eating too much, and Orfeo begins to use that representative power of human intellect, language itself–most notably demonstrated in the work's epilogue where the dog's thoughts are rendered in perfect grammar on the page. Here in *Niebla*, just as he had in *Del sentimiento trágico de la vida*, Unamuno once again turns to the Bergsonian metaphor of the cinematograph for the intellectual conception of memory. When Augusto enters the church of San Martín, he is flooded with a surge of memories that the narration describes in terms once again familiar to the reader of Bergson's work: "al poco rato encontróse sumido en un estado de espíritu en que pasaban ante él, en cinematógrafo, las más extrañas visiones" (73, see also 102 "La calle era un cinematógrafo [...]"). Even his notion of love is guided by the intellectual understanding of it as an abstract concept. To this end, his friend Víctor tells him "Porque todo tu enamoramiento no es sino cerebral, o como suele decirse, de cabeza" (61).

The original or innovative Bergsonian element of the novel, or nivola, however, is not merely the simple critique of intellectualism, for this Unamuno had already accomplished in *Amor y pedagogía*,

---

[24] Unamuno in fact was very interested in grammar and orthography as structure and system (see his writings collected in *La raza y la lengua*, OC vol. IV. In "Gramática y otras cosas" (1888) he writes that "Yo, como usted, profeso respeto a la gramática y creo en su excelencia *práctica*, pero creo no debe extremarse tal respeto" (289).

but rather the presentation of a counterbalance to intellect in the form of intuition. The vehicle for this presentation of Bergsonian intuition is the metafictive device that underlies the interaction between the novel's primary character and agonist Augusto and Unamuno's novelistic counterpart. Questioning the tenuous boundary between the fictional text and the non-fictional world of the author, Unamuno's textual double informs Augusto he is himself merely a fictional character at the mercy of the novel's creator. In the case of *Niebla*, this encounter undoubtedly serves to question the realist mode of earlier Spanish fiction (such as Unamuno's more realist first novel *Paz en la guerra* in 1897), a case that Patricia Waugh makes more generally in her masterful work *Metafiction* (1984). Nevertheless, whereas Unamuno the author may indeed want to "explore a theory of fiction through the practice of writing fiction" (Waugh 2), Unamuno the philosopher simultaneously wants to explore both a theory of life and a theory of knowledge. Given the resonance between the Spaniard's philosophy and Bergson's, the metafictional device employed in *Niebla* is then more properly understood in terms of the French philosopher's self-reflexive thought –his method of intuition.

The barrier to this intuition is the tendency of thought that Bergson labels the intellect. Intellect, as the French philosopher argues using such illustrations as the story of Achilles and the tortoise (*TFW*), the metaphor of the cinematograph (*CE*), the contrast between spatial and temporal multiplicities (*TFW*), the spatialized view of the past (*MM*), the intellect's manifestation in language (*CE*), and the distinction between static and dynamic religions (*MR*), is the tendency of the mind to treat qualitative phenomena in a quantitative fashion, to partition a moving reality into pieces and then make sense of that reality only by stitching those fragments together in an imitation of life. The problem, as Bergson puts it, is that

> Thus perception, thought, language, all the individual or social activities of the mind, conspire to bring us face to face with persons, including our own, which will become in our eyes objects and, at the same time, invariable substances. How can we uproot so profound an inclination? How can we bring the human mind to reverse the direction of its customary way of operating, beginning with change and movement, envisaged as reality itself, and

> no longer to see in halts or states mere snapshots taken of what is moving reality? (*CM*, 70)

Providing an answer to his question, Bergson suggests that we may uproot the 'profound inclination' to see static images of reality at the expense of change–discrete separation where there is only fluid connection–through the faculty of intuition. Bergson concisely defines intuition as the "direct vision of the mind by the mind" (*CM*, 42). This faculty, he writes, "exists in each one of us, but [is] covered over by functions more useful to life" (47).[25]

In order to take up the path of intuition, as the 'direct vision of the mind by the mind,' thought must turn the power of the intellect upon itself. This is to pay attention to the intellect's characteristic fragmentary approach to life, to the abstract categories through which thought selectively filters experience. It must become aware of the interested nature of the virtual action that characterizes the supposedly neutral act of perception. Through its metafictional device, the narrative of *Niebla* recounts this very process of turning intellect back upon itself in breaking down the conceptual barriers between character and author, fiction and reality, the world as it seems and as it really is, all established through traditional intellectual thought. The result is ultimately to question the structuring role that intellect plays in, not the passive reception of a world already produced, but the very active production of a world through perception that takes itself to be merely reflective of an established and solid reality. This questioning of intellect by intellect itself is the very path of Bergsonian intuition.

In *Niebla*, this Bergsonian intuition, the assessment of mind by mind itself in the form of a metafictive device that bridges the text and reality does not suddenly appear near the narrative's end, but rather has an important role that is developed through the entire

---

[25] In *Creative Evolution*, Bergson cautions that "Unless [intellect] does violence to itself, it takes the opposite course; it always starts from immobility, as if this were the ultimate reality: when it tries to form an idea of movement, it does so by constructing movement out of immobilities put together. This operation, whose illegitimacy and danger in the field of speculation we shall show later on (it leads to deadlocks, and creates artificially insoluble philosophical problems), is easily justified when we refer it to its proper goal. Intelligence, in its natural state, aims at a practically useful end. When it substitutes for movement immobilities put together, it does not pretend to reconstitute the movement such as it actually is; it merely replaces it with a practical equivalent" (155).

work. Appropriately, the author of the book's prologue–thus the person credited with mediating between the fictional narrative world of the book and the non-fictional reader of the novel–is none other than Víctor Goti, himself one of Unamuno's novelistic characters. Similarly, a key metafictional moment occurs mid-way through the novel. While in a discussion with Víctor (where the term nivola is used), Augusto is exposed to what is, in reality, the very plot of the novel he is living (93-94).[26] The most memorable use of metafiction, of course, obtains in the self-reflexivity near the end of the novel where Augusto Pérez the character travels to Salamanca in order to communicate with Unamuno, now a character in his own novel–effectively doing violence to the tidy categories of reality and fiction that structure our appreciation of novels. Yet even this decisive metafictive event is also buttressed by the novel's more consistent explicit discussion of the reality of fiction through Unamuno's incursion into the narrative voice of the novel, as well as by conversations between the characters Augusto and Víctor where Augusto questions his own existence.[27] Together with Augusto's trip to Salamanca, these narrative incursions and conversations posit that the best counterweight to the strict lines of intellect is a certain skepticism, an awareness of their abstract nature. Unamuno thus works consistently throughout the novel to critique the intellectual mode simultaneously at the levels of both form and content.

Niebla also presents a concise definition of the philosophical method shared by Unamuno and Bergson through the voice of the border-crossing character Víctor Goti who simultaneously enjoys the status of novelistic character and prologue-writer. Víctor's approach to the traditional and abstract lines drawn by the intellect, a method that he explicitly ties in with the purpose of humor, is to blur these lines, not to dispense with intellect altogether, but ultimately as Bergson advocated, to turn it back on itself: "–Y hay que

---

[26] "–Invento el género, e inventar un género no es más que darle un nombre nuevo, y le doy las leyes que me place. ¡Y mucho diálogo!

–¿Y cuando un personaje se queda solo?

–Entonces... un monólogo. Y para que parezca algo así como un diálogo invento un perro a quien el personaje se dirige.

–¿Sabes, Víctor, que se me antoja que estás inventando?..." (94).

[27] On page 116 Augusto ponders: "soy un sueño, un ente de ficción," and says "Tengo la manía de la introspección." See also 150, 160. The narrative suffers a break as Unamuno's voice takes over the narration on page 133 and again later in chapters 31 and 33.

corroer. Y hay que confundir. Confundir sobre todo. Confundir el sueño con la vela, la ficción con la realidad, lo verdadero con lo falso; confundirlo todo en una sola *niebla*. La broma que no es corrosiva y contundente no sirve para nada" (147, emphasis added). As can be seen in this statement, the title of *Niebla* points not only to the main character's aimless drifting about the city and his susceptibility to becoming wrapped up in lofty and abstract romantic ideals, but also to a philosophical method embraced by Goti, Unamuno and, of course, Bergson where the goal is to use philosophy in order to dissolve into the whole (*CE*, 191). Faced with the fragmented perspectives offered by the abstract categories of intellectual thought, this method of intuition has its challenges. As long as intellect follows its natural course, a fragmentary perspective that influences our understanding of both space and time ("Just as we separate in space, we fix in time," Bergson writes in *CE*, 163) will hide the real continuity of life.

> The truth is that this continuity cannot be thought by the intellect while it follows its natural movement. It implies at once the multiplicity of elements and the interpenetration of all by all, two conditions that can hardly be reconciled in the field in which our industry, and consequently our intellect, is engaged. (*CE*, 162-163)

The natural movement of the intellectual tendency of thought, however, prevents an intuition of continuity, offering only fragmented views of what is a continuous, if changing, whole.

In *Creative Evolution*, Bergson emphasized that philosophy has but one purpose: "Philosophy can only be an effort to dissolve again into the Whole" (191). There is, similarly, but one method of apprehending this Whole–namely intuition. Yet, because intuition involves "a certain effort which the utilitarian habits of mind of everyday life tend, in most men, to discourage" (Bergson, *CM*, 165), the intellect must turn back upon itself, holding its natural movement in check. Bergson eloquently describes intuition as the alternative to an intellectual path to knowledge.

> Let us on the contrary grasp ourselves afresh as we are, in a present which is thick, and furthermore, elastic, which we can stretch indefinitely backward by pushing the screen which masks

> us from ourselves farther and farther away; let us grasp afresh the external world as it really is, not superficially, in the present, but in depth, with the immediate past crowding upon it and imprinting upon it its impetus; let us in a word become accustomed to see all things *sub specie durationis*: immediately in our galvanized perception what is taut becomes relaxed, what is dormant awakens, what is dead comes to life again. ("Philosophical Intuition," *CM*, 129)

The metafictive device utilized by Unamuno in *Niebla* is in this sense a Bergsonian attempt to 'do violence to the mind.' More than merely questioning the process of literary representation that is implicated in the practice of writing, the incursion of the figure of Unamuno into the novel's text is an attempt to question the same limits of the abstract thought he denounced in his strictly philosophical writings.

As the complex narrative comes to an end, Augusto's encounter with Unamuno functions to free him from the intellectual prison-house of language in which he is trapped and novelistically return him to the extra-literary reality. In this way he experiences a rebirth in a sort of return to life from fiction. This return of course ends tragically–at least for Augusto as a character defined by his Bergsonian intellect–with death. Augusto's death is fitting in a sense, given Unamuno's insistence that intellectual knowledge runs contrary to the flow of life ("Para comprender algo, hay que matarlo" *DST*, 84), itself a complement to Bergson's similar insistence: "The intellect is characterized by a natural inability to comprehend life" (*CE*, 165). More importantly, it effectively illustrates of Bergson's insistence on doing violence to the mind and short-circuiting the approach of intellectual knowledge in order to return to 'grasp the external world as it really is.'

In conclusion, Unamuno and Bergson thus shared not only an historical time period but also a methodology embracing heterogeneity and contradiction. Unamuno's explicitly philosophical writings–and his novels as a manifestation of his philosophical thought–both referred to and breathed life into the same philosophical conundrums tackled by Bergson in his own works. Each philosopher relentlessly critiqued the abstract categories that, operating through intellectual forms of knowledge, encourage a fragmented approach to a reality that is, nevertheless, a fluid continuity.

JUAN BENET: RECALIBRATING SPACE AND TIME IN *REGIÓN*

> It is important to recognize that regions are 'made' or 'constructed' as much in imagination as in material form and that though entity-like, regions crystallize out as a distinctive form from some mix of material, social and mental processes.
>
> –David Harvey (*Spaces of Capital*, 2001, p. 225)

As a career-engineer turned novelist, Juan Benet (1927-1993) strongly personifies Bergson's ideal of reconciling science and metaphysics. Nevertheless, it is through the genres of the essay and the novel that the author evokes Bergsonism at its best, plunging the reader into the viscous fluidity of memory, denouncing clock-time and even recalibrating the notion of static space, now folded into a larger temporality. Most importantly–we need look no further than his own admission to find proof that Bergson profoundly influenced his work. In an interview published in *Los Ensayistas*, Nelson R. Orringer (1980) reveals novelist Juan Benet's admission that he had read Bergson's works in their entirety and consequently that they had exerted a great influence on him. Therein, Benet praises Bergson and underscores the great influence that the philosopher exerted on him as a writer in no uncertain terms:

> Esos tres nombres yo leí, digamos, por orden de aprecio: primero Bergson, que creo que lo leí en toda su extensión; a Dilthey, creo que lo leí en traducción en *Las ciencias del espíritu*; y hasta los ensayos historiológicos de Hegel, me llevó la lectura de Ortega [...] En cierto modo, si alguien me influyó en aquellos años, fue Bergson [...]. (62)

While this influence has certainly not remained unacknowledged by criticism, there are nevertheless only a handful of essays that explore the crucial importance of Bergsonism for understanding Benet's literary production at length.[1] In light of the priority allotted to Bergson by the author himself, it is important to see how the whole of his writing resonates with Bergsonian principles. This chapter thus incorporates selections from both his essays ("Un extempore," *La inspiración y el estilo*, *El ángel del Señor abandona a Tobías*) and his fiction (*Volverás a Región*, *Una meditación*, *Herrumbrosas lanzas*, *Del pozo y del Numa*) in order to underscore the Bergsonian character of his work as a whole. Through Benet's literary output there runs a perennial interest in the very topics that fascinated the French philosopher, from the limits of rationality and language to the contradiction between time as a heterogeneous inner reality (duration) and a homogeneous and infinitely divisible quantified representation (clock time). Ultimately, in his elaboration of the fictional realm of 'región,' Benet emphasizes a nuanced Bergsonian methodology that recalibrates the relationship between space and time and enfolds geography with mental processes.

Benet's Bergsonian roots are evident in his numerous essays where he decries the notion of a homogeneous time, argues (as Bergson did in *MM*) for a selective theory of memory and calls our attention to the spatialization that characterizes language, even invoking Bergson's name explicitly. Although he does not mention the philosopher by name, Benet clearly invokes Bergson's thoughts on time in an essay "Un extempore" from *Puerta de tierra*, originally composed in 1967 (Jalón 2003: 163). Begun in the wake of his brother Francisco's death, in fact on the first anniversary of his death on April 12, 1966, the essay is a more philosophical look at the passing of time and memory, which is itself appropriately "inmersa en la duración" (71). Benet contrasts the qualitative nature of memory, and thus the Bergsonian qualitative multiplicity of psychic life, with the quantitative act of marking time. In this, he revisits Bergson's notion of a spatialized time, that is, the problem of approaching a heterogeneous temporality from the perspective of a homoge-

[1] For example, Randolph Pope (1984) argues convincingly that "Benet and Faulkner find the origin of their formulations and questions in the common fascination that both declare to have felt for Bergson's philosophy" (114). See Mantiega 1984, Herzberger 1975, who also mention Bergson.

neous space which reduces it to measurable progression. For Benet, time is "la dimensión *heterogénea* con todas aquellas que hacen posible su llegar a ser" (73, emphasis added). Human beings do not merely experience the flow of time passively, as suggested by the Kantian supposition of time as an *a priori* condition of existence, but rather actively produce it, as Benet articulates:

> El hombre es una máquina de transformar tiempo en existencia: el producto transformado –lo vivido– [...] y de ahí que sea capaz de transformar lo no cuantitativo en un cualitativo cuyo depositario es, quizá, la memoria. (74; Bergson was equally critical of Kant's view of time: *MM*, *CE*)

This recalls Bergson's discussion of actualization of the virtuality of the past in present action (*MM*). Benet, echoing Bergson (*TFW*), discusses the fusion of the new ("lo nuevo") and the old ("lo habitual") that defines the present moment and draws upon his own innovative metaphor of the antique teletype (74-75; 72) to highlight the temporal dimension of novelty and the unpredictable nature of time.[2]

Benet's model of memory as discussed throughout this essay seems to be, like Bergson's, a selective one in which those memories that are irrelevant to present concerns are not actualized. In such a selective, filtered understanding of memory, forgetting plays as much of a role as remembering: "Olvido e imaginación son las dos funciones divergentes gracias a las cuales lo recordado y lo imaginado –en sus partes negativas, en sus partes de sombra, se diría– pueden ser susceptibles de volver a convertirse en existencia" (76; see McNamara 1996). Memory for Benet, presents a natural obstacle to consciousness: "La existencia –la transformación de tiempo en existencia– resulta ser una lucha constante contra la memoria, un intento de romper su cerco, una esperanza de volver a encontrar nuevas fórmulas de conversión" (76). Consciousness thus desires to produce the new, a desire which is frustrated by the call of memory that draws consciousness back to that which is already known, the familiar.

---

[2] "El tiempo que se transforma en existencia no se recuerda, no se mide, no se prevé ni se anticipa," 75; see also Bergson's "The Possible and the Real" in *The Creative Mind*, and the role of the élan vital in *Creative Evolution*.

Although Benet is not explicit regarding this point of connection, his view recalls Bergson's fusion of voluntary memory and involuntary memory. Memory, as Bergson articulates in *Matter and Memory* is never pure, but rather always mixed with perception to some degree, the latter understood as virtual action upon things, the intellect's tendency toward the outlines of matter. The co-mingling of perception and memory is reminiscent of the fusion of intellect and intuition that are the two directions of consciousness for Bergson (*CE*). It is the craving of intellect for the already known that turns thought away from the development of life in new directions. In Benet's novels, this tendency of intellect to turn from the movement of life itself frustrates his characters, whose intellectual need for stability is only intensified by the tragedy and ruin wrought of the Civil War. When real life manages to escape or overflow the designs of the intellect, even this newness, this change (remember Bergson's "Time is invention or it is nothing at all," *CE*, 341) risks being crystallized ("Un extempore," 76).

Another similarity between Benet and Bergson as revealed in the Spaniard's non-novelistic production is their common stance regarding language. The reader of Benet's fiction and essays, if there can be such a clear distinction,[3] will be familiar with the author's aversion to strict differentiations such as that which commonly obtains between language itself and conveyed meaning in the communicational model of language and a message that is sent and subsequently received. In this vein, José Hernández (1977) relates Benet's remark that "No, no es posible esa diferenciación [entre la lengua y lo que se dice]" (351). This is no offhand comment made casually during an interview, but rather a fundamental and crucial assertion that squares with similar statements found in his work *La inspiración y el estilo* (1966), itself a meditation on literary composition and criticism. Therein he refuses to distinguish between a work's form and content and similarly argues that an intuitive style envelops logical reasoning in a literary text (see also Compitello 1984). Janet Pérez (1984) also draws out Benet's reluctance to engage in traditional literary communication, stating that "Benet suggests that having clearly defined attitudes and beliefs to communi-

[3] Ken Benson (1993) writes that "Una de las características que salta a la vista al tomar cualquier novela de Benet es la interrelación continua entre pasajes ensayísticos y pasajes narrativos" (79).

cate (that is, a 'message'), may be an insuperable handicap to the writer" (19). This reluctance on Benet's part, however, is in no way an advocation of apathy nor a renunciation of thought altogether. Rather, it must be seen as an attempt to draw attention from the object of thought back to the ordinary machinations of thought themselves, an attempt to foreground the delineations of a now obtrusive and ever pernicious rationality. Benet's goal is to call attention to the way in which language works to structure and even restrict experience as thought takes on a routine and even habitual character.

Benet's acknowledgement of the insufficiency of intellectual models of language is couched in a broader critique of intellectual process that is also shared by both Bergson and Unamuno. Just as for Bergson "There are things that intelligence alone is able to seek, but which by itself, it will never find" (*CE*, 151), and for Unamuno "el más trágico problema de la filosofía es el de conciliar las necesidades intelectuales con las necesidades afectivas y con las volitivas" (*Del sentimiento trágico de la vida*, 19), one of Benet's texts reveals the corresponding idea that "el pensamiento nunca será capaz de saber lo que tras ella se esconde si no está acompañada de una ilusión emotiva" (*Una meditación*, 72).[4] Just as, for Bergson, quality always underlies quantity (see *TFW* regarding "the blows of a hammer" 121-22); for Benet, rationality is made possible only due to a preexisting chaos (see Merleau-Ponty's *Phenomenology of Perception*). In *La inspiración y el estilo*, he writes that either analysis bases itself on an enigma or else it is "una superchería que difícilmente le podía llevar al descubrimiento de cosas que no conociera de antemano" (72). This key emphasis on the limits of intellectual analysis is underscored by Bergson again and again throughout his philosophical writings. Bergson's trajectory from *Time and Free Will*, to *Matter and Memory*, and then through *Creative Evolution* exposes intellect as the tendency of thought turned toward things and toward action, toward the fulfillment of practical needs. The error of thought is to generalize from this practical basis and carry that generalization over into the realm of speculative thought. Thus while abstract categories serve a useful function in terms of meeting the

---

[4] This wording of Benet's in turn recalls statements by both Unamuno and Bergson: "Para comprender algo, hay que matarlo, enrigidecerlo en la mente" (*Del sentimiento trágico de la vida*, 84); "Of immobility alone does the intellect form a clear idea" (*CE*, 155).

practical needs of life, the intellect errs in taking them to be ontologically anterior to thought itself instead of a product of the latter.

In *El ángel del Señor abandona a Tobías*, Benet continues in this vein with a number of references to Bergson explicitly. The book launches off from Rembrandt's painting of the same name (1637) to pursue more philosophical ideas regarding language and the human being's necessarily temporal world. In *Creative Evolution* Bergson had famously denounced language for the spatialized form through which it cleaved the fluid movement of experience into qualities (adjectives), things (nouns) and actions (verbs) (298-304). Here, Benet revisits this Bergsonian idea to make the same point in the context of a philosophical exploration prompted by his discussion of the painting:

> Si la linealidad del significante procede en último término de la limitación del habla para moverse tan solo en la línea del tiempo, el arte discursivo tendrá que partir de aquella "desarticulación de lo real que consuma el lenguaje", tal como decía Bergson. Al aplicar a cada cosa y a cada acción un término significante específico la percepción lingüística fragmenta el continuo real en sus partes, la fluencia interrumpe, queda cortada la dependencia de la parte al todo y la acción secreta que el continuo espacio-tiempo desarrolla para manifestarse en quanta infinitesimalmente distanciados es suspendida y bloqueada en virtud de la fijación conceptual de los significados. (30-31)

Importantly, Benet also mentions Bergson by name elsewhere in this book-length essay (e.g. 42, 63, 111), pursues a Bergsonian line of thought when he compares human thought to a machine (47; c.f. *CE*, 306-07) and even references "duración" (65), "la paradoja eleática" (113) and "la religión dinámica" (146).

Nevertheless, the fundamental similarity between Benet and Bergson is not limited to a number of shared perspectives on diverse topics–time, language and representation, for example. Instead, the connection between the two rests on the sound base of a methodological similarity that comes to inform all of these seemingly disparate perspectives. This methodological similarity consists of the Bergsonian notion of internal difference: the distinction and interpenetration of two orders that necessarily cohabit in a complex whole. Benet shared with Bergson a methodological premise that started from two opposing yet interpenetrating multiplicities (qualitative and quantitative) only to assert their fusion in experience. In his philosophical works Bergson argued in clear prose for complex understandings of the composites he advanced fusing time and space (*TFW*), matter and memory (*MM*), instinct and intelligence (*CE*), static and dynamic religion (*MR*). For his part, as Stephen D. Gingerich (2004) brings out in an important essay, Benet also sought to reconcile the quantitative with the qualitative. Writing about Benet's work *Del pozo y del Numa*, the critic nevertheless produces a striking comment that may be applied to Benet's work considered more broadly. He states that:

> Benet creates an image of a discourse which situates itself between literature and thought by means of reconciling the difference between the two [...] For Benet, this process risks a failure to fulfill the goals of either one of them, offering neither the solid, demonstrable knowledge of science nor the mysterious vitality of literature. On the other hand, another kind of discourse emerges, which floats between the two, partaking sometimes of one and sometimes of the other. This is an uncomfortable position, resulting at times in contradiction and confusion, but valuable nonetheless. (335)

Significantly, many if not all of Benet's works, essayistic and otherwise, engage this notion of a reconciliatory discourse. With one foot in the world of the engineer and another in the world of the author, he had a unique perspective into both and was able to see the value of exploring the unitary, if variegated, folds not only between thought and literature, literature and science as Gingerich notes, but also those between history and fiction, the real and the imaginary, and ultimately geographical space and inner consciousness. Like Benet, Bergson, too, sought relentlessly to reconcile opposing multiplicities. He recognized that it is the qualitative which underlies the quantitative (*TFW* 122-23), and that the fragmenting tendency of intellection, due to its more immediately practical end, nevertheless covers over another mode of thought that is better able to address the whole of experience–intuition. For both Bergson and Benet, then, contradiction and confusion are necessary aspects of their philosophical positions and are in fact crucial in combatting the tidy and overly abstract categories that characterize the intellectual tendency of thought.

Imbuing Bergson's philosophical thought with life in his novelistic texts, Benet sought to address the conflict between intellect and intuition directly through the contradiction and confusion that are the hallmark of the stream-of-consciousness narrative style. Kumar (1962) underscores the key importance of Bergson's idea of duration and his concomitant, complex notion of memory for the stream-of-consciousness novel in general: "[T]he new novelist [...] does not conceive character as a state but as a process of ceaseless becoming in a medium which may be termed Bergson's *durée réelle*" (1).[5] He presents memory as the "essence" of the stream-of-consciousness novel, and here there is no more significant connection than that with Bergson. In *Time and Free Will* (1889) the philosopher first develops the notion of duration, squaring with William James's similar admonishment against characterizing psychic life as a series of states (*The Principles of Psychology*, 1890). This notion is not merely a reaction against a specific historical positivism but in fact, as *Creative Evolution* brings to light, a corrective to the natural tendency of the human intellect, which has molded itself to matter. The discrete nature of the material world of objects invites us to consider the life of the mind in a similarly discrete fashion, ignoring that it is the nature of life to *endure*.[6] This enduring, moving flux is indivisible.

In *Matter and Memory* (1896) Bergson gives more definition to this idea through the use of the traditional concepts of past and present. The past endures in the present. It has not ceased to be, instead it is what *is*, what continues to be. The past is all around us, a virtuality that may be actualized according to present circumstances and needs. Accordingly, grounded in the notion of duration, Bergson famously distinguishes between two types of memory–involuntary memory and voluntary memory (*MM*).[7] One is the memory in

[5] Silvia Burunat (1980) cites Kumar's study and suggests the three Bergsonian bases for understanding the stream of consciousness novel are "la duración, la memoria involuntaria y la intuición" (4-5).

[6] In this sense, Bergson is heavily influenced by the thought of Spinoza, a philosopher to whom he devoted an entire semester's Saturday class at the Collège de France (see Bistis 1996).

[7] These two types of memory were perhaps most popularized through Proust's novels, although the latter denied any correspondence to Bergson's theories (in all likelihood, he did not fully understand them), and the philosopher even objected to Proust's presentation of them. Although many casually link Bergson and Proust, the relationship between the two is not so simple. Proust believed his novels even con-

which we live and move, that by which we make sense of ourselves and our perceptions–the past that continues to be. The other is that memory conjured by an act of will that places us in the context of the different sheets of past. In the former lies our bodily memory, our habit memory, that which makes movement possible. In making use of the latter, we detach from the unfolding present and bit by bit receive the flood of past images. In the first we touch the actual whereas in the second we resurrect the virtual. What the stream-of-consciousness style allows the reader is thus a greater appreciation both of the enduring nature of the past and of the way that memory acts as simultaneously as a filter and a vital impetus for experience. For Bergson as for Benet, neither duration nor memory is homogeneous. The philosopher and the engineer-novelist thus both draw attention to heterogeneous nature of duration, memory, of consciousness as a whole and at the same time to the way this heterogeneity is threatened by the human intellect's desire toward homogenization. The chaotic flux of Benet's stream-of-consciousness narration is ultimately a complement to the philosophical (and phenomenological) return to the 'immediate data of consciousness' (as indicated in the original French title of Bergson's dissertation), *before* it has been organized by rational thought.

Another important aspect of the stream-of-consciousness style as used by Benet is its relation with Bergsonian intuition. In chapter two of his work, Kumar attempts to reconstruct "Bergson's Theory of

tradicted Bergson's theories of memory, which the former seems to have misunderstood [See Kumar (1962) 11, 27-28, for Proust's comments in this regard. Despite having read Kumar's study, Burunat (1980) seems to repeat Proust's misunderstanding of Bergson (10)]. For his part, Bergson presumably found *A la Recherche du Temps Perdu* too infused with analytical reason. Kumar (1962) writes: "Presumably, Bergson found Proust's novel, in a sense, a conceptual and therefore unmethodical representation of durational flux. The notion of *la durée* in this novel is analytically studied and formally worked into a theory of the novel towards the end of *Le Temps Retrouvé*. A real *roman fleuve*, on the other hand, would have merely presented the durational flow *méthodiquement* without directing it through the channels of reason and analysis" (18). As Bergson writes in "Introduction to Metaphysics," approaching duration analytically actually obfuscates the very object of knowledge (184-88). José Ortega (1974) continues this mistaken premise in his analysis of one of *Volverás a Región*'s characters: "La viajera se deja guiar por el impulso vital del instinto, para captar la conciencia de su pasado al que vuelve más por racionalización afectiva (Proust) que por sensación (Bergson). El retorno al pasado se efectúa mediante la apoyatura mecánica provocada por distintas sensaciones: coche (luz y sonido), el disparo, el picaporte que clausuró una época, etc." (149-150, see also 156 regarding *Una meditación*).

the Novel"[8] from observations published piece-meal across many of the philosopher's works. The stream-of-consciousness narration style is thus an approach that follows intuition rather than the intellect's tactic of objective third-person description. Through this style, the writer intuits the character's point of view and relinquishes his own in order to reach the goal of "coinciding with the person itself" ("Introduction to Metaphysics," *CM*, 160; see also *L*). This Bergsonian intuition of the character represents an implicit shift from one aspect to the other of the two cohabitating selves he discusses in *Time and Free Will,*[9] and emphasizes, as Kumar notes referencing Bergson's essay "The Soul and the Body" (*ME*), the unmediated rhythm of consciousness over intellect's limited view of experience (32). Writing, for Bergson as for Benet, thus moves away from the notion of communication as message produced within a given system of meaning and thus recuperates its role in the very production of the new (see *MR*, 242; also Benet, "Un extempore," above). The stream-of-consciousness style poses an affront to intellect, freeing thought from its assimilation to the borders of matter (*CE*), thus recovering the virtual past. Consciousness is no longer restricted by the intellect's focus on actuality, by perception's adherence to the world of things, but is instead taken off of the hinges that tether it to the world as already-given. The effect of the use of this style in Benet's novels is to underscore the devastating nature of material suffering and at the same time reclaim the possibility of a future that is open.

It is important to understand that subjective consciousness is, for Bergson as well as for Benet, merely one aspect of a complex nondual whole whose complement is objective reality. This seemingly discrete dichotomy is itself a product of the human brain and may be expressed in terms of any of a number of seemingly dualistic avatars: space and time (*TFW*), matter and memory (*MM*), intelligence and intuition (*CE*), and static and dynamic religion (*MR*). These complex models actually undermine their simple conceptual spatialization of two opposing but interrelated terms to ultimately posit that neither term may ever exist wholly in itself. The greatest achievement of *Matter and Memory*, perhaps Bergson's most impor-

---

[8] See also Kumar (1960, 1961).

[9] "Hence two different selves: (1) the fundamental self: (2) its spatial and social representation: only the former is free" (231).

tant and complex work, is that proceeding from the abstracted, dualistic and spatialized poles of perception and memory the author arrives at the notion of a perception which already includes memory, and likewise, a memory that already includes perception. This process obtains also in Benet's novels, which also incorporate Bergsonian thought by attempting to show the errors of a spatializing intellect to that same intellect. If, from one perspective, inner consciousness and outer reality are taken as the products of the human spatializing intellect, at the same time, these products are in their turn the raw materials for Benet's literary machines. This perspective asserts neither that the novel is "un anticipo de la obra pensada y trazada pero aún no ejecutada" nor is it "un texto epilogal," two compelling models entertained by José Rivero (2004). Each of these characterizations is the mirror of the other. To adopt either posture is to reify the work as an object, to uproot the novel from the varying flows which constitute it and which constitute its multiplicity of contexts. In contrast, as Bergson's philosophy does, Benet's novels function to show the errors of the intellect to the intellect itself, thus denouncing the quotidian function of the human intellect and recalibrating the relationship of space to time by subsuming the former within the latter.

Benet's first novel, *Volverás a Región* (1967), is an undervalued masterpiece of Spanish literature that relies on Bergsonian insights in order to recalibrate the relationship between space and time as it is understood by traditional intellectual thought. The novel's chaotic narrative style and multiple narrative perspectives, as noted by numerous critics, undoubtedly aid in this challenge: Esther Nelson (1979) suggests that the multiple perspectives of *Volverás a Región* obfuscate an objective perception of events, Malcolm Alan Compitello (1979) mentions the mixing of the non-focused narrator with other perspectives (16) and Josefina González (1995) further undermines the objective character of the first chapter of *Volverás* by teasing out the "tensión del lenguaje científico con el poético" that obtains in what appear at first glance to be unproblematic objectively-narrated descriptions of place (459). The novel's high degree of narrative complexity functions as a complement to the phenomenological tenet that space never exists in itself, but rather always in time as experienced, as always mediated, constructed while perceived. In fact, the book as a whole constitutes a concerted attempt to blend external space and inner reality–a reconciliation underscored by one of the narrative voices of the novel in what may be considered its distilled philosophical contribution: "La conciencia y la realidad se compenetran entre sí: no se aíslan pero tampoco se identifican, incluso cuando una y otra no son sino costumbres" (92). As in Bergson's philosophy, here Benet's main goal is not merely to problematize the act of intellection but more fundamentally to grapple with the interpenetration of qualitative and quantitative multiplicities in their various avatars: not only inner consciousness and outer reality, but more broadly even time and space.

One of the main vehicles for the novel's recalibration of the relationship between space and time is the theme of memory. Memory, of course, plays a fundamentally important role in the novelist's portrayal of lives in ruin during and after the Spanish Civil War in the seemingly fictional location of Región.[10] His characters' potential for action is overpowered by their memories, as evidenced by the fact that they often live in bewildered despair and also by the narrative itself, which frequently lacks dialogue and is best characterized as labyrinthine prose.[11] In interpretations of Benet's novels, the focus on memory has been so strong that they have unfortunately been reduced to exercises in solely internal complexity, a belief that is paralleled in the unfortunately widespread contemporary rejection of Bergson as concerned only with interior life. José Ortega (1974), for example, writes of *Volverás a Región* that "la verdadera acción tiene lugar en la vida psíquica de [los personajes]" (142).[12] Yet in both Bergson and Benet there is a thorough attempt to fundamentally reconcile spatial, material realities–conceived as external to the body, with temporal realities–conceived as internal. For Benet, as for Bergson, memory is not a self-enclosed and isolated world of its own, but rather the point of contact between space and time, two orders that are never separate in experience. Thus memory is not important in itself as a thing, but rather as a relation, for what it suggests about duration and the habitual tendency of the intellect. As such, instead of an escape from the outer world, mem-

---

[10] As many critics have noted, including Gonzalo Sobejano (1970), Benet's Región is comparable to Faulkner's Yoknapatawpha County and Gabriel García Márquez's Macondo.

[11] In the prologue to *Volverás a Región* he points out that the novel was initially rejected for lacking dialogue.

[12] Also, Sobejano (1970, 391). See also Janet Pérez (2003) regarding Belén Gopegui's work to be discussed in the next chapter.

ory in Benet's works is the starting point for the novelistic articulation of a nuanced philosophical approach to life in all of its temporal complexity.

This approach pointedly revisits what Bergson denounced as "the spatialization of time." By this he meant that the human intellect has evolved to treat temporality in spatial terms, by introducing a spatialized delay between received stimulus and response, between action and reaction (*MM*, *CE*). This character of the human intellect obtains most commonly in ordinary perception, which Bergson links to spatiality (*MM*). This is the part of thought that has molded itself to the world of things, objects with definitive spatial characteristics and discrete boundaries. Perception in this sense is merely our "virtual action on things." This spatializing tendency of thought, however, obtains not only in terms of spatial goals, locomotion, survival, but also in the more temporal aspects of life. Society in this sense institutionalizes this static character of experience at the expense of capturing real movement (*MR*). What this amounts to is that for Bergson, there are two different types of time. One is a spatialized time, such as that produced by the clock which conceives of temporal succession only through static discrete measurement, and the other is that temporal succession which is in fact the basis of experience and which cannot be divided without its changing in kind (*TFW*, see also Deleuze's *Bergsonism*). In the first perspective, the real flow of temporal experience escapes and overflows the static model by which it is represented by the intellect. In *Matter and Memory*, for example (esp. chapter IV), Bergson describes the error of this perspective through the paradox of Achilles and the tortoise. In the second perspective, although the static spatial model of movement is insufficient to explain real movement, this space is not opposed to but rather enfolded within a larger encompassing temporality.

Volverás a Región masterfully presents the conflict between these two perspectives of time, one spatialized and one rightly temporal, and suggests that the characters themselves struggle with these cohabitating, superimposed views of time. Just as will frequently occur in *Una meditación*, clock time/spatialized time is opposed to the real flow of temporal experience. Reproducing this struggle in the text, at times the word "time" is used to evoke either one perspective or the other. In fact, on the same page, the word refers both to real temporality, "un tiempo –no lo cuentan los relojes ni los calendarios, como si su propia densidad conjure el movimiento de los péndulos y los engranajes en su seno– que carece de horas y años, no tiene pasado ni futuro, no tiene nombre porque la memoria se ha obligado a no legitimarlo" (*VAR*, 93), and also to the spatialized time just negated in positing a greater unspatialized temporality, "El coche negro no pertenece al tiempo sino a ese ayer intemporal, transformado por la futurición en un ingrávido y abortivo presente" (93). The characters evoke time as "el orden odioso del tiempo" (114)–a time measured by that spatialized time Bergson documented in clocks and calendars, minutes, hours and days–while they simultaneously speak of an order outside of that time, an order which correlates with Bergson's conception of real temporality as unmeasurable and overflowing the world of space. Through their insistence on the common process of the human intellect, which severs space from its temporal imbrication and thrives on fear of the chaotic, the characters are paradoxically pushed into chaos itself, a movement only encouraged by the horrors of the Spanish Civil War which has left them in despair. The chaotic character of the novel thus not only represents the frustration of the characters' desires for stability, but also induces that very desire for the concept of stability in the reader him or herself. Here, of course, it is worth mentioning that this desire for stability has been suggested as one cause for the fascist uprising of July 18th, 1936.[13] The text denounces the very concept of stability and therefore targets the imposed official stability of "la España una, grande y libre" itself through passages that take on the house in Región (133-34), the structure of the family (137-38) and the myth of the bounded and homogeneous human community (139). The fact that Dr. Sebastián is trapped in hesitation (139-46), in a decaying house, unable to make decisions functions, is a multifaceted symbol that evokes not only an internalization of the horrors of war, but philosophically the unfortunate evolutionary "triumph" of the human intellect to delay action (see *MM*) and place itself outside of time in order to plan its action.

Significantly, Benet's first novel emphasizes geographical space and its seemingly objective character in isolation from human consciousness only to undermine such a simplistic perspective. Through reconciling the seemingly discrete categories of the real and the

---

[13] See G. Brennan (1943); Benet's "Qué fue la guerra civil" (1976).

imaginary, history and fiction and ultimately inner consciousness and external reality, Benet's fictional texts not only pursue the Bergsonian reconciliation of temporal (qualitative) and spatial (quantitative) multiplicities, but moreover act as a literary machine to recalibrate the relationship between space and time routinely simplified by the intellect. The title itself encapsulates the spatial context of the narrative in a larger notion of time–*Volverás a Región*, literally "You will return to Región" (translated to the English as *Return to Región* by Gregory Rabassa, 1985). From the fictional corner of Benet's novelistic world named 'Región' the title shifts from the focus on novelistic place to emphasize time with the awkward if not jarring inclusion of the future tense. This act, a displacement in every sense of the word, envelops the reader in a temporal flow, much as the conversational titles of the stories of Juan Rulfo (1953) did by embedding the reader in his Jalisco, México (ex: "Nos han dada la tierra") and much as the second-person narrations of Mexican Carlos Fuentes (1962a, 1962b) implanted the reader in a temporal flow that was and yet was not his or her own. Recalling the properties of a Leibnizian monad or a fractal, that is executing the same progression at any given scale, Benet's work as a whole accomplishes the same task as its title, thus restoring space to time and presenting consequences for methodological approaches to spatial practices.

The pages of *Volverás* continue to subsume the extensive spatial matter of Región in an intensive temporal flow. Moving from the work's evocative and representative title to its subsequent exposition, this transmutation of space intensifies. Criticism has appropriately signaled that the first section of the novel is devoted to exposition of the geographical space of the invented place Benet calls Región–that is to a rigorous description–tending toward the exhaustive–of its spatial dimensions and properties. Compitello (1980) charts out the novel's development of the spatial character of Región, noting a progression in the first chapter from questions of "Geography/Geology" to "Climate" to "Effects on Man," a trajectory that he asserts parallels the Brazilian Euclides Da Cunha's epic *Os Sertões* (1902). This entire first chapter of *Volverás* most approximates a third-person/zero-focalization "objective" narrator view in its depiction of a seemingly static landscape, and yet the sharp narrative changes that follow in subsequent chapters retrospectively challenge the ordinariness of this introduction. The novel's narrative shifts function to establish an initial correlation between objective narration and a homogeneous understanding of experience as spatial only to break that rigid perception through the development of a multiplicity of narrative voices (see Nelson 1979, Compitello 1979, González 1995). The effect of this shift is to assert a multidimensional view of space as the chapters progress. The reader is thus nudged away from the monolithic Kantian notion of space as a static a priori ground of experience, a notion critiqued extensively by Bergson, toward a more complex understanding.[14]

Although perhaps in the pursuit of another goal, Compitello (1979) suggests just such a complex and multidimensional view of narrative space in the novel. Discussing the anomalies of a tri-visioned narrative arrangement (16), he writes "I believe that a better image would be that of the superimposition of multiple transparencies each containing similar but not identical material, and each pertaining to one of the text's multiple narrative visions" (16).[15] With this in mind, even the region of Región understood statically –that is the Región detailed at the work's outset–is in itself a multiplicity, a production that, once again, drawing back from the mutually-exclusive either/or concepts of fiction and reality, imagination and reflection, pushes us toward reconciliation of these dualities if not toward a more thoroughly nondualistic model. Faulkner had his "Yoknapatawpha County," Columbian Gabriel García Márquez had his "Macondo" and Argentine Jorge Luis Borges had his

---

[14] Bergson rejects the Kantian description of space explicitly in *Matter and Memory* (306-09). Having done so, he then writes, "But suppose now that this homogenous space is not logically anterior, but posterior to material things and to the pure knowledge which we can have of them; suppose that extensity is prior to space; suppose that homogenous space concerns our action and only our action, being like an infinitely fine network which we stretch beneath material continuity in order to render ourselves masters of it, to decompose it according to the plan of our activities and our needs" (307-08).

[15] See also Deleuze's *Foucault* (1998): "a diagram is a map, or rather several superimposed maps. And from diagram to the next, new maps are drawn. Thus there is no diagram that does not also include, besides the points which it connects up, certain relatively free or unbound points, points of creativity, change and resistance, and it is perhaps with these that we ought to begin in order to understand the whole picture" (44). José Rivero (2004) also talks of the work in terms of superimposition: "Región y la representación cartográfica que nos propone Juan superpone las dos tramas citadas: la física y la política" (153). Of course, analysis must be careful not to limit the notion of superimposition to a finite number of maps/layers. Additionally, as the work of Henri Lefebvre and others makes clear, it may not be easy to maintain a strict opposition between physical and political maps.

"Tlön, Uqbar, Orbus Tertius"–fictional places being the hallmark of many great literary minds. Yet Benet's Región is no simple fictional place. He has not surgically carved out a place in Spain's geography where the reader enters a world contextually similar to but geographically distinct from its external referent. Rather, as Compitello (1980) suggests, Región is an intersection of two cartographies, one imaginary and the other real: "Among the place names that are a product of his imagination, Benet intersperses references to the real, if somewhat obscure locations in Spain. A check of a detailed atlas reveals that such places as Rañeces, Mampodre, Láncara and la Liébana do, in fact, exist" (44, n. 17). Even the description of the topography of Región recalls the (non)dualistic character of the human organ of intellectual thought, this mixture of quality and quantity, of time and space. As with the two hemispheres of the brain, we perceive two hemispheres in the landscape–the area from Región to the desert highlighted at the novel's outset is characterized by "dos valles parallelos" (7) and mention is made much further into the text of "la confluencia de los dos arroyos que casi por igual lo forman" (210). Like the brain's spatializing and thus dualistic process, the landscape is characterized by "la divisoria de los ríos Torce y Formigoso" (8). And yet there is also the enigma of intuition, the landscape unconquered by rationality. This is the landscape characterized as a "laberinto" (8), as an obstacle to human engineering ("hasta ahora, no ha sido posible construir una calzada," 8). Altogether, Benet creates an enduring image of the land as brain tissue, as a "serie de pliegues irregulares de enrevesada topografía" (8) in order to highlight the correspondence between inner consciousness and outer reality that constitutes the novel's distilled philosophical contribution (92, above).

Whereas the machine of the human intellect is bent on bifurcation, spatialization of what are components of a complexly articulated whole, Benet's work (re)produces the variegated union of cohabitating opposites in a regimented chaotic narrative. Space is reabsorbed by time. And yet closer inspection reveals that even the raw materials of Benet's novelistic machine, space and time, are not so segregated in themselves. Recalling the movement of Bergson's *Matter and Memory* as it regards perception and memory, the narrator's personalization of the geography of Región in the first section of Benet's novel as well as the quality and *style* of the initial spatial narration point to a space already infused with time, a quantitative realm already infused with quality (see *TFW*: "Hence it is through the quality of quantity that we form the idea of quantity without quality," 122-23). Ultimately, *Volverás a Región* functions, along with important advances in philosophy by Henri Bergson, to actually produce a complex articulation of spatial and temporal multiplicities. Departing from a perspective that, mirroring the habitual movement of intellectual thought, imagines space and time to be discrete, Benet weaves the space of Región into the chaotic psychic lives of its characters. In doing this he shows not that time trumps space, but that the former *enfolds* the latter. In this light, *Volverás a Región* must be seen as a complex work akin to Bergson's *Matter and Memory* whose effect, I insist, can similarly only be assessed through an understanding of the work as a whole.

Through the rigorous description of Región found in *Volverás*, and subsequently the similar descriptions of that place that obtain in later writings, Benet's work produces a cohabitation of the real and the fictitious thus problematizing a narrow definition of each. In so doing, the work resonates with urban geographer David Harvey's understanding that "regions are 'made' or 'constructed' as much in imagination as in material form and that though entity-like, regions crystallize out as a distinctive form from some mix of material, social and mental processes" (*Spaces of Capital*, 2001: 225).[16] As simultaneously imaginary and real, Benet's exposition of Región also recalls Bergsonian method in its reconciliation of philosophical idealism and realism (*MM*). This simultaneously imaginary and real character of Región obtains also in many of Benet's other novels, demonstrating the importance of this sort of reconciliation for the author. In particular, the many volumes of *Herrumbrosas lanzas* (1983, 1985, 1986)–themselves a sequel to *Volverás a Región* (if not its prequel)–develop this intimate and extensive entwining of historical and literary discourses further, taking the idea of region as both imagined and material to its logical conclusion and underscoring a complex model of experience in which consciousness and reality interact at a fundamental level.[17]

Perhaps the most obstinate sign that both of Benet's works share the goal of conflating the narrative worlds of Spanish history

---

[16] This assertion is strongly motivated by Lefebvre's *The Production of Space* (1974/1991) as well as Anderson's *Imagined Communities* (1983).

[17] See Guy Wood (1993) for an interesting look at the cartography of Región.

and novelistic fiction, and thus reconciling inner consciousness and external reality, are the crash of footnotes that thunder along the bottom of his pages. The footnote is the perfect tool for this goal because, contrary to what one might think, it did not merely spread from historiography to fiction. As Anthony Grafton explains in his inspired work *The Footnote: A Curious History* (1997), "Footnotes, in short, spread rapidly in eighteenth-century historiography in part because they were already trendy in fiction" (121). Footnotes achieve a particular resonance in *Volverás a Región* (and later in *Herrumbrosas lanzas*) due to their unusual function. Not only do they "form a secondary story, which moves with but differs sharply from the primary one" (Grafton 23), but they also "interrupt a narrative" (Grafton 69).[18] This function is unusually suited to Benet's multidimensional text and the reconciliation between temporal and spatial multiplicities that it advances in what it offers as a challenge to the tidy abstract divisions of intellectual thought.

In *Herrumbrosas lanzas*, just as in *Volverás a Región*, footnotes serve to interrogate the act of narration, play with the idea of linear narrative, and disrupt the traditional reading process. At times, the intent of the footnotes is more conventional, as when citations to other sources are made (470, 526, 536, 581), yet elsewhere the footnote is used to confuse, perplex and frustrate the reader, challenging him or her to question the limits of human perception and the notion of a linear and faithful memory. Often the footnotes undermine the main narrative of the volumes. Though some footnotes supply details of future occurrences (120) by describing the eventual deaths of certain persons (472, 473, 534), Benet's footnotes are likely to supplant the narrative voice of the text, leaping in only to let the reader know that there is someone else reading as if over his or her shoulder–"Si así pensaba, bien equivocado estaba" (101)–giving no more explanation. Others pose rhetorical questions (184), make editorial judgments on letters composed or discussed in the narrative's *histoire* (230, 167, 483, 573) or draw attention to disappearances that have gone unexplained in the collective memory (75, 397). The relative infrequency of footnotes (there is only one) in the

[18] The quotation continues: "References detract from the illusion of veracity and immediacy that Ranke and so many other nineteenth-century historians wished to create, since they continually interrupt the single story told by an omniscient narrator" (Grafton 69).

second part of the series can perhaps only adequately be explained by the insistence that this part most clearly "copies and simultaneously subverts the analytico-referential structures of modernist historiography" (Compitello 1991: 261) and therefore has no need for the footnote as a device that would accomplish the same goal.

Nevertheless, it is in the sequel to *Volverás a Región* titled *Una meditación* (1969, Premio Biblioteca Breve) that Benet's Bergsonism is most overt. Here, true to its title, the Spaniard's labyrinthine prose extends so far as to comprise one entire book-length paragraph. The novel builds on the complexity of temporal experience outlined in his first Región novel, denouncing spatialized clock time in favor of temporality proper and thus illustrating the flow of consciousness and the inextricable mixture of perception and memory in duration. In fact, purportedly drafted on one continuous roll of paper as a single extended paragraph of some four hundred pages, the novel itself seems to endure–seemingly almost untouched by the intellect's attempts to prioritize and organize. As is to be expected, Benet's writing has been frequently compared with that of Proust and Faulkner. Yet, despite its stream-of-consciousness narration and labyrinthine prose, *Una meditación* accomplishes a more straightforward articulation of the philosophical insights that Benet shared with Bergson concerning the intellect's habitual method that persists in the spatialization of time. By straightforward I mean to say that the work presents those insights that Benet articulated in his essay "Un extempore" (above) so directly, that in a sense, the novel is best understood as a philosophical novel in the tradition of those written by Unamuno, Baroja, and other turn-of-the-century novelists (see Johnson 1993). Considered as a philosophical treatise in itself, *Una meditación* articulates a fused vision of mental cartographies and material reality that bears remarkable resemblance to Bergson's own philosophical work. This influence is, as Benet admitted, direct, and as I explore below, substantial. The novel manages not only to incorporate aspects of Bergson's first work, but also touches on specific elements of much of Bergson's subsequent work as well. The reader of Benet's masterpiece finds direct and indirect references to the ideas Bergson explored in all of his major works: *Time and Free Will* (1889), *Matter and Memory* (1896), *Creative Evolution* (1907) and *The Two Sources of Morality and Religion* (1932). Nevertheless, it is the two-fold nature of memory itself that plays the largest role in this work. Memory becomes the point of entry into Bergson's philosophy considered as an organic whole. I want to briefly point out some of the significant connections with Bergsonism explored in the work before considering the novel's treatment of memory and time in more depth.

The philosophical connections with Bergson are more clear here than in his first novel, *Volverás a Región*. Despite the fact that Bergson is never mentioned by name, the Bergsonian notions of *durée* (279) and *élan* (vital) (373) appear in *Una meditación* italicized in the original French (and also in Spanish as "duración," 397). As with Unamuno's *Del sentimiento trágico de la vida* (see chapter two of the present work), here, too, there are embedded references to Bergson's idea of the cinematograph of the mind and its fragmented grasp of fluid reality (48, 49-50, 91; c.f. *Creative Evolution* 306-07). Here, just as in "Un extempore," Benet characterizes memory in two distinct ways. There is the memory that is inflected with intellect (which Bergson equates with perception) and the memory that reaches beyond perception into the past (which Bergson calls "recollection"). Intuition, not intellect, plays a role in the latter. Benet describes the intellect's imbrication in the former thus: "Para la memoria no hay continuidad en ningún momento: una banda de tiempo oculto es devorado por el cuerpo y convertida en una serie de fragmentos dispersos por obra del espíritu;" (45-46). Benet's text also echoes Bergson's distinction between closed and open morality, discussed at length in *The Two Sources of Morality and Religion*: "Aquellos que esperan de *una moral cerrada* el dictado de las normas particulares y casuísticas de conducta [...]" (236, emphasis added). Bergson's predilection for Xeno's parable of Achilles and the tortoise is also notably shared by Benet here as well, as the narrator returns to it on more than one occasion (92, 372). For Bergson, the paradox of Achilles and the tortoise showed illustrated the error made by the intellect upon approaching movement only through static representations of it. In Benet's novels, inclusion of this paradox works to highlight the immobilization of his central characters who, for all the pain and suffering bequeathed by the legacy of the Civil War are unable to act and are often stuck in physical structures, like the decaying house of Dr. Sebastián of *Volverás a Región*, that mirror the decay of their inner lives.

Intellectual models of language are questioned here just as they are in Benet's interviews and essays and Bergson's *Creative Evolu-*

tion where both writers note that linguistic spatialization separates fluid experience into things (nouns), qualities (adjectives) and actions (verbs) where there is only movement itself. This structured, grammatical characterization of language presents an insufficient model of communication that supplants reality with abstractions, with the concepts that are supposed to faithfully and transparently represent thought itself but ultimately constrain, if not determine, it. In *Una meditación*, Benet's narration notes explicitly that language is insufficient to explain reality.[19] It is too static to capture a fluid, moving experience of life.[20] There is nothing about the abstract nature of language that implies the successful communication of intended and received message: "Porque la abstracción es a su vez una abstracción: dos personas que hablan y se entienden haciendo uso de las mismas palabras están a menudo viendo en su interior dos espectáculos diferentes, ninguno de los cuales emerge a la vista del otro y sólo de vez en cuando dan origen a una emoción compartida y análoga" (72, see also Benet's remarks in Hernández 1977, above).

The stream-of-consciousness style employed by Benet, which indeed approaches its limit in the narratological chaos of *Una meditación*, neutralizes the typically intellectual need for abstract concepts composed along strict lines, such as those suggested by the intellect's own habitual perception of matter (see *MM*). The style is an attempt to show the intellect the pervasive nature of the way in which it structures and organizes perception. Even the highly-attentive reader struggles to find the end of one idea and the beginning of the next. Just as the form of Benet's novel denounces the abstract concepts formed by the intellect through its stream of consciousness style, its content argues against the use of static categories in philosophy. "En todo el pensamiento occidental [...] campea esa decisión de establecer de una vez para siempre un quid pro quo

[19] "No existe un verbo que defina la acción de fluir en el tiempo al conjuro de esos momentos que se arremolinan y encrespan [...]" (187), "tampoco existe ese otro verbo [...]" (188).

[20] "Por culpa de la misma simplicidad y sencillez con que un conjunto de circunstancias se resumen en una misma y única palabra que a su vez transfiere su significado emocional a una estampa fija e invariable –la que cierra el ciclo de recurrencia con una aureola de sentimientos intransferibles y malamente analizables–, el pensamiento nunca será capaz de saber lo que tras ella se esconde si no está acompañada de una ilusión emotiva" (72).

que trata de acotar, con cortaduras racionales en el campo de lo real, el continuo consciente del hombre" (279, in a letter to Carlos). This results in the overly-rational bifurcation of the real: "Hay que preguntarse por la razón que empujó al pensamiento a preferir la búsqueda de una frontera inexistente, en lugar de optar por la investigación de ese nexo único que enlaza fenómenos físicos y psíquicos y constituye la esencia del continuo consciente" (281). The problem in question stems from replacing reality with concepts, conceiving "la existencia en forma de categorías –ninguna de las cuales es real, como la gustaba decir a Cayetano Corral al distinguir entre física y psicología" (267).

Benet's second novel contests this bifurcation of a unitary, if variegated experience, into two distinct categories just as did Bergson's *Time and Free Will.* Here, the text opposes the opposing orders/multiplicities whose discreteness can only be assured by the simple designs placed on reality by intellect. There is "un primer modo del conocimiento –la serie de la conciencia" and "el segundo –la serie de la carne–" (162). This strict Cartesian duality is questioned by the text itself in the tradition not only of Unamuno's *Del sentimiento trágico de la vida* (1912) and *Amor y pedagogía* (1902) but also Bergson's *Time and Free Will* (1889; see also "The Body and the Soul," in *ME*). In every case, the emphasis is not on the divergence of body and consciousness, but on their uncomfortable union. As an important passage of *Una meditación* states, "[S]e diría que es la memoria la tierra de nadie que separa ambos modos del conocimiento y que ambos invaden en sus fútiles incursiones en busca del terreno del otro; así como la serie de la conciencia no encontrará el reposo mientras no intente elucidar los enigmas del dolor" (163). This struggle between body and consciousness, whose battleground is constituted by memory itself, is the real subject of the novel, and also the motivation for its hermetic presentation of that subject.

Here, just as in Benet's essay "Un extempore," the presentation of memory is in fact the most significant borrowing from Bergson's work. To understand how memory functions in Bergson's work and Benet's text it is necessary to dispense with the notion of memory as a closed, homogeneous concept. Memory, for both, is constituted by contradiction. For Bergson, there is one type of memory that imagines the new, and another which repeats the old (93, *Matter and Memory*). For Benet, although the term memory is sometimes used to refer to memory infused with intellect ("la memoria, [es] la facultad que controla y garantiza la repetición," 264), it is equally true that: "Tiene la imaginación su propia memoria" (182). In *Una meditación*, memory takes on a complex shape, one that is even self-contradictory, allowing the novelistic exploration of Bergson's philosophical premise.

The importance of memory is reflected in the novel's title, *Una meditación*, in the exaggerated stream of consciousness style adopted for the narration, and in the characteristic mixing of tenses that has become the hallmark of stream of consciousness writing over the course of the twentieth century. In tacit acceptance of the Bergsonian dictum that the past *endures*, the novel's narration at times describes past memories using the present tense as illustration of what Bergson called the actualization of the virtual past. The following excerpt shifts from an intellectualized representation of the distant past to its apprehension as enduring in the present:

> [...] asomó por detrás de ella con una expresión de ansiedad aquel que día a día [...] se iba configurando como prometido de la prima Mary. Se llamaba Julián y era un joven profesor de muchas cosas. Creo que la última vez que le veo está encaramado sobre la balaustrada tratando de seguir la trayectoria de una pelota de tenis que ha ido a caer en un bancal inferior, plantado de tomates (71).[21]

Here, as in the whole of the novel's single run-on paragraph, the shift is unmarked by paragraph transition or other such conventional treatment that would distance the past from the present. The effect of this is to dissolve the strict border between past and present raised by the intellectual need for discrete abstract concepts. Reminiscent of Bergson's notion of duration and its consequences for human memory, the past endures in the present, and is recognized by the degree of tension maintained by consciousness. The simplistic opposition of past and present is thus replaced by the tension

---

[21] The contrast between these two presentations of the past continues. After resorting again to the past tenses, the narration returns to the present to describe a past event: "Aún *veo* cómo su mano *acaricia* y *recorre* el copón verde cerámico [...]" (71, emphasis added).

between the virtual and the actual, and by the nuanced conflict between voluntary and involuntary memory.

Benet invokes involuntary memory as a challenge to the static and seemingly homogeneous society of the postwar period. In the novel, memory surges up unexpectedly, in the fashion of:

> esa frase musical que en una primera audición impresiona más al oído que al gusto y que una vez escuchada al poco tiempo parece borrada de la memoria que se niega a cualquier intento de repetición pero que, días después, en un momento insólito (casi siempre bajando una escalera) aflora completa y perfectamente conservada para poner de manifiesto las contradicciones de una memoria que registra y archiva pero que no recuerda ni obedece. (37)[22]

Yet this involuntary surge is accompanied by the voluntary act of recollection. It seems that Benet's narration is caught between the actual and the virtual, and between involuntary and voluntary memory.

Benet's description of the nature of voluntary recollection even recalls specific passages of Bergson's philosophy. Compare the following descriptions, the first from Benet's *Una meditación* and the second from Bergson's *Matter and Memory*. Each explores the act of directing attention toward the virtual past. As the body/consciousness adopts the appropriate attitude, the whole of the past surges forth:

> Al volver la atención sobre un recuerdo remoto que inexplicablemente vuelve a la conciencia y se actualiza, sin que haya intervenido una voluntad ajena a él y tras atravesar un extenso y sombrío plazo durante el que hubo de permanecer semiolvidado, toda un área de la existencia que envolvió a aquel momento comienza poco a poco a configurarse en una retina (porque el oído rara vez acompaña a la evocación y respeta una forma de componer la imagen, anterior a la voz, estrictamente silenciosa) en la que, emergiendo de un desordenado y azaroso ostracismo, van reproduciéndose ciertas imágenes recurrentes que se enlazan y refieren mediante una ley de continuidad que la memoria ignora pero que el sentido de lo vivido advierte. Así se produce un relato fragmentario y desordenado que salta en el tiempo y en el espacio. (*Una meditación*, 47)

---

22 Also pp. 43-44 and 45-46.

> Whenever we are trying to recover a recollection, to call up some period of our history, we become conscious of an act *sui generis* by which we detach ourselves from the present in order to replace ourselves, first in the past in general, then in a certain region of the past–a work of adjustment, something like the focusing of a camera. But our recollection still remains virtual; we simply prepare ourselves to receive it by adopting the appropriate attitude. Little by little it comes into view like a condensing cloud; from the virtual state it passes into the actual; and as its outlines become more distinct and its surface takes on colour, it tends to imitate perception. (*Matter and Memory*, 171)

These moments when Benet's writing clearly recalls Bergson's works, along with his explicit mention of Bergsonian concepts, confirm the author's own acknowledgment of Bergson's influence.

In addition to functioning as a philosophical treatise in its own right, an extension of the ideas he explores in "Un extempore," *Una meditación* is a brilliant novelistic creation whose intuitions regarding philosophy are manifest in the work's most captivating and pervasive leitmotif–clocks. In its capacity as a novel of memory, *Una meditación*'s single most important symbol is the clock. For Bergson, the division of fluid time into discrete, measurable units was suspect, the act of an overly rational intellect that does not organize so much as distort experience. During the nineteenth century, the increasing demands of a rapidly industrializing world were met by the machine-like regularity of temporal partitions. These partitions affected not only the hourly work day, but also the human geography of the earth as the 1880s saw the surface of the globe divided into time zones. In the face of this increasing desire to treat time as a homogeneous plane to be broken apart by the intellect, Bergson argued that this spatialization of time was suspect–qualitative multiplicities cannot be understood through quantitative means. Although some 80 years had passed from the publication of Bergson's first major work, *Time and Free Will* in 1889, to Benet's philosophical masterpiece *Una meditación* in 1969, this critique of spatialized time is actualized novelistically during a moment in which Spain itself is experiencing what many critics have pointed to as a crucial transition into modernity. Applied economist José Luis García Delgado's (1995) characterization of three periods of the evolving Spanish economy under Franco, the autarky (1939-1950), an opening to the exterior (1950-1960) and the exposure to international economic development (1960-1974), supports this view of rapid and palpable change.[23] In this social context, the clocks in *Una meditación* are evocative of the spatialization of time understood simultaneously as both a philosophical and a socio-economic problem. In the latter case, the stopped clocks signify a critique both of the stagnant nature of Spanish society under a dictatorship that touts conservative traditions and enforces limited, static ideals of citizenship, and also of the overly-regimented dependence on clock time requisite of the advanced capitalist countries during and after the Second World War. Thus clocks are at once a critique of both the Spain that has been and still endures, and the new Spain that lies beyond the horizon of Franco's dictatorship.[24]

Throughout the novel, the homogeneous nature of clock time, that is, measured time, is contrasted with heterogeneous, experienced nature of time. The "tic-tac" regularity of time's measurement juxtaposes with the description of passing of time as "un espasmo," "un susto," or "un santiamén" (112). To the positivist notion of incremental progression, *Una meditación* counterposes the unpredictability of experienced time and the instantaneous unformulaic aspect of change (94-95), thus recalling the vital impulse of Bergson's *Creative Evolution* and even the paradigm shifts written about by Thomas Kuhn in his *Structure of Scientific Revolutions* (1962). The novel equates real moving time with freedom whereas measured time reflects that which can be understood by

---

[23] "La economía española durante el franquismo tiene tres etapas bien diferenciadas. La primera es la etapa de la autarquía (1939-1950), caracterizada por la depresión, la dramática escasez de todo tipo de bienes y la interrupción drástica del proceso de modernización y crecimiento iniciado por el Gobierno de la República. En la segunda etapa (1950-1960) se produce una vacilante liberación y apertura al exterior que genera un incipiente despegue económico, aunque muy alejado del ciclo de expansión que disfruta el resto de Europa debido a las políticas keynesianas. Por último, entre los años 1960 y 1974 la economía española se ve favorecida por el desarrollo económico internacional, gracias al bajo precio de la energía, a la mano de obra barata, y a las divisas que proporcionan emigrantes y turistas." (www.vespito.net/historia/franco/ecofran.html)

[24] In this sense the dual critique made by Benet has as its precursor the figure of Mariano José de Larra, along with others of his generation, who in essays such as "Vuelva usted mañana" lampooned both the conservative monarchic backwardness of Spain and the over-eager industrializing French and their *afrancesado* counterparts.

the intellect: "El tiempo era ahora más real, más absoluto, más independiente de las manos y del celo del amo; completamente ajeno a la capacidad métrica del reloj" (113). To reduce real qualitative movement to quantity is to make time "intelligible."[25] In "Un extempore" Benet had already written of this mania for measuring temporality quantitatively through infinitely divisible clock-time:

> Que cuentan, no tiene duda; que saben que cuentan, es otro cantar. [...] en definitiva cuenta [el hombre] por miedo e ignorancia, cuenta en cada transacción, cuenta por diferencias, cuenta sustractivamente como esos chiquillos poco habituados al dinero que entran en el comercio, y van escogiendo objetos sosteniendo en la mano una moneda que no saben para cuánto les ha de llegar. (73)

This mania for measuring time is derided as childish as Benet's simile (above) also deftly highlights the connection of homogeneous partitioned time with the world of commerce.

The mania for measurable time in *Una meditación* is rivaled only by its overt critique through the depiction of broken clocks, which abound. Benet's central character Cayetano Corral spends his time attempting to restore movement to clocks and other mechanical objects (108). The stopped clocks are not an indication that the people live beyond or outside of time, but rather that the domination of time by spatialization, which arrests movement, introduces static structures into the fluid passage of time (Achilles and the tortoise), is now total. The qualitative movement of time has been reduced, arrested completely and totally by the bourgeois mentality entrenched after the war (see *Una meditación*, 120-21). The characters have not renounced the quantitative designs of intellect for the openness of intuition, but rather remain transfixed by the quantitative measurement of time, and even crave to subject the movement of life to its logic.

Ultimately, both *Volverás a Región* and *Una meditación* should be seen as the novelistic development of philosophical intuitions

---

[25] "Que una pasión tan vehemente se convirtiera en pocos meses (aunque la explicación de tal mutación hubiera que buscarla muchos años atrás) en esa tranquila, solemne y escéptica aceptación de un acontecer sin sobresaltos era algo que ni siquiera el reloj podía comprender" (111).

that he shared with Bergson and explored through his essays, a connection made all the more appropriate following Benet's own admission that the French philosopher's thought exerted a great influence on him. If his is a project of reconciliation, Benet's literary production also foreshadows the work of Spanish novelist Belén Gopegui. As the following chapter will explore, Gopegui's first novel, *La escala de los mapas* (1993), is arguably underpinned by a Bergsonian philosophy that even resonates with the focus of recent spatial theorists on the union of mental and material processes.

BELÉN GOPEGUI:
MENTAL AND CARTOGRAPHIC SPACE

> The dilemmas of space appear to lie in the way we relate to it: the way we understand and therefore transform, it. The debates between absolute and relational space, the dilemma between physical and social space, between real and mental space, between space and mass, between function and form, between abstract and differential space, between space and place, between space and time, can all be seen as indicators of a series of open philosophical questions: how do we understand space and relate to it? Does it exist beyond our cognition or is it conditioned by it? Do we relate to it by our reason or our senses? Is space a collection of things and people, a container for them, or are they embedded in it? Is it representing openness or fixity? Do we understand and transform space individually or socially? How do we relate space and time? In our response to these questions, we find ourselves divided between rationalism and empiricism, between materialism and idealism, between objective and subjective understanding, between reason and emotion, between theory and practice, between uniformity and diversity, and between order and disorder.
>
> –Ali Madanipour (*Design of Urban Space*, 1996, pp. 28-29)

THROUGH her many intriguing novels and film scripts,[1] Belén Gopegui (1963-) has established an enviable reputation as one

[1] These include: *La escala de los mapas* (1993); *Tocarnos la cara* (1995); *La conquista del aire* (1998)–on which the script for Gerardo Herrero's *Las razones de mis amigos* (2000) was based; *Lo real* (2001); *El lado frío de la almohada* (2004); and the script for Gerardo Herrero's *El principio de Arquímedes* (2004).

of Spain's most talented and successful writers of fiction. In fact, her debut novel *La escala de los mapas* (1993) won the Premio Tigre Juan in 1993 and the Premio Iberoamericano de Primeras Novelas in 1994. This important novel itself blurs the boundaries between fiction and essay building on a long-standing critical and philosophical tradition of Hispanic fiction–recalling such important works as Miguel de Unamuno's *Amor y pedagogía* (1902) and Juan Benet's narratives of the Civil War starting with *Volverás a Región* (1967), among many others. More than just a prize-winning story, Gopegui's Janus-faced narrative investigates the fictional world of its narrator-protagonist Sergio Prim at the same time that it examines the philosophical underpinnings of our treatment of geographical space–proving to be an insightful look into the intimate connection between mental and cartographic space. In effect, the work responds to a methodological crisis in geography[2] focusing on how space is produced–a crisis that divides unflinching materialists from entrenched immaterialists. Reconciling both approaches with one another, and finding the inadequacies inherent in each, *La escala de los mapas* asserts that a thorough answer to our interrogations of space must acknowledge "a notion of the material that admits from the very start the presence and importance of the immaterial" (703), as Alan Latham and Derek McCormack express so succinctly in their article "Moving Cities: Rethinking the Materialities of Urban Geographies" (2004).

Gopegui's novel proposes that we question the notion of an objective and static geographically spatial dimension and, in so doing, underscores an idea most clearly articulated in Henri Lefebvre's watershed opus *The Production of Space* (1991).[3] The novelist leads the reader precisely towards the Lefebvrian idea of space as a *process* that envelops both the notion of materiality and that of immateriality. I argue that an awareness of Henri Bergson's philosophical writings on space, time and consciousness–and the relevance of those writings to Lefebvre's project–most clearly illuminates the

[2] Academic geography has arguably been in methodological crisis since its inception in late Victorian England–see Alain Reynaud's *La Géographie entre le mythe et la science: Essai d'épistemologie* (Reims: Institut de Géographie, 1974).

[3] Lefebvre's work has influenced many more contemporary thinkers such as David Harvey (1989, 1990, 1996, 2000), Edward Soja (1996), Michael Dear (2000), Ali Madanipour (1996), Don Mitchell (2000), and David Thorns (2002) among many others.

novel's contribution to this understanding of a simultaneously mental and cartographic spatiality. Readers who are more familiar with the term 'space' as it is used in Physics or more specifically by Einstein may need to shift their perspective, as the notion of space used throughout this chapter will be a synthesis of Bergson and Lefebvre's ideas (explored in more depth in chapter eight of the present volume). To wit, it certainly bears repeating that Bergson attempted to dialogue with Einsteinian physics in his *Duration and Simultaneity* (1922), ideas which Einstein did not entertain at length, and that the volume *Bergson and the Evolution of Physics* (1969) offers an intriguing reconciliation of Bergson's interpretation of the physical sciences which "remains one of the least understood, least discussed and least appreciated aspects of his thought."[4] Nevertheless, the goal of this chapter is not to interrogate space from the perspective of physics (either in Bergson's time or its contemporary state) but rather to reconcile Gopegui's novel and Bergson's writings with the notion of space as it is being dealt with by theorists across the humanities and social sciences, namely Lefebvre himself.

Concomitantly, as I will show, *La escala de los mapas* places great importance on ideas of space and the in-between; therefore, I think it necessary to first explore the very construction of a discourse of the in-between, or what underwrites the latter–the concept of the interval. Because of the absolutely crucial role played by tropes of space and distance in the novel (the "between" and "empty" space), I will first interrogate the very concept of the interval, or the gap, in both common parlance and in seminal works of Anthropology by Arnold Van Gennep (1909) and Victor Turner (1969) before subjecting Gopegui's novel to a deep reading informed by the fusion of Bergsonism and geographical theory. As above, this is not the interval of general relativity, but an interval understood more generally as a space between things. In general relativity, for example, the 'distance' between two points in space-

[4] The volume includes republished writings by numerous physicists including even Louis de Broglie, the originator of the wave theory of matter, and its essays reconcile Einstein's method of intelligence with Bergson's method of intuition (210), Einstein's critique of Newtonian physics with Bergson's critique of static views of motion (214), among numerous others, suggesting even that "physicists ought to study Bergson's concept of time as a challenge" (229). Although it does not speak to Bergsonism, Peter Galison's book *Einstein's Clocks, Poncaré's Maps* (2003) offers a more readable take on Einstein's theories.

time is measured in intervals which are absolute and not relative. Here, as is appropriate given the present interest in Bergson's philosophy, we are dealing with the complex interaction between physical and mental space–primarily a non-scientific psychological negotiation of the material world that owes more to the spatial theories currently being explored in the humanities and social sciences than it does to Einstein's work.

As Bergson instructs, it is only possible to understand the concept of the interval from the perspective of a homogenous space whose nature is divisibility. This means that the discourse of the interval assumes the recognition of this divisible homogenous space and ignores that this recognition is only a view taken by mind. In emphasizing one tendency of a unitary experience, one part of a composite space-time, the focus on space necessarily severs another temporal tendency of experience, with grave consequences for understanding not only the production of space, but the possibilities and manner of constructing a world different from the one which currently exists.

Within the wider interdisciplinary realm of cultural studies, Bergson's philosophical-phenomenological methodology proves of great importance to concerns of spatial production. Culture is no longer to be considered merely another object *in* space. Rather, space (as that which is *in* things–Bergson 1889; Harvey 1996; Hewitt 1974) is now properly understood as constitutive of works of literature at the same time that it is constitutive of their reception and subsequent interpretation. As Deleuze and Guattari rightly assert in *Capitalism and Schizophrenia* (1987), there is no longer a tripartite world-book-author division, nor is there space "between" the world in which the book is written, the book which is written in the world, and the critic who as another object in the world performs an act of interpretation. Or rather, this division is a *production* that leads to false conclusions. The view (of intellect) that the world is a series of separate and distinct objects leads to the necessity of *creating* connections, a cutting and stitching together of a world that suits certain interpretations and leaves others to assert themselves by the strength of their inclusion or the deficit of their marginality. If, instead the world is understood to be a unitary, if variegated, experience, in which the relationship of each thing to every other is the starting point rather than the conclusion of investigation, then analysis of the boundaries and divisions that human societies have traced into the world (that is analysis of the production of space–the latter understood as difference) yields the very method through which exclusion is produced. In short, the posture we take on questions of ontology influences the questions we ask of methodology.

This suggests that between writing and world there is indeed no interval. In explaining the immanence of writing to world, there are several meanings of the word interval with which we must grapple:

> **interval** [...] *intervallum* space between ramparts [...] **1 a:** a space of time between states or events **b** *Brit* **:** INTERMISSION **2 a :** a space between objects, units, points, or states **b :** difference in pitch between tones **3 :** a set of real numbers between two numbers either including or excluding one or both of them **4 :** one of a series of fast-paced runs interspersed with jogging for training (as of a runner). (613)[5]

Unpacking these definitions necessitates the dismantling of erroneous conceptualizations of space. In the above meanings of interval we see a definite use of that spatialized time, the use of staticity to represent flow, denounced by Bergson and characterized by a trope of presence and absence, something and nothing, more and less. If there is to be a space in-between two things, objects or ideas, this use of the word space is made operative only by the concept of the void, the vacuum, emptiness, in short, the idea of nothing.

In his treatment of false philosophical problems (*CE*) Bergson asserts that the idea of nothing is in fact more, and not less, than the idea of something–that it includes the idea of something, plus its negation, plus the motivation for that negation. A similar manifestation of this false problem of nothing obtains in the use of a homogeneous space by human perception which is presumed divisible so that the body might insert action into a dynamic flux. The notion of nothing is created by the intellect in order to accomplish an act which necessitates the relevance of only that which interests us. That is, when we adopt a certain posture to things, others cease to exist–the idea of nothing is literally a place holder for whatever is not of interest to our task. A "space" of time between states or between events is only a space because we have first isolated the states

---

[5] From *Merriam-Webster's Collegiate Dictionary* (10th ed.).

or events that are of interest to us. In this "space" there doubtless continue to be other events, things, and potentialities which may be actualized as events or things. It is only that these are not of interest to our present intention. If we consider an "interval" of real numbers as such, it is only to the extent that we judge the boundary numbers as spatial frames. Over the interval of 1-10, the numbers "in-between" do not immediately interest us, whereas the numbers 1 and 10 in fact do. A "space" between ramparts is only nothing insofar as we focus our perception on the ramparts, that is if we extract the ramparts from a shifting temporal flux and infinitely populated material reality. To continue, the example of a "space" between musical notes is badly-framed, as it is the nature of each note (understood as part of a heterogeneous succession that Bergson calls duration) not to stop before the other begins but rather to *endure*. This example, too, is already imbued with the spatializing of time, for it is the will of the intellect to see staticity where there is none.

In contrast to what the above definitions of "interval" may claim, there is neither a "space" between musical notes nor is there empty room between objects in space (*TFW*). As Bergson contends (with Harvey 1996 and Hewitt 1974) things are not *in space*, but rather space is *in things*. Synthesizing the Bergson's conclusions in both *Matter and Memory* and *Creative Evolution*, the fact that we nevertheless perceive space "between" things is due to the fact that there is one intellectual tendency of perception that has molded itself to things, both evolutionarily and situationally, but not deterministically. The notion of interval as a "space between" is a practical one relevant not to our thought but to our action in the world, one which presumes a given intent and its corresponding division of a produced homogeneous spatial plane. The "space between" things cannot exist independently of a given predisposition.

The notion of interval in its capacity of empty space is of extreme interest here for the association that may be made with the anthropological notion of liminality. Most talk of "the liminal" today can be traced to Anthropologist Victor Turner's seminal study *The Ritual Process: Structure and Anti-Structure* (1969) wherein he famously defines it as "betwixt and between" (95). Before Turner, of course, there was Arnold Van Gennep whose study of rites of passage (1909), as Gustavo Pérez Firmat (1986) notes, presents a difference in scope from that of the former:

> Modern discussion of liminality begins with Arnold van Gennep's *Les Rites de passage* (1909), where the liminal or marginal moment marks the interstitial stage in the three-step process of ritual initiation (separation, margin or limen, and reaggregation). For van Gennep, then, liminality is a phase, a fleeting, ephemeral moment destined for supersession. More recently, Victor Turner has expanded van Gennep's definition by adding a synchronic dimension to the concept. According to Turner, liminality should be looked upon not only as a transition between states but as a state in itself, for there exist individuals, groups, or social categories for which the liminal "moment" turns into a permanent condition. Turner, in effect, supplements van Gennep's temporal, processual view of liminality with a spatial one. While for van Gennep the limen is always a threshold, for Turner it can also be a place of habitation. (xiii-xiv)

It is important to approach this description of liminality in spatial and temporal terms carefully. If Turner's affirmation of liminality is both temporal and spatial, Pérez Firmat is not clear from the outset about the process by which one is separated from the other. In the one case, the intellect represents a sequence of presumably temporally distinct stages. In the other case, the same faculty represents an array of presumably spatially distinguishable identities. In both cases, intellection must fix staticity where there is only movement. It of course needs be acknowledged that this spatializing intellect is indeed that which has produced the very ritual process identified by Van Gennep and Turner itself. Even so, the notion of liminality, be it temporal or spatial, is an opportunity to see the outcome of the process of intellection through the cleavage of space from time and the presence of immanence in representation. If the stage labeled by Van Gennep and the state of a people permitted by Turner are indeed liminal, this is only so with reference to an implicit overarching notion of structure. Liminality and structure are both tendencies that encroach upon the other, thus Turner's notions of structure and anti-structure. In a sense, what Van Gennep ignores and what Turner successfully recovers is a notion of liminality that escapes the spatialization denounced by Bergson. Liminality is no longer itself a thing, but like Bergsonian difference is present in all things as a tendency, complementing structure and cutting a diagonal through social hierarchies and geographical dispersions or spatial fixity. In short, structure from the outset constitutes the very liminality that is said to dispense with the former. Liminal bodies appear only at the end of two successive moments of structural production. Just as instinct and intellect, matter and memory, space and time inhabit each other, the liminal and the structural cohabitate. Just as there is a spatialized liminality and liminality as a tendency co-constitutive of structure, there is the notion of a spatialized interval that denotes a false model of difference and the notion of interval as internal Bergsonian difference.

Bergson uses the word interval to deal with the nature of the brain as telephonic exchange and also as intrinsic to the method of division where the interval exists not between objects of the same nature of multiplicity, but rather between co-constitutive multiplicities themselves. In this last capacity, interval is merely differentiation by tendency. First I will explain what Bergson says of the evolutionary function of the brain. In *Matter and Memory*, he imagines the brain as the interval between the afferent and efferent, the centripetal and centrifugal, nerves. In this capacity, the brain exists merely as an exchange between received stimulus and response. As an interval it has the capacity to delay, but not change the response embodied in action.[6] Yet the space or time between received sensation and performed action is of course only a liminal space conceived from the perspective of a sensory-motor structure. It is also necessary to point out that in this usage of the term interval, Bergson is necessarily using the vocabulary of an intellect whose activity is of an entirely spatializing nature. Nevertheless, the true difference to which the notion of interval applies is the difference in kind between tendencies which Bergson articulates as the whole of his methodology. This interval is neither the distance between objects nor subsequently the difference between concepts as objects of thought, but merely the difference in nature between two tendencies that cohabitate. As Merleau-Ponty explains in *Phenomenology of Perception*:

> Even the unity of ordinary things, which a child may handle and move about, does not amount to establishing their substantiality.

[6] This idea is clearly relevant to Deleuze as Gregory Flaxman's (2000) volume shows, and as we find in *Cinema II: The Time-Image* where the "time-image" is itself a breakdown in the Bergsonian sensory-motor scheme of the mobile body. I will be able to devote more time to this filmic discussion in chapter five of the present work.

> If we set ourselves to see as things the intervals between them, the appearance of the world would be just as strikingly altered as is that of the puzzle at the moment when I pick out "the rabbit" or "the hunter". There would not simply be the same elements differently related, the same sensations differently associated, the same text charged with a different sense, the same matter in another form, but in truth another world. (18)

The interval presents two directions which may be followed, but in the tracing of each direction we move further and further away from their convergence, from their cohabitation as indivisible tendencies, and it is thus that we reify each tendency as an object of thought. The notion of liminality in this way works against the static lines drawn by spatializing thought. It does not represent the distance between things or states, as does the notion of the interval in a general sense, but instead provides the opportunity to assess the limitations of fixed structures and perspectives and to reconcile worlds which are seen as being discrete.

Much criticism is fascinated by the notion of an interval between writing and world which it never questions. It drives either to investigate what has happened in the space between author and text, or what has occurred between text and reader. This is the effect of an analytical gaze, to devise a plan, to impose a structure, and thus to separate a plane of production off from a plane of reflection. But reflection *is* production. The method of approaching literary texts I appropriate in this meditation, then, is driven not by the need to interpret, not to merely show *what is there* in the works, nor to show what *is placed there* by the act of analysis. Each of these paths, in diverging from the other, creates an imbalance where there can only be coexistence. Rather, I hope to trace the natural lines of articulation in the works being manipulated as Plato's good cook, for the real object of enquiry cannot be the books themselves, but the very way of perceiving the works. In this sense, interpreting/producing literature is no different from interpreting/producing city-space. In either case it is the same movement of intuition that must be brought to bear upon the natural bent of the intellect, not so that we can reach a better interpretation of a finished work, or a finished city, but rather so that we understand how it is that we produce the same problem in the means of a solution, how process itself is indivisible and how the human act of intellection partitions an immanency of space-time.

In apparently juxtaposing Sergio Prim, the interval-seeking narrator and Brezo Varela, his unattainable love, Gopegui's novel sets up a straw-man philosophical dichotomy between affect and action, between subjectivity and objectivity, between the purely theoretical poles of ideal and real consciousness, ultimately to affirm Bergson's maxim that "all consciousness *is* something" over Edmund Husserl's weakened version–"all consciousness is consciousness *of* something" (Deleuze, *Cinema 1: The Movement-Image*, 56). More importantly, the Bergsonian idea that existence is an unceasing movement occurring in an ever-expanding duration takes shape amidst a discourse of geographical processes and scales centered on Madrid. Gopegui's resulting elegant take on the production of space highlights the notion of spatial process as a movement at once material and symbolic, with implications regarding whose mental maps achieve cartographic form. Ultimately the novel successfully negotiates those very questions important to the study of cultural and urban geography–inquiring into the very nature of space as well as the method through which space is simultaneously shaped by both action and thought itself.

Although I will focus more specifically on the link that Gopegui's text realizes with questions of cultural geography, the present examination of novelistic form and philosophical methodology is meant to evoke larger questions of perception and even consciousness itself. The questions that Bergson asked of consciousness through his works are by no means relegated to the dustbin of the history of philosophy, but are themselves indicative of the *enduring* nature of the Bergsonian conception of past itself. In an article that appeared in the *New York Review of Books* (January 15, 2004) titled "In the River of Consciousness," Neurologist Oliver Sacks, in fact, returns to Bergson's *Creative Evolution* (1907) in order to explore the renewed interest in theories of perception which posit a discontinuous apprehension of reality.[7] As Sacks, Bergson

[7] This philosophical problem of the discontinuous apprehension of reality is at the core of Bergson's writings. This spatialization of reality is in fact the tendency of life which has obtained evolutionarily in the function of the human intellect (although as he explains as part of both in *Creative Evolution* and *Matter and Memory* this tendency exists in the whole of duration itself). As Bergson explains, this spatialization is caused by the fact that the human intellect has continuously molded itself to matter. My more-than-passing interest in the writings of Sacks leads me to suggest that the whole of his approach to the mind-body-world problem squares

and Gopegui are aware, however, admitting that we may perceive reality in a discontinuous manner does not mean that reality is itself discontinuous. Rather, our experience in and production of a shared reality is tied in great measure to our perception of the world through static images, models and mechanisms. *La escala de los mapas* seeks to draw attention to the way these mechanisms influence our understanding and production of personal, social and even urban space.

I will first show how the novel sets up the binary structure of subjectivity and objectivity, of affect vs. action, through the characters Sergio and Brezo, respectively the literary representations of these oppositions. I will then explore the Bergsonian metaphor of the cinematograph of the mind as it presents itself in the text in order to draw attention to the false divisions created by the mind–divisions which for Bergson are the very essence of a false spatiality abstracted from and imagined as distinct from temporality. Subsequently I will show how, through the concept of the "intervalo" or "hueco," Gopegui constructs a narrative attentive to the problem of uniting affect and materiality and yet unwilling to accept the very way this question is posed. The protagonist's conception of a space *between* the mental and the cartographic illustrates what for Bergson is a spatializing tendency of perception. Notably, Gopegui's novel reveals the insufficiency of this tendency much as the philosopher's *oeuvre* does. Moreover, I will emphasize that the geographical content of the novel highlights the appropriate application of Bergson's ideas on space to geography. Ultimately, the triple fusion of Gopegui's *La escala de los mapas*, Bergson's philosophy and geography constitutes a unique call for the way in which we perceive space, now neither wholly mental nor purely material, but a process from which the human intellect extracts either one or the other, forming those very simplistic dichotomies that drive the novelistic Sergio Prim to anguish.

Simply put, *La escala de los mapas* is the story of geographer

---

quite well not only with phenomenological philosophy and psychology but perhaps more specifically with the writings of Bergson on consciousness. To explore this connection more adequately, however, would be to adopt quite a different focus than that of the present chapter. Nevertheless, let me conclude this diversion by stating that there is still support Bergson's musings on memory (see McNamara 1996). Readers may wish to consult the discussion on Sacks's article by Benjamin Libet et al. and also appearing in the *New York Review of Books*, April 8, 2004.

Sergio Prim's longing for his love interest, Brezo Varela, also a geographer. The former character documents his yearning through a continual surge of emotions, thoughts and memories, ultimately seeking a gap in space through which he would be able to finally connect with the object of his passions. These memories, thoughts and emotions all but completely eclipse the action of the novel understood in the traditional sense of a sequence of events. This is a direct result of the narrator's (Sergio's) clear desire to immerse himself in his own ruminations at the expense of the world around him. In the last chapter he clearly reveals how he has been attempting to hide from reality–"Brezo, aunque la realidad me busque, no podrá dar conmigo. Para esconderse, ahora lo entiendo, conviene elegir el sitio donde nadie supondría que nos íbamos a esconder" (229). It is somewhat problematic to summarize the plot of Gopegui's novel further for the reader. This difficulty is not solely a function, as I will have chance to explore, of the narrator's insistence upon what might all too easily be termed mental or psychic activity–the constant flux of emotions and memories that pervade and organize the work–although this is perhaps the primary obstacle. Rather, creating a short synopsis of the work is made more complex by the text's nuanced and clever narrative structure. At the risk of introducing this narrative complexity before it is entirely appropriate to do so, let it suffice to state that the novel's action–the part that exceeds the protagonist's important mental involutions–is to be read only secondarily, and that the largely (but not wholly) first-person narrative style precludes a so-called 'direct' apprehension of the novel's events at the level of plot. In lieu of a chapter-by-chapter summary of the work, then, I hope to give a sense of its trajectory by means of the text's presentation of its major characters through the philosophical opposition of reality to ideality. This opposition, as I will show, is undeniably emphasized throughout the work–and yet as I will argue, the effect of the novel is ultimately to question this dichotomization.

Few previous studies have taken on the complex philosophical core of *La escala de los mapas*.[8] When the novel has been mentioned it has proved tempting to limit discussion of the novel's two (necessarily one-dimensional) protagonists to notions of fixed dichotomies.

---

[8] Nevertheless, Judith Drinkwater (1995) unites body and space in an excellent reading of the novel as part of her essay.

One such example is to be found in Janet Pérez's "Tradition, Renovation, Innovation: The Novels of Belén Gopegui" (2003). The critic sets out to explain Gopegui's novels, including *La escala de los mapas*, in terms of "the dichotomy of dreams or illusion versus reality" (128). She explicitly calls attention to problems of ontology, and shows convincingly how one or another of these poles comes to be predominant in the novels under consideration, thusly finding the novel to be examined here an example in which idealism obscures realism. Yet, I would like to expand Pérez's discussion of ontology in order to focus on the very division between the real and the ideal. In ignoring that this dichotomy is created by a certain tendency of the intellect, the split serves to affirm the ontological status of its avatars, namely affect/action and mental/cartographic space. This limitation ignores that Gopegui's novel indeed seeks to challenge these very boundaries, and thus leads to the mistaken conclusions that "Readers have no objective external referent, no third-person omniscient narrator, no other narrative voice or character's judgment to help them distinguish between what happens in reality and what exists only in the mind of the protagonist" (120) and "Although Gopegui presents the urban landscape in realistic fashion together with contemporary social and historical attributes of the metropolis, interaction between this setting and the characters of *La escala* is minimal: the important 'action' is psychic, occurring largely within enclosed spaces, often within the characters themselves" (119). I disagree, and would offer that these conclusions are in fact already given at the moment one severs affect from action, internal mind from external reality, memory from matter.

On the contrary, releasing these constructed separations, and finding the complex cohabitation of one in the other provided by Bergson's phenomenology, reveals the text as a rich commentary on reality, on matter, and on the production of space. In *Matter and Memory* (1896) Bergson writes on the inadequacy of the real/ideal dichotomy:

> The realist starts, in fact, from the universe, that is to say from an aggregate of images governed, as to their mutual relations, by fixed laws, in which effects are in strict proportion to their causes, and of which the character is an absence of center, all the images unfolding on one and the same plane infinitely prolonged. But he is at once bound to recognize that, besides this system, there are *perceptions*, that is to say, systems in which these same

> images seem to depend on a single one among them, around which they arrange themselves on different planes, so as to be wholly transformed by the slightest modification of this central image. Now this perception is just what the idealist starts from: in the system of images which he adopts there is a privileged image, his body, by which the other images are conditioned. But as soon as he attempts to connect the present with the past and to foretell the future, he is obliged to abandon this central position, to replace all the images on the same plane, to suppose that they no longer vary for him, but for themselves and to treat them as though they made part of a system in which every change gives the exact measure of its cause. (14-15)

Bergson argues that these two poles of consciousness, the real and the ideal, the consciousness in things and the consciousness in living beings as indeterminate centers of action, are necessarily and intimately connected. This relationality becomes concretely symbolic in Gopegui's work through the two characters, Sergio and Brezo, whose relationship constitutes a literary metaphor for that very relation between the consciousness of things and the consciousness of living beings.

As is made quite clear in the text, Sergio represents the pole of ideality, an abstracted, receptive center of affect; Brezo is the pole of reality, the distant center of indeterminate action. Sergio Prim is identified with the pole of ideality through metaphors that weaken his physical, and thus corporeal, real presence. He is described as "pequeño" (19, 145). His body is puny, weak and "casi ficticio" (12-13). He is "un hombre tan pasivo" (38). Metaphors of interiority heighten this identification. His narrative is filled with memories, he seeks mental escape (52), seeks to "recolectar imágenes" (70) as an outward projection of his internal memory collector, he envies the *action* of his peers (51), he is "un ser de emoción" (53). The text underlines his "intimidad poblada" (87) in opposition to "los cuerpos venidos del exterior" (20-21). He is a small Sergio (65), a Sergio "imaginario" (65) who prefers to surround himself with "una difusa constelación afectiva" (29). Though he lives in affect, he is unable to exteriorize his feelings or to act (27, 153). His movement in space is clumsy (23), he doesn't calculate the distance between himself and objects well (44), and not surprisingly he is "el único estudiante de geografia que no le gustaba viajar" (44). He even rants against materiality explicitly:

> Contra la fisiología. Contra esta humana dependencia de ser abrazado, tocado, lamido con minúscula delicadeza por una lengua exacta. Me gustaría escribir contra la fisiología, porque la fisiología es imposible. No quiero salir a la vida, no quiero bajar a las tiendas a comprar latas ni arroz, tú eres mi concha, Brezo, quiero quedarme en ti. (58)

His lack of camaraderie with material things is revealed in his need for glasses to focus or magnify the physical world (21) and the centrifugal connection he has with reality within which he feels the sensation of smoke *before* noticing others smoking (21)–affect and sensation before perception. His is not the world of things but that of his own "feraces jardines imaginarios, el ensueño" (62). His is a universe closed and enveloped by an affect that desires itself: "que mi pasión no se repliegue, amiga, que mi pasión fluya por un espacio blanco y libre de realidad, por esta ruta apaisada que voy trazando" (91). In many instances he explicitly opposes himself to reality (87, 102, 105, 138, 172). He is the second half of the book title he shows Brezo: *La realidad y el deseo* (30), a being of desire living in "el peligroso mundo de las sensaciones" (170) as his boss Doña Elena describes it. He toys with the intellect itself as others might play chess (51), needing of course no physical pieces.

Likewise, Brezo Varela is the abstracted pole of reality, movement, action upon things. Her materiality is expressed in the physical term of 'agility' (16, 19); she needs to know the whereabouts of *things* (87). Sergio notes that "[Brezo,] tú mandas sobre los objetos" (152). She is the reality opposed to Sergio's musings on Berkeley's idealist philosophy (89, 135, 155, 169). Sergio describes her as action incarnate:

> El mundo quiere pruebas, flor traída del dueño, dinosaurio. El mundo, por lo general, detesta la retórica, desconfía de los verbos mentales: recordar, creer, pensar, suponer, fantasear, representarse. Esas gentes extravertidas que atruenan con su claridad en absoluto prestan oídos a la imaginación. *El mundo y tú, Brezo, que estabas en el mundo, exigíais actos, estabais en tratos con la realidad.* (183, emphasis added)

His association to intellectual verbs such as "to remember," "to believe," "to think," "to suppose," "to fantasize" and "to represent" contrasts with Brezo's links with reality, actions, and the world. Due to his imprisonment is his own mind, his perception cannot capture real movement but rather only catches a jump shot of Brezo's action in the world: "En el último rincón estabas tú, pero ya te habías levantado, venías hacia mí" (26). By the time he mentally captures and processes Brezo's location at one instant, she has already moved to another. She is a corporeal presence identified with objective things, supposedly uninflected by that desire to which Sergio clings. In the following quotation, Brezo is clearly identified with this physical movement, while Sergio links himself instead with mental flow:

> Brezo, tú eres el énfasis que no tuve, eres la alacridad puesta delante de mi monotonía. Yo soy un hombre introvertido, manantial subterráneo, corriente prisionera, mientras que tú, catarata, te extroviertes pintando de blanco empapado fragmentos de la atmósfera. Tú desconoces la palabra reserva, el acto de acumular imágenes, emociones para el invierno. (59)

Brezo is not equipped to express emotions, but rather only "un relato inconexo de su vida sentimental" (64).

Together, Sergio and Brezo represent in human sexual union the relational union of material and idea, "yo era lo ajeno, y ella me habitaba" (20), "Ella existió en mí" (19). Problems between the two, often glossed in terms of communication, engender the encounter between the mental and the material. Sergio "exigía que el gesto ratificara siempre al sentimiento, que el enunciado fuera reproducción exacta del mensaje interior" (89) while Brezo's connection with the sentimental remains unexplored. Sergio is thus imagined as a subjective experience cut off in many ways from action itself while Brezo is pure movement, lack of reflection and sensation. The ideal consciousness that presents itself in the human organism as a center of indetermination or a screen between received action and its corresponding delayed action (Sergio) contrasts with the real consciousness of things themselves, discussed by Bergson as a plane of images where each interacts with all the others constantly on all of their sides (Brezo). If the realization of this theoretical model is problematized through the appearance of each pole in a distinct novelistic human consciousness this is only an effect of the literary metaphor that Gopegui employs to represent the cohabitation of real and ideal consciousnesses on what Deleuze, following Bergson's nondualistic ontology, terms the 'plane of immanence' through a human relationship.

That their relationship is a failure is attributed to the fact that the pole of individual consciousness has been cut off from action. The implication is that to give in to affect, or to sever affect from action is to attempt to interrupt the ever-changing flow that is duration. It is not that affect without action is not real. In fact, undermining Sergio's own implicit claims to the contrary, the reader is convinced that affect as expressed by Sergio's self-absorbed narrative has very real properties (and one cannot exist without the other). Rather, as Lefebvre's (1991) triadic model of the production of space outlines, space is experienced, perceived and conceived–spatial practices, representations of space and spaces of representation all engender the real movement of spatial processes (33). There is no thought without action, no action without thought. Sergio and Brezo are thus necessary foils for one another, whose separation illustrates the practice of a false spatiality described by Bergson in *Creative Evolution* (1907) using the metaphor of the "cinematograph of the mind."

Bergson argues in *Creative Evolution* (1907) that the function of the human intellect, of a necessarily "spatial" character, is to insert indeterminate action into the continual movement of experience. This is done by fragmentation, as this oft-quoted passage explains:

> We take snapshots, as it were, of the passing reality, and, as these are characteristic of the reality, we have only to string them on a becoming, abstract, uniform and invisible, situated at the back of the apparatus of knowledge, in order to imitate what there is that is characteristic in this becoming itself. Perception, intellection, language so proceed in general. Whether we would think becoming, or express it, or even perceive it, we hardly do anything else than set going a kind of cinematograph inside us. We may therefore sum up what we have been saying in the conclusion that the *mechanism of our ordinary knowledge is of a cinematographical kind.* (306, original emphasis)

Nevertheless, as Bergson emphasizes, matter does not present itself as fragmented snapshots. These intellect-snapshots divide the flow of movement, separating qualities from things from actions, adjectives from nouns from verbs, affect from action and thought from the material world (298-304). Bergson shows that qualities fade into other qualities, that thingness vanishes, that adjectives and nouns thus cannot capture movement. He writes in *Matter and Memory* (1896) that affect is a material process, that centripetal and centrifugal movements of the nervous system are continuous and that the brain merely introduces an interval between the two in order to act. This interval, this cinematographic character of the intellect, this tendency, however practical it may be considered, to introduce separations into what is but flux is what readers of Bergson may recognize as the "spatialization of time," a notion which the philosopher never ceases to denounce, but which is just as frequently misunderstood as it is recognized. The prevalence of references to the cinema in the novel makes clear Sergio's mania to divide and to "spatialize," thus abstracting objectivity from subjectivity and closing off action from affect. At the same time, these references lead the wary reader, or the reader familiar with Bergson's phenomenology, to question such easy compartmentalizations. The cinema thus appears explicitly in the novel in three ways: as seemingly trifling detail, as symbol for memory and most of all as structure–the latter paradoxically evocative of Bergsonism.

As detail, it deceptively appears to warrant little attention. Sergio describes a kiss from Brezo to her father as a "beso de cine mudo" (43), her haircut as "su peinado de actriz de cine" (53) and her gait as "una invención cinematográfica" (82). He seeks asylum in the "sombras móviles de una película" (48) and laments the times when "no había cine" (50) while Brezo works "el cine" innocuously into a conversation about one of the many avatars of the "hueco" to be discussed below (55). Other seemingly innocuous appearances of the cinema are frequent throughout the novel as Sergio indexes it in recalling names of screen Indians (34), comparing the size of a window to a movie-screen (112), ruling out future meeting places for Brezo and himself (177), and foretelling his own disappearance (229).

Yet Sergio's referencing of the cinema is not limited to such seemingly insignificant details. A more technical cinematic vocabulary finds its place in his description of moving light on the shower curtain as "sucesión de fotogramas" (59). The cinema becomes equated with the mind through its use as a metaphor for human perception and memory, recalling Bergson's denouncement of the cinematic apparatus. Consider Sergio's meditation that "el hombre es un ser con dificultades para la comunicación, muere con su película de sensaciones detrás de la frente" (180-81), or the use of the phrase "el proyector de su película daba marcha atrás" (42) as a segué into Brezo's memories as perceived by Sergio-narrador. Elsewhere he mentions that her eyes "contemplaban una filmografía interior" (56). Note the language used in his dream that "la película de tus deseos y la de mis carencias, ambas han dejado de rodar" (194). Sergio insists that reality "[t]iene vísceras corrientes, lacias mejillas que el celuloide no refleja. Su vida, en fin, depende del proyector que suena como lluvia, de la oscuridad de la sala, de la corriente eléctrica. Y hay tantos cines, Brezo, y es tan raro que mis imágenes coincidan con las tuyas" (224). In novelistic expression of Bergson's cinematograph of the mind as false spatiality, for Sergio the perception of each individual is thus likened to a cinematic apparatus. Sergio's unfulfilled longing for connection is phrased in precisely these terms, reinforcing the metaphor: "cómo va a incorporar [a un individuo] sobre su corta cinta, sobre su sino nada duradero, una película ajena" (181).

Yet if the cinema is associated with division and separation for Sergio, as well as for the Bergson of *Creative Evolution*, the reader must be more attentive to discern the cinematic structure which pervades the novel. Understanding this structure calls for a recuperation of the cinema from Bergson's derision in order to understand how the philosopher might have better used it to his advantage.[9] As Sergei Eisenstein said, one must remember that the cinema is not only the camera but also montage. It is the juxtaposition of images–it is collision. As Pier Paolo Pasolini (1988) has

[9] In this way, it is unfortunate that Bergson denounced the cinema when later he might have learned to praise it. This is in fact Deleuze's argument in *Cinema 1: The Movement-Image* (1-3). Fragmenting a real movement at a rate of 24 per second, the frames of the cinematic apparatus cannot themselves reproduce this real movement as a whole. Between every two frames there are an infinite number of intermediary frames not captured by the camera. It is for this reason that the Bergson of *Creative Evolution* had decried the cinematic apparatus as illusion, but as Deleuze asserts, it is the projection of the frames that restore (albeit through an illusion) to the captured movement its real continuity. Attempting to explain the contradiction between Bergson's philosophical tenets and his rejection of the cinema, Deleuze writes: "The essence of a thing never appears at the outset, but in the idle, in the course of its development, when its strength is assured. Having transformed philosophy by posing the question of the 'new' instead of that of eternity (how are the production and appearance of something new possible?), Bergson knew this better than anyone. For example, he said that the novelty of life could not appear when it began, since when it began life was forced to imitate matter. . . . Is it not the same with the cinema?" (3).

shown, it is also the semi-subjective; it is the visual and auditory representation of the free indirect discourse (see Voloshinov 1973) analyzed by Bakhtin in the written text of the nineteenth century Russian novel. The cinema gives this discourse enunciation through the oscillation between subjective and objective poles, or by a camera that is neither within nor outside of the character but merely *with* him or her. It is evident that what Pasolini understands as the semi-subjective has much to do with Bergson's phenomenological rejection of the purity of such notions as reality and ideality. In *La escala de los mapas*, a markedly non-homogenous narrative style that turns unceasingly from the first person "Sergio-yo" to the third person "Sergio-él" and back again betrays both Sergio's feelings of isolation as well as the concomitant philosophical concepts of fixity and closed systems. Although it is beyond the scope of this essay to assess the frequency of these twists and turns, the following excerpt may be taken as typical:

> Brezo, *mi* vida estuvo llena de cifras inexactas, *me confundía* en las sumas, tachaba y era en vano, los errores nos siguen siempre. De un lado *estaba Sergio e iba perdiendo* caballos, peones, torres; del otro, la realidad intacta, sedienta. Fue cuando subiste a *mi* casa [...] *Pude haber eludido* tu presencia [...] *Pude haber permanecido* solo [...]. (my emphasis, 87)

It is certainly possible to believe that this narratological choice is best interpreted as the self-speech of a disturbed individual who describes himself in the third-person and not, in fact, as the near-cinematic oscillation between subjective and objective perception. Yet to do so would be to deny, on the whole, not only the prevalence of the cinematic indexing described above, but also the very prevalent philosophical concern of the novel. This concern is the investigation of the connection between desire and reality, between inner and outer space, between affect and action, all implicitly mediated through the relationship Sergio-Brezo.

As a whole, then, the cinematic indexing and semi-subjective narration work together to posit various dualities, the juxtaposition of affect and action as well as that of real and ideal consciousness, and then record their collision. Just as in *Matter and Memory* Bergson is interested neither in pure perception nor pure memory but their cohabitating indiscernibility, just as he merely abstracts affect from action for theoretical reasons and then joins them as part of an indivisible movement, here Gopegui's work is focused neither on Sergio nor Brezo, but on their connection. This connection, the goal of the first-person narrator's search, is imagined as a *space*. Within the confines of his mind, and with cinematic imagery, Sergio imagines that he invites Brezo into that space: "ven y quédate conmigo entre la gota de luz y la pantalla" (42). This is metaphorically the Bergsonian gap between action and reaction formed by the human brain, the theoretical meeting place of real with ideal consciousness. This is the point of collision that expresses Sergio's desire to connect with Brezo. This is the interval. It is in reference to this concept, one which is all too easily misunderstood, that Bergson's work most illuminates my reading of *La escala de los mapas* and provides a subsequent necessary correction to the philosophical basis of current explorations in cultural geography.

The prevalence of the idea of the interval as a *space between* in the novel, as a nexus between affect and action, as a gap or a space betwixt and between desire and reality, between ideal and real consciousness, testifies to the power of Sergio's mistaken spatialization of flow, a process of division whose over-application Bergson denounces as the tendency of the intellect (*MM*). It is the goal of the novel's protagonist to inhabit this gap, thereby being able to transmit emotion into action, a possible connection manifested through the amorous relationship between Brezo and himself.

From the first chapter, Sergio's obsession with the opening crank or "manivela" of a window (9, 88, 168, 216-17, 227) becomes a metaphor for the interval between himself as a creature of affect and an outer reality. This gap, also a connection, is more ubiquitously referred to as a "hueco" and even explicitly, in some cases, an "intervalo," though it is elsewhere described in terms of "pausas," "fallas" and is implicit in recurrent symbolism of portals such as windows and doors.[10] If Bergson comments that "[t]here are inter-

[10] As "hueco" on 11, 13, 80, 82, 90-91, 101, 106, 109, 111, 116, 120-122, 125, 137, 141, 148, 156-57, 153, 160, 164-68, 170, 174, 176, 179, 183, 191-92, 196, 199-200, 205, 207, 210, 218-19, 227 and 229; as "intervalo" on 85, 120-122, 139, 159, 173, 176 and 229. The explicit source given in the text for the use of the word interval is Nabokov's *Ada o el ardor* which Sergio finds it necessary to quote at greater length than what appears below: "No los golpes recurrentes del ritmo sino el vacío que separa dos de esos golpes, el *hueco* gris entre las notas negras, el Tierno

vals of silence between sounds" (*MM*, 259), Sergio complements this with a quotation from Debussy "La música no está en las notas, sino entre las notas" (55). Sergio, then, is seeking this gap, as he terms it "un puente levadizo [...] un lugar suspendido entre dos mundos, el de la desnudez [el material] y el otro [el ideal]" (26). The "hueco" is "*el espacio* que va desde la acción del uno al sentimiento del otro: un tramo firme, un puente no inconsútil sino hecho de sólido granito transitable" (157, emphasis added). Through this utopian gap the isolated protagonist hopes to access a world he considers to be outside of himself.

For Sergio, this idea of the hueco, the space between, comes into being to correct a teratological error of a spatializing intellect. Instead of renouncing this intellect (through a method akin to Bergson's) and recovering the phenomenological ground of existence, that is, instead of recovering the indivisible presence of the objective in the subjective and likewise of the subjective in the objective, Gopegui's protagonist follows the tendency of intellect and creates yet another abstraction. This need to partition space calls his attention to the "margín"–a mystical number situated between seven and eight discovered in Cádiz in the XVIth century (27-28), to the birthday gift that a young Brezo asks her father for–"una barra espaciadora [. . .] que sirva para la vida. Si yo la aprieto dentro del cine, por ejemplo, empiecen a aparecer asientos vacíos entre mi butaca y la de al lado" (55). The "hueco" is, of course, a symbol for the relationship between Sergio and Brezo themselves. It is "un lugar de descanso en donde transcurrir contigo sin cometer equivocaciones" (90), "el canal que comunica los objetos entre sí" (91).

Yet Sergio's greatest error is assuming that the "hueco" really exists as he perceives it–that is, as a space in between things. One of the core assertions of Bergson's philosophy is precisely that space between things is a view taken by mind, and that we err in limiting our conception of the universe to this view. Bergson's first thesis in *Matter and Memory* is that one cannot equate a movement with the

---

Intervalo. La pulsación misma no hace sino recordar la pobre idea de medida, pero entre dos pulsaciones acecha algo que se parece al verdadero Tiempo" (my emphasis, 120). It is not out of place to say that Gopegui's Sergio sees in Nabokov's Van Veen a fellow entity of affect, a memory-diver whose ability to feel and think also heavily outweighs his ability to act.

distance covered by that movement.[11] In fact, in a moment of lucidity, Sergio tells himself that the "hueco" is only a metaphor (137). This is exactly what Bergson tells us–that although in one sense language makes a community of action possible, it allows us to erroneously separate the continuous flow within space into qualities (adjectives), things (nouns) and movements (verbs) when there is only movement, only change itself. There is no empty space between objects. Sergio misunderstands the continuity of space and instead believes in the body as ontologically-given separator of affect and action. Yet, instead, as Bergson notes, perception is virtual action, and affect is real action occurring where it is felt. Movement is continuous, and the body is one of many abstractions that can never, in reality, be separated from the system of images that interact each on the others on all their sides simultaneously. From Sergio's perspective, this remark that the "hueco" does not exist conveys his doubt that he will ever be able to negotiate the gap between affect and action, and in fact he will not, provided he persists in his divisive intellectual oppositions.

Moreover, Bergson's implication that the barriers between inner and outer space are *not* strong ones is mirrored in the text subtly, in details that consistently evade Sergio's conscious knowledge. Not until late in the book does he admit his "problemas limítrofes" (209). After a conversation with his psychologist's secretary, he takes offense at her desire to continue working instead of chatting with him. This moment delivers a notable shock to his fixed ideas of limits, "[E]ntre el punto donde aquella mujer pronunció la ironía y el punto donde la recibí, no había separación. Me sentí maltratado de repente. Como un pequeño animal retráctil, *sin membrana, soy*. Y por eso mi corazón se encoge, es un calambre de corazón que duele, y tú percibes mi dolor, y por eso resulta tan difí-

[11] The proof of this assertion lies in the deconstruction of Zeno's example of Achilles and the tortoise. If Achilles runs ten times faster than the tortoise, and the tortoise is given a ten-meter head start, then by the time Achilles runs the initial ten meters, the tortoise will have moved another 1/10 meter. When Achilles runs the 1/10 meter, the tortoise will have moved another 1/100 m. and so on. Thus, Zeno concludes, Achilles will never catch up with the tortoise. Nevertheless, and as Bergson correctly assumes, the flaw in this reasoning is that while the space traveled may be divisible, the movement is not. Movement cannot be equated to the distance covered because it is pure duration, continual becoming, the eternal moment where the past bleeds into, even recreates itself in, the present. Achilles will indeed surpass the tortoise.

cil relacionarse conmigo" (209, emphasis added). Questioning that which he has taken for granted at other times in the novel, he asks Doña Elena, his boss, "¿dónde está el límite entre la vida exterior y la interior?" (169). Similarly, windows consistently evoke the "delgado límite [...] entre los radiadores y el mundo, entre la habitación concreta y el exterior oscuro, interminable" (113), a stand-in for the meeting place of affect-action. His disappearance at the end of the novel, presumably into the "hueco," into the very spaces between the words of his memoir (229), indicates that his problem has not been caused by an inability to relate to his environment, but rather by renouncing himself to a debilitatingly-advanced affective sense. It is precisely that the inner and outer worlds are *too connected*, and not that they might not be connected enough, that causes his anguish. Bergson is right,

> [a] body, that is, an independent material object, presents itself at first to us as a system of qualities in which resistance and colour–the data of sight and touch–occupy the centre, all the rest being, as it were, suspended from them. On the other hand, the data of sight and touch are those which most obviously have extension in space, and the essential character of space is continuity. There are intervals of silence between sounds, for the sense of hearing is not always occupied; between odours, between tastes, there are gaps, as though the senses of smell and taste only functioned accidentally: as soon as we open our eyes, on the contrary, the whole field of vision takes on colour; and, since solids are necessarily in contact with each other, our touch must follow the surface or the edges of objects without ever encountering a true interruption. (*MM*, 259-60)

Not only are all things in space connected with no gaps, but also sensation, just as perception, is extensive, only that it *takes place* inside the body where it is felt (*MM*, 45-49). Sergio sees barriers where there are only transitions, staticity where there is only constant movement and change in the whole. His feelings are real, yet he is incapable of turning affect into action. This is of course one of the primary problems facing urban studies, how to look at the city and see what's really there (Bunge and Bordessa 1975), how to create spaces of hope (Harvey 2000), how to combat the uneven geographical distribution of a pernicious capitalism and assure "the right to the city" (Lefebvre 1968, D. Mitchell 2003).

In the novel, the interplay between Sergio and Brezo, between affect and action, evokes another movement between mental and cartographic space, between physical and mental maps (56, 88). Without collapsing idealism and realism, without sacrificing idea to action, Gopegui's novel articulates the link between the two in purely geographic terms. The book's spatial vocabulary leaves no mental or physical state untouched. Sergio imagines that his interior world will grow "como península emanada, como margen de río o bastión inatacado por los otros" (87). He is Castilla and Brezo is Aragón (95). He is "un pueblo de Burgos cuando nieva, territorio aislado" (135), he is Albania (29): "En mi república se practica la autarquía de repliegue: producir para autoabastecerse y permanecer inmodificado, al abrigo de influencias extranjeras. Porque habitar con los otros es la guerra y me destruye, he preferido rodearme de una difusa constelación afectiva" (29). If interior spaces are compared with geographical forms, the reverse is also true. A map of the Baltic Sea is said to have "forma de hombre arrodillado" (40). A discussion of a geographical study bleeds into a question of a personal nature: "El resto de la mañana lo pasé corrigiendo las consecuencias de un error de escala en un estudio de impacto: cómo instalar una estación espacial en las estribaciones del parque de Monfrague sin perturbar el equilibrio. ¿Cómo instalar a una mujer de ideas fijas en mi vida prudente y lograr que los dos saliéramos incólumes?" (24). Sergio is sure that the emotive forces in which he is drowning are real, and he is not wrong. His conclusion is thus that they occupy space. Implicitly affirming Bergson's idea that sensation *takes place* where it is felt and thus that it is extensive, in supporting that all consciousness *is* something, Sergio is led to speak of his emotions in geographical terms: "Brezo, toda la noche estuve pensando que existía la emoción y era geográfica: ocupaba un sitio, tenía longitud y diámetro como la barra del metro, yo podía aferrarme a ella para no caer" (180). Whether he does this in order to deceive himself as to the debilitating nature of his affective sense or as a preparatory step in his intent to link his mind and world, subjective and objective consciousness, idealism and realism (note that he claims "estoy dispuesto a pasar a la acción" (209)) matters not. What is important is that the geographical metaphor for body gives emotions a real and extensive character. The implication is that there is a fundamental link between mental and cartographic space.

Yet Sergio persists in imagining this link as a space, instead of recognizing the immanence of mind to cartography, instead of realizing that both one and the other are simplified abstractions. Consider the development of this linkage as it is explored through Sergio's discussion of the geographers of perception:

> Me hallaba particularmente interesado en los geógrafos de la percepción, una corriente que apenas había merecido un epígrafe en el programa de la asignatura, pero entre cuyas aportaciones figuraba el "mapa mental". Oh deliciosa idea. *Oh concepción tripartita del mundo.* No hay un dentro y un afuera, no hay un hombre en su casa y abajo la superficie de avenidas y paseos que consignan los planos, sino un hombre en su casa, una urdimbre de aceras en las calles y, *entre los dos*, un mapa mental o *filtro* que modifica el paisaje, el desnivel de las cuestas, las escalas... Con un dibujante cartógrafo a su servicio, cada individuo podría plasmar las imágenes de su mapa mental en un papel. Veríamos entonces cambiar la geometría de las plazas, multiplicarse o reducirse la distancia entre la Cibeles y la Puerta del Sol, crecer la densidad de población de Africa, la extensión de China, la altitud del Retiro. Con un cartógrafo a su disposición, Sergio Prim hubiera acertado a descubrir ángulos como heridas de un papel doblado muchas veces, pues no ignoraba que había fracturas en su mapa mental por donde cabía irse. ¿Pero cómo accederse a los mapas mentales ajenos? ¿Cómo señalarlas allí? (85, emphasis added)

Using a tripartite structure and the idea of a space "between" proves problematic for Sergio. In defining mental and cartographic space as inherently distinct he creates the necessity of a bridge between the two. And yet his vocabulary points to the city-space imagined by the Situationists. For Guy Debord and Asger Jorn, the apparently Cartesian-gridded space of the city existed not as a planar totality but rather always mediated by the experience of the individual. Any individual, then, with the help of a cartographer could reconstruct an experiential map of the living city, no longer a reification subject to the spectacle of modern capitalist practice, but, in Bergsonian terms, a circuit formed by the continuous flow of ideal consciousness into real consciousness and back again. For all his differences with the Situationists (see Harvey 1991: 429), it is this very circuit that Lefebvre delineates in *The Production of Space* (1991). Space is a process, a relation, just as Marx's revolution was to define capital as a relation. A radical understanding of this idea involves a more complex articulation of spatial praxis than Sergio's dualistic affect-action model, no more complete for the inclusion of a "hueco" connecting space.

It is just such a complex articulation of space that has been taking hold amongst theorists working with the issue of space across various disciplines. Theorists are once again recognizing the constructed nature of what was previously thought of as statically given, the mutually constituted nature of the previously isolated spheres of culture and of material landscape. David Harvey (2000) looks "From Place to Space and Back Again." Charles Tilly (1999) advises us to go "toward relational analyses of political processes" (419). Bob Jessop (1999) asserts that the boundaries between the economic and the political are of cultural origin (380). Michel Foucault (1975) looks at the way disciplines originate at the level of the individual and take on the form of repeated spatial practice. Tim Mitchell (1999) argues that the "state effect" arises from the material and provides a framework for a "double-articulation" between the Foucaldian notion of disciplines ascending to more global constructions of power. Sallie Marston (2004) calls for recognition of the "'nexus' among" and "mutually constitutive nature of the categories" of state, culture and space (38). In "The Social Construction of Scale," Marston (2000) presents an incisive and convincing look into how ideas of scale, itself not ontologically given, become shaped by social practice.

In fact, as Gopegui's novel suggests despite the insistence of its mistaken narrator-protagonist, scale is a matter not only of global, supranational, national, regional, and local, but also of individual concern. It is no wonder that the psychologist who advises Sergio, Maravillas Gea, has written her thesis on "la pérdida del espacio en los esquemas mentales: un análisis del sentimiento de desaparición" (177); geographical space and mental space are intimately entwined in the embodied mind, or as Sergio states in a rare epiphany, "todo está comunicado" (131, 182), itself an echo of what Waldo Tobler in 1970 called the First Law of Geography: "everything is related to everything else, but near things are more related than distant things."[12] Like the protagonist of John Cheever's "The Swimmer"

---

[12] Tobler sought to recalibrate space. His online paper posted at www/geodyssey.com/papers/tobler93.html titled "Three Presentations on Geographical Analysis and Modeling" drives at a more complex model of travel across space. For

who, in using an "ojo de cartógrafo" (129) as Gopegui's text mentions, finds that he can get home by tracing a path through the pools of his suburban wasteland, both the reader and the protagonist of *La escala de los mapas* discover that a movement exists which envelops both psychic and geographical space. Sergio links the geographical with the psychological upon declaring "las escalas no son patrimonio de los geógrafos. En realidad, todo el mundo las utiliza" (33). The partitioning of reality into levels of abstractions called scales finds a complement in the discussion of the layering of minerals (69) and the profound and simple structures of both emotions and extra-corporeal facts (89). In fact it appears that "todo es cuestión de escalas" (227).

This connection between mind and geography, phrased in scalar terms, manifests itself in an equivalence between maps and books. Essentially, Sergio points out, "el mismo sistema que rige para la tierra y sus mapas, rige para los hombres: escalas y signos, representación. Los mapas de los hombres son los libros" (127). Completely debilitated by an overdeveloped affective sense, the question for the interval-seeking protagonist is how to convert affect into action. He complains that "Nadie me puso ejercicios para aprender a trasladar lo imaginado a lo vivido" (169). His affective sense is so self-indulged that his emotions have the power to cloud the perception of space. In the following passage, Sergio touches Brezo affectionately and finds the world around him distorting itself, eventually disappearing. "En el instante en que puse mis manos en su cuello comenzó la dispersión de los objetos, se marcharon aceras y cabinas y espejos retrovisores. Como se interrumpe el río en la cascada cesó el día" (156). Like emotions, books also have this power to immerse Sergio completely in the idea (127).[13] This temporal metaphor works alongside the prevalent spatial metaphor of the "hueco" to signify the nexus between desire and reality manifest also in the space between books and reality. The reader wonders how Sergio will turn the imagined into lived experience. This at times takes a

---

an enlightening forum on Tobler's First Law of Geography, the reader may wish to consult the *Annals of the Association of American Geographers* Volume 94, June 2004 Number 2 for a series of seven authors' comments including a reply by Tobler himself.

[13] The idea of stopping the world, a philosophical tenet explored in Deleuze and Guattari's *A Thousand Plateaus* (1987: 139) and taken from the works of Carlos Castaneda (1968), appears in Gopegui's novel as well ("detener el mundo" 139, 170; "detener el espacio" 176).

personal tone focusing on the small scale–Sergio modifies the space of his office to reflect his isolation (84). Yet, given the geographical context, the reader simultaneously must ask questions of a larger scale–how, for example, do ideas of city-space become social praxis?

The novel caters to these larger questions as Madrid and its surrounding areas are implicated by the numerous studies of environmental impact performed by the novel's geographers. Even Sergio's group is contracted to "evaluar el suelo no urbanizable de quince municipios periféricos" (46), and Sergio himself leads a study of the impact of "un helipuerto militar" (80) in Alnedo, "un pueblo de la serranía alta de Cuenca" (102). Despite his insistence to the contrary, he is in intimate connection with reality, taking part in the production of space. Nevertheless, Sergio's personal isolation and the fact that he carries with him a mental map of Madrid (127) have consequences not only for his relationship with Brezo, his other half, the reality to his subjectivity, the matter to his memory, but also for his relation with city space. Losing a connection with Brezo, with his outer reality, will leave a flexible mental map that will soon become unmanageable. "Brezo, piano mío, te callarás y entonces Madrid sea infinito, laberinto sin puertas, y no volveremos a coincidir" (177). Yet it is not that this connection might be lost, but rather that it will be clouded by the power of his affective sense.[14]

With the above reading, we find that Sergio's mistake is creating an interval between things where there is none. That at the end of the book Sergio dissolves into the "hueco" between the words of his testimony (229) means that the intellectual division between affect and action, books and reality, mental maps and cartographic maps has come to an end. Sergio is a mere vehicle for showing the absurdity of the divisions the human mind thinks into reality. Only by seeing these products of thought as such can we truly see space as a process, as Bergsonian real movement. We are then faced with

[14] Here Gopegui has inverted traditional social gender roles with an end to emphasize larger questions of spatial process. If the story had been told with Sergio as the active reality and Brezo as the passive subjectivity, it would have been tempting to read the novel through constructions of gender – either as affirmation or critique of the societal roles continually negotiated by individuals. Yet Gopegui's reversal of a traditional and ill-formulated dichotomy that links affective with feminine and extensive with masculine pushes us away from this interpretation, instead presenting an illustration of a standard dichotomy of spatial production.

"el problema del después" (25), with the real problem of how to put our capability for indeterminate action to work. We find ourselves riding the wave of the eternal Bergsonian transition of the past into the present "como quien vive en lo que está a punto de ocurrir" (92).

The link between representations of places and those places themselves, between mental maps and cartographic maps, between the individual and the city, between the small and the large scale has an ample and accessible bibliography. Theorists working across many disciplines such as Dear (2000), Foucault (1975), Harvey (1989; 1990; 1996; 2000), Jessop (1999), Latham and McCormack (2004), Lefebvre (1974), Madanipour (1996), D. Mitchell (2000), T. Mitchell (1999), Marston (2000; 2004), Soja (1996), Thorns (2002) and Tilly (1999) ask trenchant questions of the relationship between the mental and the cartographic. Taken as the philosophical basis for the understanding of the production of space, Bergson's works caution against simplifying the interaction of both material and immaterial processes and are more relevant than ever to geographical inquiry.[15] Gopegui's *La escala de los mapas* provides a notable opportunity to assess the relevance of these two approaches to spatial process. Sergio Prim's strict dichotomies (of affect vs. action, of subjectivity vs. objectivity, of idealism vs. realism) serve to warn us of the dangers inherent in partitioning the movement of spatial production into material and immaterial components. Scholarship must be able to reassess its intentions in order to see how these categories become abstracted out of the flux of experience only

[15] The philosopher, in fact, may be experiencing a new wave of attention in critical theory as a recent issue of the journal *Culture and Organization* (9.1, 2003) shows, to name just one example. In their essay "Time Creativity and Culture: Introducing Bergson" Stephen Linstead and John Mullarkey (2003) argue for the relevance of Bergson's work to the analysis of culture (see also Linstead 2002). Alexander Styhre's "Knowledge as a Virtual Asset: Bergson's Notion of Virtuality and Knowledge Organization" (2003) shows the importance of Bergson's thought to a theory of knowledge as process. Sean Watson attempts to bring Bergson to bear on the analysis of both literature and social groups in his "Bodily Entanglement: Bergson and Thresholds in the Sociology of Affect" (2003). Antoine Hatzenberger's "Open Society and Bolos: A Utopian Reading of Bergson's 'Final Remarks'" (2003) likewise finds great relevance of Bergson's ideas to current and alternative social organizations. Carl Power's "Freedom and Sociability for Bergson" (2003) suggests that "we need to re-evaluate the relevance and value of Bergson's thought today" (71). Bergson's importance for Deleuze is evident not only in the cinema books but also in *Bergsonism* (2002) and in two essays of *Desert Islands* (2004).

through the work of the human intellect. Ultimately, the fusion of Cultural Geography, Bergsonism and Gopegui's text suggests, as do Latham & McCormack (2004), that "we need to consider more fully how the process of abstraction actually allows us to draw out, and also to become implicated in, the excessive force of materiality" (707).

Along with the previous one on Juan Benet, this chapter has argued that Bergson's philosophical writings have had a direct, acknowledged effect on the contemporary novel in Spain (Benet) and also a more indirect yet nonetheless significant effect (Gopegui). As such this concludes the first half of the present work. Up until now, the purpose of the previous chapters has been to argue for the importance of Bergsonian philosophy on Spanish letters in an historical sense. The book's next two parts will focus instead mainly on the methodological legacy of Bergson's philosophy. While the connections developed in these subsequent chapters tend to be, on the whole, less direct, the approaches to both film and urban space outlined in following chapters should be understood as having a significant Bergsonian component in returning from static snapshots to movement, from abstract concepts to the concrete flow of life.

PART II. FILM STUDIES

FROM BERGSON TO DELEUZE: DURATION AND MULTIPLICITY IN TWO SPANISH FILMS

THE philosophy of Henri Bergson has always been intimately entwined with the development of the cinema. His three major works (*Time and Free Will* 1889, *Matter and Memory* 1896 and *Creative Evolution* 1907) were published in close proximity to the decade in which the cinema exploded on the scene–the 1890s. *Creative Evolution* even famously evoked the cinema as a metaphor for one tendency of human consciousness, the Bergsonian intellect:

> We take snapshots, as it were, of the passing reality, and, as these are characteristic of the reality, we have only to string them on a becoming, abstract, uniform and invisible, situated at the back of the apparatus of knowledge, in order to imitate what there is that is characteristic in this becoming itself. Perception, intellection, language so proceed in general. Whether we would think becoming, or express it, or even perceive it, we hardly do anything else than set going a kind of cinematograph inside us. We may therefore sum up what we have been saying in the conclusion that the *mechanism of our ordinary knowledge is of a cinematographical kind.* (306, original emphasis)

Although he arrived at this metaphor in his third major work, Bergson's use of the cinema was consistent with the larger goals of his philosophical project to denounce the characteristic spatialization of time that he had emphasized since the publication of his doctoral thesis in 1889. Even so, the idea he evoked of the cinema in this larger project was not a positive one. Bergson denounced the cinema in order to point out the flaws of intellection in general. For him, cinema spatialized time by fragmenting it into static images which were then strung together on a false becoming. In the same way, the intellect approached the process of becoming–that is, living, fluid realities–only through static/immobile snapshots. He concluded that both the cinema and the intellect were similarly unable to grasp movement and change.

Nevertheless, Bergson's philosophy itself contrasts with his stated denunciation of the cinema. Philosopher Gilles Deleuze (1925-1995) has shown convincingly that the whole of Bergson's philosophy might yield quite a different understanding–Bergsonism in fact forms the basis for Deleuze's two works on cinema *The Time-Image* (1983) and *The Movement-Image* (1985). His explanation of the distance between his view of Bergsonism's relevance to the cinema and Bergson's own argues that, although the Bergson of *Creative Evolution* had decried the cinematic apparatus as illusion, it is the cinematic *projection* of the static frames that restores (albeit through an illusion) the continuity of the original fluid reality. He explains Bergson's rejection of the cinema by means of his assertion that

> The essence of a thing never appears at the outset, but in the idle, in the course of its development, when its strength is assured. Having transformed philosophy by posing the question of the 'new' instead of that of eternity (how are the production and appearance of something new possible?), Bergson knew this better than anyone. For example, he said that the novelty of life could not appear when it began, since when it began life was forced to imitate matter. . . . Is it not the same with the cinema? (*MI*, 3)

Thus Bergsonism might serve to reinvigorate film studies today not only because Bergson's philosophy was contemporary to the cinema, but also because of Deleuze's reworking of Bergsonism in his *Cinema* books (not to mention *Bergsonism* 1966).

Although Bergson had denounced the cinema in *Creative Evolution*, Deleuze rightly restores to Bergsonian philosophy its open and revitalizing approach to cinema. Though for Bergson the cinematographic character of consciousness manifested itself as a truncation, as a testimony to the error of viewing flow through staticity, Deleuze succeeds in recovering the virtual resonance of the 'seventh art' with the whole of Bergson's philosophy of becoming. In his two cinema books, Deleuze actualizes that detailed synthesis of philosophy and film which Bergson had insinuated, in spite of the latter's intent to use the "cinema" as a metaphor for the divisions made by the intellect in the apprehension and production of reality. He elaborates a theory of film that is simultaneously a commentary on the production of concepts and a philosophy of life, thus recuperating the Bergsonian spirit. Deleuze applies Bergson's conception of movement to the cinema at the levels of both frame and shot, brings his predecessor's idea of difference to bear on filmic montage, reiterates that perception is in things and that thought is virtual action, and articulates the notion of the open as a diagonal which runs through closed sets and their relations, emphasizing the produced nature of signification and forever blurring the boundary between given and not-yet-given.

From Bergson's oeuvre, Deleuze thus extracts three theses relevant to cinema: that 1) movement is distinct from the space covered, 2) attempts to recompose movement proceed from either privileged instants or any-instant-whatevers, and 3) just as an instant is an immobile section of movement, movement is a mobile section of duration that expresses change in the whole. This first thesis, that movement is distinct from the space covered, is developed by Bergson with reference to Zeno's paradox of Achilles and the tortoise. The paradox finds that if the tortoise, which moves at 1/10 the speed of Achilles, is given a 10 meter head start, Achilles will never catch it. For first he will have to travel 1/10 of the distance (1 meter), in which time the tortoise will have also moved another 1/100 of the distance, then 1/100 vs. 1/1000, 1/1000 vs. 1/10,000, and so on. As Bergson shows, this paradox is caused by the mistaken idea that movement is equivalent to the space covered. Nevertheless, he asserts, whereas the space covered may seem infinitely divisible, the process of movement itself is indivisible. The space covered by movement is then a view taken by mind, a production of Bergson's "intellect," while real movement escapes the designs placed on it by the latter. Opposed to a homogeneous and divisible space there is an inclusive and heterogeneous time, the two cohabiting multiplicities whose fusion Bergson establishes as early as *Time and Free Will*. Mistaking one for the other – that is, taking a static view of movement – is thus not to grasp the movement itself, but merely the way the intellect represents movement (*CE*, "We take snapshots...").

The second Bergsonian thesis recuperated by Deleuze in the *Cinema* books posits that in mistakenly recomposing movement from staticity, or space covered in the previous example, there are two paths. The first or ancient/classical method of reconstituting movement proceeds by connecting privileged instants or poses which are representative of a certain segment of motion, the peaks or valleys of a flow, which evoke an absent transcendent form. The second or modern/scientific method of reconstitution involves the stringing together of unprivileged instants, or any-instant-whatevers–as illustrated by the equidistant shots of E. Muybridge's motion studies and the functioning of the mechanical claw punches of the cinematic apparatus, for example. Nevertheless, Deleuze (1983) points out that "cinema seems to thrive on privileged instants" (5), presenting a contradiction that he resolves by declaring that cinema is neither strictly art nor science in this sense. The radical property of cinema for Deleuze lies precisely in that "When one relates movement to any-moment-whatevers, one must be capable of thinking the production of the new, that is, of the remarkable and the singular, at any one of these moments; this is a complete conversion of philosophy" (7).

The third thesis, that movement is a mobile section of duration that expresses a change in the whole, revisits Bergson's critique that movement is more than just translation in space. Movement does not merely involve a change in location of the parts of a closed set, but moreover is the expression of a qualitative and innovative change in the whole. Movement is thus a recreation of elements of the old at the same time it is a creation of something which has never before been. The error of old/ancient and new/modern science, says Deleuze, is to take the whole as already given. In contrast, Bergson's method is to always look beyond the closed system to the possibility of newness at every moment.

Thus, as Deleuze summarizes, "(1) there are not only instantaneous images, that is, immobile sections of movement; (2) there are movement-images which are mobile sections of duration; (3) there are, finally, time-images, that is, duration-images, change-images, relation-images, volume-images which are beyond movement itself" (*MI*, 11). This Deleuzian theorization of the movement-image and the time-image is an attempt to reconcile film with philosophy in a way that had never been done before, and, as one critic points out, is still far from being realized.[1] Of course, part of the reason for this is that Deleuze's work, as always, explicitly turns away from the tendency toward systemic precision. Like Bergson before him, he is not driven to give definition to closed categories that will settle into the rote forms of doctrine, but rather to open up the act of thinking. Both Bergson and Deleuze underscore the distinction between reflexive, reactive thought and truly creative and innovative thought. Deleuze thus develops Bergson's philosophical writings on thought and applies them explicitly to the cinema–not to advocate the proper direction of film studies as a cohesive discipline, but rather to see what this new application yields for the understanding of thought itself as a temporal process.

The intriguing connection between Bergson and Deleuze points to two concepts of great importance to film studies–duration and multiplicity. The remainder of this chapter will take on each in turn through a look at two Spanish films. First, Víctor Erice's film *El sol del membrillo* visually demonstrates that film is a superb medium for expressing Bergson's philosophical insights regarding duration/ *durée* and the interpenetration of quantitative and qualitative multiplicities. Subsequently, reading Alejandro Amenábar's film *Abre los ojos* through a Bergsonian/Deleuzian perspective on internal difference/multiplicity explores the possible disconnect between a film's simultaneous narrative and non-narrative meanings.

Despite having made only three full-length films over the span of three decades, Víctor Erice is still one of the most celebrated contemporary Spanish filmmakers. Although as a hybrid of documentary and fictional film styles *El sol del membrillo* (1992) represents a departure from his ealier films *El espíritu de la colmena* (1973) and *El sur* (1983), it nevertheless continues the director's interest in issues of temporality, which in the latter two films takes the form of the aftermath and enduring legacy of the Spanish Civil War.[2] Even in

[1] Claire Perkins (2000) notes that "Despite the first volume having been published for nearly twenty years, film theory hasn't found a way of absorbing the *Cinema* books–in a testament to Deleuze's inventiveness we are still very much 'out of our element'" (no pag.).

[2] Marsha Kinder (1997) considers the film a straight-forward documentary, while Linda C. Ehrlich (1995) notes "Erice's editing, which transfers the film from the realm of documentary to that of storytelling" (23). Erice explored temporality explicitly in his earlier films through the trope of memory. Interested readers should consult Arocena (1996) and Ehrlich (2000) for monographs on Erice's work.

articulating his conception of the cinema itself as a whole Erice underscores the importance of memory, and thus temporality: "Never [...] did we imagine that with the passing of years cinema would become an essential element of our memory, the container capable of holding the images that best reflect the human experience of the century that has just died."[3] Seen in this light, *El sol del membrillo* offers the director's most focused and insightful attempt to grapple directly with temporality itself, as both a concept of key philosophical importance and a concrete, if fluid and ever-changing, reality.

The central concern of Erice's film is an attempt by the famed Spanish artist Antonio López to paint a quince tree from his garden in Madrid, beginning on September 29, 1990. This attempt is not necessarily a successful one given that the painter's desire to capture the quince tree in the fall's vibrant sunlight is repeatedly frustrated by an unusually rainy and cloudy season (thus the significance of the translated English title *Dream of Light*). As Linda Ehrlich (1995) has noted, the film dialogues insightfully with the Bodegón painting tradition and with specific masterworks of the western tradition. The film is notable, too, for addressing the issue of painting more generally in its incorporation of not only artists Enrique Gran and María Moreno but also three Polish housepainters who come and go, and two Chinese visitors who question López about his work. As Gran and López reminisce about their shared past as students of art, time gains a personal inflection. As Kinder (1997) states, this is a film about the importance of subjectivity, yet it is also more than that. As María paints a picture of López in bed, the film cleverly shifts back and forth between her painting and the image in order to problematize representation itself. News reports emanating from López's portable radio are repeatedly incorporated throughout the film and draw our attention to important events such as the official dissolution of the GDR and problems in the Middle East. Running throughout all these seeming distractions is the ostensible subject of the film, which is, as Adrian Danks (2003) appropriately signals, "a preoccupation with light, observational detail and the subtle patterns and differences wrought by the passing of time" (no pag.). It is clear that the film is

[3] The quotation is from an article authored by Erice and published in *Rouge* titled "Writing Cinema, Thinking Cinema ..." (1998; www.rouge.com.au/4/cinema.html).

a sophisticated attempt to grapple with the passing of time right down to the details of the conversations taking place on screen in which López and Gran reminisce about their days in school together and photographs of days gone by–even conversations in which López's attempt to paint the tree is framed as a race against time. The preoccupation with temporality is indeed central to the film, and it is clear that Erice's *El sol del membrillo* offers visual reinforcement of a Bergsonian understanding of time's fluid nature.

Although the fluidity of time underlies all of Bergson's philosophical assertions in one way or another, he approaches the subject more directly in his dissertation, *Time and Free Will* where he differentiates between a model of discrete states of consciousness and what he calls 'pure duration.'

> Pure duration is the form which the succession of our conscious states assumes when our ego lets itself *live*, when it refrains from separating its present state from its former states. For this purpose it need not be entirely absorbed in the passing sensation or idea; for then, on the contrary, it would no longer *endure*. Nor need to forget its former states: it is enough that, in recalling these states, it does not set them alongside its actual state as one point alongside another, but forms both the past and the present states into an organic whole, as happens when we recall the notes of a tune, melting, so to speak, into one another. (*TFW*, 100, original emphasis)

Whereas the practical aspect of our thought, which Bergson terms the intellect, encourages us to think in static terms, life nevertheless consists of changes–changes that are not strictly delineated and which endure. Consciousness is thus best approached not as a series of changes that can be divided and in a sense quantified, but rather as a real movement which must be understood as a whole. Although we routinely consider time quantitatively–spatializing it into segments (hours, days, months, years; even time zones)–for Bergson this is a quantitative division that covers over what is the basic enduring and fluid nature of temporality. As is to be expected given the film's focus on the process of painting, *El sol del membrillo* hammers home this point regarding the enduring, fluid nature of time. In fact, the film deals not with one temporal process, but with two such processes at once–fusing the process of painting the tree with the ongoing growth of the tree itself as a living thing. Moreover, an even more complex picture of duration is delivered via the film as Erice complements these twin temporal processes (of painting, of tree growth) with a Bergsonian nod to a larger temporality that enfolds them both.

When time is seen in the light of its philosophical importance, even what seem, at first, to be mere either distractions from the documentation of López's painting or contextualizations to better highlight the film's depiction of Spanishness (Kinder 1997) are in fact crucial to Erice's foregrounding of time. The film's numerous intercalated quotidian happenings–the repeated radio sequences detailing current world events, the Chinese visitors, the Polish workers, the coming and going of the dog, the discourses on art, reflections on youth–all help to create the filmic image of a larger temporality which enfolds others, a larger time that is comprised of, but not defined by, smaller times. This appropriately reflects Bergson's idea of a temporality that, far from being one-dimensional, is multi-faceted and complex. In *Duration and Simultaneity*, he wrote of duration that:

> When we are seated on the bank of a river, the flowing of the water, the gliding of a boat or the flight of a bird, the ceaseless murmur in our life's deeps are for us three separate things or only one, as we choose. We can interiorize the whole, dealing with a single perception that carries along the three flows, mingled, in its course; or we can leave the first two outside and then divide our attention between the inner and the outer; or, better yet, we can do both at one and the same time, our attention uniting and yet differentiating the three flows, thanks to its singular privilege of being one and several. Such is our primary idea of simultaneity. We therefore call two external flows that occupy the same duration "simultaneous" because they both depend upon the duration of a like third, our own; this duration is ours only when our consciousness is concerned with us alone, but it becomes equally theirs when our attention embraces the three flows in a single indivisible act. (36)

As if inspired by Bergson's meditation on temporality, Erice's film nudges us magnificently from the time of the process of painting and the time of the tree's growth toward a larger duration upon which they both depend. Those sequences that at first appear peripheral to the topic of time in fact resonate profoundly with the idea of complex temporality that enfolds others.

One of the sequences that most helps to develop this notion of an enduring and complex temporality is constituted by a repeated pattern of curious establishing shots that capture the still images of the exteriors of neighborhood buildings. At various points throughout the film, the viewer is shown a series of visual landmarks, from the 142-meter tall Moncloa communications tower in Madrid's Argüelles district to a variety of rooftop views of streets, distant shots of city skylines and ground-level shots of the exteriors of buildings. These sequences consist of short shots, from 2-4 seconds each, which, while brief, are long enough to allow a glimpse of time's unfolding: a train rolls by, the images on a television visible from outside change, a light turns on in a building, the noise of traffic is heard, dogs bark, and so on. As the film progresses, a shot of the Moncloa tower captures it lit-up at night, emphasizing the flow of time and paralleling the subtitles that advance the film by contextualizing the passing of calendar days (sábado 29 de septiembre, domingo 30 de septiembre, lunes 1 de octubre…). When seen in terms of the film as a whole, these sequences constitute an attempt to grapple with time more directly such as that signaled by Deleuze (above).

A similar repeated pattern of establishing shots are used in another film that deals with simultaneity also from the early 1990s –Jim Jarmusch's *Night on Earth* (1991). Yet whereas Jarmusch's mostly silent establishing shots are more conventional in that they introduce each of that film's five mini-stories (in Los Angeles, New York, Paris, Rome and Helsinki), rooting the viewer in the specificity of place, Erice's shots are in effect stripped of this establishing or introductory function. In every case he gives us shots of Madrid that mark no change whatsoever in the narrative line of the film. Moreover, the repetitive nature of the images–we are dealing not with repetition but with similar images of the same place at a different time of day–serves not to orient us spatially, but to give us, in the Deleuzian sense, a direct image of time itself. Extending Juan F. Egea's (2007) Deleuzian analysis of the 'still lifes' that Erice intercalates as adjacent to the film's narrative (of the painting, the artist's tools, the plumb line, a table), these exterior shots of buildings similarly constitute "weak linkages" in the "sensory-motor schemata" described by the French philosopher of cinema (Egea 171-72). To the degree that these sequences are adjacent to–if not outside–the conventional narrative of the film they reflect the Bergson-inspired Deleuzian notion of "time-images, that is, duration-images, change-images, relation-images, volume-images which are beyond movement itself" (*MI*, 11). They do not 'advance' the narrative through the exploitation of sensory-motor connections but instead approach duration itself as "images that claim some independence of meaning" (Egea 172). In this way they come to constitute a complement to the constant and almost obsessive use of fades that obtains in Erice's editing. Both techniques discourage the division of time into strict sections, what Bergson called the 'spatialization of time,' in order to encourage the viewer to intuit a whole that lies beyond the limited process of representation, yet to which we all have immediate access. As Bergson was aware, we have direct experience of the reality of the passing of time–and it is this experience that lies at the heart of the film.

Erice's concern with the enduring nature of the passing of time becomes even more overt toward the end as *El sol del membrillo* takes on the tenor of a more fictional film. The images that precede the film's final oneiric sequences evoke a sense of closure: the viewer realizes that the act of painting has come to a definitive end as the infrastructure necessary for López's artistic process disappears (canvas, the tent that covers the tree, etc.). Likewise, a Polish worker washes the paint marks off of a membrillo at the sink and a group of women gather membrillos from the tree to carry away and eat elsewhere. Although the sequences which follow have been interpreted as a dream sequence, they must be read in terms of the main thrust of the film as a whole.[4] This thrust is a concern with the qualitative nature of time and thus with a notion of wholeness, of fullness. A casual remark by López and Gran underscores this as they reminisce how it took years–another testament to the unfolding nature of time–to understand an art lesson by their former teacher who prompted them to paint everything 'más entero.' In the final sequences Erice manages to branch off from the main emphasis of the film, shifting from explicitly tracing the full arc of the life of an artistic process (the birth, development and even death of López's project) in order to focus more poignantly on the life-arc of

[4] The oneiric qualities of the final images have been noted by Fernando Bayón (2000a).

the artist as a human being. With this in mind it becomes clear that the film manages to suggest even the final change wrought by López's (fictional) death.[5]

The film suggests the (fictional) death of the painter as the everyday documentary feel of Erice's film yields abruptly to a more stylized sequence characterized by a faster-pace, non-diegetic music and voice-over narration. While his wife María is painting her picture of López on the bed, a tense suspenseful thread of music is heard as he goes limp–seemingly anticipating sleep. Even though at this very moment he drops a crystal from his hand as it relaxes, the loud noise resulting from its hitting the floor does not stir him. After María turns off the lights in the room, Erice returns to a series of familiar still-camera exterior shots and ends with a shot of the lights illuminating the grandiose Moncloa tower similarly being switched off. What follows is a captivating image that functions as a metaphor not merely for sleep, but in fact, given the film's focus on the full arc of both artistic and living processes, for death. We see a film camera set up to the side of the quince tree and its fallen fruit, a bright light shining directly on the decaying membrillos. In this sequence of shots, Erice lays bare the film's artifice, setting the camera's tripod legs up at the nails by the tree precisely where López placed his feet. The whirring of the camera exaggeratedly underscores the identification the shot makes between the temporal process of painting and that of filming itself. Even the machine's whirring dies out slowly as if another cinematic metaphor for death, coming to constitute a visual metaphor for the end of human life–especially if thought itself is imagined to be, as Bergson imagined it, a cinematographic mechanism (*CE*). The cinematic light set up beside the tree fades off and the silence that follows comes to connote not the quotidian, as it had in earlier parts of the film, but rather a marked end to the everyday.

Music evoking tragedy, quite unexpected given the documentary style Erice pursues in the earlier part of the film, soon accentuates the visually austere interior shots of sculptures and paintings in their places under the glow of the moonlight which streams in through windows–artistic products without their producers–ending with the striking image of what might even be a recent death mask.

[5] Domènec Font points out the importance of death in the latter part of the film.

The voice-over narration, spoken by López over a shot of his own unmoving body, stirringly returns to the image of membrillo trees as it evokes not merely the oneiric qualities of the dream, but that dream of all dreams, the death of the human body. As if describing the final image-memories that occur in the moments before death, López describes a highly metaphorical scene:

> Estoy en Tomelloso, delante de la casa donde he nacido, al otro lado de la plaza hay unos árboles que nunca crecieron allí. En la distancia, reconozco las hojas oscuras y los frutos dorados de los membrilleros. Me veo entre esos árboles junto a mis padres acompañado por otras personas cuyos rasgos no logro identificar [...] Nadie parece advertir que todos los membrillos se están pudriendo bajo una luz que no sé cómo describir, nítida, y a la vez sombría, que todo lo convierte en metal y ceniza.

Beautiful images of the decaying membrillos, filmed in close-up as they blister and rot–no longer on the tree's branches but at its base–visually establish a parallel between the human life of the artist and the life of the fruits (remember López's earlier comment: "yo voy acompañando al árbol"). Yet after even the finality of this implied death, time flows onward. Appropriately, the closing shots of the film juxtapose the still rotting fruits with blossoming flower buds and the newly forming fruits of the spring–even the emphasis on death thus fades in order to capture new life being born. Fernando Bayón (2000b) aptly writes that time in the film "no entiende la muerte ni como exterminación ni como liberación, simplemente como la memoria inesquivable de un nuevo nacimiento, de un crecimiento nuevo." The final dedication of the film "A Paco Solórzano, in memoriam" emphasizes the enduring nature of time through the importance of memory (*MM*) and gives a personal inflection to the film's late focus on the full arc of human life itself.

Still, when the film is subjected to a thorough analysis it resonates not merely with Bergson's notion of duration–a fluid time which *endures*–but, in a more complex way, even with his methodological premise itself. Although Bergson's meditations on time are often condensed to a simplistic opposition (space vs. time) by pointing out that he denounced what he called the 'spatialization of time,' his method of highlighting internal difference in fact calls for recognizing the complex differences between a space and a time that are never found in isolation from one another (*TFW*). This method extended also to the complex distinctions he makes between instinct and intelligence (*CE*), matter and memory (*MM*), static and dynamic religion (*MR*) in an attempt to replace clearly delineated ontologies with the notion of a composite in which opposing multiplicities interpenetrate one another. In *Time and Free Will* he clearly points out the importance of recognizing the complex fusion of quantitative and qualitative multiplicities.

> What we must say is that we have to do with two different kinds of reality, the one heterogeneous, that of sensible qualities, the other homogeneous, namely space. (97)
> In short, we must admit two kinds of multiplicity, two possible senses of the word "distinguish," two conceptions, the one qualitative and the other quantitative, of the difference between *same* and *other*. (121)

Bergson's discussion of quantitative and qualitative multiplicities emphasizes the interconnection of each, and, ultimately, the primacy enjoyed by the qualitative over the quantitative: "Hence it is through the quality of quantity that we form the idea of quantity without quality" (122-123).[6]

In *El sol del membrillo* this complex imbrication of the quantitative and the qualitative is omnipresent. During the numerous sequences where we watch López as he sizes up the tree, Erice has wonderfully highlighted López's strategy of marking individual quince fruits, the tree's trunk, branches and leaves, with white paint. As the tree grows, his subsequent markings reflect the changing visual center of the objects his eye seeks to represent on his hand-made canvas ("yo voy corrigiendo"). Returning to these markings again and again, Erice not only gives us a glimpse of the dual temporal process mentioned above (of painting/tree-growth) but more importantly draws our attention to the interplay between quantitative and qualitative aspects of these processes. Ehrlich (1995)

---

[6] Bergson: "And yet we cannot even form the idea of discrete multiplicity without considering at the same time a qualitative multiplicity. When we explicitly count units by stringing them along a spatial line, is it not the case that, alongside this addition of identical terms standing out from a homogenous background, an organization of these units is going on in the depths of the soul, a wholly dynamic process, not unlike the purely qualitative way in which an anvil, if it could feel, would realize a series of blows from a hammer?" (*TFW*, 122).

has pointed out that the painter's approach, while artistic, "is equally mathematical" (24). To wit, as López sets up his painting area in the garden, we witness what could be described as a sacred mathematical rite: he frames the tree with lines of string and uses plumb line with its dangling weight in order to center his vision and anchor his perspective ("es el centro de lo que yo veo"), he drives nails into the ground where he will consistently position his feet as the days pass, and he uses a large straight-edge with measurements when initially marking his canvas. Along with the paint marks on the tree itself, the painter even goes so far as to draw multiple chalk lines on the brick wall beyond it so as to better assess the tree's growth.

This quantitative aspect of López's artistic process (his mathematical markings) is highlighted not only visually by the camera but also in conversations with the Chinese visitors and most pointedly a conversation between two formally-dressed men who inspect the painter's work area before he arrives on the scene with a larger group. Noting the markings on the walls specifically, the two men discuss López's approach to the work in detail commenting on his proximity to the tree, the nails where he places his feet, the string lines and more. Yet their most revealing comment regarding López's artistic process cuts to the heart of the film's central proposition: "es que aquí está unido perfectamente el sentimiento y... y el orden [...] la razón y la intuición." Just as in Bergson's philosophy, the apparent mania López has for orderly work (one man comments: "éste tiene que ordenarlo todo") does not reflect an entirely quantitative endeavor. Instead, his ordering of physical space constitutes a sort of superstructure on the more basic qualitative nature of his artistic process. At the base of this process there is the brute attempt to reach out with his qualitative consciousness to coincide with the tree's duration: as he explains to the Chinese visitors, "yo voy acompañando al árbol," "siempre voy... paralelo al desarrollo del árbol." As in any artistic process, a supra-added layer of rational technique comes to inform the original artistic inspiration, but this rational technique cannot stand on its own (as Juan Benet points out in *La inspiración y el estilo*, see chapter three of the present work). The key reflection by López and Gran on their former teacher's insistence that they paint "más entero," fully, more completely, drives home the film's point that details are merely a surface whereas the true goal of painting lies beyond what can be taught.

Just as for Bergson philosophy was "an effort to dissolve again into the Whole" (*CE*, 191), in painting too, it is the whole that matters.

Ultimately, López is frustrated in his attempt to represent the tree on his canvas due to the fluid nature of time. The sunlight wanes, the rain comes, he switches from paint to charcoal and starts over, the tree continues to grow, its fruit fall to the ground, and, as Erice's overt fictionalization at the end of the film signals, the painter himself ages. The struggle between the man and the tree is eclipsed by the ongoing, unpredictable nature of a larger time that enfolds them both. Simply put, time just will not stand still for the act of representation. With his career-spanning concern for temporality, Erice has here consciously created a film that exploits what the cinema offers as a temporal medium (see Ehrlich 1995: 26) to confront temporality head-on. As Santos Zunzunegui (1995) writes, the film "se propone el acuerdo mítico entre cine y pintura, y sobre todo, entre el tiempo concreto de la filmación y el tiempo 'abstracto, intelectual e imaginario' del montaje" (73). Ultimately, the film's focus on time–in both the concrete and the abstract–functions as a complement to Bergson's rigorous philosophy. Resonating with the French philosopher's clear prose, Erice's easily-underestimated stylistic simplicity belies a complex meditation on the multifaceted notion of a time which *endures* and the Bergsonian methodological premise that process enfolds both quantitative and qualitative multiplicities.

Alejandro Amenábar's fantastic science-fiction thriller *Abre los ojos* (1997) is another film that, although it may be easily written off as a Spanish science-fiction blockbuster, nevertheless presents a complex model of temporal multiplicity that runs against the grain of its more standard narrative aspects. Before discussing the complex role of the real and the imaginary in the film, however, particularly as presented simultaneously in both its narrative and non-narrative aspects, it is first necessary to return to the connection between Bergson and Deleuze. Whereas the complexity of Bergson's philosophy was lost on many critics who took him to be either an idealist escaping from materiality or a champion of time who disregarded space completely, it was not lost on Gilles Deleuze. The idea is perhaps widespread that *Bergsonism* (1966), Deleuze's now classic rendering of Bergson, is merely a tribute to the former's ingenuity alone, and that the challenge for such an avant-garde thinker was precisely to breathe life into a stagnant and unsalvageable philosophy from the early twentieth century. Nevertheless, the work does not reflect Deleuze's ingenuity alone. Instead, it summons the complexity of Bergson's original works forth to a more contemporary time, as Deleuze infuses his predecessor's novel ideas with his own voice, reproducing a newly streamlined critique of philosophical method.

In two of his earliest essays from the 1950s titled "Bergson, 1859-1941" and "Bergson's Conception of Difference" (later published in English as part of *Desert Islands*, 2004), Deleuze concisely presents the complexity of Bergson's method and its consequences for thought:

> there will not be in Bergson's work anything like a distinction between two worlds, one sensible, the other intelligible, but only two movements, or even just two directions of one and the same movement: the one is such that the movement tends to congeal in its product, in its result, that which interrupts it; and the other turns back and retraces its steps, rediscovers in the product the movement from which it resulted. ("Bergson, 1859-1941," 23-24)

Given the complex, or better said composite, nature of movement, Deleuze foregrounds the key notion of Bergsonian philosophy as the notion of "difference" ("Bergson's Conception of Difference," 32). This difference is *internal.* This statement in fact sums up Bergson's complex stance on ontology–things are not in space, rather space is in things.[7] The key question is not one of the distance *between* things but one of the difference *within* things. It is this premise, not created by Deleuze but instead notably extracted or distilled by him from Bergson's thought, which obtains throughout the whole of Bergson's writings. Above all else, Bergsonian philosophy deals with the interpenetration/cohabitation of spatial and temporal multiplicities: "In short, we must admit two kinds of multiplicity, two possible senses of the word 'distinguish,' two conceptions, the one qualitative and the other quantitative, of the difference between *same* and *other*" (*TFW*, original emphasis, 121)–this is Bergson's quotation and not Deleuze's (although the latter cites it in his own *Bergsonism* 1966).

---

[7] This is an idea embraced not only by Bergson 1889 but also more recently in geography by Harvey 1996 and in physics by Hewitt 1974.

No doubt influenced by this complex mode of internal differentiation that he took straight from Bergson's text, Deleuze uses cinema to develop a theoretical posture that prioritizes the cohabitation of opposing multiplicities. "According to Deleuze, modern cinema develops a mode of perception that makes it possible to sense virtual worlds, that is, worlds divorced from space-time built on the logic of practical action, worlds containing simultaneously the past, present, and the future, the imaginary and the real" (Kovács 2000: 162-63). In the taxonomy developed by Deleuze throughout his two cinema volumes, *Cinema 1: The Movement-Image* and *Cinema 2: The Time-Image*–both rooted explicitly in Bergson's works, there are two tendencies operating through films. Some fit squarely within the sensory-motor connections of the movement-image, thereby allowing only an indirect image of time, blocking thought from plumbing time's depths and thus cleaving the "real" from the "imaginary." This is the tendency of the movement-image.[8] Others arguably present a direct image of time, thereby allowing for a passage from the virtual to the real and emphasizing the connection between the "real" and the "imaginary." This is the time-image. Deleuze's concept of the time-image, and the fluid connection it evokes between such abstract categories as the 'real' and the 'imaginary' is meant to highlight that an entirely new thought may erupt into consciousness at any-instant-whatsoever, if only one prepares for it dispositionally. Coterminous with the "intellectual" tendency of thought present in the movement-image, the tendency of thought present in the time-image resists discrete division. This tendency of thought, which Bergson notes is subordinated to "intellect" in evolution and in common practice, is that

[8] The movement-image manifests itself in three ways, either as perception-image, as action-image, or as affection-image, and Deleuze elaborates quite a bit on the way these avatars close the set and open onto the whole each in its peculiar fashion. These monikers correspond, of course, to Bergson's description of the human brain, as that which creates a gap, an interval, between perception and action (*MM*). That interval is affection, which subtends and envelops both sides of the gap between received stimuli and reaction. But of course, as Bergson argues, perception is virtual action, and being such, the brain operates only to prolong the reaction indeterminately. The movement-image in this sense, is thought as it is involved in sensory-motor connections, and thus as it is implicated in dividing a presumably homogeneous space. Yet this thought, understood as the Bergsonian tendency of space, is only a tendency–albeit one which the developments of social life and the evolution of the organism itself have privileged.

part which resists sensory-motor connections, or rather which persists despite those connections. For Deleuze, the time-image tends towards "a point of indiscernibility of the real and the imaginary" (*TI*, 12), which represents a "collapse of traditional sensory-motor situations" (*TI*, 12).[9]

Importantly, Deleuze's taxonomy of the movement-image and the time-image is based on the same notion of internal difference he borrows from Bergson. The time-image cannot exist outside of movement-images, nor the latter outside of the former. The two regimes that he contrasts are not bounded totalities, but are in fact the Bergsonian Two which differ in nature but which cohabit in the One. What Deleuze manages in the cinema books is a Bergsonian nondualism of movement-image and time-image. Films with a face open toward the latter tend toward either a cinema of the body or one of the brain, but each differs only in tendency from the other–for in fact, "Landscapes are mental states, just as mental states are cartographies" (*TI*, 206-07; see chapter four of the present work). It would be an error to conclude that the films Deleuze mentions in his books, those of Rosselini, De Sica, Fellini, Godard,

[9] In presenting his own novel understanding of the cinematic time-image Deleuze, however, draws directly upon Bergson's thought extensively theorized in *Matter and Memory*.

> And consequently, those particular images which I call cerebral mechanisms terminate at each successive moment the series of my past representations, being the extreme prolongation of those representations into the present, their link with the real, that is, with action. Sever that link,–and you do not necessarily destroy the past image, but you deprive it of all means of acting upon the real and consequently, as we shall show, of being realized. (*MM*, 88)

In differentiating the movement-image from the time-image, the organic regime from the crystalline regime, "a kinetic regime from a chronic regime" (126), "a lived hodological space and a represented Euclidean space" (128) from what Deleuze alternately calls Reimanian, quantum, probabilistic and topological, or crystallized spaces (129), the film/philosopher is seeking to inflect the questions asked not only of cinema, but of life, time and space, with a decidedly Bergsonian trajectory. The question is not, "Why is there something instead of nothing?" but rather "Why this instead of something else?" (a question at the heart of Bergson's *Creative Evolution*). The time-image is, then, designed to make salient both the revolutionary moments of film and also those revolutions of all movement itself. It underscores the importance of extracting from a cycle of action-reaction that indivisible and unpredictable any-point-whatever that is a forking of time, the point of stillness in which thought severs its links to sensory-motor determinants and takes on its proper role to produce the new, that point where it is allowed to become fully conscious of its own operation.

Resnais, Antonioni, Pasolini, etc., possess an essential quality that permits the viewer a direct image of time, of the whole. If he chooses these directors, it is because in their works, the time-image as a tendency is greater, for he speaks not of essences, but as did Bergson, merely of tendencies. The time-image subtends the movement-image, even makes the movement-image possible, in the sense that we have now found "temporality as a state of permanent crisis" (*TI*, 112). Through this permanent crisis of temporality, Deleuze seeks to demonstrate that "the Whole can only be thought" (*TI*, 158). This is not a temporality merely of cinema, but temporality as lived, perceived and imagined in the broadest sense–an ongoing process. What Deleuze underscores in Bergson is the coexistence of the virtual with the real. What he expresses in the concept of the time-image is the necessary release of a sensory-motor paradigm to allow the emergence of a real thought, a thought which is not merely tied to the real and thus destined to recapitulate its pre-packaged definitions of problems and their corresponding solutions, but which may now delve into the imaginary to explore and actualize the virtual.

Read in this context, Amenábar's *Abre los ojos* offers an exercise in thinking through the problematic relationship of the "real" and the "imaginary" as conceived from two distinct ontological positions. The way in which we make sense of the play between the two concepts and of the protagonist's final choice in the film speaks volumes regarding both the way in which our spatializing "intellectual" thought operates and the possibility of producing a world other than the one which we have currently produced. This section will briefly address previous analyses of the film before discussing what it achieves when considered from a Bergsonian/Deleuzian perspective rooted in contradiction and the complex relationship of the real and the imaginary. This view on the film suggests the need to return space and time, the material and the immaterial, the real and the imaginary, to the same variegated world–itself a Bergsonian proposition.

Although the struggle to define the difference between the real and the imaginary lies at the heart of the film's form and content, some takes on in the film have not completely done justice to this relationship. Rob Stone's analysis of the film in *Spanish Cinema* (2002), for example, an otherwise enviable work, fails to address it.[10] His position on the film seems best expressed in the following quotation: "It may be argued that the film is an anonymous exercise in genre, whose Hitchcockian references cannot disguise a lack of substance; but that is missing the point of a film which deals with themes of anonymity and conformity in contemporary Spanish society" (202). Despite the lucid connection Stone makes with Hitchcock,[11] the film seems quite far indeed from dealing with anonymity and conformity in contemporary Spanish society. César's disfigurement on the one hand seems a necessary plot device that drives the fantastic events discussed below, and on the other contributes greatly to the development or depiction of his defining characteristic, his vanity. Sandra Robertson (2001), however, quite appropriately explores the connection of Amenábar's film to age-old metaphysical discourses on reality and dream using Calderón's "La vida es sueño"–thus providing a starting point for more thoroughly interrogating the philosophical basis of this distinction itself. What is needed is an understanding of the very real and tangible consequences of this displaced metaphysical division–for the existing and possible productions of city-space. Malcolm Compitello (2001) convincingly and coherently argues for the importance of cityspace to *Abre los ojos*, highlighting the portrayal of Madrid's built environment in the film and suggesting that the latter can be read as emphasizing "the necessity of opening one's eyes to place." Although he does not talk of the real or imaginary *per se*, his approach, based as it is on works by Henri Lefebvre and David Harvey, implicitly acknowledges the need both for entwining the material with the immaterial and for recovering the iconic nature of film as Prince (1993) suggests (see chapter six of the present work).

Nathan E. Richardson's (2003) analysis of the film specifically foregrounds these ontological questions relevant to the production of space. He takes on "the question of national history and memory as posed within a context increasingly influenced, if not defined, by

---

[10] This perhaps owes to the fact that the film is mentioned only under a section heading of "Penélope Cruz," hidden in a chapter titled "Seeing Stars." Strange too, is first that the author does not support his assertion, and secondly that the little space allotted to discussion of the film should contrast so ostentatiously with the photograph of its final scene's prominent location on the front cover of the book.

[11] For those interested, Anne M. White (2003) explores the many references to classic European cinema and popular Hollywood films added to the remake of *Abre los ojos* as *Vanilla Sky* (2002).

visual, virtual, and spatial properties" (328) and does well in recognizing the "local specificity" (331) that may be found in the film as well as its spatial logic (333)–the latter as expressed in the initial dream-like vision of the Gran Vía which produces a Madrileñan cityscape uprooted from history and society where signifier has been severed from signified. Yet although he ultimately believes the film to restore history to Madrid, space to time, his very analysis divides space and time, contrasting an older historiographic sensibility with a new spatialized youth culture, even if he regards definition of the latter as problematic (328, 328 n. 1). Nevertheless, rather than pursue a discussion of the degree to which a contrast between an older memorializing generation and a new dehistoricizing spatially-oriented youth culture is appropriate, this section investigates the philosophical basis of the very possibility for dehistoricization. I want to explore the consequences of the spatial logic of the film, not by emphasizing space as a tool of either one generation or another, but by using the Bergsonian methodology continued by Deleuze in the *Cinema* books that understands space, separation, severed connections as a limitation placed on the reality of change. I agree with Compitello that it is important to recognize the film's presentation of space as undoubtedly *Madrileñan* space and not just as a mere symbol or metaphor for city-life. I likewise concur with Richardson that "*Abre los ojos* here foregrounds these questions [of history, memory, identity] as space rather than time, geography rather than history, and the visual rather than the temporal become its focus" (337). Yet I believe that the film's thematic focus warrants an extended analysis of the ontological concerns that underwrite the division between material and ideal that is so central to the production of city-space itself (see Part III of the present work).

There is much of interest in Amenábar's film. At its core it addresses the coexistence and interpenetration of differing sheets of past centering around the character of César, an upper class, vain, rich entrepreneur for whom the addiction of acquisition trumps even the value of his best friend. From an opening sequence presenting a dream narrative that cinematically mirrors César's morning routine closely down to the level of shot, a cinematic statement is made emphasizing the incompossible, forking nature of time. There are many virtual worlds, the film starts to suggest, from which only one is actualized, but which nevertheless continue to exist as simultaneously evolving possibilities: César's face is disfigured from a car-crash/suddenly it is not disfigured, his face is repaired/it is not repaired, César kills himself/he does not kill himself. At first glance these alternatives are represented only spatially in the film, by contrasting and definitive cuts between sequences, cuts represented through props such as the bars used by the Life Extension representative to illustrate César's dualistic predicament.[12] To the degree that these incompossible worlds are left irreconcilably discrete, the film presents a thoroughly spatialized vision of the real from the imaginary. When the film is approached from a narrative perspective, what is, in essence, an explanation of the film's plotline by the character working for Life Extension effectively constrains the power of the imaginary. Yet at work within this strictly spatial narrative ontology there is another breaking through, just as for Deleuze the time-image had always been breaking through the movement-image (*Cinema 2*).

The two incompossible worlds of the real and the imaginary are not *only* spatialized in *Abre los ojos*. Instead, as the film progresses they actually begin to overlap and even cohabitate. Through the purely spatial tendency of reality that is underscored by the film's narrative logic there can be seen another tendency operating, even if in a subordinated position. The equivalent of that nondiegetic image and sound superimposition on Norman Bates at the end of Hitchcock's *Psycho* (1960), which Angelo Restivo (2000) correctly identifies as a "virtual doubling characteristic of the time-image" (182), is here arguably recreated more directly as connections between seemingly incompossible worlds or differing sheets of past (*Cinema 2*) are actualized through a mataxis of character, prop, or speech act. For example, the question "¿Crees en Dios?" appears in scenes with both Nuria and the psychiatrist, a subtle point of connection between two realities that the viewer has been coaxed into separating spatially. Pictures of Sofia become pictures of Nuria as Sofía / Nuria becomes Sofía becomes Nuria.[13] Another mataxis: the TV commercial for Life-Extension appears in the scene at Sofía's apartment where she and César draw portraits of one another, in

[12] The representative uses one small plastic bar representing César's life and another representing his 'virtual' life to explain how Life Extension has done just that, extended his life virtually.

[13] Regarding this doubling Amenábar has remarked in an interview that *Abre los ojos* is "una especie de Vértigo, pero al revés" ("Interview with Carlos Heredero," 109).

César's psychiatrist-guided drug-induced hypnotic recall session, and in the psychiatric ward communal room. The "Frenchman" from Life-Extension appears in two bar scenes with César, drawing the latter's attention to a point of contact between the world he believes to be experiencing and another world, outside of his full grasp, but nonetheless real. Following this line of thought, the scene where César and the "Frenchman" from L.E. speak in the bar shows that underneath the sensory-motor connections of the film in its capacity as movement-image there is a time-image seeking to break through. As César exclaims "Lo que quiero es que se callen" the restaurant extras freeze and become silent. Taken together with the opening shot of the movie which shows a near lifeless image of the Gran Vía emptied of all car and pedestrian traffic, this similar scene of frozen action yields to the time-image in its disruption of sensory-motor connections.

Thus there are two possible solutions to the problem of these two incompossible worlds. The first is to accept a problematic distinction between the "real" world and the "imaginary" world–a spatialized version of difference that the narrative plot of the film underscores through its underlying and coherently progressing chronological story that culminates in the solution given by the Life Extension organization. The second is to admit the presence of one world in the other–a Bergsonian/Deleuzian version of internal difference. In this sense, the film's chronological story contrasts sharply with the philosophical premise regarding the confusion between real and imaginary that itself drives the film's narrative. Of these two incompossible solutions, the first severs body from mind, reality from representation and immaterial thought from the material world–thus limiting and understanding of how space is produced and undermining struggles to produce a world other than the one that exists from the outset. The second restores body and mind, reality and representation, thought and action, in short ideality and materiality, to one and the same world–thus recovering the very possibility of change even if this means recognizing the difficulty of achieving it.

Far from precluding one interpretation at the expense of the other, the distance between the narrative logic of the film and its non-narrative aspects, *Abre los ojos* actually presents a choice for interpretation at the same time that it presents a choice for César's character. This choice is reflected in the narrative action of the film during the final culminating scene in which he converses with the Frenchman on top of a building with a 360 degree view of Madrid's urban space. Either reading of the film–that is, either the simplistic chronological narrative guided by the discrete worlds of the real and the imaginary or the underlying confusion of real and imaginary that gives force to that narrative itself, is possible. Yet as Compitello (2002) suggests, speaking not only of *Abre los ojos* but also Fernando León de Aranoa's *Barrio* (1998) and Alex de la Iglesia's *El día de la bestia* (1995), "If we *open our eyes* we can perceive the ways in which these films afford varied responses that contest hegemonic capital's control of the urban process" (no pag., my emphasis). We can either view the production of space as somehow outside of our control, severing imaginary space from real space, or reclaim the immanence of one to the other. When César jumps off of the building, we may choose to understand that he leaps from one possible world into another thus reifying the very notion of the real as distinct from the imaginary and ultimately inaccessible, or we can see that making a decision requires the movement of the body and mind in unison and uncover the foundational possibility that a world quite different from the one that now exists may be created through our action. Pursuing the first interpretation involves merely in accepting one of three pre-scripted solutions–either César wakes up in the same imaginary 'virtual' world, or in the year 2145, or in a real 1997 where the entire film has been a dream. In every case, the strict ontological barrier between the purportedly discrete realms of the real and the imaginary persists, the consequence of which is the depiction of a closed world in which action does not express a qualitative change in the whole, in which action is merely translation in space, a world in which the possibility for social change is negligible indeed. The opportunity, however, as this reading of the film has shown and as Bergson and Deleuze both argued, is to find the future as a decisive possibility contained within the present and yet unexpressed in it.[14]

Like Erice's *El sol del membrillo*, Amenábar's *Abre los ojos* also engages aspects of a combined Bergsonian–Deleuzian approach to film through the use of narrative and non-narrative techniques in

[14] Amenábar's film *The Others* (2001) does a similarly beautiful job of showing the existence of one world within another, although to discuss it here would be distracting, if not an aberrant spoiler.

order to present a complex understanding of temporality. In both cases, the medium of cinema is exploited to problematize the spatialized notion of a monolithic time that consists of discrete units. Nevertheless, the interdisciplinarity of Bergson's thought and his overall attempt to return thought to life (and Deleuze's attempt to use Bergsonism to revolutionize our approach to film) require that we venture beyond the boundaries of traditional film analysis in order to more thoroughly reconcile the cinema with the world in which films are made and viewed. As the next (sixth) chapter will explore, this necessity to return film studies to an extra-filmic reality turns to the Bergsonian elements of existing non-structural film theories in order to exploit the iconic and indexical aspects of film. This reconciliation will, in turn, make possible an interdisciplinary conversation between film studies and urban geography as the subsequent seventh chapter will explore through a look at Carlos Saura's *Taxi*.

FILM AS THE REDEMPTION OF REALITY: THE IMPORTANCE OF ICONICITY/INDEXICALITY

> The cinema contains all three modes of the sign: indexical, iconic and symbolic. What has always happened is that theorists of the cinema have seized on one or more of these dimensions and used it as the ground for an aesthetic firman.
>
> –Peter Wollen (*Signs and Meaning*, 1972, p. 125)

A crisis has long been brewing in film theory. In response to a new wave of cultural theory that no longer views the film as merely an isolated cultural artifact–reflecting an individual author's vision or containing one monolithic meaning–criticism is beginning to emphasize cinema's positioning as an opening onto the whole of society. From this perspective, the 'seventh art' not only reflects cultural norms and margins but also simultaneously constitutes and shapes culture in turn as part of a larger process of cultural production. In a departure from perspectives that view the film as an object constructed through the language of art, whose meaning is waiting to be deciphered by the properly trained critic, this chapter prepares the ground for a notion of filmspace that ultimately eschews static representation in favor of the reconciliation of two disciplines in particular: film studies and geography. This is ultimately to call for a redemption of reality in film studies through emphasizing the cinema's iconic and indexical meanings.

A timely fusion of geography with film studies has undeniably broadened the type of questions asked of film, linking film-text with city-text and reconfiguring both formalist interpretation and urban investigation to comment on the ills of a systemic and variegated spatial production (see especially Aitken and Zonn 1994, Clarke

1997, Cresswell & Dixon 2002, Dear 2000, Hopkins 1994). Unfortunately, however, theories of film have to contend with a deeply entrenched representational and symbolic bias that is present not only in the auteur tradition but also in the linguistic roots of filmic analysis. Following Saussure's spatialized model of linguistic signification in which the signifier is displaced from the signified, much film theory of the twentieth century was unable to recover the iconic/indexical–and thus *motivated*–basis of cinema. Nevertheless, as suggested by the Bergsonian aspects of the film theories explored in this chapter (Béla Balázs, Siegfried Kracauer, Stephen Prince, Pier Paolo Pasolini, Peter Wollen), film cannot solely be a static product of the artistic endeavor to communicate an idea to an audience. In addition to the cinematic 'language' of montage there is the undeniable fact that film works to produce meaning, not merely through the intentional systemic encoding of visual data, but through the expressive *qualities* immanent to the image itself (Balázs). Thus films are not, as much popular and theoretical discussion of film suggests, merely objects constructed through the language of art.[1] When the iconic/indexical aspect of filmic signification is given priority, film analysis is able to *redeem* physical reality and recapture the "flow of life" (Kracauer).

Stephen Prince's important article, "The Discourse of Pictures: Iconicity and Film Studies" (1993) draws upon a body of work by film philosophers and provides a theoretical basis for recapturing film studies from a decidedly linguistic bent. He succeeds in questioning the preeminence of symbolic or arbitrary signification in film analysis. This questioning is crucial because, although iconic/indexical signification in film operates simultaneously with more arbitrary, symbolic and socially conventional forms of signification, the iconic/indexical dimension of its representation is what motivates a critical geography of film and as such is wholly necessary in order to reconcile filmspace with extra-filmic city-space. This reconciliation is a crucial part of what I imagine the essentially Bergsonian-inspired view of film to be–film studies must be recon-

---

[1] As Susan Sontag (1964) noted in her seminal essay "Against Interpretation" where she critiques a purely mimetic theory of art "what is needed is an erotics of art" (23). In subverting the representational bias of much structuralist film theory, the indexicality/iconicity of film contributes to answering Sontag's call for an erotics of art by returning the film to the fluid and corporeal life from which representational models have distanced it.

ciled with life, particularly a life that, as urban geographer David Harvey writes, is increasingly dominated by the twin urbanization of capital and the urbanization of consciousness (Harvey 1985).

The idea that film is a product of artistic language is not only an incomplete picture, as Stephen Prince (1993) suggests, but also ultimately, as the next chapter will show by exploring the disconnect between filmspace and urban space in the on and off-screen productions of Madrid's Retiro Park in Carlos Saura's film *Taxi*, one that obfuscates the role capital plays in the production of space by encouraging the view of film as a thing in itself. In order to prepare for the following chapter's concrete analysis of Madrid's Retiro Park as simultaneously both a space of representation and a representation of space (Lefebvre 1974: 33), this chapter asserts that films should be understood not as a representation of reality but as part of reality itself. Beginning with a discussion of the Bergsonian dimensions of the film theories of Balázs and Kracauer, this chapter argues against the common erroneous perception of film as only a product of the language of art (the grammar, the arbitrary linkages, Eisenstein's montage) in order to subsequently call for a Bergsonian-inspired redemption of reality in film studies. Squaring with Prince's perspective, I will then argue that the paucity of studies that privilege the iconic/indexical in film is rooted in the under-recognized role of the iconic/indexical aspects of language itself. Finally, the issue will then be raised of the iconic/indexical nature of film (Pasolini, Wollen) and its importance for a critical geography of film.

Two notable theorists who have sought to reconcile film as art and as reality, Béla Balázs and Siegfried Kracauer, also implicitly bring the thrust of Bergson's philosophy to bear on the cinema, emphasizing a Bergsonian return from the abstract realm of concepts to the concrete flow of life. Importantly, Balázs was actually a student of Bergson's in Paris (Koch 1987: 167; also 1990: 165; Loewy 2006: 61-62) and, like Bergson, he was denounced for his supposed "mysticism" (Carter 2007: 94). As Hanno Loewy (2006) argues, his first novel and diary entries even invoke specific Bergsonian ideas on space, time, memory and duration (62). For his part, Kracauer thoroughly, if implicitly, articulates a Bergsonian perspective on film. Taken together, the work of these two film theorists gives an idea of what Bergson's contribution to film studies might have been had he not written the cinema off from the outset in his famous remark denouncing the "cinematograph of the mind" (*CE*, 306-07; see chapter five of the present work).

It is important to note that critics have generally painted a picture of Balázs's cinematic writings that is wholly in tune with Bergsonian philosophy. Gertrud Koch (1987) notes explicitly that "Balázs's film theory remains under the spell of his early teachers, Simmel and Bergson" (168) and implicitly recalls Bergsonism in stating that the Hungarian's is not a closed system (174), that it exalts the expression of subjectivity (169) and the emotional potential of film (174), and that it approaches film less as a reflection and more as an invention (171; remember Bergson's dictum that "time is invention or it is nothing at all," *CE*, 341). Bergson's work was clearly driven to question the suspect nature of the intellect's representation of reality. In order to prepare our action on things (*MM*), the intellect had assimilated to the apparently bounded shape of matter (*CE*) and mimicked the discrete nature of objects even when dealing with ideas–thus the "cinematographic" nature of thought. Balázs's film theory retains this Bergsonian skepticism regarding the cut, in essence the Bergsonian intellectual tendency of thought, having even incurred the wrath of Sergei Eisenstein who once remarked "Béla, Don't Forget the Scissors!"–i.e. remember the importance of montage (Koch 175). Yet the Hungarian also moves beyond Bergson, coming to appreciate film on its own terms. Balázs writes against the representational understanding of film as an art form constructed to communicate a single message:

> Film images are not supposed to *signify* thoughts but to create and stimulate them. These thoughts arise in us as inferences rather than as symbols already fully articulated in the image. If montage becomes little more than the reproduction of a prefabricated rebus, it is no longer productive. (original emphasis, cited in Koch 1987: 175-76; see also Loewy 2006: 86)[2]

Balázs's view of film not only criticized its "cinematographical"/intellectual montage but also echoed Bergson's intuitions regarding time and the qualitative coming to criticize the static nature of landscape shots (see Marcus 2006: esp. n. 48) and concomitantly em-

---

[2] Originally from Béla Balázs, *Schriften zum Film II* (1926-1931), ed. Wolfgang Gersch, Munich: Hanser; Berlin: Henschel; Budapest: Akadémiai Kiadó, 1984: 89.

phasizing the qualitative nature of the close-up and the microphysiognomy of things, as his book *Theory of the Film* (1945) so masterfully testifies.

This shared critique of the intellect and of the quantitative concommitantly expresses a critique of abstract concepts and denounces the tradition of a philosophy that had always placed supposedly disinterested knowledge over the body's imbrication in the world. In this way, reconciling mind and body in a complex relationship, Bergson strove to advocate a theory of knowledge that was also a theory of life (*CE*, xiii). Difference was not something that existed between objects (externally to them), but within them (internally). He argued compellingly that relations must supplant things if the mind is to more properly think the movement that characterizes life as it really is. From this Bergsonian position, being understood as a mere snapshot of becoming (*CE*). Although critics mistakenly understood Bergson's position to be one of dualism, his philosophy (like Unamuno's, see chapter two of the present work) was an attack on simplistic dualist models of experience that, over time, had been privileged by traditional philosophy. Locating his own work in this anti-philosophical tradition, Balázs critiques this driving dualist principle of western thought in applying it to the interpretation of art:

> A basic principle of European aesthetics and art philosophy from the ancient Greeks to our own time has been that there is an external and internal distance and dualism between spectator and work of art. This principle implies that every work of art by force of its self-contained composition, is a microcosm with laws of its own. It may *depict* reality but has no immediate connection and contact with it. The work of art is separated from the surrounding empiric world not only by the frame of the picture, the pedestal of the statue, the footlights of the stage. The work of art, by force of its intrinsic nature, as a result of its self-contained composition and own specific laws, is separated from natural reality and precisely because it depicts the latter, cannot be its continuation. Even if I hold a painting in my hand, I cannot penetrate into the painted space of the picture. I am not only physically incapable of this, but my consciousness cannot do it either. It should be said here, however, that this feeling of insuperable distance was not always and everywhere present in all nations. For instance the Chinese of old regarded their art with a different eye [...]. (*Theory of the Film*, 49-50, original emphasis)

Reconciling the work of art with the world in which it is produced, Balázs's view of the cinema recalls the phenomenological reconciliation of body and mind in general (see Maurice Merleau-Ponty's *The Phenomenology of Perception*), and the overarching Bergsonian critique of the dualism characteristic of western philosophy as a whole. As Erica Carter (2007) notes, "The influence of the vitalist argument for 'being as time, which is a constant flux of creativity, difference and becoming' was already evident in Balázs's early essays" (95).[3]

But Balázs's work also more specifically evoked Bergson's idea of the image. The view of the image advocated by Bergson in *Matter and Memory*, became in fact a condensed point of expression for the whole of the Frenchman's philosophy by reconciling the traditional views of realist and idealist philosophical systems: "by 'image' we mean a certain existence which is more than that which the idealist calls a *representation*, but less than that which the realist calls *a thing*,–an existence placed half-way between the 'thing' and the 'representation'" (*MM*, xi-xii, original emphasis). The reconciliation of thing and representation was a refusal to accept the problems posed by intellectual perception of the world at the same time that it was an expression of the methodological fusion of subjectivity and objectivity, materialism and idealism and the other spurious concepts opposed to one another by the intellect. The image was, for Bergson (*MM*), the object itself minus all that which does not interest us. As such, our perception, already interested and selective by its very nature (just as Bergson's model of memory was in part selective), presents us with a necessarily reduced view of things. Balázs testifies to the importance of this Bergsonian thought as well as its underlying reconciliation of disparate philosophical postures when he writes that

> Every object, be it man or beast, natural phenomenon or artifact, has a thousand shapes, according to the angle from which we regard and pin down its outlines. In each of the shapes defined by a thousand different outlines we may recognize one and the same object, for they all resemble their common model even if they do not resemble each other. But each of them expresses a different

[3] Carter cites Jan Campbell (2006) and Hanno Loewy (1913: 62-74; 108-97) as evidence of this assertion.

> point of view, a different interpretation, a different mood. Each visual angle signifies an inner attitude. There is nothing more subjective than the objective. (*Theory of the Film*, 90)

Bergson is explicitly mentioned in Balázs's most famous work only once (61-62) in a discussion of melody (see also *TFW*). Nevertheless, in the author's assertion of the primacy of the qualitative nature of film over the quantitative nature of the spatialization of montage, he arguably provides the philosophical underpinnings of the work as a whole.

Although he may have had his differences with the Hungarian-born filmmaker,[4] Kracauer's *Theory of Film* (1960) was not so far from Balázs's own theory of film. Koch notes that Kracauer's work is a "strange synthesis" of Balázs's work (1987: 173), and Carter (2007) reports that Kracauer welcomed "Balázs's formulation of film's 'inner aesthetic'" (91). For Kracauer, film was an extension of photography: "where photography ends, film, much more inclusive, takes over" (1960: 299). The subtitle of what is arguably his most important contribution underscores the importance of viewing film not as a privileged art form but as part of the continuity of life: *Theory of Film: The Redemption of Physical Reality*. Kracauer asserts that it is precisely through externality that inner life must be reached.[5]

> Perhaps our condition is such that we cannot gain access to the elusive essentials of life unless we assimilate the seemingly non-essential? Perhaps the way today leads from, and through, the corporeal to the spiritual? And perhaps the cinema helps us to move from 'below' to 'above'? It is indeed my contention that film, our contemporary, has a definite bearing on the era into which it is born; that it meets our innermost needs precisely by exposing–for the first time, as it were–outer reality and thus

[4] For one, he challenged Balázs's political commitment (Carter 2007).

[5] Kracauer: "They [filmic images] seem to be the more cinematic, the less they focus directly on inward life, ideology, and spiritual concerns. This explains why many people with strong cultural leanings scorn the cinema. They are afraid lest its undeniable penchant for external might tempt us to neglect our highest aspirations in the kaleidoscopic sights of ephemeral outward appearances. The cinema, says Valéry, diverts the spectator from the core of his being. Plausible as this verdict sounds, it strikes me as unhistorical and superficial because it fails to do justice to the human condition in our time.

> deepening, in Gabriel Marcel's words, our relation to 'this Earth, which is our habitat'" (x-xi).

Importantly, in Kracauer's call for a 'redemption of physical reality' there is a Bergsonian conceit. While Valéry contends that film is merely superficial, external, and that it compels us to pay far more attention to outer life than inner life (Kracauer 285), in his denunciation of superficiality/externality, Valéry is displacing and subsequently reifying the process of thought. For Bergson, it is the intellect that discourages the contemplation of inner worlds–whereas inner worlds are heterogeneous, qualitative and indivisible (*TFW*), the intellect approaches them only in terms of immobility.

As Bergson's wholesale rejection of transcendental forms suggested, there is nothing transcendant about the world of ideas. The latter are not opposed to corporality, but imbricated with materiality. It is the complex relationship between consciousness and things that allows us to reach the inner life through, or perhaps despite, the object. Both Bergson and Kracauer refuse to see the material world as purely material in a simple sense. There is a relationship between the material and the immaterial that, recalling the language used in Bergson's *Time and Free Will*, both describe in terms of "indeterminacy." Bergson's discussions of the "image" (*MM*, above) as between the thing and representation reveal the multiplicity characteristic of the physical world. For Bergson, objects are not as simple as our intellect represents them–from which a parallel can be established with Kracauer, who writes in prose reminiscent of Bergsonism that "Natural objects, then, are surrounded with a fringe of meanings liable to touch off various moods, emotions, runs of inarticulate thoughts; in other words, they have a theoretically unlimited number of psychological and mental correspondences" (68). The film theorist's position on screen images displays a conscious attempt to reconcile this philosophical/ontological position with film: "screen images tend to reflect the indeterminacy of natural objects. However selective, a film shot does not come into its own unless it incorporates raw material with its multiple meanings" (69); also "the film maker will wish to exhibit and penetrate physical reality for its own sake. And this calls for shots not yet stripped of their multiple meanings, shots still able to release their psychological correspondences" (69). Here Kracauer approximates Balázs's critique of the limits of Eisenstein's praise for the scissors/editing (above). Ultimately, for these two Bergsonian film theorists a film does not merely signify something or communicate just one meaning (Kracauer 46-48)–it is a vehicle for creating multiple meanings.

Refusing to reduce film to an artistic representation or to mere signification, Kracauer's view of cinema presents the possibility of seeing the spatialization of our every thought for what it is–in a way the very possibility for a Bergsonian intuition that turns back upon intellect itself. Although many critics have denounced the externality or superficiality of the filmic image, it is Kracauer who so magnificently saw this not as a reduced or limited world, but rather as an evocation of the same multiple possibilities as the extra-filmic world. Thus he writes "If film is a photographic medium, it must gravitate toward the expanses of outer reality–an open-ended, limitless world [...]" (x), and also "The cinema seems to come into its own when it clings to the surface of things" (285). Thus the cinema for Kracauer is–and here he is actualizing what Bergson's view of film might have been–not merely an art, not merely stuck in the trap of representation, but "an approach to the world, a mode of human existence" (xi). Film in this sense, like philosophy for Bergson, is an opening onto the whole of life. And this approach to the world, as Bergson might have recognized, rightly privileges movement, or as Kracauer writes in undeniably Bergsonian language, both the "flow of life" and the "primacy of inner life" (285).

> The concept "flow of life," then, covers the stream of material situations and happenings with all that they intimate in terms of emotions, values, thoughts. The implication is that the flow of life is predominantly a material rather than a mental continuum, even though, by definition, it extends into the mental dimension. (It might tentatively be said that films favor life in the form of everyday life–an assumption which finds some support in the medium's primordial concern for actuality.) (Kracauer 71-72)

This flow of life is, for Kracauer just as it was for Bergson, a complex fusion of material and immaterial forces. In the call for a return to "everyday life," Kracauer's analysis squares with not only Bergson's philosophical return from concepts to movement but also Henri Lefebvre's study of the rhythms of everyday life (see chapters eight and nine of the present work).

Thus the concreteness of film encourages the concreteness of thought and, paralleling Bergson's writings, does nothing to validate the use of abstract concepts in themselves. In the tradition of the philosophical thought of both Bergson and Unamuno, film reminds us that there is no transcendent world of meaning, that all the inner meanings of things are to be found right here in the material world (on the immaterially material, see Latham and McCormack 2004). Here it is interesting that Kracauer turns to the writings of one of the mid-twentieth century's most important urban critics, Lewis Mumford, in order to underscore this property of cinema: "Without any conscious notion of its destination, the motion picture presents us with a world of interpenetrating, counterinfluencing organisms: and it enables us to think about that world with a greater degree of concreteness" (299, original citation in Mumford 1934: 340). Kracauer's denunciation of those who criticize film for its presentation of a purely outer world (Valéry, Georges Duhamel, Nicola Chiaromonte; see Kracauer 286) reinforces a Bergsonian understanding of the interpenetration of consciousness and things. The faulty implication–that narrative takes us further into inner life than photography and film–is certainly anathema to the Bergsonian perspective that sees language itself as an expression of the characteristic spatialization of intellect (*CE*, 298-304). Kracauer's work in fact hinges on an implicitly Bergsonian refashioning of the traditional philosophical dichotomy of the abstract concepts material/ideal, things/consciousness, space/time in order to reconcile each with the other and ultimately to recover film's potential, going beyond both the artistic fallacy that limits film to representation and the simplistic realism that severs objective external realities from subjective inner realities.

Thus although Balázs and Kracauer may have had their differences, they shared with Bergson a desire to return the focus of analysis to quality instead of quantity, to multiplicity instead of intended and received signification, to movement, to life–in short, they both sought to reconcile film with reality. Each film theorist accomplished this reconciliation largely outside of the structuralist view of film that gave priority to editing and also saw the film as merely the product of an artistic endeavor.

Through their emphasis on the iconic/indexical aspects of film, what amounts to a continuation of Balázs and Kracauer's shared project to reconcile film with reality, theorists like Pier Paolo Pasolini and Peter Wollen (epigraph, above) have seen that traditional film analysis was guided by a bias toward symbolic signification at the expense of the other aspects of the filmic image. In the alternative tradition articulated by Pasolini and Wollen, film is not only constituted through the language of art, but shares in what Bergson identified as the multiple nature and the "indeterminacy" characteristic of reality. Thus it is not sufficient to view film solely through the language of cuts, the close-ups, the realist long takes/deep focus, hand held camerawork and the false eyeline-matches used to unsettle the viewer or create a sense of irony. In this view of film as constituted by filmic language, the notion of a juxtapositional and arbitrary formal grammar is contrasted with a base-level content which it then trumps in importance. Although it is the system of arbitrary and symbolic signification that historically captured the attention of film analysis throughout much of the twentieth century, this system downplays the *motivated* nature of the filmic sign itself.

Unlike written texts, which arguably depend predominantly (but not only) on arbitrary systems of signification, filmic texts are based predominantly (but not only) on iconic/indexical representation. Thus, in line with Kracauer's thinking, films tend toward the concrete and the particular. As filmmaker and theorist Pasolini notes:

> [The filmmaker] chooses a series of objects, or things, or landscapes, or persons as syntagmas (signs of a symbolic language) which *while they have a grammatical history invented in that moment*–as in a sort of happening dominated by montage–*do, however, have an already lengthy and intense pregrammatical history.* [...] This is probably the principal difference between literary and cinematographic works (if such a comparison matters). The linguistic or grammatical world of the filmmaker is composed of images, and [filmic] images are always concrete, never abstract. ("The 'Cinema of Poetry,'" 171, original emphasis)

As products of the multiple yet *concrete* process of reality, films can never express the same degree of abstract signification that one finds in, for example, the novel. One would never experience the abstract or generalized sign "tree" in a film as one can in a book. No such generality can ever exist on the screen–a "tree" is always a "pine tree" or an "orange tree," for example. Iconic and indexical signs in film clearly possess a concreteness that arbitrary signs lack.

This concreteness has consequences for a critical geography of film as the next chapter will explore. Since Madrid's Retiro Park plays a large role in the following analysis of Carlos Saura's film *Taxi*, it is fitting to begin there. The signifier "park" or the image of a park as described in a novel may play up the class-mediated symbolic, arbitrary, conventional social and cultural meanings of relaxation, leisure, monumentality, for example. Nevertheless, when you see, Madrid's Retiro Park on the screen, for example, you see an *iconic/indexical* manifestation of the Retiro Park in Madrid. While the park retains its place in the filmic structure, the particular message that may have been encoded by the director/editor through montage that plays upon the symbolic aspect of this place, the image has an indexical/iconic meaning that is insufficiently understood through the symbolic language of social convention and directorial intent alone. In a movie filmed on location there can be no generalized sign "park." Indexical/iconic representation in such a film is always connected to concrete place, and thus also to its substantial *pregrammatical history* and to all its attendant conceptions of meaning.

It is not hard to see that the lack of interest in the role of indexicality/iconicity in film studies is predicated on a lack of interest in the iconic in language itself. This aversion to the indexical/iconic, itself extant in the study of all visual and oral/aural languages, is perhaps most a consequence of the domination of the field of linguistics first by Saussure, who merely referenced onomatopeya as a footnote in his *General Course on Linguistics* then and pressed on to emphasize the arbitrary, and second by Noam Chomsky, whose supposedly universal grammatical concern ignores iconicity, or in the words of Peter Wollen (1972), "banishes the ungrammatical into outer darkness" (124). Yet this conception of language that reduces it merely to grammar or structure, as symbolic and socially-negotiated meaning is strongly entrenched. It does not originate merely with Saussure or with Chomsky, but rather reflects a longstanding tradition. Michel Foucault notes the sea-change that occurs, as regards the perception of linguistic functions, in the passage of the 16th to the 17th century. In *The Order of Things: An Archaeology of the Human Sciences* (1971), he writes of the change in the nature of sign. The sign, the word, at one time was conceived of as somehow resembling (read iconically) what it represented. A disconnect in co-existing modes of signification led to the primacy established in the 17th century of an arbitrary conception of the relationship signifier-signified. The debate on iconicity vs. arbitrariness, of course, goes back even further to the Cratylus, a dialogue written by Plato discussing the origin and meaning of names.

Revisiting this debate in the context of more contemporary linguistics, many researchers have emphasized the crucial role of iconicity and indexicality in language. As Ivan Fónagy (1999) states, "Iconicity, far from being a marginal kind of verb play, is a basic principle of live speech, and more generally, of natural languages" (3). Roman Jakobson and Linda Waugh have made some of the most significant contributions in this area.[6] They are thus pushing beyond the limits of Saussure's off-hand comment and assert that not only is there onomatopoeia in language, the most frequently recognized iconic form of language, but there is also phonesthesia (word groupings ending in -ash, crash, bash, flash, stash, for example, all share the characteristic of quickness). Iconicity, in fact, occurs at all scales of spoken/written language, from the level of phoneme/ grapheme through that of syntactical structures.[7] Furthermore, the meaning of spoken language is highly dependent upon visual cues not generally taken to be a grammatical part of spoken/written languages. As Pasolini writes, "In fact, a word (lin-sign or language sign) spoken with a certain facial expression has one meaning; spoken with another expression it has another meaning, quite possibly its opposite" ("The 'Cinema of Poetry,'" 167).[8]

Nevertheless, the same understanding of language that underscores the (Saussurean) bias toward the arbitrary, conventional, structural, and grammatical aspects of language has even, strangely enough, marginalized the signed/visual languages of the deaf precisely by considering them (incorrectly) to be *too* iconic/indexical. These languages, although they might display iconicity/indexicality

---

[6] Jakobson (1965), Jakobson and Waugh (1979), and Waugh and Newfield (1995) serve as good introductory readings. Waugh and Newfield (1995) is particularly concise and informative regarding the presence of iconicity in the lexicon.

[7] *Syntactic Iconicity and Linguistic Freezes: The Human Dimension* provides many examples of this type of iconicity. Among them is the classic example stemming from Jakobson (1965): veni vidi vici. Joseph H. Greenberg writes that this sequence is "the mapping of succession in language with succession in real time. [...] the act of seeing follows the act of coming and the act of conquering follows the act of seeing." (59)

[8] The study of facial expression and gesture was termed "kinesics" by Ray Birdwhitsell. He and Paul Ekman, as Prince notes, are point of entry to the field. See Birdwhitsell's *Kinesics and Context* (1970) and *Approaches to Emotion* (1984), ed. Klaus R. Scherer and Paul Ekman.

in a more apparent way than spoken/written languages, use not only iconic/indexically motivated meanings but also arbitrary/conventional ones. With the iconic/indexical aspects of language in general being so historically maligned, hearing and deaf linguists–particularly William C. Stokoe, a hearing researcher at Gallaudet credited with leading the charge for recognition of signed languages as languages in their own right in the 1960s–have fought long and hard so that the arbitrary and internally-consistent grammatical structures of signed languages might be recognized. Just as iconicity/indexicality exists both in spoken/written languages and the visual field, so too, arbitrariness exists also in languages in the visual modality: ASL (American Sign Language), LSE (Lengua de señas española), and LSC (Llengua de signes catalans), for example. Although it is a common misperception that there is a universal sign language, these are distinct natural languages that have their own syntax and lexicon which are subject to change over time. As such, they do not merely consist of iconic representational "gestures" but rather arbitrary signifiers that operate in the same way as spoken languages, only this time in the visual field.[9]

Unfortunately, the lack of both 1) adequate recognition of iconicity/indexicality as a part of language and signification in general and 2) sufficient understanding of the value of iconicity/indexicality where it has been recognized somewhat simplistically (as in the case of signed languages) has carried over from studies of language to studies of film. As both Balázs and Kracauer saw in their critiques of montage, and as Deleuze recognized in his attempt to break out from a theory that equates film with language, film studies has been severely crippled by Saussurean concepts of language. That iconicity is of little or no importance in film studies is not only caused by the absence of study of the iconic in natural languages, but also by

[9] For more information in this area, the reader may consult *Seeing Language in Sign: The Work of William C. Stokoe* (1996) by Jane Maher for the biographically driven historical view of acceptance by hearing linguists of ASL as a language, *Linguistics of American Sign Language: An Introduction* (2000) by Clayton Valli and Ceil Lucas for a discussion of ASL phonemes and syntax and *The Mask of Benevolence* (1992) by Harlan Lane for an understanding of the cultural colonization of the deaf by the hearing. For an interesting take on iconic and non-iconic forms in signed language, see "Spatial structure as a syntactical or a cognitive operation: Evidence from signing and nonsigning children" by Filip Loncke in *Syntactic Iconicity and Linguistic Freezes the Human Dimension* (1995). I have written on Deaf culture in *Sign Language Studies* (2007).

the presence of a Saussurean take on the sign, one which not surprisingly privileges the arbitrary over the iconic and the indexical.[10] Prince's illuminating essay charges correctly and succinctly that:

> Film theory since the 1970s has tended to place great emphasis upon what is regarded as the arbitrary nature of the signifier-signified relationship, that is, upon the purely conventional and symbolic aspect of signs. What this focus has tended to displace is an appreciation of the iconic and mimetic aspect of certain categories of signs, namely pictorial signs, those most relevant to an understanding of the cinema. This stress upon the arbitrary nature of semiotic coding has had enormous consequences for the way film studies as a discipline has tended to frame questions about visual meaning and communication. (99)

As relations to the fusion of film studies and geography, because films often make use of pre-existing concrete places, the meanings inscribed in these concrete places will necessarily have bearing on their interpretive possibilities in film. If a film's importance is to be found only in the arbitrary, the symbolic or the conventional, this severely limits the capability of film analysis to comment on systems of injustice whose meanings, due to the uneven geographic development characteristic of capitalism, are inscribed in space, concretely then, in place. Signs are in fact involved in a triadic model of signification involving not only arbitrariness but also iconicity and indexicality. Wollen (1972) powerfully comments on these processes of signification and their involvement in film in his seminal work:

> The cinema contains all three modes of the sign: indexical, iconic and symbolic. What has always happened is that theorists of the cinema have seized on one or more of these dimensions and used it as the ground for an aesthetic firman. [...] In the cinema, it is quite clear, indexical and iconic aspects are by far the most powerful. (125, 140)

Here, the critic signals an important direction for film theory to take, correcting an error of earlier film analysis and also highlight-

[10] Just as interesting as the idea that film analysis has been shaped by Saussurean linguistics is the idea that the bias towards arbitrariness inherent in Saussure's model of language might itself be a consequence of literary attitudes.

ing that which is unique to film as compared with the written text.[11] As a visual image that in some sense captures or redeems reality, film should draw our attention to attitudes that shape and are shaped by that reality.

In the words of Pasolini, the semiotic code of cinema is not the semiotic code of *language*, but rather is the semiotic code of *reality*.[12] Acceptance of this idea is crucial for a critical geographical analysis of film. Moreover, it is important to note that this does not preclude the film critic in any way from commenting on social structures or systems. Pasolini writes:

> Because, in fact, the "gaze" of a peasant, perhaps even of an entire town or region in prehistoric conditions of underdevelopment, embraces another type of reality than the gaze given to that same reality by an educated bourgeois. Not only do the two actually see different sets of things, but even a single thing in itself appears different through the two different "gazes." ("The Cinema of Poetry," 177)

These two gazes use the same code to approach reality; it is only that their positions regarding that reality differ. And reality, as Deleuze's writings on multiplicity, Bergson's formulation of the "image," and Kracauer's redemption of materiality suggest, is not monolithic, but is instead the terrain of contestation, the product of the mixture of material and immaterial forces. Pasolini's statement that "the semiotic code of cinema is the semiotic code of reality" is

---

[11] To some degree, the focus on the arbitrary nature of the filmic sign at the expense of its coexisting iconic and indexical aspects seems to be a consequence of trained formalist literary scholars unfairly transposing their modes of analysis from the linguistic code of narrative to the visual text. The bias that language is the pre-eminent system of signs through which to interpret all others is an easy sale for critics of written texts who can, by the very nature of their work (their object of study is undoubtedly constructed by language), thus place themselves at the center of an hermeneutic paradigm. Consider also the Tartú School (most notably I. Lotman and J. Uspenski), whose analyses posited language as a primary modeling system and all other sign systems as secondary modeling systems dependent on the first.

[12] From "Living Signs and Dead Poets" (1967). This idea is also found in Christian Metz who states that, in the semiotic sense of the word, the images of cinema are always motivated. This motivation is the semiotic process of iconicity and not that of the arbitrariness of spoken/written language. Though perhaps Metz and Pasolini agreed on this point, they had their differences–namely regarding the double-articulation of the cinematic image.

absolutely crucial.[13] It is inappropriate that arbitrary signification would seriously outmuscle iconic/indexical representation in cinematic analysis. This way of viewing film privileges form (or artistry) over content (image) instead of linking the two in a single conception of cinematic message that is at once structural/arbitrary and iconically/indexically-motivated. The result is that viewers are encouraged to interpret film texts in terms of their fictive artistry, that is, in overarching generalizations detached from the specific nature of place. At their worst these generalizations are images of "the universal plight of the working man" or trite depoliticized metaphors for the "human condition" or "the ephemeral nature of love." A theory of cinema must recognize its iconic/indexical nature, that is, its specificity of concrete place, first and foremost, integrating this with or even reading this against a given film's artistry to produce meaning (in the next chapter I pursue the latter direction).

It deserves repetition that this is not a rejection of arbitrary signification altogether. The iconic/indexical nature of film is coexistent with embedded arbitrary meanings. This fact is shown quite succinctly and in such a clear manner by Jeff Hopkins that an entire paragraph is worthy of reproduction here:

> For example, let us imagine one frame in a documentary film depicting a wide-angle shot of a city skyline. Is the film image an icon, an index, or a symbol? How strong might be the impression of an "almost real" film city, and how much effort might be required to "willingly suspend" one's disbelief that the film city is merely a projected image of light and shadow rather than an actual city? The film city is signified by all three semiotic processes. The projected image is an iconic sign because it convincingly represents or resembles what viewers visually experience, or might expect to experience, as a city in the everyday material world. The image is also an index because it has causal

[13] There are admittedly some flaws with this idea that are not fully addressed by Pasolini–we have in film only the illusions of motion and three-dimensionality as well as the complete absence of olfactory and tactile modes of sensing. Nevertheless, taking as an assumption that iconicity is a sliding scale, dependent to some degree on technological advances, the film medium is the most iconic/indexical mode of representation available (barring virtual reality experiments that are surely just over the horizon). This idea of a scale of iconicity is implicit in Prince. "Moreover, iconic representation is appropriately understood in terms of degrees of resemblance rather than the all-or-nothing terms of arbitrariness or identicality. A photograph, for example, exhibits a higher degree of iconicity than a line drawing" (102).

> connection to the material world. The skyline on the screen has been created by light reflecting off a "real" city and hitting raw film stock to produce a representation on the film of the city. The city image may also be read as a symbol of any one of a number of socially constructed conventions: adventure, mystery, progress, temptation, and so-forth. Because it is a documentary film, a so-called "live-action" authentic record of actual events using real people and objects in an actual space and time [...], spectators are more apt to accept the film city as real, which will lesson the effort necessary to suspend their disbelief. (53)

To usc Hopkins's example, film studies has tended to focus on the city skyline as a symbol thus privileging an arbitrary mode of signification. Yet the iconic/indexical aspects of the skyline are just as important. In a documentary, the iconicity/indexicality gives a sense of the specificity of place locating the film's message concretely along the axes of time and space. Chris Marker's *Le joli mai* (1963), for example, comments not only on the human universals of peace, war, love and money, but also on the specific economic and social conditions that existed in Paris in 1962 as a consequence of the Algerian War. To accept this argument in a documentary, as does Hopkins, is one thing. To see that the same process goes on in supposedly fictional films is somewhat of another matter, although a quite necessary and important one. Discussing the issue further will necessitate reassessing our notions of narrative, fact and fiction.

Fictional films, just like documentaries, are nevertheless representations of or comments on concrete locations in time and space. The overlapping of fictional and non-fictional narratives has been discussed by Linda Hutcheon (1980), Hayden White (1987) and Félix Martínez-Bonati (1992), among others. The distinction between history and fiction in the written text has been shown to be cloudy at worst, and at best, a false distinction between narrative modes that legitimizes a given authority. To bring this distinction into the study of cinema is to wrongly privilege the documentary over the fictional film. The documentary is no more a "truth" than the historical text. Both the documentary and the fictional film, as are the historical text and the fictional text, are ways of contesting or legitimizing ideology. This ideology is always tied to a sense of place. This is true even of the fantasy film, with less on-location filming, where place is evoked through the representation of community. Consider *Star Wars I: The Phantom Menace* where questionable ideas of community and place are arguably evoked through suspect presentations of accent and phenotype. But this is most true of an on-location urban film, such as *City of Angels* that in addition to representing community, inevitably place-bound, evokes a recognizable cityscape (Los Angeles). These films, predominantly the big-budget blockbusters, are designed to evoke in the viewer a reaction of superficial identification or recognition–"That is the hotel Bonaventure in Los Angeles," "Those are the twin towers of New York," "That is the Eiffel tower in Paris." There is an overlap, in this sense, of the narratives of cinema and tourism, something not surprising once we admit that the semiotic code of cinema is the semiotic code of reality (Pasolini 1988). This recognition works predominantly visually and caters to an aesthetic that is too often depoliticized.

Yet this must not necessarily be so. Consider Alex de la Iglesia's film *El día de la bestia* (1995), whose iconic representation of urban space in Madrid, as Malcolm Compitello (1999) shows, lends itself to an anti-capitalist interpretation.[14] It is not that analyses of arbitrary signs in film cannot be political. Take for example Marvin D'Lugo's (2002) analyses of Medem's *Amantes del Círculo Polar* (1998) and Almodóvar's *Todo sobre mi madre* (1999) where the critic is successfully able to extrapolate from the film to issues of the construction of national identity through a synecdoche seeing Medem's Otto and Ana as a metaphor for Spanishness (83). Yet unlike that of Compitello, such analyses are insufficient to explain power as rooted to space in scales other than the national. To explain the uneven geographical development of capitalism at the local and city/urban scales an iconic geography of film is imperative. This undertaking is even more important given the fact that cinemas function to sell place or create or legitimize ideas of place that feed into patterns of tourist consumption and economic development.

To recognize the importance of iconic/indexical signification in film–to acknowledge that the semiotic code of film is the semiotic code of reality–is to acknowledge that the space of cinema is the

[14] See "From Planning to Design: The Culture of Flexible Accumulation in Post-Cambio Madrid" (1999) by Malcolm Alan Compitello for an article that uses iconic references to the built environment in Madrid as a basis for analysis of the film's message.

space of tourism. It is undeniable that narratives of tourism play themselves out on the global screen. The increasing global character of the film industry and market has created a forum in which the practice of viewing films is more and more akin to sedentary tourism–especially since cinema is a commercially viable way to package otherness and cultural specificity. This squares with what semiotician Iuri Lotman has written about a "two-fold experience" where the film's observer participates in "simultaneously forgetting and not forgetting that the experience is imaginary in origin" (Hopkins 57; reading Lotman 1976: 17). Hopkins writes:

> By juxtaposing signs signifying other times and spaces, therefore, film promotes expansions and compressions in the viewer's temporal and spatial sensibilities; boundaries of time and space may become permeable and blurred. The viewer is simultaneously inside and outside the film, construing both fantasy and reality, switching back and forth across distances, visiting various settings and times, experiencing what Fell has termed a kind of 'geographic omnipresence' (1975, p. 63), without ever leaving his or her seat. (57)

The language that Hopkins uses to explain both Lotman (and Fell) piques our interest because of the contrast between the seemingly discrete pair of "fantasy" and "reality." This language almost seems to undermine his point, mainly that there is a confluence of two places and times which both serve equally to constitute the reality of the spectator. The phrase "without ever leaving his seat," which recalls the research method of the armchair anthropologists of the nineteenth century, is crucial to an understanding of how the cinematic experience is at once a visual spectacle and a virtual act of tourism. Within the theater, and mirroring the cohabitation of form and content, metaphor and metonymy, the two geographies of the theater and surrounding areas and that presented on the screen, collapse into one, if variegated, semiotic field.

It must not be overlooked that the role of iconicity/indexicality becomes more important given the union of a globalized film industry and a globalized tourist economy both focused on selling place (see Philo and Kearns 1993). Consider the iconic/indexical filmic representations of Madrid's Retiro Park and Hopkins's skyline examples mentioned earlier. They both have arbitrary meanings–the first leisure and freedom, the second modernity and progress. Yet in an industry in which film has to successfully negotiate the local and the global to make a profit, they also become, through their place-rooted iconicity, a way for international viewers to come to conceptualize the specificity of place–a place that importantly already has a substantial pregrammatical history.

In conclusion, despite a long semiotic history that has marginalized the iconic and indexical in favor of the arbitrary mode of signification, iconic and indexical signs necessarily play a large role in interpretation of films. It is not that the formalist tendency to fixate on arbitrary patterns of meaning is incorrect or unnecessary, but rather that a film's meaning must be approached taking into account Bergson's theory of the image, Deleuze's Bergsonian emphasis on multiplicity, Prince's defense of iconicity/indexicality, Pierce's triadic model of the sign, Balázs's and Kracauer's return to qualities and reality in the cinema, Wollen's critique of the myopic arbitrary/symbolic interpretation of films, and Pasolini's dictum regarding the semiotic code of reality–in short, film studies must redeem reality. The iconic and indexical are particularly important in reconciling film with geography. A geographical analysis of film is, moreover, imperative in combating the spatial hegemony of late-capitalism. This analysis may at times contradict a formal analysis of a film or it may at other times support it.

One must remember that filmic images, as Pasolini rightly says, are always concrete, and never abstract. This concreteness has two faces, one which frames the imagined place of pre-production, and the other which opens outward on the post-production viewing place. As the next chapter will explore, supplying an iconic/indexical corrective to a film theory traditionally biased, just as linguistics, toward arbitrary/conventional meanings will allow a better articulation of the key questions of film theory with the key questions of the rapidly urbanizing world.

CARLOS SAURA'S *TAXI*: RECONCILING FILMSPACE AND URBAN SPACE

> The cinematic landscape is not, consequently, a neutral place of entertainment or an objective documentation or mirror of the 'real', but an ideologically charged cultural creation whereby meanings of place and society are made, legitimized, contested and obscured.
>
> –Jeff Hopkins ("Mapping of Cinematic Places," 1994, p. 47)

INSTEAD of approaches that limit film as *only* representational, symbolic, metaphorical, what is needed is a perspective that methodologically balances the film on one side and the world outside film on the other–one that seeks to incorporate cinema's iconic/indexical nature as well as its manipulated structure. Michael Dear's theory of filmspace as articulated in *The Postmodern Urban Condition* provides such a perspective, strongly asserting the interrelation between both film and city. In refusing to limit cinema as a simple reflection of urban realities, his theory from the outset seeks to fold film into the built environments for both production and consumption. Although he gives his model spatialized form on the page (190), drawing what are apparently isolated boxes representing the "film text," "place of production," "production of place," and "consumption in place," these boxes are best understood, in the Bergsonian tradition as abstractions wrought of a unitary experience. These abstractions in effect serve as so many socially constructed scales (see Marston 2000) from which to view a singularity of movement that enfolds both cinema and city. Restoring iconicity/indexicality to a film theory historically driven by symbolic concerns and arbitrary connections recovers the relevance of the material problems of city-space to the (purportedly) purely symbolic nature of film.

The importance of this reconciliation has become clearer as scholars from various disciplines have explicitly developed the connections between Film Studies and geography. Volumes such as *Engaging Film: Geographies of Mobility and Identity* (Eds. Cresswell and Dixon, 2002), *Place, Power, Situation, and Spectacle: A Geography of Film* (Eds. Aitken and Zonn, 1994), *The Cinematic City* (Ed. Clarke, 1997), and *Cinema and the City* (Eds. Shiel and Fitzmaurice, 2001), among others, have linked spatial and temporal multiplicities and prioritized the question of method, thus reviving questions explored by Bergson himself. Bergson's original philosophical premise thus resonates across a web of inquiries that incorporate linguistics, film theory and finally geographical theory in an effort to "dissolve again into the Whole" (*CE*, 191). Ultimately, no word better sums up Bergson's philosophical contribution to the study of film today than "filmspace." This word, although not of Bergsonian origin, connotes a desire to reconcile the abstract concepts routinely used by analysis and to return the film as object of representation to the fluid moving reality it supposedly represents. This means, in my estimation, a return to the notion of the production of space–to the notion of geographical process.

This chapter explores this idea of filmspace–the reconciliation of on and off-screen space, of film studies and urban geography –through its application in interpreting one particular Spanish film. Although *Taxi* was made by one of Spain's most successful and prolific directors, Carlos Saura, it did not receive the attention some of his others have, and it in many ways displays the plot elements typically found in a blockbuster movie: a high dose of action, chase scenes, drugs, violence, the tension between indoctrination and striking one's own path by doing what's right. By choosing an otherwise relatively unnoteworthy film, I hope to emphasize that this process of reconciling film and geography can be applied to any film whatsoever. Most important is that the film's action culminates in an uplifting scene staged in one of the most recognizable areas of central Madrid–the Retiro Park. Reconciling both the on-screen role of the Park with its off-screen role, and thus both film studies and urban geography, the place of production and the production of place (Dear 2000) and the symbolic and the iconic/indexical, this chapter will chart out an important reconciliatory direction for film studies. This direction seeks to revisit what Raymond Williams (1986) described as the central concern of cultural studies, "the refusal to give priority to either the project or the formation–or, in older terms, the art or the society" (152).

Given the fact that Spain has been more fully engaged in the intercity competition requisite of capitalist accumulation strategies following the death of Franco on November 20, 1975, film theorists must reassess the relationship between on-screen space and off-screen space. This endeavor is framed by the work of theorists who have sought a more intimate connection between mental and physical space. In his first work, philosopher Henri Bergson declared famously that "Things are not in space, but space is in things" (1889), arguing for the conceptualization of space not as a mere container of events but as a complex method of division or differentiation at once mental and physical. This idea forms the implicit basis for spatial theorist Henri Lefebvre's watershed work *The Production of Space* (1991[1974]), wherein the latter links spaces of representation and representational spaces, and has been subsequently taken up by urban geographer David Harvey (1996; see also 1989, 1990, 2000) in the Lefebvrian tradition. Attempting to reconcile geography and cinema, Michael Dear (2000) has linked the filmic production of place with its place of production. In an attempt to show how the meaning of on-screen spaces must be tied to the production of off-screen spaces, this section will investigate the pivotal role of Madrid's central Retiro Park in Carlos Saura's film *Taxi* (1996) at the same time that it looks into the off-screen battles over the park. This park is significant not only because of its historical role and central location, but also because it has been the focal point of much Madrileñan literature[1] and film.[2] This discussion of Madrid's

[1] Naturally, in its capacity as Madrid's green lung, an important central meeting place and most recently a tourist attraction, the Retiro park has played a role in quite a few novels. In Pío Baroja's *El árbol de la ciencia* (1911), Andrés Hurtado frequents the Retiro in order to escape from his classes in medicine (33), with his family (50), with his friend Montaner (58), with Antonio Lamela (73), and with Lulú and her mother (123). The park is also central to his 1933 novel *Las noches del Buen Retiro*. In Luis Martín-Santos's *Tiempo de silencio* (1961), Retiro (38), and Cartucho, novio of Florita and eventual killer of Dorita, throws stolen objects into the Retiro's lake (139).

[2] As Jean-Claude Seguin notes in his *Historia del cine español* (1999), Benito Perojo filmed his 1914 *Fulano de tal se enamora de Manón* in the Retiro park. Yet

Retiro Park constitutes a case study illustrating how Bergsonism, through its indirect appearance in film theory, can be used to signal the false problems of an urban criticism not cognizant of its philosophical premises, thus calling for a change in the production of urban space through action and not through application of the standard dichotomies popular in academic scholarship.

In pursuing the link between the on-screen battle over the park and its off-screen companion space, this discussion will start from inside the film itself and work toward the extra-filmic space of the Retiro Park. Initially it will be important to place the film within the context of director Saura's cinematographic tradition. I will first briefly outline the successful critique of the bourgeois family that Saura achieves in *Taxi*–a hallmark of a number of his earlier films. Those he directed under the dictatorship such as *La caza* (1965) and *Jardín de las delicias* (1970) certainly functioned as an important, if subtle or guised, critique of the deployment of Franco's power and its concomitant and problematic persecution of marginality and difference. From this auteur perspective, and within the tradition of Saura's larger work, *Taxi* functions as a harsh invective against the fascist ideology that took root in Spanish culture under the dictatorship.

While this is certainly a valid approach, it insufficiently grapples with the iconic/indexial meaning of the film images and ultimately conflicts with a reading of the film from a perspective grounded in urban theory. A closer look at the portrayal of urban space in *Taxi* shows the extent to which Saura's traditional metaphors fail to comment on the more recent production of urban inequalities across the city-spaces of post-dictatorial Spain. This alternative reading of the film allows an assessment of the disconnect between the emphasis on structure/montage in the traditional/auteur-oriented film analysis and the consideration of film as part of the extra-filmic process of selling place. Although Saura launches a substantial critique of the fascist ideology operating prior to the transition to democracy, the film's abrupt and easy solution to the complex problem of social and cultural difference severs mental ideas of space from their simultane-

more importantly Seguin goes on to acknowledge the park as "[un] decorado constante de las películas de la época" (14). Alex de la Iglesia's *El día de la bestia* closes with a shot of the park's statue to the fallen angel, evoking a powerful commentary on the ills of capitalist production of the built environment.

ous counterpart–the physical built environment of Madrid's Retiro district. In effect, the film leaves the viewer thinking that to get rid of the fascist holdovers from the dictatorship is to end the persecution of the marginal in Madrid. Ultimately, engaging the spatial practices of post-cambio Madrid requires a more sophisticated understanding of capital's role in the formation of the modern city than *Taxi* is prepared to offer.

This sophisticated model of capital can be found in what David Harvey (1989) terms the twin processes of the urbanization of consciousness and the urbanization of capital. Reading the use of the park in the film requires delving into the production of the off-screen park, from the progressive gentrification of the Retiro district throughout the twentieth century to the police interventions and historic preservation of the 1990s. From a perspective that sees film as a mere reflection or metaphorical commentary, detached from extra-filmic social processes, *Taxi* is certainly a successful denunciation of institutionalized marginalization. Yet if film is returned to the social context in which it is produced, viewed and interpreted–in an approach that attempts to reconcile the filmic space of the Retiro Park with the extra-filmic urban space of the Madrid of the 1990s–Saura's product has quite another meaning indeed. The fact that it was filmed in the Retiro Park during a time in which the park itself was closed at night, and during the day being cleansed of racial difference for sale to transnational capital, allows an interesting study of the jarring contrast between the production of on-screen and off-screen space.

This section thus suggests two valid interpretations of *Taxi* that are at odds with one another. The first–the auteur approach–reveals that the film successfully denounces an insular construction of Spanish identity. The second–what might be called the urban approach–, in reconciling the film with its extra-filmic counterpart, raises new questions about how Spanish film might be understood in a post-dictatorial context. This second approach requires that theory find some way of returning questions of artistry to the social world in which identities and places are constituted through images and their underlying cultural and economic processes. Rather than merely finding fault with Saura, to put it bluntly–i.e. declaring the director either a bourgeois or progressive filmmaker in the tradition of Walter Benjamin's speech "The Author as Producer" of 1934–I want to emphasize the opportunity his film offers to dwell on the spatial problems of the city and on questions of representing social struggle in urban films. Such films, like all cultural processes, are not mere containers for one incontestable monolithic truth, but instead are subject to those very battles over the construction of meaning that regulate the selling of identities and places for tourist consumption. Ultimately, it is important that a film criticism attuned to struggles over urban space reframe questions of directorial intent in terms of the spatial problems that a given film makes visible–or those that it obscures.

Perhaps miming its straight-forward ideological critique of Fascism, *Taxi* develops a chronological plot whose narrative structure is squarely conventional. There are no extended breaks of place or time. There are no ambiguities as to the events themselves–such things being quite frequent among the films of younger directors of the 1990s.[3] It is to Saura's credit that this very bourgeois class of people forms the central family and focus of his film. In *Taxi*, a group of accommodated middle-class *taxistas* use their profession to facilitate the realization of their fascist ideology–roughing up blacks, throwing addicts off bridges, and persecuting anyone that does not conform to a heterosexual norm. Before taking a closer look at the film itself and the way in which Saura's presentation of Madrid is informed by struggles over difference, I would like to briefly discuss Saura's focus on the bourgeois family itself, which is certainly nothing new to *Taxi*. In fact, the director has frequently and powerfully used a bourgeois friend group or family as a synecdoche for the class that benefited from the Spanish Civil War (1936-39).

Starting out with what Virginia Higginbotham (1988) terms realist aims (77), Saura soon turned to slightly veiling his criticism of the civil war and the Franco regime. This critique has often found expression in a group or family that allegorically models larger social struggles. Higginbotham gives the example of *La caza* (1965), where Saura used the three businessmen Paco, José and Luis to represent the class ideology that came to power in the post-war years. Another example is *Jardín de las delicias* (1970), in which José Luis López Vázquez plays Antonio Cano, an industrialist suffering from amnesia as a result of a car accident. His family tries

[3] For example, Alejandro Amenábar's *Abre los ojos* (1997) and Mateo Gil's *Nadie conoce a nadie* (1999).

to bring back his memory through a series of dramatic recreations of significant episodes of his life. Their goal, ultimately, is to induce him to remember the number of his Swiss bank account. Cano is clearly representative of a Spain whose amnesia reflects the repression of the Franco era. His family, similarly, is a Spain witness to Franco's declining health. As Higginbotham states, "López Vázquez achieves an almost iconographic importance in the countermyths of Carlos Saura" (86). The critic fruitfully extends this analysis to include other films by the director: *Ana y los lobos* (1972), *La prima Angélica* (1973) and *Cría cuervos* (1975). The family of *Taxi* is another perfect example of this tradition of the filmmaker's. Here there is no nuclear or extended family, but rather of a group of *taxistas*, only some of whom share blood relationships. Extending Marvin D'Lugo (1991), these taxi drivers are the logical continuance of the Spanish bourgeois characters that Saura has depicted in films since *La caza* (1965), wearing "the mask of modernity, while mentally and spiritually rooted in the past" (67). The family in *Taxi*, while similarly mentally and spiritually rooted in the past, is, however, in some sense a modern family–an urban family. It is this tension between Spain's past and present, Madrid's persecution and possible acceptance of marginality that Saura's film attempts to resolve.

While *Taxi* continues what can be seen as Saura's traditional critique of the bourgeois family, the film also innovatively directs the viewer's attention to the negotiation of both city-space and urban issues. The taxi is itself a very important choice of title and theme by Saura that emphasizes his modern, urban focus on Madrid. The taxi leitmotif of the film highlights patterns of movement through and access to urban space.[4] The prominent experience of the taxi-ride in the film encourages a view of the city as a product constructed by notions of difference and focuses on the taxi as a vehicle for viewing the urban. In navigating the city as space of urbanized capital, we are forced to ask questions of the concomitant urbanized consciousness–not only "Who has access to space?" but also "Who has the right to the city?" (Lefebvre 1968; D. Mitchell 2003). The taxi-ride seems to offer a respite, however ephemeral, from the out-

[4] In this sense there is an interesting comparison to be made with Jim Jarmusch's *Night on Earth* (1992) which tells the stories of five taxi drivers in five large cities across the western globe.

side world and its issues of power–it almost seems a space of liminality, betwixt and between point of departure and destination. Yet in arriving at this conclusion there is something quite rotten–as Saura's inflection of the *taxistas* with fascism instructs the viewer. As the film suggests, this sense of liminality cannot be sense of neutrality. Interests of class, gender, and race are no more invisible inside the taxi than they are throughout the city as a whole–there can be no politically neutral space. Conflicts of class, gender and race are played out even inside the taxi, as the rear-view mirror is used to negotiate space between passenger and driver, and dialogue either challenges or necessarily reinforces the issues of power that root themselves in less transitory institutions.

In Saura, the taxi serves as a vehicle for the direct confrontation of fascism with marginality. Here, the purportedly neutral although ephemeral spatial qualities of the taxi become the direct instruments of violence. Saura's family of *taxistas* steps in to fill the gap left by the Franco dictatorship and continue its early fascist aims of cleansing within a new context–perhaps akin to the "*Limpia Madrid*" gangs of Alex de la Iglesia's *El día de la bestia* (1995) who set fire to the homeless in the street. Calero, the most vehement leader of Saura's group of *taxistas* sums up this attitude while staring down at a *chabola*, "Negros, maricones, drogadictos, delincuentes internacionales… Ellos tienen la culpa de todos los males que padece este país...". Calero's list of the scapegoats for Spain's supposed ills forms an equally accurate summary of the movie's most brutal scenes.

As part of the opening sequence of the movie, the camera pans downward from a hotel directly to a woman vomiting into a trash can. As a taxi approaches her, the *taxista* notices a needle on the ground next to the woman. She is subsequently disposed of by the male members of the "*familia taxista*" for being a drug-addict by being thrown off of a bridge. A switch from successive mid-shots to a decisive low-angle long shot that frames the bridge from below just after the moment of the woman's release directs the viewer's attention to the connection between the isolated event and larger issues of the city. In the next episode,[5] an upper-class black passenger is on his way to the Hotel Palace via taxi. His request of destination

[5] Which recalls the Paris segment of Jim Jarmusch's *Night on Earth* (1992). See also Mahoney (1997).

is met with the *taxista*'s racist reply "Desde cuándo admiten negros en el Palace." After the passenger gets out, he spits on the hood of the taxi, and the driver leaps out and begins to rough him up on the hood while launching an insular and racist invective at him. The violence is only stopped by a chance police car driving by, which gives the passenger the chance to escape. In one of the more extended segments, the *taxistas*, armed with baseball bats, go to a *chabola* to destroy that which they see as being responsible for, as above, "todos los males que padece este país"–ultimately setting fire to the shanty-town.

Saura's intent here is to echo the bourgeoisie's instrumental support of Franco during the Spanish Civil War. Following from Gerald Brenan (1960), tired of a history of violent worker strikes and brutal repressions, many members of the bourgeoisie in Spain were easily persuaded to a fascist ideology that promised illusions of unity and an end to conflict. While denouncing Francoist ideology, the film also expertly reproduces the evils of bourgeois mobility. Contrary to the taxi drivers of Jim Jarmusch's *Night on Earth* (1992) or even Martin Scorsese's *Taxi Driver* (1976) who are clearly working class, here the mobility of the *taxistas* likens them to the middle class. Their taxis, indicative of their middle-class access to space, facilitate their arrival at, and more importantly, their quick getaway from the *chabola* after they have beaten its habitants and set fire to their dwellings and possessions.

The camera emphasizes the connection of these class-based atrocities to the city, and thus to an increasingly urbanized, though not uniquely Spanish, consciousness. Larry Ford (1994) documents that "the role of cities in film gradually changed over time from serving as mere background scenery to acting as the equivalent of major characters in many stories (119). This is most certainly the case in Saura. Throughout the movie, lighting and camera angle are manipulated to capture the reflections of buildings and the urban on the windshield of the taxi. The effect is such that, in looking at the *taxista*, the viewer cannot visually separate them from the superimposed reflections. Person and city are cut from and constructed by the same fabric. Moreover, this city is itself produced in the image of the bourgeoisie. The family formed by the *taxista* Velasco (played by Ángel de Andrés López), his wife and their daughter Paz (Ingrid Rubio), who is the main protagonist of the movie, is solidly middle-class. Shots of the daughter's room clearly depict bourgeois space. Innumerable outfits fill her closet. Mirrors line many surfaces in the room as a metaphor for the bourgeoisie's wide-angled access to space, extending the visual space of the room for both Paz and movie-goer alike. A poster on the wall depicts a palm-treed tropical scene of bourgeois escape, the image of a possible vacation-destination equally at home in Manuel Vázquez Montalbán's *Los mares del sur* (1979). Paz, however, although a product of her bourgeois family environment, is seemingly interested in progressive causes, carrying around a lighter upon which is written "*Lucha por la paz*," which eventually gets Dani (Carlos Fuentes), her stock love interest in trouble.

Dani, the youngest *taxista*, plays a less peripheral role in the brutality. Although he urinates on someone he calls a *maricón* in a dance club bathroom and beats one of the members of the *chabola* with a baseball bat, he is nevertheless portrayed–unconvincingly–as politically on the fence. He waffles from racially insulting a black peddler in a bar to purportedly apologizing to him later on and even purchasing a gift from him in order to prove his love to Paz. The violence instigated by Dani and the entire family of *taxistas* is simultaneously an attempt by fascists representing an accommodated bourgeois class to reclaim the city as their own space. These attempts take on a special meaning since they are perpetrated against infiltrations of otherness, in terms of class, race, gender and sexuality made more poignant by Spain's increasing involvement in a global economy. In contrast to *Jardín...*, *Taxi* represents a move out of the isolation of the Franco period to encompass themes of more relevance in a globalized world–issues of contemporary immigration and difference.

Despite this successful and direct denunciation of fascist beliefs, Saura's *Taxi* simplifies the way in which the battle over city-space is dominated–not merely by ideological precepts considered separate from economic factors motivating the production of space–but by the laws of flexible capital accumulation and their support by the Spanish bourgeoisie. Lacking from the film is a substantial critique of these laws that unerringly presents capital, and not just its culturally-based lackeys, as the prime player in this battle over space. Ultimately, Saura's film portrays ideology as a mere mental form superimposed upon a pre-existing city-space. This ideology, the film argues, has played no role in the construction of the city itself. Thus to rid Madrid of the Francoist fascist hold-outs–which is indeed the film's finale–is to cleanse the city itself of inequality, and to immediately restore to marginalized peoples the right to negotiate city-space as they please. An exploration of the interesting parallel between the key role of Madrid's Retiro Park in the film and its role in struggles over difference in Madrid during the 1990s will bring out the insufficiency of Saura's critique of ideology. Although from the auteur perspective the film succeeds, from the urban perspective, Saura is blind to the way in which his own filmic representation of the city projects a space that is–to use the words of Walter Benjamin–a mere "object of comfortable contemplation."

The Spain of the 1990s faced new questions of cultural and national identity under the globalized nature of the world economy. In recent decades, Spanish film has been in an important position to comment upon these questions of changing identity. Though the Franco regime itself became more invested in entering the world economy even before 1975, most of all due to its anti-communist position during the Cold War, Spain is now in a position to participate more fully in a system dominated by corporate multinationals and governments cooperating to sell place as never before. This selling of place has been facilitated by and reflected in the Spanish cinema despite a transparent effort to disguise the process in patriotic rhetoric. In 1982, Barry Jordan notes:

> Government policy reaffirmed the PSOE's [Partido Socialista Obrero Español] pre-electoral commitment to the concept of a subsidized national cinema, defining the cinema not simply as a commercial product but as a 'cultural good' ('bien cultural'), which formed part of the people's cultural heritage ('el patrimonio del pueblo') and served as an instrument of emancipation ('instrumento de liberación') (Hopewell, 1989, p. 400; Gubern et al., 1995, pp. 400-01). (181)

Yet despite this decree that cinema was "not simply a commercial product," the film industry, especially during the 1990s, became subject to the desires of its financers. These financers, as Jordan continues, were more and more dominated by "foreign transnational capital, which demands projects that promise a commercial return" (190). The appearance of corporate American product-placement–in the form of a Coca-Cola vending machine in one scene of *Taxi*–testifies to Spanish cinema's involvement in these global and commercial practices which, having been almost absent under Franco, are becoming more and more an integral part of filmmaking, not to mention the viewing experience itself.

The present discussion of space in the city and its corresponding cultural and cinematic forms is informed by the theory of cultural geographer David Harvey. The parallel processes that Harvey terms the "urbanization of capital" and the "urbanization of consciousness" work to shape specific interests that in turn police the city. This consciousness is a negotiation between and amongst five loci of power: individualism, class, community, the state, and the family, all of which interact with capital to form and reify the way in which we conceptualize the city. As capital and consciousness become increasingly urbanized in the uneven geographical development of capitalism, the city becomes the playground of those trying to decrease turnover time. Turnover time can only be accelerated through the production of space and long-term investments. Capitalists and local, state, and federal governments work together to create spaces of long-term investment that will make money, but that will do nothing to minimize the disparity between what the upper tier earns and what the underclass brings home. Harvey (2000) illuminates the distinctively capitalist production of space:

> Capitalism thereby builds and rebuilds a geography in its own image. It constructs a distinctive geographical landscape, a produced space of transport and communications, of infrastructures and territorial organizations, that facilitates capital accumulation during one phase of its history only to have to be torn down and reconfigured to make way for further accumulation at a later stage. (54)

As sections of the city fall prey to urban renewal schemes, working class areas are gutted, spruced up, resold, in the hopes that more affluent populations will turn dumps into booming downtowns.

These processes intensify in the city that necessarily engages in interurban competition–Madrid, as I will show, is a prime example of this intensification. As capital becomes urbanized it is also globalized, and the idea of selling place in a global economy becomes a city's main focus. To be sold, places must undergo a minimization of difference. As Harvey (1996) writes, drawing on Boyer (1988):

> Investment in consumption spectacles, the selling of images of places, competition over the definition of cultural and symbolic capital, the revival of vernacular traditions associated with places as a consumer attraction, all become inflated in inter-place competition. I note in passing, that most of postmodern production in, for example, the realms of architecture and urban design, is precisely about the selling of place as part and parcel of an ever-deepening commodity culture. The result is that places that seek to differentiate themselves as marketable entities end up creating a kind of serial replication of homogeneity. (298)

Class conflict must be erased from the landscape, written out of that place's history. Cities strive to attract international businesses that are all too pleased to set up shop in an area in which the infrastructure of what Marx denominated the "second circuit of capital" is already provided for them. The nature of capitalism's "spatial fix," or its uneven geographic development, necessitates that these corporations seek out the most advantageous business location. The interpretation of the city, and of all its representations both in cultural products, filmic and otherwise, necessitates a negotiation of the twin processes of the urbanization of capital and that of consciousness, and of their particular spatial manifestations. How, then, should the cultural critic interpret the presence or absence of these connections in filmic representations of the city?

On this point Walter Benjamin's "The Author as Producer" appears to offer direction. Addressing the Institute for the Study of Fascism in Paris on 27 April 1934, he distinguishes between two types of authors, the bourgeois and progressive:

> You believe the present social situation forces him [the author] to decide in whose service he wishes to place his activity. The bourgeois author of entertainment literature does not acknowledge this choice. You prove to him that, without admitting it, he is working in the service of certain class interests. A progressive type of writer does acknowledge this choice. His decision is made upon the basis of the class struggle: he places himself on the side of the proletariat. And that's the end of his autonomy. He directs his activity towards what will be useful to the proletariat in the class struggle. (85-86)[6]

---

[6] Though these comments were made in an era of the fascists' rise to power, their force does not diminish when related to today's context. Consider the asser-

Still key is Benjamin's designation of bourgeois production as that which "transforms the political struggle so that it ceases to be a compelling motive for decision and becomes an object of comfortable contemplation." The political struggle, though it has gone considerable mutations from Benjamin's pre-war context to Harvey's late-twentieth century urbanized consciousness, is still an appropriate lens through which to view cultural products. Under Benjamin's formulation, the authors of contemporary film have a responsibility to speak out against ideological injustice.

Yet there is a gap between those filmmakers that approach injustice as a mental construct detached from the built environment and those who present mental ideologies as intimately tied to the production of city-space. An approach that undertakes to reconcile film studies with urban geography requires investigation of the link between the ideological premises that frame capital-accumulation and the physical space of the city. The nature of capitalist intercity competition requires the modification of Benjamin's argument to account for the somewhat more subtle deployment of privileged categories of difference that actualize themselves in the modern city. If urban space is a simultaneously mental and physical product, as Lefebvre and Harvey argue, then it is methodologically suspect to denounce, on one hand, the mental idea without its corresponding spatial configuration, or on the other hand, a spatial configuration without the idea of space through which it is actualized.[7] Melding Benjamin's important statement with recent urban theory suggests that Harvey's (1989) connections between the "rules of capital accumulation" and the "ferment of social, political, and cultural forms" are either explicitly present, as in the work of a progressive filmmaker, or ignored, as in the case of a bourgeois filmmaker. Using this reformulated criterion for evaluating a film's political stance reveals that *Taxi* does not sufficiently critique the connection between capital accumulation and social, political and cultural forms.

---

tion by Michael Parenti (1989) that "US policymakers use fascism to protect capitalism" (52). Though there is no space here to discuss the fascist nature of contemporary capitalist injustice, it should suffice that injustice exists tied to capitalist processes of wealth concentration.

[7] Harvey (1989) writes that: "The conquest of space first required that it be conceived of as something usable, malleable and therefore capable of domination through human action. A new chronological net for human exploration and action was created through navigation and map-making" (176).

Perhaps the most important location filmed in the movie is *El Parque del Retiro* in Madrid, which occupies a central place in its narrative. The viewer witnesses night scenes of the *Palacio de Cristal*, lit-up in splendor, and the water's edge monument to Alfonso XII. It is this monument that forms the location for the movie's climactic final confrontation between Paz, Dani, and Calero. In this scene, Calero is worried about Dani's increased predilection for the notorious political fence-ride due to his non-fascist love interest, Paz, and determines to kill her. Paz, also worried about Dani's choices, arrives at the *Parque del Retiro* to escape and sits meditatively under the statue of Alfonso XII at the water's edge. Calero arrives with a gun, and Dani enters the monument from another side, forming a triangle. In a stock love-interest-sticks-up-for-girl move, Dani says that Calero will have to kill him first. Calero shoots Dani, conveniently enough in the shoulder. Dani knifes Calero, and as Calero is about to knife him back, Paz shoots Calero several times with his own gun. Dani, supposedly cleansed of his military ingrained life-long fascist prejudices, walks out of the park, limping alongside Paz, along the tree-lined path that leads to the water's edge. With the leader of the fascist family killed, the persecution of marginalized city-dwellers will end. Thus the park's space has supposedly been reclaimed for all.

As I will discuss, this solution is an all-too-easy one which ignores the way the Retiro Park was already enmeshed in webs of capital accumulation before the filming of *Taxi*. Its important role in the accumulation of tourist and business capital increased substantially throughout the 1990s, even during and shortly after the filming of *Taxi*. In ignoring the reality of this extra-filmic Retiro Park, Saura's film can be accused of a certain negligence following the lines of Benjamin's thought–newly informed by urban theory. Despite the erroneous assertion made by Harvey (1989) that film is "in the final analysis, a spectacle projected within an enclosed space on a depthless screen" (308), there is, indeed, an interaction between the medium of film and the city. Rob Lapsley (1997) writes of the oft-quoted cliché that "the city is constructed as much by images and representations as by the built environment" (187). Both city and film are, in a sense, reifications of processes engendered by the distinctively urban nature of consciousness and capital. Both share a capacity if not a propensity to present dominant discourses of power as natural. And as the writing of Jeff Hopkins (1994) shows, film, too, has the power to construct a façade of neutrality over that landscape of power–"The cinematic landscape is not, consequently, a neutral place of entertainment or an objective documentation or mirror of the 'real', but an ideologically charged cultural creation whereby meanings of place and society are made, legitimized, contested and obscured" (47).[8] This realization necessitates a discussion of *El Retiro* off the screen.

Madrid's Retiro Park, comparable in many ways to New York's Central Park and situated behind the renowned Prado museum, is a large green royal legacy in the center of the city and at the heart of a recent battle over public and private space. The park's most recent manifestation, as a space in continuous production by both material and ideological forces, has been fraught with simultaneous historical restoration, increased privatization, subsequent police intervention and the production of what Steven Flusty (1994) terms "crusty space"–"space that cannot be accessed, due to obstructions such as walls, gates and check points" (17). At issue is certainly the question "who has the right to the city?" (Lefebvre, 1968: reformulated in D. Mitchell, 2003). Faced with the all too one-sided struggle for power that underlies the cleansing of the park and surrounding areas, whose collective image is being sold to transnational interests and dominated by the intercity competition requisite of a local, regional and national tourist-centered economy, the answer to the question "who has the right to the city" would seem to be: the urban developers who are given priority in shaping space and contingent privileges of race and class. Delving into the place-bound history of the park and surrounding areas reveals a curious intersection of on and off-screen narratives. The doubled *Retiro* and its surrounding areas, in both the on-screen and the off-screen Madrid, proves to be a space progressively claimed by the Spanish bourgeoisie for use in selling the city to tourism and transnational capital.

As María Jesús Vidal Domínguez notes, at the beginning of the 20th century, housing in older sections of the zone known as *El Retiro* was originally directed to working or popular class peoples. Yet, the middle class soon occupied these dwellings. In the 60s and 70s, the same pattern emerges nearby. The zone known as *Niño Jesús* was first directed to middle class professionals, but was occu-

[8] This citation appears also in Dear (1999: 182).

pied by the more accommodated middle class who installed pools and gardens among other renovations characteristic of their class privilege. Housing in *Estrella* was constructed for lower middle class families but was soon placed in demand by middle class professionals. *Fuente del Berro*, too, underwent a change from lower-middle class to solid middle class residents. A familiar pattern emerges in which the underclass is pushed to the outer rim of the city or from one place to another as cities try to secure a safe haven for transnational capital. This capital, tied to tourism, would rather see homogeneity than the real wealth disparities created by practices of flexible accumulation that now greatly inform the global production of city-space.

The park itself has long-time ties with class privilege. "Lugar predilecto de los reyes ya desde la época de Felipe II, fue Felipe IV el que impulsó su creación y en 1868 se convirtió en propiedad del municipio."[9] Contrasting with one of the goals of the Revolution of 1868, which sought to bring the location under public control, the 1990s saw the increasing privatization of the park's supposedly public space. An attempt to close the park at the start of the '90s did not fully succeed due to the lack of perimetral barriers. In 1995, before *Taxi* was released, the park's closing was announced "por razones de seguridad y para evitar el gamberrismo" (Blasco, *El Mundo*, 1 Feb 2000). The rhetoric of protecting the public disguises a need to remake the park in the bourgeois image, and is a reformulation of the same attitudes that have sought to homogenize space in Spain since at least the start of the twentieth century, if not since even earlier.

On the screen, Saura's bourgeois fascist characters strangely enough have unfettered access to the park. There is no evidence of the night-time *gamberrismo* that has motivated talk of its closings. Instead, the violence therein is the product of the same particularly bourgeois fear and hatred that characterized support of the Civil War Nationalists and accompanied Spain's integration into a global economy in the Post-Franco era. *Taxi* presents a homogenized view of public space idealized by a bourgeois mental cartography. It is this urbanized consciousness, present in Madrid before *Taxi*'s release as well as in Saura's film itself, that has engulfed *El Retiro* and surrounding areas in class struggle even after the film's release.

---

[9] See <http://www.madridhoy.net/ciudad/parques.htm>.

During the 1990s, the park increasingly became the site of a battle over the privatization of space–a battle that seems to be dominated by governmental legislation under the rule of the more conservative Partido Popular (PP) that beat out the socialist PSOE in 1996. This legislation seems, more than ever, to focus on attracting tourism and business. Chris Philo and Gerry Kearns (1993) describe three ways in which history is used to attract these very things, or in other terms, "sell place."

> The first occurs when local authorities and local entrepreneurs self-consciously draw upon the economic and social history of a particular place as a source of pride and inspiration for the present [...] The second and related possibility here entails the use of 'heroic' imagery surrounding historical processes as a lever for money-making and persuasion in the present [...] The third possibility here involves the planned adoption of all manner of historical references, particularly architectural references, in the fabric of the built environment, so as to foster the 'cosy' ambience of a place that is basically familiar. (6)

As recent urban projects have sought to sell Madrid in the realm of interurban competition, they have used all three of these methods. The park and surrounding areas have become part of efforts to restore Madrid's patrimony, to seek out the false shadow of historical accuracy, and also to police bourgeois space to secure the interests of transnational capital.

Madrid also experienced a massive campaign to restore historical monuments. In the last few years, restorations have been performed on over 182 statues, 174 sculpture groups, 397 fountains, and 17 doors and arcs (Esteban, *El Mundo*, 10 Jan 2001). Slated for restorations, even the top of the statue of Alfonso XII at the water's edge was closed to the public stating in 1990 (*El Mundo*, 16 March 2000). Documentation of the clean-up was even organized into a museum exposition itself, on the assumption that "Los madrileños no tienen conocimiento suficiente del patrimonio monumental del que disponen," according to Sigfrido Herráez, Concejal de Vivienda y Rehabilitación Urbana (Esteban, *El Mundo*, 10 Jan 2001). As regards the bourgeois production of space it seems there is always a need to document, and in this case, document in a museum the documentation that already exists in the park, itself a museum.

Furthermore, the *Retiro* metro stop, declared a Monumento Histórico Nacional in 1997, was also remodeled in an attempt to sell Madrid's urban space. Homogenization of corporate interest has taken precedence over that of small businesses. As Sandra Commisso writes of the station: "Los quioscos y locales que se instalaron sin respetar la estética del lugar serán reubicados de acuerdo con la idea original. En fotos antiguas conservadas en el Museo Ferroviario se puede apreciar que la farmacia, la fiambrería y la bombonería, mantenían el mismo estilo de la estación" (*Clarín*, 26 Oct 2000). Here as elsewhere in the world of globalized capital, historic preservation serves as a smokescreen for the consolidation of corporate interest as small businesses are pushed out for "not fitting the style we had in mind."

The same interests apparent in the restoration projects above have resulted in increased policing of the *Parque del Retiro* itself. The reasons given for the privatization of this supposedly public space have been the usual–prostitution, drugs and stigmatized undesirables. Sound like *Taxi* yet? Yet underneath these conservative rationalizations lie larger systems of capital and the social injustice that always accompanies them. Non-governmental organizations such as SOS Racismo have denounced the increased policing of the park. Rosa M. Tristán describes the presence: "Policías a caballo, en coche, en moto. Decenas de agentes recorren cada día, durante horas, el parque de El Retiro a la caza del inmigrante." As Tristán notes, pedestrians of African or Arab appearance were routinely and systematically stopped and asked to produce papers. Even if the papers were in order, they were told to leave (*El Mundo*, 15 Aug 1998). During June and July 1998, she continues, the municipal police identified 990 people as suspicious. Of these 911 had no result whatsoever. The operation, part of the aptly named Turista 98, found: "[...] 16 decomisos de pequeñas cantidades de droga; una navaja; un indocumentado; tres personas sancionadas por consumir algún tipo de estupefaciente en público y 56 intervenciones menores, que incluyen desde pasear suelto al perro hasta la pérdida de un niño o una multa de tráfico por circular el parque" (*El Mundo*, 29 Aug 1998). In real life, as in the movies, we see once again the homogenization of public space. The persecution of otherness in the park is not a hold-over from the Franco era as is the violence that Saura embodies in his *taxistas* so much as it is a presumably valid method to be used in policing investment of capital. In this case the capital takes the form of restoration of a national patrimony that Madrid uses to make money through selling itself to global tourism. One can see a familiar process–capitalist intercity competition must play up the history of a given place. The history of that place must be as inoffensive as possible, as bland as possible, and be presented in as supposedly neutral a manner as possible. The idea of a "neutral" history is, however, quite preposterous. Instead of calling attention to the history of persecution of immigrants, the park celebrates the history of the bourgeois control of space. The spaces of this bland monumental history must then be policed and deemed "safe" for capital.

It is important to note that attempts to reclaim that space from the interests of bourgeois supported capital have been made. The monument was the site of many pro-immigrant protests. On July 23, 2000, for example, various immigrants rights and human rights groups assembled by the monument to protest the PP's 1985 offensive Ley de Extranjería. Under this law, in the words of the organization Papeles para Todos, "los inmigrantes que lleguen a España no serán personas con reconocimiento legal y derechos, sino 'ilegales obligados a aceptar cualquier condición de trabajo, a ocultarse, a callar ante las injusticias'" (*El Mundo*, 24 Jul 2000). The interests of these immigrants are not being served by the aforementioned large-scale historical restoration projects. Rather these urban projects reconstruct space to accommodate a larger influx of multinational money.

In the context of the above place-bound history of *El Parque del Retiro* and its surrounding areas, I return once again to the climactic ending of *Taxi*. The characters' free movement in the park at night, seen in this light, reflects their privileged status and their appearance as non-immigrants. Their mobility goes unchecked, in marked contrast to the fact that by the filming of this scene, there had already been much discussion surrounding the closing of the park and the marginalized people who occupied its presumedly public space. In an inversion of the discourse advanced by the *taxistas* in the movie, the strange occupants of the park are the middle class themselves. The "*gamberrismo*" cited in 1995 as the reason for wanting to close the park takes the form of the racially privileged and fascist-leaning Calero, who is shot dead. Yet, it is too easy to conclude that justice has been served. As Paz and Dani march out of the park toward the rising sun, the movie would have one believe that Calero's fascism is a characteristic of a generation gone by–that a new generation marches forward, rejecting racism, homophobia, and the marginalization of women. With Calero dead, we presume, Dani will be deprogrammed and metaphorically seek out the "*Lucha por la paz*" lighter that became emblematic for his struggle. The problems posed by the use of *El Parque del Retiro* in *Taxi*, however, are not easily packaged as Francoist ideology, but rather as I have attempted to show, by the marked construction of space around the ideology of selling Madrid in a globalized economy. It is this ideology that is only hinted at through Saura's movie. He does not unravel the link of the *taxista* attitudes to global business, but rather displays the social ill without its corresponding economic counterpart. The Hollywood ending is reproduced here in all of its glory as a new day dawns, love and drying blood are in the air, and the lovers' passage through the park goes unchallenged.

Ultimately, Saura's traditional critiques and metaphors seem unlikely to capture the issues surrounding space in an epoch of flexible accumulation. Despite functioning on one level as a harsh commentary of insular Spanish attitudes, on another, *Taxi* merely functions to sell place with its focus on the monumental history of the Retiro Park and its final over-dramatic crane shot taken of the rising sun from the statue of Alfonso XII. The relationship of capital to its corresponding socio-cultural manifestations is not fully developed, and what development exists is disappeared in the final scene as we are dealt an all-too-familiar ending. Will a viewer of the movie see use of the park as anything other than that which appears in a tourist brochure? The park information easily found on the web can serve just as easily as a summary of the movie itself.

> Se trata de uno de los parques más animados de Madrid. Desde la entrada norte se baja por un paseo arbolado hasta el lago, donde se pueden alquilar barcas de remos, en un lado del estanque se levanta una columnata semicircular con la estatua ecuestre de Alfonso XII. Recomendamos un paseo por este parque, uno de los sitios emblemáticos de Madrid.[10]

As class history gets erased from the landscape of globalized capitalism it, too gets erased from popular memory. The most em-

---

[10] See <http://www.rodamons.net/espamadrid.htm>.

blematic sites of a city, in tourist parlance, become those that express a false image of class homogeneity. The most economically successful movies do the same. As Spanish film gains a wider international market and more distance from the Franco era, there is a danger that it will become even less critical and more bourgeois. As cultural artifacts, films play an important role in class war, either affirming or protesting capitalist claims on the landscape, either pointing out injustice or contributing to it through omission. A key challenge for Spanish film studies in this post-dictatorial context will be to assess the gap between the perspective of traditional auteur analysis and urban theory regarding the struggles over city-space. This assessment requires the twin investigation of how urban space is used in film as well as of how the film is used in urban space–ultimately a return to Raymond Williams's conception of cultural studies as "the refusal to give priority to either the project or the formation–or, in older terms, the art or the society" (152).

PART III. URBAN THEORY

FROM BERGSON TO LEFEBVRE: TOWARD A PHILOSOPHY OF THE URBAN

> The philosopher and philosophy can do nothing by themselves, but what can we do without them? Shouldn't we make use of the entire realm of philosophy, along with scientific understanding, in our approach to the urban phenomenon?
>
> –Henri Lefebvre (*The Urban Revolution*, p. 64)

> The relation between time and space that confers absolute priority to space is in fact a social relationship inherent in a society in which a certain form of rationality governing duration predominates. This reduces, and can even destroy, temporality.
>
> –Henri Lefebvre (*The Urban Revolution*, pp. 73-74)

ALTHOUGH Henri Lefebvre (1901-1991) publicly and consistently eschewed the philosophy of Henri Bergson (1859-1941), his writings in effect made great use of the latter's key ideas and method. Like Bergson's philosophy, Lefebvre's urban criticism denounced the spatialization of time and gave priority to lived experience over the abstractions employed by static intellectual or traditionally analytical models of experience. Throughout *The Urban Revolution* (1970), *The Production of Space* (1974), *The Critique of Everyday Life, Vol. 1-3* (1947, 1961, 1981) and the writings posthumously collected in *Rhythmanalysis* (1992), Lefebvre's urban philosophical project appropriated the ideas Bergson advanced in his three major works, *Time and Free Will* (1889), *Matter and Memory* (1896) and *Creative Evolution* (1907), through their *application* to the problems of social life–a *de facto* collaboration that Bergson never lived to appreciate and that Lefebvre would never recognize.

This connection is important not only as a corrective to the scant attention paid to Lefebvre's work by philosophers (Elden 2001, 2004), but also because it reinforces both thinkers' own emphases on interdisciplinarity and on reconciling theories of knowledge with theories of life.

Lefebvre's early explicit rejection of Bergson's philosophy[1] might have one or many causes–the anti-Bergsonian bias of the time,[2] the widespread misunderstanding of Bergson's ideas even among philosophical circles,[3] Lefebvre's inability to see the value of philosophical work in itself,[4] or perhaps the necessary and brute rebellion of youthful iconoclasm. Yet whatever the cause, Lefebvre's facile explicit dismissal of Bergson's philosophy is at odds with his texts' uneasy, if implicit, relationship with Bergsonism's tenets. Lefebvre's later unacknowledged and unexplored application of the key ideas of Bergson's anti-philosophy, more than merely evident, deserves some scholarly attention. In fact, the fundamental position

---

[1] Stuart Elden considers this early rejection, divulged in a work by Lefebvre himself, as important to the contextualization of Lefebvre's oeuvre, in two key locations drawing the reader's attention to it quite quickly in two works: a) in the "Introduction" to *Rhythmanalysis* (2006): "Lefebvre later recounted that they were concerned with challenging the dominant philosophy of Bergson" (x). (From Henri Lefebvre, *La somme et le reste*, Paris: Méridiens Klincksieck, 3e édition, 1989 [1959] pp. 383-4), and b) in the "Introduction" to *Understanding Henri Lefebvre* (2004): "This journal [*Philosophies*] was founded [by Lefebvre and others] with the belief that a challenge to the dominant philosophy of Bergson was necessary" (2), reference as above.

[2] In the Foreword to the Second Edition of the *Critique of Everyday Life, vol. 1*, Lefebvre offers the following concise contextualization of the book's initial reception: "At that moment, in 1946, French philosophy had suffered a series of shocks from which it was only slowly recovering. The war and the Occupation had killed off several important currents of thought, notably Bergsonian anti-intellectualism, compromised by a vague relationship with German irrationalism, and Léon Brunschvicg's intellectualism, which was poorly equipped to resolve the new problems" (5).

[3] Fraser ("The Difference Space Makes," 2006) offers a concise survey of the ways in which Bergson's work was misunderstood at the time.

[4] David Harvey writes that early on, Lefebvre "became one of a small group of *jeunes philosophes* who, revolting against what they saw as the anachronistic and politically irrelevant establishment philosophy of the time (personified by Bergson), sought, largely through the pages of the radical journal, *Philosophies*, to redefine philosophical endeavors [...] Lefebvre and his companions refused to see philosophy as an isolated or wholly specialized activity" (426). Yet, while Bergson was content to engage with philosophy largely within traditional disciplinary boundaries, his philosophy itself was anything but traditional, and in fact, as the reader will have the chance to assess, paved the way for Lefebvre's analyses of society and the urban, even if the latter chose not to acknowledge this connection.

occupied by Bergson's methodological premise in Lefebvre's urban theories is simply astounding given Lefebvre's initial and explicit rejection of Bergson and the subsequent superficial dismissal of his philosophy. It is quite curious indeed that Lefebvre's approach to urban life rests solidly on such Bergsonian ideas as the rejection of "the spatialization of time," the critique of the intellectual/analytical view of living processes and movement, the generally suspect nature of thinking itself/of confusing living and knowing, the insistence on multi- or interdisciplinary approaches, and the qualitative nature of difference. Seeking a new relationship between space and time other than that offered by more traditional philosophy, both thinkers prized lived temporalities and worked to uproot the immobile intellectual (for Bergson) and analytical (for Lefebvre) representations of those complex realities. Both thus refused to cede terrain to that mode of conceptualization that reduces the heterogeneity of temporal experience to a unitary and homogeneous spatialization. Whereas Bergson struggled against the faulty premises of philosophy from within philosophy itself, it is Lefebvre who in effect appropriated Bergson's work in the act of *applying* it astutely to the whole of social life.

It must not be overlooked that "Lefebvre hated Bergson's guts" (27) as Andy Merrifield puts it in a recent and laudable work, *Henri Lefebvre: A Critical Introduction* (2006). Since there is no reason to believe that Merrifield has overstated Lefebvre's contempt for Bergson,[5] there is no other option except to expose Lefebvre's own hatred to be misdirected–or at least more appropriately directed to a false idea of Bergsonism, one that nevertheless has proved popular for no less than 100 years. Contemporary research into Bergson's ideas has proved them to be far more complex than previously understood, and more adaptable to other disciplines than Bergson himself was prepared to articulate.[6] Lefebvre, in fact, falls prey to

---

[5] As evidence, Merrifield cites Lefebvre's own autobiography: "In *La Somme et le Reste* (*Tome II*, p. 383), he writes, pulling no punches, 'If, during this period [1924-26], there was a thinker for whom we (the young philosophers group) professed without hesitation the most utter contempt, it was Bergson. This feeble and formless thinker, his pseudo-concepts without definition, his theory of fluidity and continuity, his exaltation of pure internality, made us physically sick'" (27-28).

[6] See Antliff (1993), Burwick and Douglass (1992), Deleuze (1966, 1983, 1985, 2004), Hatzenberger (2003), Kennedy (1987), Kumar (1962), Linstead (2003), Linstead & Mullarkey (2003), McNamara (1996), Mullarkey (1999a, 1999b) Olkowski (2002), Papanicolau & Gunter (1987), Power (2003), Watson (2003).

the common misconception that takes Bergsonism to dispense with space altogether in a romantic exaltation of pure temporality–what amounts to the reduction of complex spatio-temporal multiplicities to a simple and untenable idealism or subjectivity–a view rejected by Bergson himself (see *MM*, 14-17).

It is perhaps a uniquely obstinate error of Lefebvre's misreading to conclude that Bergson's notion of time was easily equated with the homogeneous and continuous narrative of history. This error is most apparent in Lefebvre's own articulation of his theory of moments (see *CEL, Vol. 2*, 342), and even in Merrifield's understandably Lefebvrian misreading of Bergsonian time as "linear" (2006: 27-28).[7] What Lefebvre denounces as Bergsonian time is in fact what Bergson himself denounces as the spatialization of time, that is, time understood as linear, a continuous historical narrative in which one event follows another, a plane of homogeneity ripe for partitioning by human thought. Time, for Bergson, is neither linear, nor homogeneous, nor reducible to periods. It is not unitary in the simple sense, an erroneous conception of Bergsonism shared by Lefebvre and Bachelard,[8] but only unitary by means of difference (see *TFW*, Deleuze *B*). All this while Lefebvre had much in common with Bergson: both decried philosophical finalism (Lefebvre,

[7] Merrifield refers to Bergson's use of the example of the arrow's path in supporting this idea that time, for Bergson, is linear. Nevertheless, the path of the arrow that Merrifield refers to, much like the example of Achilles and the tortoise which this essay will discuss below, is not used by Bergson to show the linear nature of time, but rather to show the problems of the intellect upon reducing real movement, that is, temporality, to the space this movement covers. It is space, for Bergson, that is linear, while it is time that is undirected creativity, thus the title of one of his works, *Creative Evolution*. Each exists with the other. Lefebvre's intent to praise the discontinuities, the possibility inherent in his exploration of the "moment" is what Bergson expressed in his dictum that "*Time is invention or it is nothing at all*" (*CE*, 341, original emphasis). Bergson explores the philosophical error inherent in the concept of linear time in his essay 'The Possible and the Real,' published in *CM*, 91-106.

[8] Elden (2006) explains that "*Dialectic of Duration*, is the book where Bachelard discusses rhythms most explicitly. Here Bachelard suggests that the notion of duration made famous by Bergson, is never as unitary and cohesive as Bergson suggested, but fragmentary and made up of disparate elements. It is the notion of continuity above all that Bachelard wishes to critique. Lefebvre took much from this critique" (xiii). This view of Bergson's philosophy is reductive. One does not have to have read Deleuze's (1966) formulation of *Bergsonism* to disagree, the evidence is there in Bergson's own texts: *Time and Free Will, Matter and Memory, Creative Evolution* present a complex articulation of space and time, quantity and quality. This has rarely been understood by Bergson's excessively numerous critics.

UR, 67-68; Bergson, quite extensively along with mechanism, *CE*, esp. 39-53), both dismissed the idea of space as a container (Lefebvre, *UR*, 40; Bergson, *TFW*, chapter two; *MM*, esp. 307-09; *CE*, esp. 157), both denounced the static character of human thought (Lefebvre, *R*, esp. 20-21; Bergson, *TFW*; *CE*, chapter four), both rejected any attempt to articulate time without reference to space (Lefebvre, *PS*; Bergson, *TFW*, *CE*), and both exposed the objectionable consequences of spatializing time, even if these were explicitly political for Lefebvre and only virtually so for Bergson (Lefebvre, *CEL*; Bergson, *TFW*, *MM*, *CE*).

This chapter does not take it upon itself to discern how conscious Lefebvre may have been of these connections. He was not, and moreover they most likely would have infuriated him. Neither does it seek to establish the indirect route he may have taken in coming into contact with Bergsonian ideas, after all, Lefebvre's works do not provide evidence of a direct contact. Rather, the act of articulating the work of each with that of the other has not an historical motivation but a methodological one–to bolster the common project whose continuation Bergson never lived to appreciate and whose inheritance Lefebvre never overtly recognized. Moreover, acknowledging the Bergsonism in Lefebvre's later work–which is at once to recognize the philosophical debt to contemporary urban theory–works to correct what has been denounced as a reduction of the philosophical aspect of Lefebvre's work.[9] Finally, consistent with the stated aims of both thinkers, exploration of this connection provides strong evidence for reassessing the way problems of life–or more specifically those of urban life–are conceived and represented by more traditional disciplinary approaches. Both thinkers advocated interdisciplinarity. Bergson has been quoted as saying "We gauge the significance of a doctrine of philosophy by the vari-

---

[9] Stuart Elden wrote of the "recent attention to Lefebvre's work" that "much [...] has been in the field of geography, or related areas such as urban sociology or cultural studies. Little attention at all has been paid by political theorists or philosophers. This should be cause for inquiry, given that Lefebvre described himself, not just as a Marxist, but as a Marxist philosopher on several occasions. It is also cause for concern" (2001: 809). Three years later, the force of Elden's assertion had not waned: "As I have argued at greater length elsewhere, one of the problems of recent appropriations and interpretations of Lefebvre in the English-speaking world is the narrowness of the reading that has been given. The focus from fields of geography, urban sociology and cultural studies has largely been at the expense of interest from political theorists or philosophers" (2004: 6).

ety of ideas which it unfolds, and the simplicity of the principle it summarizes" (Chevalier 74).[10] Lefebvre gives a nod to Jane Jacobs's articulation of the urban as a complex problem akin to those of the natural sciences[11] and spends many pages arguing for an interdisciplinary approach to the urban (*UR*, chapter three "The Urban Phenomenon," esp. 53-55). In *Rhythmanalysis*, he once again argues explicitly for interdisciplinarity (20). More than merely explicit, the importance of interdisciplinary methods for both Bergson and Lefebvre is evident from the content of their texts and the shared refusal to narrowly define the problems each took on.

The first section of this chapter will investigate Lefebvre's unacknowledged return to Bergsonian ideas starting from the framework for spatial analysis outlined in *The Production of Space* (1974). It is here that Lefebvre, in spite of his stated intention, reveals the fundamentally philosophical nature of his understanding of space and of the relationship between space and time. In the *Critique of Everyday Life, Vol. 3* (1981) he continues to work with Bergsonism without calling it by that name, and later in *Rhythmanalysis* (1992) in many ways a stronger, more intensely philosophical, manifestation of the project outlined in *The Production of Space*, he in fact realizes Bergson's call for an intuitive grasp of experience and the reconciliation of a theory of knowledge with a theory of life. That this connection might have provoked Lefebvre's anger does not make it any less significant.

One of the key problems of cultural geography, and of Marxist praxis, concerns the reconciliation of that perennial philosophical dichotomy that cleaves space from time in its various and sundry avatars–the material and the immaterial, movement and representation, the particular and the universal, the real and the imaginary and the concrete and the abstract. Although these oppositions cannot be reduced to one another, the conceived distance between space and time helps to shape our understanding of each of them to some degree. In an article published in *Progress in Human Geography*, Alan Latham and Derek McCormack (2004) have stated quite

---

[10] The note beneath this epigraph from Chevalier's text reads "From the preface written by Henri Bergson for G. Tarde's *Extracts*, published in the series *Les grands philosophes* (Paris, Michaud, 1909)."

[11] *UR*, 45; on 19 of the same work he speaks favorably of Jacobs by name; Jacobs addresses this character of the problem of urban life in her classic *Death and Life of Great American Cities*, C. 22 "The kind of problem a city is," 428-48.

concisely what has been the goal (in many cases, even if the failure in others) of much recent geographical work: interrogations of space must acknowledge "a notion of the material that admits from the very start the presence and importance of the immaterial" (703). Henri Lefebvre's watershed text *The Production of Space* (1974) in fact addresses this very central philosophical problem of geography, even though he discourages the reader from seeing it for what it is. It is here that a deep understanding of Henri Bergson's anti-philosophical project reveals the hidden Bergsonian premise of Lefebvre's work. I must insist that exploration of the connection between these two French thinkers undermines the work of neither one. Instead, the Bergsonian approach to space can be read as both a precursor to and an extension of Lefebvre's substantial and important work on spatial practice. This view of Lefebvre's work is additionally important as it seeks to correct what has been seen as a reduction of the philosophical complexity of Lefebvre's work (Elden 2001, 2004). I plan to underscore Lefebvre's important contribution to discussions of space in order to suggest new paths of investigation that retain the vital impetus of his work and make possible its extension to a wider range of cultural processes. *The Production of Space*, then, places the philosophical question of space as preeminent, seeks to reconcile space and time with one another considering each in itself as an abstraction, and even relies on Bergson's critique of the idea of "nothing." Drawing attention to these important connections of Lefebvre's work with Bergsonism will provide the context for the subsequent discussion of the Bergsonian refutation of the "spatialization of time" that obtains in Lefebvre's *The Critique of Everyday Life* and motivates the "new science" of rhythmanalysis in his later writings.

Lefebvre's epic treatise *The Production of Space* is clearly concerned with space in a broad sense and more importantly the way in which we apprehend and make sense of it. It undeniably suggests that philosophical assumptions play a role in our understanding of space, even if the author himself lamentably chooses not to pursue this significant motivation for his investigation, and subsequently discourages this approach. Early on in the text, Lefebvre, in spite of himself, lays claim to the importance of philosophy for his project, strangely enough, through its dismissal. The following quotation, although lengthy, is essential to understanding of this paradox:

> What term should be used to describe the division which keeps the various types of space away from each other, so that physical space, mental space and social space do not overlap? Distortion? Disjunction? Schism? Break? As a matter of fact the term used is far less important than the distance that separates 'ideal' space, which has to do with mental (logico-mathematical) categories, from 'real' space, which is the space of social practice. In actuality each of these two kinds of space involves, underpins and presupposes the other.
>
> What should be the starting point for any theoretical attempt to account for this situation and transcend it in the process? Not philosophy, certainly, for philosophy is an active and interested party in the matter. Philosophers have themselves helped bring about the schism with which we are concerned by developing abstract (metaphysical) representations of space, among them the Cartesian notion of space as absolute, infinite *res extensa*, a divine property which may be grasped in a single act of intuition because of its homogeneous (isotopic) character. This is all the more regrettable in view of the fact that the beginnings of philosophy were closely bound up with the "real" space of the Greek city. This connection was severed later in philosophy's development. Not that we can have no recourse to philosophy, to its concepts or conceptions. *But it [philosophy] cannot be our point of departure.* (14, emphasis added)

In this passage, Lefebvre denounces philosophy itself as suspect. Philosophy, in the sense of a traditional metaphysics, is deemed responsible for the schism between the concepts of "ideal" space and "real" space. Although he suggests a decentering of the philosophical question and not its eradication, he is at this point working against the very interdisciplinarity that he will so strongly espouse in *Rhythmanalysis* (see also *UR*, 53-55). Most importantly, he minimizes the role of this philosophical question in the process of human thought–something appreciated and written extensively about by Bergson. It is this question that Lefebvre, despite himself, will return to in *The Critique of Everyday Life* and *Rhythmanalysis*, and it is this question which in fact motivates *The Production of Space*.

By the time of publication of *The Production of Space*, this traditional metaphysical division between ideal space and real space, the space of mental categories and the space of social practice, had already been denounced by none other than Bergson himself–a good half-century before Lefebvre's opus, in fact. In pointing out the cohabitation of space and time, in describing the intimate connection between physical and mental realities, between matter and memory, between things and consciousness, Bergson hoped to dislodge the Kantian understanding of space and time as abstract and prior to lived experience (see esp. *CE*, chapter four). In *The Production of Space*, Bergson is mentioned only twice in passing (21-22, 73), yet it is precisely because of the fact that Bergson's is an *anti-philosophy* –one which calls traditional philosophical categories into question and which takes it upon itself to explain the origin of philosophical error–that his works are of such great relevance to Lefebvre's goal to arrive at a "[...] unitary theory of physical, mental and social space" (*PS*, 21). What Lefebvre is at a loss to name ("Distortion? Disjunction? Schism? Break?", ibid.) is in fact the Bergsonian idea of "space" itself–a method of division, of carving up reality which in itself produces not only physical space, mental space and social space but also their conceptual division from one another. I believe that Lefebvre's dismissal of Bergsonian methodology, when in fact it would most behoove him to explore it, is itself predicated on a common misunderstanding of Bergson as a philosopher of "time" interested in the immediacy of consciousness at the expense of material/spatial realities (see Lefebvre 1974, 21-22; Fraser 2006 delves concisely into some effects of these misunderstandings).[12] These misunderstandings prove as detrimental to contemporary scholars interested in questions of space as they did for Lefebvre. Just as Bergson sought to correct the errors of a traditional metaphysics that cleaved space from time, Lefebvre, without the support of the philosopher's works, sought to correct the way those same errors had influenced our understanding of space.

---

[12] This century-old misunderstanding appears even in recent scholarship. Consider Doreen Massey's otherwise impressive essay on "Philosophy and the Politics of Spatiality: Some Considerations" (1999) in which she argues that Bergson's error was to not have envisioned space as equally open as time, not to have seen that space is also a realm of difference and multiplicity. I insist that Bergson's ontological claim concerning space is much more nuanced than the dualist space vs. time argument attributed to him by his detractors. For Bergson, space was not a "dimension" (Massey, 32) but a view taken by mind (*CE*, 157). It is just as egregious to consider Bergson a "philosopher of time" (and not space) as it is to see Lefebvre as interested in space at the expense of time. Neither the philosopher nor the urban critic had such a simplistic understanding of difference or multiplicity. That said, although Massey's use of Bergson is problematic (I find Elizabeth Grosz's view of Bergsonism much more accurate; see esp. Grosz 2004, 2005), her analyses are superb.

In the three works that are commonly judged to be his most important, *Time and Free Will* (1889), *Matter and Memory* (1896), and *Creative Evolution* (1907), Bergson dissolves from provisional dualisms (of space and time, matter and memory, intellect and instinct) in order to emphasize their union as a composite. The composite is wrought of two tendencies which cannot be isolated from each other. Put most succinctly, the nondualism is one between "two different kinds of reality, the one heterogeneous, that of sensible qualities, the other homogeneous, namely space" (*TFW*, 97). Although language invites us to consider time and space as distinct or opposed facets of reality (this aspect of language is addressed in *CE*, 298-304; later challenged by Lefebvre in *CEL, v. 2*, 342, where he speaks opaquely of a "disintegration of language"), it does not encourage us to think about how it is that our intellect separates one from the other (the form of thought), nor does it clarify how each is implicated at every moment of our experience. Time and space are, for Bergson, neither abstract ideas nor concrete things, but two ways of thinking about experience, two entry points to a temporally-spatial whole. Each one suggests a certain way of differentiating this whole. Put a different way, there are "two kinds of multiplicity, two possible senses of the word "distinguish," two conceptions, the one qualitative and the other quantitative, of the difference between *same* and *other*" (*TFW*, 121, original emphasis).

More important than this first maneuver in which Bergson references the two multiplicities, the two tendencies that are themselves abstracted from a unitary if variegated space-time, is the way he brings up their interpenetration (see also *MM*, 72):

> And yet we cannot even form the idea of discrete multiplicity without considering at the same time a qualitative multiplicity. When we explicitly count units by stringing them along a spatial line, is it not the case that, alongside this addition of identical terms standing out from a homogenous background, an organization of these units is going on in the depths of the soul, a wholly dynamic process, not unlike the purely qualitative way in which an anvil, if it could feel, would realize a series of blows from a hammer? [...] In a word, the process by which we count units and make them into a discrete multiplicity has two sides; on the one hand we assume that they are identical, which is conceivable only on condition that these units are ranged alongside each other in a homogeneous medium; but on the other hand,

> the third unit, for example, when added to the other two, alters the nature, the appearance and, as it were, the rhythm of the whole; without this interpenetration and this, so to speak, qualitative progress, no addition would be possible. Hence it is through the quality of quantity that we form the idea of quantity without quality. (*TFW*, 122-23)

Here it can already be seen how quality plays a role in quantity, intensivity in extensivity, inclusive succession in simultaneity, duration in matter, time in space. This is akin to what Lefebvre posits in analyzing the *production* of space. It is not a static moment (space) that deserves attention, but rather the process of creating what at any moment may be taken *by the intellect* as staticity (space-time). This is to rightly deal with process, not product–and process, as Lefebvre and his proponents in cultural geography (Harvey 1989, 1990, 1996, 2000, for one) are aware, is by no means strictly spatial. Just as Bergson (and for that matter self-proclaimed phenomenologists such as Merleau-Ponty)[13] emphasized the interaction between space and time, matter and memory, the quantitative and the qualitative, Lefebvre delves into these same reconciliations in the name of what he calls "social space." This "social space" is both a "field of action" and a "basis for action", both "actual" and "potential," and, approximating most clearly Bergson's own use of language, both "qualitative" and "quantitative" (*PS*, 191).

For Bergson, the qualitative and quantitative are intimately con-

---

[13] Maurice Merleau-Ponty (1982, 2000a, 2000b, 2000c, 2004) often returned to the idea that "the hand that touches is also the hand that is touched." Space and time were not separable abstract concepts: "We must therefore avoid saying that our body is *in* space, or *in* time. It *inhabits* space and time" (Merleau-Ponty, *The Phenomenology of Perception*, p. 161, original emphasis); "I am not in space and time, nor do I conceive space and time; I belong to them, my body combines with them and includes them" (Merleau-Ponty, *The Phenomenology of Perception*, 162). In this sense, Lefebvre can be said to have brought phenomenology to bear explicitly on social production. He writes: "Can the body, with its capacity for action, and its various energies, be said to create space? Assuredly, but not in the sense that occupation might be said to 'manufacture' spatiality; rather, there is an immediate relationship between the body and its space. Before *producing* effects in the material realm (tools and objects), before *producing itself* by drawing nourishment from that realm, and before *reproducing itself* by generating other bodies, each living body *is* space and *has* its space. [...] This thesis is so persuasive that there seems to be little reason for not extending its application–with all due precautions, naturally, to *social* space" (*PS*, 170-71, original emphasis). See also Simonsen (2005), who splendidly recovers Lefebvre's contribution to the literature of the body/phenomenology.

nected, as are memory and matter, consciousness and things, time and space; yet it is the role of the intellect to perceive quality only through quantity, to reduce consciousness to a thing in order to act upon it, to perceive time only through space. As I will have chance to discuss further in the next section, to the degree that human thought follows the tendency of the intellect it carves fluid reality into bits and pieces through representation. Lefebvre's own triadic model of spatial production ("Spatial practice, representations of space, representational spaces," *PS*, 33; see also Harvey 1990: 218-19) is a testament to the power of this tendency of thought to divide and partition, even as it attempts to undermine this very practice and restore movement to the conceived image of a static spatial field. That said, it is quite a narrow view indeed to assume that Lefebvre's work on space prizes space over time.[14] As the title itself indicates, his work treats *The Production of Space*, that is the way in which space is implicated in a larger temporal process–the way that temporality permits the formation and reformation of spaces. Recalling the complex relationship between space and time that Bergson takes great care to develop in his works,[15] Lefebvre explicitly asserts that "Time is distinguishable but not separable from space" (175). Space and time are for Lefebvre, as they were for Bergson, only separable in "a view taken by mind";[16] "time is known and actualized in space, becoming a social reality by virtue of spatial practice. Similarly, space is known only in and through time" (*PS*, 219). Lefebvre goes on to discuss how capitalism has produced a particular relationship between space and time, thus his famed dictum that

[14] Elden (2004) similarly confronts this possible misunderstanding head-on: "In other words, Lefebvre did not replace temporal with spatial analysis, but thought the relation between space and time, and in the process rethought both concepts. It is crucial to remember that they must be thought together, and yet cannot be reduced to the other. Space and time are the indispensable coordinates of everyday life, and therefore a rethinking of them essential to that overall project" (170).

[15] This complex relationship between spatial and temporal multiplicities, between differences of degree and differences of kind, is treated with great care and precision in the work of Gilles Deleuze, esp. *Bergsonism* (1966). Deleuze also works with Bergsonism extensively in his two *Cinema* volumes (2002a, 2002b) and in two essays posthumously published in English as part of *Desert Islands* (2004).

[16] In *Creative Evolution*, Bergson writes that "This space [a homogeneous and empty medium, infinite and indefinitely divisible] is therefore, preeminently, the plan of our possible action on things, although, indeed, things have a natural tendency, as we shall explain later on, to enter into a frame of this kind. It is a view taken by mind" (157).

capitalism has survived through the twentieth century "by producing space, by occupying a space" (1973: 21). Whereas for the philosopher Bergson it is the tendency of the intellect to prioritize space over time, for the urban critic Lefebvre it is the tendency of capitalism to do so (*PS*, 219). Reading both Bergson and Lefebvre together produces the interesting question of the relationship between the spatial nature of Bergson's "intellect" and the spatial nature of capitalism as discussed in Lefebvre (and Harvey). The key to understanding this relationship involves the two thinkers' shared critique of the "spatialization of time." Before moving on to discuss their common use of this concept in relation to everyday lived experience, it is necessary to touch upon one more similarity involving the theorization of space.

In addition to the shared redefinition of the relationship between space-time, another important philosophical premise shared by Bergson and Lefebvre is that of the idea of nothing, the void, empty space.[17] Common sense representations of "nothing" claim that it is less than something. The idea of a stack of papers on my desk is, for common sense, more than the same idea minus the stack of papers. Yet for Bergson, the idea of nothing is in fact more than the idea of something–it is the idea of something plus its negation (*CE*, 272-98). This discussion, comprising many pages indeed, is tied into Bergson's extensive critique of the intellect and of traditional philosophy. As might be expected of the philosopher's philosopher, he does not directly tie this faulty premise into social life. And yet, once again, we find evidence for the assertion that Lefebvre's work consists, in part, of the rigorous, if unconscious, *application* to social life of Bergson's philosophical corrections. In *The Production of Space*, Lefebvre's writing at times almost appears to base itself on Bergson's discussion of nothing as an unfaithful if not illusory concept. He writes: "The notion of a space which is at first empty, but is later filled by a social life and modified by it, also depends on this hypothetical initial 'purity,' identified as 'nature' and as a sort of ground zero of human reality. Empty space in the sense of a mental and social void which facilitates the socialization of a not-yet-social realm is actually merely a *representation of space*"

[17] Bernard Pullman's *The Atom in the History of Human Thought* (1998) explores the rich history of the opposed theories of the universe as either an empty container or a full field.

(*PS*, original emphasis, 190; see also *UR*, 40). Although Lefebvre's discussion, because of the priority extended to the application of philosophical concepts, lacks the philosophical rigor of Bergson's, he has in a sense given life to Bergson's somewhat dry but nevertheless astute observation.

It should now be apparent that both thinkers shared the concern of reconciling the abstract realms of space and time with one another. In *The Production of Space*, Bergsonism is present in the philosophically-grounded framework used by Lefebvre to approach space, one that eschews static and abstract concepts to apprehend fluid experience. Yet it is in *The Critique of Everyday Life* that one finds Lefebvre relying implicitly Bergson's philosophy with more consistency and in more detail. The following discussion will allow a more in-depth discussion of what both men denounced as the "spatialization of time." It bears repeating that in reconciling Bergson's philosophy with Lefebvre's later works, it is the aim of the present section to rediscover Lefebvre's original intention, even if in doing so it must defy the explicit instructions of Lefebvre himself, as evidenced in *The Production of Space* (above) and take on the philosophical understandings that constitute our spatial experiences and practices. This intention was to correct two entwined problems of philosophy. The first was what Lefebvre saw as the insular character of philosophical speculation–he thought it should be applied to the lived world in accordance with Marxist praxis, the reconciliation of thought and action. The second was the faulty philosophical problem of using static categories to understand a mobile world. In addition to grounding our understanding of the struggles over urban space, ultimately Bergsonian methodology allows us to take Lefebvre's analysis where it is just beginning to venture, not only into philosophy, but into all of the humanities, social sciences and even the sciences, for that matter.

One of Lefebvre's greatest contributions has been this three volume work in which he seeks to return to the concrete, to reconcile thought and life, to expose the intimate connection between thought and action and to recover the fundamental possibility for radical social change–a work he aptly titled *Critique of Everyday Life*.[18] This focus on the everyday needs be seen as the complement

[18] Trebitsch (1991) supplies a concise rendering of the events and motivation leading up to this project.

to Bergson's philosophical project.[19] Bergson worked to dismantle from within philosophy the very traditional abstract philosophical concepts which Lefebvre later eschewed in his concrete and applied analyses. Philosophically, Bergson questioned the very conceptualization of movement in static terms, explaining how movement seen/represented by the intellect was quite another thing entirely from real movement itself. In this three volume work Lefebvre consistently proposed "starting out from actual experience, and elucidating it in order to transform it–as opposed to starting from the conceptual in order to impose it" (*CEL, v. 3*, 76), a continuation of his insistence in *The Production of Space* that "spatial practice is lived before it is conceptualized" (34). First let us see how Bergson placed lived experience at the center of his effort in order to be better equipped to discuss the Bergsonian critique of the "spatialization of time" inherited by Lefebvre.

For Bergson, the role of the intellect was to "spatialize time:" to partition a fluid reality, to create divisions in that reality even, especially, through the "simple" act of perception. Even the evolution of the intellect was geared toward preparing the body's action upon things.[20] As such, the intellect developed as the part of the body geared toward matter, the world of things.[21] To the degree that the intellect was the form of thought that most adhered in social life, social life itself consisted in the imposition of static forms: "And the essential object of society is to introduce a certain fixity into universal mobility. Societies are just so many islands consolidated here

[19] In the third volume of the *Critique*, Lefebvre explicitly denounces traditional philosophy with prose that is reminiscent of Bergson's: "The originality of the project with respect to traditional philosophy has already been underscored. It regarded daily life neither as the non-philosophical, nor as raw material for some possible construction. It did not regard it as the thing from which philosophy distances itself in order to embark upon either a phenomenology of consciousness, or a logic, or ethics, or aesthetics. It sought to show that the confused character of lived experience, as of daily life, betokened not their poverty but their richness" (17).

[20] In *Matter and Memory*, Bergson repeatedly refers to perception as the "virtual action of things upon our body and of our body upon things" (309).

[21] In the following quotation, Bergson explains this in form of suggesting an alternative to the Kantian understanding of time and space. "This alternative consists, first of all, in regarding the intellect as a special function of the mind, essentially turned toward inert matter; then in saying that neither does matter determine the form of the intellect, nor does the intellect impose its form on matter, nor have matter and intellect been regulated in regard to one another by we know not what preestablished harmony, but that intellect and matter have progressively adapted themselves one to the other in order to attain at last a common form" (206).

and there in the ocean of becoming" (*CM*, 82; see also *MR*). In this vein, one of the comments most widely attributed to Bergson is his characterization of the functioning of this intellect. For this characterization, he employed, as did others of the time, the newly-burgeoning seventh art form as a metaphor. Likening the intellect to the cinema he famously wrote that:

> We take snapshots, as it were, of the passing reality, and, as these are characteristic of the reality, we have only to string them on a becoming, abstract, uniform and invisible, situated at the back of the apparatus of knowledge, in order to imitate what there is that is characteristic in this becoming itself. Perception, intellection, language so proceed in general. Whether we would think becoming, or express it, or even perceive it, we hardly do anything else than set going a kind of cinematograph inside us. We may therefore sum up what we have been saying in the conclusion that the *mechanism of our ordinary knowledge is of a cinematographical kind.* (*CE*, 306, original emphasis; see also Deleuze *MI*, *TI*)

The intellect, like the cinema, partitions reality into snapshots, it understands real movement only through static images. One may perhaps think of the famous photographic motion studies of Eadweard Muybridge as a visual accompaniment to Bergson's metaphor. Bergson himself, elsewhere, critiqued the Eleatic philosopher Zeno's example of Achilles and the tortoise to illustrate this teratological error of the intellect. If Achilles runs ten times faster than the tortoise, and the tortoise is given a ten-meter head start, then by the time Achilles runs the initial ten meters, the tortoise will have moved another 1/10 meter. When Achilles runs the 1/10 meter, the tortoise will have moved another 1/100 m. and so on. Thus, Zeno concludes, Achilles will never catch up with the tortoise. Nevertheless, and as Bergson correctly assumes, the flaw in this reasoning is that while the space traveled may be divisible, the movement is not. Movement cannot be equated to the distance covered because it is pure duration, continual becoming, the eternal moment where the past bleeds into, even recreates itself in, the present. Achilles will indeed surpass the tortoise. Here Bergson has illustrated that temporal phenomena cannot be understood by the spatializing process characteristic of the intellect. To put it another way, lived experience, for Bergson is not reducible to the static designs of thought.

Lefebvre relentlessly advocated this philosophical premise, as discussed above, through its *application* to urban life in his three volume *Critique*, especially in the last volume. Now in the position to reflect most perspicaciously upon the project's entirety, he writes:

> [K]nowledge must proceed with caution, restraint, respect. It must respect lived experience, rather than belabouring it as the domain of ignorance and error, rather than absorbing it into positive knowledge as vanquished ignorance. [...] Understanding lived experience, situating it, and restoring it to the dynamic constellation of concepts; 'explaining' it by stating what it *involves*–this was how the meaning of the work and project was expressed. (*CEL, v. 3*, 17, original emphasis)

Now in the role of respecting lived experience, knowledge has to relinquish its addiction to representing fluid experience through static concepts. In Bergsonian terms, this means that the tendency of intellect in human thought must give way to intuition–that is, to "a certain effort which the utilitarian habits of mind of everyday life tend, in most men, to discourage" (Bergson, "Introduction to Metaphysics," 165). Recognition of the "spatialization of time" is a key part of the movement of practicing intuition–which Bergson calls metaphysics, philosophy (see "Introduction to Metaphysics," esp. 188-93; compare with the idea of "metaphilosophy" as articulated by Lefebvre in *UR*, 64-68). For Lefebvre, this recognition is also of great importance.[22] At one point he criticizes traditional Marxism's approach to rhythms by stating: "The general problem here is the spatialization of temporal processes" (129). This Bergsonian lan-

[22] Although Bergson sees this rift as an innate tendency of human thought he calls the intellect, Lefebvre historicizes the rift between knowledge and life, attributing it to the "silent catastrophe" (46) of modernity's beginning. Lefebvre places the advent of modernity at around 1910: "One continued to live in Euclidean and Newtonian space, while knowledge moved in the space of relativity. Comparatively straightforward, Euclidean and Newtonian space still seemed absolute and intelligible because it was homogeneous and had nothing to do with time. As for time, it remained clock-time, and was itself homogeneous" (47). Interesting in this regard, is the fact that Bergson's three major works, *Time and Free Will*, *Matter and Memory*, and *Creative Evolution* were all published before 1910. Also, while controversy surrounds the work to this day, Bergson engaged his philosophy with Einstein's physics in 1922 with *Duration and Simultaneity*–an effort which, judged successful or not, produced entanglements still worthy of consideration (see Durie 2002).

guage, although perhaps unconscious and definitely unacknowledged, is not used lightly. Underlying Lefebvre's understanding of the rhythms of life is an explicit rejection of the way that the qualitative nature of time has been made linear and homogenous, the way living processes have been reduced to quantities. In Bergson, this critique is purely philosophical and only virtually political. In Lefebvre, however, the philosophy is brought into relation with the capitalist mode of production by his actualization of the critique Bergson left unexplored.

> On a watch or a clock, the mechanical devices subject the cyclical–the hands that turn in sixty seconds or twelve hours–to the linearity of counting. In recent measuring devices, and even watches, the cyclical (the dial) tends to disappear. Fully quantified social time is indifferent to day and night, to the rhythms of impulses. (130)[23]

The consequences of the quantification of the qualitative, the spatialization of time, the "splintering of space and time in general homogeneity, and the crushing of natural rhythms and cycles by linearity (135) are, for Lefebvre, disastrous–thus the illusion of time as reversible, and from that illusion, the suppression of tragedy and death (133) and the rampant colonization/commodification of daily life. "Time is projected into space through measurement, by being homogenized, by appearing in things and products" (133; see also *CEL, v. 2*). Thus asserts itself the need for restoring the irreversibility of time, Lefebvre argues, through music, dance, the festival; in short, the themes of everyday life. Lefebvre has rescued time from the "social relationship" (see the Lefebvre epigraph, above) through which it is managed by capitalist spatialization.

Despite his insistence on redefining philosophical premises from within the discipline of philosophy itself, Bergson, too, sought a philosophy that would be more precisely attuned to life itself, to the ways in which the time of life is cut up, partitioned, managed by the intellectual representation of it. Thus his persistence in suggesting that "*theory of knowledge* and *theory of life* seem to us inseparable. [...] It is necessary that these two inquiries, theory of knowl-

[23] *Inner Time* (1993), by Carol Orlock, provides a fascinating discussion of biological cycles that I believe would have intrigued Lefebvre in this regard.

edge and a theory of life, should join each other, and, by a circular process, push each other on unceasingly" (*CE*, xiii, original emphasis). In imbricating his philosophical revolution with the evolution of life as he did (especially) in *Creative Evolution*, Bergson perhaps thought that he had achieved this goal. The result has nevertheless proved unsatisfactory for Lefebvre and others. In his critique of everyday life, Lefebvre, too, thought he had reconciled theory of knowledge and theory of life. He had brought philosophical problems out of the ivory tower to their social application. And yet might philosophers bemoan Lefebvre's explicit rejection of philosophy (see *PS*, above)? Whereas each thinker succeeded on his own terms and perhaps failed regarding the priorities of the other, there can be no doubt that together this search for a unified knowledge/life was realized. The following discussion will pass on to Lefebvre's rhythmanalytical project. It is here that I believe Lefebvre's work would have most pleased Bergson–the project is intensely philosophical, and is methodologically grounded in the realities of lived experience. It is not the intellect that obtains in rhythmanalysis, but intuition, a mode of thinking that attunes itself to movement and not static forms. For Lefebvre, this movement, this lived temporality opposed to linear trajectories, escaping from yet coexisting with the colonization of daily life (*R*, 73), is rhythm.

To the extent that Lefebvre's rhythmanalytical project–articulated most directly in the posthumously-published volume *Rhythmanalysis*–is a logical continuation of his distaste for traditional philosophy, it is already foreshadowed in *The Production of Space*,[24] and in *The Critique of Everyday Life* where he even terms it "a new science" (vol. 3, 130).[25] He rejects the static approach of traditional analysis, recalling Bergson's denunciation of the intellect as "cine-

[24] "Naturally, the history of space should not be distanced in any way from the history of time (a history clearly distinct from all philosophical theories of time in general). The departure point for this history of space is not to be found in geographical descriptions of natural space, but rather in the study of natural rhythms, and of the modification of those rhythms and their inscription in space by means of human actions, especially work-related actions. It begins, then, with the spatio-temporal rhythms of nature as transformed by social practice" (*PS*, 117).

[25] "Rhythmanalysis, a new science that is in the process of being constituted, studies these highly complex processes. It may well be that it will complement or supplant psychoanalysis. It situates itself at the juxtaposition of the physical, the physiological and the social, at the heart of daily life. [...] Compared with the existing sciences, it is multi- or interdisciplinary in character" (130).

matographical" knowledge. Whereas intellection apprehends movement only through static images, something akin to the effect of Muybridge's motion studies, the method of the rhythmanalyst is altogether different:

> For him [the rhythmanalyst] nothing is immobile. He hears the wind, the rain, storms, but if he considers a stone, a wall, a trunk, he understands their slowness, their interminable rhythm. This *object* is not inert; time is not set aside for the *subject*. It is only slow in relation to our time, to our body, the measure of rhythms. An apparently immobile *object*, the forest, moves in multiple ways: the combined movements of the soil, the earth, the sun. Or the movements of the molecules and atoms that compose it (the object, the forest). [...] He thinks with his body, not in the abstract, but in lived temporality. (Lefebvre, *R*, 20-21)

In the tradition of Bergson, who declared that intellect was the static, speculative tendency of consciousness that had attenuated itself to matter in order to act upon it (*MM*), Lefebvre is seeking to escape the tropes of an historically disinterested theoretical knowledge divorced from moving, living realities. To unite thought and action, thought must escape the static images of movement, and mold itself to (nonlinear) rhythms.

This concept of rhythm is at the same time, a conscious acceptance of the phenomenological project and its concomitant rejection of the knowledge that imagines itself noncorporeal. Bergson's aim was to dispense with the simplistic representations of lived realities offered by realism and idealism, by extreme objectivity and extreme subjectivity. Lefebvre, in this fashion, held a similar belief that the body was at once mental and physical, yet subject to reduction and/or abstraction by the mainstream political and philosophical imagination.

> One could reach, by a twisty road and paradoxically beginning with bodies, the (concrete) universal that the political and philosophical mainstream targeted but did not reach, let alone realize: if rhythm consolidates its theoretical status, if it reveals itself as a valid concept for thought and as a support in practice, is it not this concrete universal that philosophical systems have lacked, that political organizations have forgotten, but which is lived, tested, touched in the sensible and the corporeal? (Lefebvre, *R*, 44-45; see also 67)

This acknowledgement of the primacy of the body (one thinks of Merleau-Ponty's *Primacy of Perception*) makes it possible to unhinge thought from its visual bias. Analysis of the rhythm, although it does not completely lack a visual element, downplays it. Lefebvre subverts the hegemony of the visual field, embracing the tactile, embracing sensations and especially sound, the act of listening (esp. 19-20, 22, 60). This de-emphasis of the visual accomplishes a comparable thing to what Bergson envisioned with his insistence that perception was our virtual action upon things (*MM*, 307-09). Thought must release its speculative character, it must relinquish the preconceived designs through which perception operates, it must turn away from intellect. For Bergson, who succeeded where Kant failed, this was possible through intuition. In advocating that the rhythmanalyst think "with his body" (20), Lefebvre in effect calls attention to the speculative character of intellectual thought. One might compare this bodily-thinking with the thought likened by Quantum physicist David Bohm to bodily "proprioception", the self-perception of the body by the body (*Thought as a System* 1992: 121-30).

Intuition, like Lefebvre's bodily-thinking, acts in turning away from the abstract categories habitually employed by the intellect in perception and thought. Intuition restores thought to the world of lived experience. Just as intuition, for Bergson, is not ignorant of intellect, but intensely aware of it, aware of its mechanical nature, so too, for Lefebvre, is rhythmanalysis aware of the rhythms that have been instilled in time by capitalist production (see *R*, 69). A moving, living reality requires a mode of knowledge that is also mobile, capable of moving with it yet not becoming assimilated into it. It is this form of knowledge that, for Lefebvre, can approach the lives of those modern people who "not only move alongside the monster [that is capital] but are inside it; they live off it" (54-55). This mobile knowledge would make it possible to discern the qualitative difference between the rhythms imposed on life and the rhythms of life itself.

Such a mobile knowledge is exactly what Bergson strove to articulate. Whereas his idea of analysis was closely tied to his view of the intellect and the apprehension of static forms, intuition was more carefully attuned to movement. In "Introduction to Metaphysics," he contrasts intuition with analysis:

> We call intuition here the *sympathy* by which one is transported into the interior of an object in order to coincide with what there is unique and consequently inexpressible in it. Analysis, on the contrary, is the operation which reduces the object to elements already known, that is, common to that object and others. Analyzing then consists in expressing a thing in terms of what is not it. All analysis is thus a translation, a development into symbols, [...] [an] ever incomplete representation. (161-62, original emphasis)

Lefebvre comes to find Bergsonian intuition and to politicize it on his own terms. In "Introduction to Metaphysics," Bergson articulates what philosophy should be. In *Rhythmanalysis*, Lefebvre actually *does* Bergsonian philosophy–something he may very well not have wanted to hear.

I propose that seeing the common thread of Bergson and Lefebvre's work is not just of historical interest, but of methodological significance as well. The force of their combined emphasis on real movement, on lived realities, on the insufficient nature of abstract concepts in understanding fluid experience, on the reconciliation of space and time, on the spatializing nature of the intellect and on capitalism's spatializing reduction of rhythmic processes–their call for a return to the body and thus to action and their firm commitment to interdisciplinarity; all of these commonalties give philosophical strength to current understandings of urban life as a dynamic process (see Harvey 1996, Madanipour 1996, 2001, 2003). The union of Bergson-Lefebvre points to the importance of three interconnected points that, while they have been addressed by theorists in turn, have yet to be sufficiently imagined as part of one unitary, if complex, problem of urban criticism. Each of these points need be seen as part of a larger philosophical project, understanding philosophy in the Bergsonian sense–"Philosophy can only be an effort to dissolve again into the Whole" (*CE*, 191). This idea of the Whole, of totality, is not that of a monolithic whole, but, like the Bergsonian notions of durée/duration (1889), creative evolution (1907), the élan vital (1907) and the open society (1932), one that is multiple, constantly changing, unpredictable and even alive. Although the struggles over social space, over mental categories, over the spatialization of time characteristic of contemporary capitalism (Harvey's "spatial fix") may be struggles at a certain place at a certain time, they are in effect struggles over the whole of a social life. Seen as an attempt to "dissolve again into the Whole" (above), philosophy is thus a refusal to accept the compartmentalizing conceptual divisions that the intellect introduces into the world through its assimilation to the apparent boundaries of matter (Bergson) just as it is critical of the reification inherent to contemporary capitalism (Lefebvre). The whole is this sense can in no way be an abstract concept but rather a concrete, complex and expansive living reality. The first point suggested by Bergson-Lefebvre thus involves the use of abstract categories in approaching reality. Significantly, much current research in human geography and cultural studies shares the desire to return from abstract intellection to concrete lived realities and thus to acknowledge the importance of a renewed call to reconcile theory and practice, knowledge and life. Numerous studies have emphasized the insufficiency of static intellectual concepts for the analysis of urban life by, to give just a few examples, problematizing the definition of public versus private space (Brown 1999, Staeheli 1996, Fraser 2007a), noting the complexity of the urban process (Jacobs 1961, Delgado 1999, 2007, Fraser 2007b), and bridging the perceived gap between material and immaterial realities (Steinmetz 1999, Latham and McCormack 2004, Marston 2004). This problematization of abstract concepts must be understood in terms of both Bergson's overarching critique of intellect, one which has evolved by assimilating to the hard-lines of matter thus attuning itself more and more to deal with things instead of with relations (*CE*, 206), and also the Marxist critique of reification. This two-pronged critique is not altogether new as Lefebvre eschews abstract categories and even David Harvey agrees implicitly with Bergson when he writes that things are not in space, space is in things (Harvey 1996, Bergson 1889, also Hewitt 1974).

The second point, which in fact follows from the first, involves interdisciplinarity. The very notion of discrete disciplines is a product of the abstract "intellectual" concepts denounced by Bergson and the "analytical" thought discarded by Lefebvre in favor of a bodily thinking. A challenge for researchers across the disciplines has been to recognize the socially-constructed as nonetheless materially-real and to, in turn, see the material world as socially-constructed–to see experience, just as Marx saw capital, as a relation (see Harvey 2000: 28). In short, just as things are abstracted out of relations, disciplinary knowledge is an abstraction of the Whole –this knowledge is no less an abstraction for having a practical application. Disciplines are, just as matter/space was for Bergson, also "a view taken by mind" (*CE*, 157). With this implicit philosophical motivation, many astute studies, to give just a few examples, have sought to bridge the socially-constructed and the materially-real (Marston 2000), material and immaterial realities (Latham and McCormack 2004), culture and the state (Steinmetz 1999), and culture and the economy (Jessop 1990). The current state of research, in cultural studies and human geography, as well as film studies and literary studies, places a high value on interdisciplinarity and has in fact implicitly employed Bergsonian tenets in dislodging the primacy of the object long characteristic of academic scholarship. To this end, Kitchen and Dodge (2007) suggest that even maps, traditionally seen as static and representational objects, need be understood as a practice of "creating, rather than simply revealing, knowledge" (332). There is an interdisciplinary drive for process to replace the product, for relations to replace things. Bergson's disruption of the facile designs of the intellect not only squares with the critique of capitalist mechanism, but also becomes an ally of cultural studies, for example, in challenging film studies' insistence on the self-contained importance attributed to the individual text (see Turner 2000). In this tradition, there have been many recent attempts to reconcile film studies and geographical concerns that come to rest implicitly on the very philosophical upheaval represented by Bergson-Lefebvre (Aitken & Zonn 1994, Clarke 1997, Cresswell & Dixon 2002, Dear 2000, Hopkins 1994). Neither abstract categories nor disciplinary knowledge is sufficient to take on the relations that constitute the movement of life.

The third point highlighted by the union of Bergson-Lefebvre is the importance of mobility. Interestingly, Bergson's call to return to movement, to lived experience, a call–it must be noted–echoed by Lefebvre's work on process, everyday life and rhythm, has been answered by a whole emerging tradition of scholarship that necessarily cuts across traditional disciplinary boundaries. It is likely that the contemporary interest in mobilities (e.g. Urry 2000, Hannam, Sheller and Urry 2006, Brenner 2004, Cresswell 2006, Blunt 2007, Lorimer 2007) would not have been possible without an implicit grounding in the modern philosophical work of Lefebvre, and before him, that of Bergson.[26] Although Lefebvre called for the use of philosophy in investigation of urban phenomena (epigraph, above), few authors have thoroughly grappled with the philosophical basis for this approach. At times, those studies that purport to establish such a basis end by misreading and subsequently rejecting Bergson only to reclaim him from other sources.[27] This connection with philosophy is important not merely as another new area to be studied (thus not mobility merely as content or topic: e.g. [im]migration, tourism, travel, information technology, etc.) but rather because there is no area of contemporary life that lies outside of the characteristic channeling or reduction of complexity into simple formula or manageable system. In its contemporary manifestation, the increasing drive of capitalism to accelerate turnover time coincides with a pervasive emphasis on the spatialization of time and the "intellectual" nature of thought as cities are carved up, development is projected, daily life is subjected to simplified schemes, and human rhythms and movement are increasingly subjected to mechanical reproduction.

This pervasive spatialization of time, seen through the combination of Bergson-Lefebvre is not merely a "natural" tendency of the intellect (Bergson), nor is it solely an "historical" creation of the capitalist mode of production (Lefebvre). Understanding the philosophical basis of the purportedly discrete categories of the material and the immaterial realities, that is, acknowledging the complex and process-driven model of reality shared by both Bergson and

[26] "The analysis of spatiality and spatial restructuring is one area of social science that began to bring out the significance of mobilities (Soja 1989; Harvey 1989), yet in some ways has not fully taken this step [...] in their search for spatial *ordering*, the social sciences have still failed to fully recognize how the spatialities of social life presuppose, and frequently involve conflict over, both the actual and the imagined movement of people from place to place, event to event" (Hannam, Scheller, Urry 2006: 4, original emphasis).

[27] Richard G. Smith (2003), for example, maintains that space and time cannot be separated (578 n. 8) and yet opposes this view to Bergson's stating that the Bergsonian idea "subordinates space to time in its movement from a space that is solid, discontinuous and concrete to a space that is a continuous abstract extension (mathematical time)" (563). He goes even further in allying himself with a critic of Bergson who "relies on arguing that this duality of space is no more than a product of different degrees of abstraction" (563). The view of a combined space-time which he espouses, noting its polymorphous and multiple nature, is in fact not merely a Deleuzian conceit but comes also from the "Bergsonians" he criticizes early in the essay (563). If nothing else, this example testifies to the unfortunate legacy of denouncing Bergson without a full understanding of his thought.

Lefebvre, relieves scholarship of the need to oppose the "natural" solution to the "historical" solution. It is not that new terrain needs to be conquered, that the "study of mobilities" needs to be tackled as a discipline in its own right with its own unique method and originally-defined set of problems. Rather, the emerging research on mobilities, rhythms and flows, that is, research into what Bergson called the "real movement" of life, needs to acknowledge at once both the historically situated spatialization of capitalism and the teratological spatialization of intellect. As the key question facing the study of mobilities, this must involve an encounter with a philosophical problem of method that both Bergson and Lefebvre confronted, each in his own way.

In summary, in spite of his declared refutation of Bergsonian philosophy, Lefebvre's actual relationship with it was significant–although uncomfortable, unconscious and certainly unacknowledged. His urban project relied on rejecting traditional philosophy, denouncing the spatialization of time, escaping the vision of space as a simple container for activity, reconciling knowledge with life, and departing the realm of static abstract concepts for the lived realities of temporal experience–all aspects of Bergson's philosophy now applied to a scintillating critique of the capitalist mode of production. Bergson hoped to discern the lived realities underlying their representation by the intellect. Lefebvre exposed the living urban realities that are obfuscated by the cloud of a negligent urbanism. Conceived as a relational totality, the work of both thinkers provides a compelling philosophical base for the study of urban life conceived as a process. The composite of Bergson-Lefebvre provides a philosophically interdisciplinary understanding of movement and process –of mobilities and rhythms–, that is useful in side-stepping the complicity of scholarship in the spatialization of time characteristic of contemporary capitalism. Together, the two philosophers provide a compelling basis for a philosophy capable of approaching the urban as process. The next and final chapter will explore how this same philosophical base informs the work of Manuel Delgado Ruiz.

MANUEL DELGADO RUIZ: THEORIZING THE LIVING CITY

> Though all the photographs of a city taken from all possible points of view indefinitely complete one another, they will never equal in value that [multi]dimensional object, the city along whose streets one walks.
>
> –Henri Bergson (*The Creative Mind*, pp. 160-61)

THE previous chapter has tackled the significant, if uncomfortable, relationship between Bergson's philosophical postures and Henri Lefebvre's theorization of the urban. It has argued that, taken as a whole, the ideas of both thinkers bolster each other in a compelling presentation of the urban as process and a concomitant denunciation of the spatialization of time. It is this very view of the urban that Manuel Delgado Ruiz (1956-), titular professor of anthropology at the Universitat de Barcelona, embraces in his many written works. Delgado, certainly one of the most outspoken critics of urbanism in Spain, is important to a study of the Bergsonian legacy in Spain both for his explicit acceptance of a Lefebvrian understanding of spatial production but moreover for his frequent implicit and infrequent explicit incorporation of Bergsonian ideas in his writings. This final chapter will thus document his incorporation of Bergsonism through his contact with Bergson's ideas themselves as well as his contact with them through their reformulation by Lefebvre. Ultimately, Delgado Ruiz uses a process philosophy derived from Bergson-Lefebvre to underscore the living character of our cities.

Although Delgado's explicit references to Bergson and Lefebvre can be more or less briefly enunciated, the legacy of their thought arguably underlies the whole of his work. He mentions Bergson less frequently than Lefebvre, but nevertheless when he does so he does so with respect, refusing to indulge the entrenched and yet superficial misunderstandings of Bergsonism as mere subjectivity that in fact obtain in Lefebvre's merely obligatory references to his work (1974: 21-22, 73). In *El animal público* (1999) Delgado Ruiz references not merely Bergson's "élan vital" but also the notion of a "moral abierta" (110), thus signaling that he is familiar not only with Bergson's popular *Creative Evolution* (1907) but also his less popular *The Two Sources of Morality and Religion* (1932). In one of his presentations titled "Memoria y lugar" (2001), he refers again to Bergson, this time of course in reference to the latter's writings on memory which remain among his less controversial and thus more easily digested ideas.[1] In his most recent book titled *Sociedades movedizas: Pasos hacia una antropología de las calles* (2007), however, there is not one single reference to Bergson. Nevertheless this omission is conspicuous given his consistent, if infrequent, mention of the philosopher in his other works. As suggested by Bergson's discussion of time itself, these past references persist and endure in Delgado's present work even though they are not made explicit. Moreover, it is through the mention of Lefebvre and even Deleuze that Delgado most significantly connects to the Bergsonian legacy.

While the Lefebvre's critical tradition is notably evident in the earlier works of Delgado Ruiz as well (1999, 2001), here it contextualizes his most recent *Sociedades movedizas* from the first page of the work's introduction. The urban critic builds on a crucial, if complex, distinction between "the city" and "the urban" he has explored in his previous works (1999: 23, 2001: 9), here citing Lefebvre explicitly (2007: 11). Thus Delgado again picks up on the importance of this distinction for an understanding of the urban as a process. In his previous assessment of Lefebvre's contribution, one sees a crucial acceptance of process and multidimensionality: "La premisa lefebvriana es que el espacio social no puede reducirse a

[1] "Los grandes teóricos pragmáticos del recuerdo –G. H. Mead y *Henri Bergson*–, y los epistemológicos constructivistas después, han distinguido dos tipos de memoria: una memoria en sucio, por así decirlo, constituida por la totalidad almacenada de evocaciones posibles, y otra memoria extremadamente selectiva, que escoge entre todas las imágenes del pasado disponibles, entre todas las historias posibles, aquellas que mejor se adecúan a los intereses prácticos del presente" (2001: 20-21, emphasis added).

unidad alguna, puesto que responde a una pluralidad múltiple y en cierto modo innumerable, cada uno de cuyos elementos constitutivos se yuxtaponen muchas veces de forma imprevisible unos sobre otros" (2001: 39). In *Sociedades movedizas* he once again provides similar explicit references to Lefebvre, referring, for instance, to the latter's insistence that "Only the bulldozer and the Molotov cocktail can modify existing space" (2007: 179-80),[2] and mentioning the "*derecho a la calle*" (2007: 196, original emphasis)[3] which he attributes to Lefebvre and extols.[4] Lefebvre is present also through frequent mention of the rituals of everyday life (2007: 41) such as the festival (2007: 61, 70, 159) and through the continuation of his project through the work of Michel de Certeau (2007: 61, 68, 69, 70, 177, 180). The last pages of the work even see an attempt to tie Lefebvre in to notions of "el espacio infantil" and "el espacio adulto" (267).

Whereas elsewhere (Fraser 2007b) I have dealt briefly with the similarities of Delgado's work (1999, 2001) with Bergson and Lefebvre in a general sense, here I will place an emphasis on his most recent *Sociedades movedizas* (2007) and from there begin a point by point exploration of his work's relevance to geographical theory. In this way I hope to show the importance of Bergsonism for his contemporary understanding of urban process, both supporting his ideas and also extending them. Thus this section will take on key points of the legacy presented to contemporary geography by the union of Bergson-Lefebvre-Delgado: the priority given to enigma with regard to rational systems, the importance of recognizing indeterminacy, an acknowledgement of the problematic legacy of urban planning, the problematic nature of the abstract categories (such as public and private) in approaching the urban, and

---

[2] "Henri Lefebvre veía en la barricada un instrumento espontáneo de renovación urbana, la expresión de una voluntad absoluta de modificar no sólo el espacio físico, sino también el espacio social: 'Sólo el bulldozer y el cóctel molotov podrían cambiar el espacio existente.'" (179-80). A footnote in Delgado's text cites "H. Lefebvre, *La production de l'espace social*, Anthropos, París, 1974, p. 68."

[3] "No se ha pensado lo suficiente lo que implica este pleno *derecho a la calle* que se vindica, como concreción de aquel derecho a la ciudad que reclamara Henri Lefebvre" (196, original emphasis).

[4] "Desde el punto de vista de la teoría política, la manifestación de calle concreta el derecho democrático a expresar libremente la opinión, derecho personal ejercido colectivamente" (163).

ultimately the question of method and the importance of recognizing mobility in the study of spatial practices. To read Delgado is to reinvent Bergsonism just as it is to reformulate the legacy of twentieth-century anti-urbanism as seen through figures such as Henri Lefebvre and Jane Jacobs.

Although at first the relevance of enigma to Delgado's work may seem somewhat trivial and unclear, it is nevertheless of great methodological importance to his perspective and may be considered, in fact, the central trope of his approach. His writings place an emphasis on the fundamental role of the unknown, the mysterious nature of everyday life as opposed to the orderly designs of the rational systems that attempt to constrain it. The starting point for Delgado's mobile theory of the urban is a philosophical question explored most extensively by Bergson throughout his works. This is the question of freedom, the question with which the French philosopher concludes first *Time and Free Will* (1889)[5] and later *Matter and Memory* (1896).[6] Bergson's approach to this question of freedom in fact reveals the priority of the enigmatic nature of time itself in understanding spatial practices.

Bergson writes that this question of freedom has been badly posed.[7] Nevertheless, freedom is evident from the mobile nature of consciousness.[8] With movement, for Bergson, comes choice. Free-

[5] "The problem of freedom has thus sprung from a misunderstanding: it has been to the moderns what the paradoxes of the Eleatics were to the ancients, and, like these paradoxes, it has its origin in the illusion through which we confuse succession and simultaneity, duration and extensity, quality and quantity" (240).

[6] "Thus whether we consider it in time or in space, freedom always seems to have its roots deep in necessity and to be intimately organized with it. Spirit borrows from matter the perceptions on which it feeds, and restores them to matter in the form of movements which it has stamped with its own freedom" (332).

[7] "I believe that the great metaphysical problems are in general badly stated, that they frequently resolve themselves of their own accord when correctly stated, or else are problems formulated in terms of illusion which disappear as soon as the terms of the formula are more closely examined. [. . .]" (*CM* "The Possible and the Real," 95; see also Deleuze's *Bergsonism*). Also: "The truth is that in philosophy and even elsewhere it is a question of *finding* the problem and consequently of *positing* it, even more than of solving it" (*CM*, 51, original emphasis). The link with urbanism is made clear by similar acknowledgements of Marx ("Frequently the only possible answer is a critique of the question, and the only possible solution is to negate the question," *Grundrisse*, 127) and Jane Jacobs ("Merely to think about cities and get somewhere, one of the main things to know is what *kind* of problem cities pose, for all problems cannot be thought about in the same way," *The Death and Life of Great American Cities*, original emphasis, 428).

[8] Delgado, too, notes that for Robert Park of the Chicago School, which he

dom is obliterated by closed systems of thought, whereas from the perspective of open systems it is a brute reality. In one of Bergson's more notable essays, "The Possible and the Real," written after having already received the Nobel Prize, he describes how he responded to someone asking him to make a prediction regarding the future of literature. As in his earlier writings where he stated that "claiming to foresee an action always comes back to confusing time with space" (*TFW*, 191), here he reframes the debate surrounding the questions that surge from a position that claims time merely as a fourth dimension of space. "[T]ime is something," he writes.

> Therefore it acts. What can it be doing? Plain common sense answered: time is what hinders everything from being given at once. It retards, or rather it is retardation. It must, therefore be elaboration. Would it not then be a vehicle of creation and of choice? Would not the existence of time prove that there is indetermination in things? Would not time be that indetermination itself? (*CM*, 93; see also *MM*, 332)

It is time that is creation, choice, indetermination itself, as he famously states in *Creative Evolution*: "Time is invention or it is nothing at all" (*CE*, 341). It is the spatialization of time that reduces change to mere mechanism, movement to mere static poses, consciousness to things. In his contention that "Claiming to foresee an action always comes back to confusing time with space"–time itself is identified as an enigma, that which cannot be known all at once. Thus time is not predictable.[9] In his essay Bergson writes, "We must resign ourselves to the inevitable: it is the real which makes itself possible, and not the possible which becomes real" (*CM*, 104). The new does not spring mechanically from the old, but refashions this relationship with the old as it creates something that has never before been.[10] Freedom is enacted at every moment and is rooted in the very nature of consciousness. Nevertheless this freedom is impeded, it is covered over, by that aspect of consciousness that is

---

mentions frequently throughout not only *Sociedades movedizas* but also *El animal público*, "La conciencia no es sino un incidente de la locomoción" (2007: 66).

[9] "Hence it is a question devoid of meaning to ask: Could or could not the act be foreseen, given the sum total of its antecedents?" (*TFW*, 189).

[10] See the section titled "Determinism and Freedom" from Bergson's lecture at the Ateneo in Madrid, appendix, this volume.

most implicated in social life, the intellect–manifest, also, in the realm of urban planning as will be discussed below. In the philosophical sense, then, a recognition of temporality is a recognition of freedom and of indeterminacy. This is to fundamentally recognize that things as they are might have been different, that they might still be different in ways that cannot be foreseen. The primary enigma of temporal experience is never fully limited by spatialization, by territorialization, by the designs of a totalizing urbanism understood in the broadest of strokes. The old, for Bergson, holds back the new, but does not determine it. A full recognition of the enigma of time requires, as Bergson is well aware, a rejection of the teleological inadequacies posed by both mechanism and finalism as he documents in *Creative Evolution*. Delgado, too, embraces indeterminacy explicitly in *Sociedades movedizas*, penning an appropriate rhetorical question: "¿Y si reconociésemos el papel que juega en las relaciones humanas la indeterminación, la disolución que las prácticas le imponen a las pautas culturales más presuntamente sólidas?" (84).

This philosophical primacy of enigma, of chaos, over rationality, the brute fact that the open enfolds the closed is the starting point for Bergson's philosophy just as it is, subsequently, for Maurice Merleau-Ponty's *Phenomenology of Perception* (1945) and later in Spain even Juan Benet's approach to literary production (see chapter three of the present work). Thought is, for Merleau-Ponty, the passage from the indeterminate to the determinate (36). Chaos is the basis of experience (65-66).[11] For Benet, who was greatly inspired by Bergson's philosophy (Orringer 1980), inspiration comes to an author only when he has a style. As he explains in *La inspiración y el estilo* (1966), a style is not rational, although it includes rationality. A style is "una zona de sombras" that is not reducible to a "razonamiento matemático" like that professed by

[11] "The experience of chaos, both on the speculative and the other level, prompts us to see rationalism in a historical perspective which it set itself on principle to avoid, to seek a philosophy which explains the upsurge of reason in a world not of its making and to prepare the substructure of living experience without which reason and liberty are emptied of their content and wither away" (65-66). Yet as a student of Bergson's, Merleau-Ponty is reformulating an idea that was already central to Bergson, the idea of a return to experience, the idea that intellect is an insufficient view onto the world, the idea that life overflows the designs placed upon it by thought.

Edgar A. Poe in *La filosofía de la composición* (1848; Benet's reference, 72). First comes imagination, and later comes analysis–which can never completely explain its object. Either analysis bases itself on an enigma or else it is "una superchería que difícilmente le podía llevar al descubrimiento de cosas que no conociera de antemano" (72). In shifting the discourse to the question of style, out of which form and content are inevitably abstracted by the intellect, Benet underscores the primacy of the unknown in the construction of the literary text and points out the limits of a traditional, rational literary criticism which seems ill-equipped to deal with that "zone of shadows" that is the object of its analysis.

What the philosopher, the phenomenologist and the engineer-novelist have in common is a similar conception of the relationship between the open and the closed. Bergson writes that "Now, from the limited to the unlimited there is all the distance between the closed and the open. It is not a difference of degree, but of kind" (*CE*, 263). For Benet there is a difference in kind between imagination and analysis–it is the former which makes the latter possible. It is freedom that comes first, followed by constraint. For Delgado the difference in kind is that between the enigmatic nature of the urban and the apparent predictability characteristic of urbanism. The qualitative freedom manifest in the city-streets finds its place in Delgado's work through his underscoring the indeterminate mystery of everyday city life in his emphasis on the pedestrian as "Un enigma que camina" (2007: 201). He implicitly activates Bergson's understanding of time as invention and creativity (*CE*, 341) by returning time and again, here explicitly and there implicitly, to Jane Jacobs's depiction of the life of the sidewalks as dynamic and creative. Jacobs is famous for having articulated this dynamism through recourse to a metaphor of the movement of the fine arts, one to which Delgado repeatedly returns (1999: 19, 38, esp. 74; 2001: 27; 2007: 129, 135, 245). For Jacobs, who is the origin of what is now a basic precept of urban criticism, the life of the sidewalks is a ballet, a dance (1961: 50, 96, 153).[12]

---

[12] Jacobs writes of the complex order of the city-streets: "It is a complex order. Its essence is intricacy of sidewalk use, bringing with it a constant succession of eyes. This order is all composed of movement and change, and although it is life, not art, we may fancifully call it the art form of the city and liken it to the dance–not to a simple-minded precision dance with everyone kicking up at the same time

It is important to note that Jacobs's metaphor is no attempt to turn life into representation, for she states explicitly that "a city cannot be a work of art" (1961: 372). Instead, the metaphor highlights the multidimensional nature of city-life, its mobile, fluid and necessarily complex nature. As part of his attempt to underscore the living character of cities, Delgado Ruiz references this metaphor explicitly in *El animal público* (74), and then in *Sociedades movedizas* builds on it implicitly: "Cabe insistir en la ya apuntada –y vieja– analogía entre las actividades peatonales y una determinada forma de coreografía" (2007: 135).[13] The sidewalks are a site of negotiation, creation and movement.[14] And yet, as Delgado takes great pains to elaborate, the enigma of the life of the city-streets, the indeterminacy of human spatial practice, the Jacobsian "ballet," the very Lefebvrian "right to the city" (1968) is constrained upon on a daily basis. For Delgado, speaking particularly of the figure of "the immigrant" but relevant to all, the right to the city is precisely the

---

twirling in unison and bowing off en masse, but to an intricate ballet in which the individual dancers and ensembles all have distinctive parts which miraculously reinforce each other and compose an orderly whole. The ballet of the good city sidewalk never repeats itself from place to place, and in any one place is always replete with new improvisations" (50).

[13] The citation continues: "En efecto, el baile expresa a la perfección ese lenguaje de reciprocidades multiplicadas, a veces microscópicas, proclamaciones de una extrema levedad, vigilancias mutuas –con frecuencia de soslayo– y otras actividades visuales manifiestas, que producen una diversidad de realizaciones y de formatos socio-organizativos en los espacios urbanos. La danza es ese tipo de creación artística que se basa en el aprovechamiento al máximo de las posibilidades expresivas del cuerpo, ejerciendo su energía sobre un tiempo y un espacio, tiempo y espacio que podría parecer que ya estaban ahí antes de la acción humana, pero que en realidad es de ésta de la que emanan. El baile lleva hasta las últimas consecuencias la somatización por el actor social de sus iniciativas, la comprensión en términos corporales de la interacción que mantiene con su medio espacial, con las cosas que le rodean y con los demás humanos, la interpelación ininterrumpida entre persona y mundo. El cuerpo-energía-tiempo del danzante expresa todas sus posibilidades en una actividad cotidiana en marcos urbanos en que las palabras suelen valer relativamente poco en la relación entre desconocidos absolutos o parciales y en la que todo parece depender de elocuencias superficiales, no en el sentido de triviales, sino en tanto actos que tienen lugar en la superficie, que funcionan por deslizamientos, que evitan o extraen el máximo provecho de los accidentes del terreno, que buscan y crean las estrías y los pliegues, que desmienten cualquier univocidad en la piel de lo social" (135-36).

[14] "Las aceras, como espacios urbanos por excelencia, deben ser consideradas por tanto terreno para una cultura dinámica e inestable, elaborada y reelaborada constantemente por las prácticas y discursos de sus usuarios" (129). Also "De la calle podría decirse que es ante todo un lugar peregrino, un espacio-movimiento" (129).

right to be unknown, to be anonymous. He enumerates these rights in compelling prose that approaches the form of a bill of rights for pedestrians:

> su derecho a ser un desconocido; derecho a no dar explicaciones; derecho a existir sólo como alguien que pasa, un tipo que va o que viene –¿cómo saberlo?– sin ver detenida su marcha ni por unos que de uniforme les pidan los papeles, ni por otros que se empeñen en "comprenderle" [...] Derecho a la indefinición, al distanciamiento, a guardar silencio. Derecho a ser clasificado por los demás como los demás [...] Derecho a personaje ignoto [...] Derecho a dejar atrás un sitio y dirigirse a otro, atravesando para ello lo que debería ser una tierra de nadie y por ello de todos. [...] Derecho a devenir viandante: a un mismo tiempo el elemento más trivial y más intrigante de la vida urbana. Un enigma que camina. (201)

Delgado's evocation of the social constraint placed upon enigma, anonymity and ambiguity recalls the spatial control over temporality manifest in the Lefebvrian production of space. The struggle between these two movements becomes the basis for Delgado's work as he carefully approaches (as did Bergson) the complex entanglement of opposing forces that differ in nature but are entwined in experience.

Both the philosophical priority given to enigma and the indeterminate and the subsequent material and immaterial struggle to constrain this indeterminacy through the production of the built environment figure into Delgado's characterization of the urban as *process* in the crucial, even foundational and certainly explicit Lefebvrian distinction he makes between the city and the urban–"La ciudad no es lo urbano" (2001: 9). This key distinction "the city" and "the urban" in fact contextualizes his *Sociedades movedizas* from the first page of the introduction.

> Por doquier, constantemente, podemos dar con pruebas de la actualidad de un viejo contencioso inherente a la historia misma de la ciudad moderna: el que opone el conjunto de maneras de vivir en espacios urbanizados –la cultura urbana propiamente dicha– a la estructuración de las territorialidades urbanas, es decir la cultura urbanística. La manera de formular esa apreciación es deudora de la fundamental distinción entre *la ciudad* y *lo urbano*

> que propusiera Henri Lefebvre. La ciudad es un sitio, una gran parcela en que se levanta una cantidad considerable de construcciones, encontramos desplegándose un conjunto complejo de infraestructuras y vive una población más bien numerosa, la mayoría de cuyos componentes no suelen conocerse entre sí. Lo urbano es otra cosa distinta. No es la ciudad, sino las prácticas que no dejan de recorrerla y de llenarla de recorridos; la "obra perpetua de los habitantes, a su vez móviles y movilizados por y para esa obra". (11, original emphasis)[15]

This difference between the city and the urban, a definition he returns to after having already discussed it in previous works (1999: 23, 2001: 9), is here explicitly and directly credited to Lefebvre (above). But nevertheless, as I have argued in the previous chapter, this distinction on Lefebvre's part is best understood as an uncomfortable and unacknowledged if not wholly unconscious *application* of Bergson's complex philosophical distinction between space and time. Just as space and time for Bergson, or spaces of representation and representations of space for Lefebvre, for Delgado, the city and the urban are best understood as two tendencies of one movement–one tendency material and the other immaterial. The city for Delgado is "una composición espacial," whereas the urban is a process "sin marcas ni límites definitivos" (2000: 23). The interaction between these material and immaterial tendencies, as the reader familiar with urban theory, or philosophy, or literary analysis for that matter is well aware, is nothing short of complex.

Somewhat paradoxically, the urban–although indeed a process–is a process that produces a certain kind of regularity in thought and in material spaces. There is a distinction between the urban process and urbanism, although the latter forms part of and contributes to the former. Far from being merely the "raw material" for urbanism, the urban is a qualitative, heterogeneous enigma. The view of urbanism is that this enigma can be controlled, subjected to static representations and ultimately linked to the accumulation of wealth as cities vie for capital. Delgado thus moves us to understand urbanism in the following way: "en última instancia como una

---

[15] The footnote to this citation reads "(de H. Lefebvre, *El derecho a la ciudad*, Península, Barcelona, 1978, p. 158. Sobre la distinción entre la ciudad y lo urbano véase también su *Espacio y política*, Península, Barcelona, 1972, pp. 70-71)" (cited in n. 1, Delgado 11).

máquina de homogeneizar y clarificar el medio ambiente urbano" (2000: 11). Urbanism seizes upon this indeterminate, enigmatic, multidimensional, qualitative, unlimited, heterogeneous and ever-changing flux of the urban and seeks to reduce it, constrain it, limit it, define it in quantitative and wholly spatial terms. Yet taking on this perspective of urbanism–that is, the perspective of this machine seeking to homogenize and clarify urban space–requires that one makes a speculative identification between the form of space and the content of space, between the active elements of the production of a given space and the subsequently prescribed activities that will take place within it. It is this machine that urban planners are able to harness to their speculative interests. Delgado denounces this speculative activity characteristic of the limiting action of urbanism through recourse to the distinction between form and content[16] (as have other critics; see Fraser 2007b) and argues for a recognition of the urban not as a structurally determined coherent system but rather as

> una proliferación de marañas relacionales compuestas de usos, componendas, impostaciones, rectificaciones y adecuaciones mutuas que van emergiendo a cada momento, un agrupamiento polimorfo e inquieto de cuerpos humanos que sólo puede ser observado en el instante preciso en que se coagula, puesto que está destinado a disolverse de inmediato. (2007: 12)

In this return to the key issue of a mobile complexity, one which he advanced throughout *El animal público* (1999) where he advocated his vision of an "urban anthropology" (12),[17] Delgado Ruiz revisits the central concern of Jane Jacobs's process-oriented theory. In *The Death and Life of Great American Cities* (1961) Jacobs famously wrote that "Cities happen to be problems in complexity, like the life sciences,"

---

[16] Delgado denounces this speculative activity: "Todo ello requiere que el proyecto busque sobre todo la congruencia entre forma y actividad, y lo haga a través de la estereotipación y la esquematización de los entornos" (2001; 11–see also Staeheli 1996).

[17] "Una antropología urbana, en el sentido de lo urbano, sería, pues, una antropología de configuraciones sociales escasamente orgánicas, poco o nada solidificadas, sometidas a la oscilación constante y destinadas a desvanecerse enseguida [...] una antropología de lo inestable, de lo no estructurado, no porque esté desestructurado, sino por estar *estructurándose* [...]" (1999: 12, original emphasis).

> They present "situations in which a half-dozen or even several dozen quantities are all varying simultaneously *and in subtly interconnected ways.*" Cities, again like the life sciences, do not exhibit *one* problem in organized complexity, which if understood explains all. They can be analyzed into many such problems or segments which, as in the case of the life sciences, are also related with one another. The variables are many, but they are not helter-skelter; they are "interrelated into an organic whole." (433, original emphasis)

In effect, Jacobs has actualized a notably Bergsonian perspective on the complexity of life and movement and has applied it to the urban phenomenon. Just as Bergson sought to underscore the contradictory nature of the interpenetrating forces of composites such as those entwining matter and memory, things and consciousness, intelligence and instinct, the closed and the open, he emphasized the movement as indivisible in order to point out the irreducible heterogeneous *quality* of life–thus his extensive attempt to reconcile the problems of biology with the problems of philosophy in *Creative Evolution* and elsewhere. His signaling the importance of time was not a turn from space but a call to fold it back into time, thus: an acknowledgement of complexity, a denunciation of the static designs and abstract categories characteristic of intellectual thought. His work as a whole moves contrary to the intellectual movement to define and make precise, what amounts to the tendency of the closed (*MR*), and instead advocates the open through the complex articulation of difference. Living things, he tells us, consciousness, temporality itself, is nothing short of complex. It is this Bergsonian legacy, what amounts to a powerful condemnation of spatialization as both mental and material process, that has obtained in the perspectives of Henri Lefebvre and Jane Jacobs, and it is this Bergsonian legacy that subtends Delgado's *Sociedades movedizas* from the first page to the last in his conceptualization of the urban as fluid and mobile qualitative heterogeneity. One of the most poignant and original contributions of this most recent work, especially when compared with his earlier writings (1999, 2001), is Delgado's more conscious discussion of the ills of urban planning.

Delgado's contribution to studies of space is in fact an enfolding of Bergson's non-dualistic spatial and temporal philosophy and of Lefebvre's triadic model of spatial production. This amalgam of paradigm shifts, digested as they are from the realms of anthropology, geography and philosophy, suggests as much for the study of space as it does for the reconceptualization of the very idea of "space" itself. Incorporating the phenomenological questioning of perceiver and perceived into a superb materialist critique of capitalist spatial practices, Delgado draws together the imagined and physical aspects of our spatial production much as recent theorists in cultural geography have attempted to reconcile material and immaterial forces.[18] The consequences of this type of scholarship cannot be overemphasized given the contemporary accelerated drive for capital accumulation through the production and reproduction of cityspace (Harvey 1990, 1996, 2000).

In this context, Delgado has succinctly characterized the teratological problem of urbanism as its fundamental opposition to and reduction of difference, enigma and ambiguity. Urbanism suffers, in Delgado's (2001) words, from the need to "arquitecturizarlo todo"–"[c]omo si la tarea en última instancia colonizadora del urbanista tuviera como su peor enemigo la tendencia que todo espacio socializado experimenta hacia la ambigüedad, hacia la indefinición, como consecuencia de la propia naturaleza indeterminada de los usos que registra" (8). Grappling with the urban process, then, means grappling with this very act of homogenizing space–treating space as a homogeneous medium which may then be sectioned off into innumerable parts–this very act of organizing space.[19] Thus for Delgado, just as for Lefebvre (1974) before him, "Todo espacio estructurado es un espacio social, puesto que es la sociedad la que permite la conversión de un espacio no definido, no marcado, no pensable –inconcebible en definitiva antes de su organización– en un territorio" (1999: 177). If space is experienced as already organized–if space is experienced in fact *through* its very organization, then the problem of cityspace cannot merely be a spatial problem. It is a temporal problem just as much as it is a spatial problem. It is a question of the relation of the temporal to the spatial, the relation of the immaterial to the material, the relation of mind and matter, consciousness and things–a question not merely of space but of the *production* of space.

[18] Most importantly Latham and McCormack 2004. The previous chapter on Bergson-Lefebvre discusses this tradition in more detail.

[19] Delgado points out that "una división clara entre público y privado" (179) is quite important to this process. More on this anon.

The legacy of modern urban planning demonstrates, above all else, a proclivity for an intellectualization–in the Bergsonian sense–of space, thus a spatialization of time and a reduction of qualitative to the quantitative. To the degree that urban planners approach the city as a work of art or as a blank canvas from which to start as if from nothing, they reproduce a philosophical error denounced by Bergson most directly in *Creative Evolution*–an error that concerns the idea of nothing. To concisely summarize this argument, one which occupies quite a few pages (272-98), will take only a few sentences here. The idea of nothing, it is said, is less than the idea of something. It is lack, the void; it is the empty glass. To get something from nothing, the error of this common sense continues, one must proceed by addition, adding something that was not there before. Nevertheless, as Bergson argues, this common sense approach is flawed. The idea of nothing, he writes, is actually the idea of something plus its negation. Thus, there is more content in the idea of nothing than in the idea of something. In the idea of nothing, we have all that which is in the idea of something, plus an added negative act of mind. This is quite important to understand when approaching the method that commonly obtains in urban design.

Let us look at what happens: the act of positing parts of the city or the city as a whole as a blank canvas eradicates all the voices of the city save those that the thinker has maintained through his or her own caprice. Before this act of mind, this negation on the part of thought, the city is there, the urban is there in all its qualitative heterogeneity. It is a sidewalk ballet that escapes representation, a multidimensional and complex problem (if indeed it is appropriately considered a problem at all). After this act of mind, after this negation, it is a conceived and contrived smooth space, homogenous, bounded and ready to receive the thought-ink of urban design. In short it has passed from a cacophonous and mobile multiplicity to the simple state of a thing. But surely, one might protest, if the thinker through rational means can gather all the appropriate information before-hand, assemble all the data, they will take into account this or that voice. But, and this is a matter of principle, a matter of intellectual thought, and not merely a question of having adequate means and desire at one's disposal, however fair and balanced the assessment might be, he or she will *never* manage to recompose the totality of this complex qualitative movement of the urban through stitching together isolated fragments.[20] Although urban design may tend to envision space as a homogeneous and purely extensive medium upon which it can act, this type of space is a poor representation of the movement characteristic of urban life. Bergson wrote that this idea of a homogeneous and indefinitely divisible space was a "view taken by mind" (*CE*, 157).[21] It is this view that actually produces a space that is indefinitely divisible. This view represents the quotidian functioning of a particular kind of thought that Bergson termed the "intellect." This intellect routinely reduces movement to static snapshots (*CE*, 306-07) and sees quality only through quantity where it is the reverse that is true (*TFW*, 122-23). Yet beyond this view there is the fundamentally indivisible reality of urban life. As Bergson writes, "Though all the photographs of a city taken from all possible points of view indefinitely complete one another, they will never equal in value that [multi]dimensional object, the city along whose streets one walks" (*CM*, 160-61; epigraph, above).

Bergson in fact made one other explicit attempt to reconcile his critique of spatialization with the organization of the city, one that must be considered absolutely crucial to the present effort. This attempt calls attention to the importance of privileging relations over things. Relations, and not merely things, were of utmost priority for Bergson just as they were for Lefebvre (1974), Harvey

[20] "The whole of matter is made to appear to our thought as an immense piece of cloth in which we can cut out what we will and sew it together again as we please" (*CE*, 157). Nevertheless, this is the appearance of matter, and as such is insufficient to explain the relations out of which things are abstracted.

[21] Bergson appropriately takes this "view taken by mind" of "an immense piece of cloth" to task. It is the power to imagine a homogeneous space that is at fault. He continues: Let us note, in passing, that it is this power that we affirm when we say that there is a *space*, that is to say, a homogeneous and empty medium, infinite and indefinitely divisible, lending itself indifferently to any mode of decomposition whatsoever. A medium of this kind is never perceived; it is only conceived. What is perceived is extension colored, resistant, divided according to the lines which mark out the boundaries of real bodies or of their real elements. But when we think of our power over this matter, that is to say, of our faculty of decomposing and recomposing it as we please, we project the whole of these possible decompositions and recompositions behind real extension in the form of a homogeneous space, empty and indifferent, which is supposed to underlie it. This space is therefore, preeminently, the plan of our possible action on things, although, indeed, things have a natural tendency, as we shall explain later on, to enter into a frame of this kind. It is a view taken by mind (*CE*, 157). See also the last chapter of the work where Bergson relates this view of space to Kant's misunderstanding.

(2000) and of course Marx (see Harvey 2000: 28, also 1989). In *Creative Evolution* there is an uncharacteristic reference to the realm of cities that provides a point of departure for connecting the supposedly disparate realms of philosophy and urban geography. Bergson writes:

> Each being cuts up the world according to the lines that its action must follow: it is these lines of *possible action* that, by intercrossing, mark out the net of experience of which each mesh is a fact. No doubt, a town is composed exclusively of houses, and the streets of the town are only the intervals between the houses: so we may say that nature contains only facts, and that, the facts once posited, the relations are simply the lines running between the facts. But, in a town, it is the gradual portioning of the ground into lots that has determined at once the place of the houses, their general shape, and the direction of the streets: to this portioning we must go back if we wish to understand the particular mode of subdivision that causes each house to be where it is, each street to run as it does. (*CE*, 367-68, original emphasis)

In this important quotation, Bergson anticipates many of the later critiques of urbanization made throughout the twentieth century and succeeds in signaling the importance of a philosophical basis for urban criticism. It is the thought of urban planning that posits a flat spatiality of already given things, the houses, and the strictly materialist distance between them as another thing, the intervals. All these, for the urbanist are considered things. Nevertheless, as Bergson points out wonderfully, these things are merely a "view taken by mind" (*CE*, 157), and the flat spatiality that reduces heterogeneity to homogeneity must be seen as an abstraction, an extraction from the movement characteristic of the production of space. Stepping back from this moment of abstraction, he asks what is the dialectical relationship that has produced the given relationship between these apparent facts of the landscape? It is the dynamic movement of "portioning" that has determined what is, for the intellect, the apparent discreteness of these city-things, the streets and houses.

This inadequacy of the intellect's approach to city space signaled by Bergson is reproduced in Jane Jacobs's critique of the reduction of the complexity of city life to static views or abstract plans. "The sidewalk," Jacobs states clearly, "is an abstraction" (1961: 29). The implication is that urban life overflows the idea one has of it and is thus insufficiently represented by this abstraction. Although she might have eschewed such a pointedly philosophical take on urban life, there is, operating throughout her epic work on the city, a critique of traditional ontology quite reminiscent of Bergson's. She fundamentally rejects the idea of the city as a thing or as a group of interchangeable or replaceable parts.

Yet it is precisely this idea of the city as blank canvas whose homogeneous space may be indefinitely subdivided that has obtained in the projects of urban design. To give an example that Jacobs herself points out, in a tradition going back to Ebenezer Howard, modern urban planners have confidently designed parks into city-space, believing that the mere existence of park space itself will determine the activities that take place within it.[22] Yet, on the contrary, as Jane Jacobs's *The Death and Life of Great American Cities* shows, open park spaces frequently play a role in the deterioration of neighborhoods–and not necessarily their regeneration. Jacobs thus supplies an important corrective to the utopian ideals of the parks movement: "Conventionally, neighborhood parks or parklike open spaces are considered boons conferred on the deprived populations of cities. Let us turn this thought around, and consider city parks deprived places that need the boon of life and appreciation conferred on *them*" (89, original emphasis). The focus for Jacobs is not on things but on relations, and relations cannot be altered by merely constructing a park. Neither can a system of relations be changed by conceiving of the city as an art project, by conceiving of buildings as works of art–a proposition that ignores the class-character of much contemporary urban architecture which indeed takes this view. Architectural critic Diane Ghirardo does well in reminding us that, "At its core, architecture today is supremely elitest, drawing most private and public commissions from various elite groups" (2007[1997]: 170). Furthermore, a park is not, nor is any other parcel of city-space, a piece of a puzzle. The city is not a puz-

---

[22] For a discussion of the complex motivations for the constructions of parks in the American context, see Roy Rosenzweig's *Eight Hours for What We Will: Workers and Leisure in an Industrial City, 1870-1920* (1983). See also Fraser (2007a).

zle whose pieces can be reshuffled until the right arrangement is found. Such a view is the urban equivalent of either the finalism or the mechanism denounced by Bergson in *Creative Evolution*. Instead, as Delgado's depiction of the urban as fluid and enigmatic, Jacobs's definition of cities as a complex problem akin to the life-sciences, Lefebvre's understanding of the urban as process and Bergson's characterization of life as a movement all demand, we must recognize urban life as a moving reality that subtends and overflows the insufficient designs of abstractions and static categories.

For Delgado Ruiz, one of the most important static categorizations to dismantle before approaching the city as a living process is the distinction between public and private. It is not by chance that his award-winning book was titled *El animal público* (1999). Significantly, Delgado employs an implicitly Bergsonian argument in suggesting that this so-called public space is not a space at all, but rather a movement.[23] Within this process, public space itself is seen as a negotiation (Delgado 2001: 35), with the real movements of people constituting and reconstituting a shifting and *produced* boundary between public and private. Whereas he entertains the notion of public space, a public sphere such as that famously extolled by Hannah Arendt (1958) and Habermas (1989), both of whom he cites explicitly (2007: 49, 67, 197, 245, 260; 172, 191, 197, 234), he recognizes that such an image of space is problematic and counters Arendt's conception pointedly:

> Pero tal imagen no es más que una quimera. Cabe insistir de nuevo, ese espacio público en que se concreta la realización del republicanismo kantiano al que Habermas dedicara una brillante reflexión, no existe. Ese espacio público accesible a todos se disuelve en cuanto los controles y las fiscalizaciones desmienten su

[23] "El espacio público es pues, un territorio desterritorializado, que se pasa el tiempo reterritorializándose y volviéndose a desterritorializar, que se caracteriza por la sucesión y el amontonamiento de componentes inestables. Es en esas arenas movedizas donde se registra la concentración y el desplazamiento de las fuerzas sociales que las lógicas urbanas convocan o desencadenan, y que están crónicamente condenadas a sufrir todo tipo de composiciones y recomposiciones, a ritmo lento o en sacudidas. El espacio público es desterritorializado también porque en su seno todo lo que concurre y ocurre es heterogéneo: un espacio esponjoso en el que apenas nada merece el privilegio de *quedarse*" (1999: 46).

> vocación democrática o cuando el sistema de mundo que padecemos hace de ellos espacios no para el uso, sino para el consumo. (2007: 197)[24]

This opposition of public and private, although much discourse may take it to be an ontological truth, is an abstraction, "Lo privado y lo público existen en tanto que modalidades de *nosotros*" (2007: 54, original emphasis). As an abstraction, an intellectual one in the Bergsonian sense, the distinction has been subject to the claims that urbanists have made upon it often with private interests in mind. In a recent article from *El País* Delgado reminds us that "Para el urbanismo oficial, *espacio público* quiere decir otra cosa: un vacío entre construcciones que hay que llenar de forma adecuada a los objetivos de promotores y autoridades, que suelen ser los mismos, por cierto" (29 May 2006).[25] Ultimately, Delgado underscores the complicity of this abstract category with the perspective of a pernicious urbanism. Public space comes to be conceived as "[un] lugar en que se materializan diversas categorías abstractas como democracia, ciudadanía, convivencia, civismo, consenso y otras supersticiones políticas contemporáneas" (2006).[26] Delgado suggests that discrete and static categories, abstractions such as public and

---

[24] Lynn Staeheli's (1996) lucid critique is also a necessary corrective to the simplistic enlightenment rhetoric of theorists such as Arendt (1958) who argue for a genuinely public "space of appearance." Most importantly, her bottom line (which for the Hispanist may call up remarks by Mariano José de Larra) underscores the difficulty confronted by the desire for social change. Staeheli writes, definitively, that "the idea of a unitary space (metaphorical or material) for politics in which individual interests are set aside is impossible" (617). Consider also Larra–"Before all else, the public is the pretext, the cover, for the private needs of each man" [1832/1975]. I look more closely at this issue of public and private space in Fraser 2007a.

[25] The quotation continues: "No en vano la noción de espacio público se puso de moda entre los planificadores sobre todo a partir de las grandes iniciativas para la especulación, el turismo y las demandas institucionales en materia de legitimidad."

[26] The full citation reads: "En este caso, el *espacio público* pasa a concebirse como la realización de un valor ideológico, lugar en que se materializan diversas categorías abstractas como democracia, ciudadanía, convivencia, civismo, consenso y otras supersticiones políticas contemporáneas, proscenio en que se desearía ver pulular una ordenada masa de seres libres e iguales, guapos y felices, seres inmaculados que emplean ese espacio para ir y venir de trabajo o de consumir y que, en sus ratos libres, pasean despreocupados por un paraíso de amabilidad y cortesía, como si fueran figurantes de un colosal anuncio publicitario" (Delgado 2006).

private space, are not only ontologically suspect but that they also lend themselves to abuse by proponents of urban design.

Delgado's (and Lefebvre's) primary distinction between the city and the urban, however, is no such discrete category but rather an attempt, in the Bergsonian tradition of the composite, to portray a more complex relationship of interpenetrating opposites. The complexity of this distinction, however, is precisely what urbanists have ignored in their attempt to subject urban life to mere mechanism. Whereas it is the heterogeneity of the urban that is irreducible to a static plan, it is precisely this heterogeneity that urbanists have taken upon themselves to control.

> Así pues, no cuestiona aquí la necesidad y hasta la urgencia de planificar las ciudades. Las ciudades pueden y deben ser planificadas. Lo urbano, no. Lo urbano es lo que no puede ser planificado en una ciudad, ni se deja. Es la máquina social por excelencia, un colosal artefacto de hacer y deshacer nudos humanos que no puede detener su interminable labor. En cambio, en todo el mundo se pueden constatar las evidencias de que el proceso que se sigue es exactamente el contrario. Se planifica lo urbano –la calle y la vida que se despliega en y por ella–, pero no la ciudad, que es vendida para que el más feroz de los liberalismos la deprede y haga de ella un negocio. Se estimula la propiedad, pero se restringe la apropiación. En realidad, una cosa es consecuencia de la otra: la renuncia de la administración pública a planificar la ciudad, para entregarla al desorden especulador y a su conversión en producto de y para el consumo, sólo es posible manteniendo rigurosamente vigilados los espacios por los que transcurre una vitalidad urbana contemplada siempre como obstáculo para el buen marketing urbano y como fuente de desasosiego para cualquier forma de poder político. (2007: 19, see also 13-14)

What comes out of the act of reading of Delgado's most recent work through its implicit Bergsonian and explicit Lefebvrian roots is that urban planning is committing an error of methodological nature. This error has its roots in a faulty conception of temporal process, and a pernicious accompanying reduction of time to space, quality to quantity, heterogeneity to homogeneity, the movement of city-life to static poses. What urbanism lacks today, as Delgado's work suggests, is, as Jacobs stated so poignantly, precisely what it lacked in 1961:

> As long as city planners, and the businessmen, lenders and legislators who have learned from planners, cling to the unexamined assumptions that they are dealing with a problem in the physical sciences, city planning cannot possibly progress. Of course it stagnates. It lacks the first requisite for a body of practical and progressing thought: recognition of the kind of problem at issue. (439)

The kind of problem at hand is a dynamic and complex one that is insufficiently addressed and in fact aggravated by overly rational, spatial, intellectual approaches. In this sense, the most important question for urban studies is, as it was too for Bergson in the realm of philosophy, the question of method.

In approaching the living city methodologically we must start with the "immediate data of consciousness" as Bergson titled his first work (1889–in the original French *Essai sur les données immédiates de la conscience*, also Bernard 1865, Bergson 1934). We must redeem physical reality, see the material as already infused with immaterial process and return to "the flow of life" (Kracauer 1960, see also Latham and McCormack 2004). This is to return to our experience, to our lived realities (Lefebvre 1974), to the real movement and process of life. This dynamic methodological premise rejects the idea that knowledge must be conceived in static terms and instead reconciles knowledge and life (Bergson 1907: xiii "theory of knowledge and theory of life seem to us inseparable"; also see Harvey 1989: 7). As Jane Jacobs points out, "Because we use cities, and therefore have experience with them, most of us already possess a good groundwork for understanding and appreciating their order" (1961: 376).

The methodology advocated by Delgado is one tied to the concrete nature of experience (Bergson) and the struggle over the production of space (Lefebvre). Delgado writes that "Se defiende, pues, que nada debería justificar una renuncia a *la observación directa de los hechos sociales* y al intento honrado de –con todas las limitaciones bien presentes– explicar posteriormente lo observado, en el doble sentido de relatarlo y advertirlo en tanto que organización" (2007: 112, emphasis added; also 124). This "direct observation of social data" (Delgado) recalls Bergson's emphasis from his first work (1889, above) and is consciously tied to the ills of contemporary urban planning through Delgado's more conscious engagement with the early-twentieth century philosopher's ideas than that which is found in Lefebvre. Space is, for Delgado as for Bergson and later Lefebvrian geographer David Harvey no mere container for social action (Delgado 2007: 13; also Bergson 1889, 1934; Harvey 1996).[27] The question is not merely that of a static space such as that provided by the Bergsonian intellect, a "view taken by mind" (*CE*, 157), but that of a movement that is insufficiently represented by such static views:

> la idiosincrasia functional y sociológica del espacio urbano no está –no puede estar– preestablecida en el plan, no puede responder mecánicamente a las direccionalidades y los puntos de atracción prefigurados por los diseñadores, puesto que resulta de un número inmenso e inmensamente variado de movimientos y ocupaciones transitorias, imprevisibles muchas de ellas, que dan lugar a mapas móviles y sin bordes. (2007: 13)

Thus the speculative plan–the urbanist's static representation of the city–cannot capture or incorporate the mobile nature of urban praxis (13).[28]

> La empresa que asume el proyectista es la de trabajar a partir de un espacio esencialmente *representado*, o más bien, *concebido*, que se opone a las otras formas de espacialidad que caracterizan la labor de una sociedad urbana sobre sí misma: espacio percibido, practicado, vivido, usado, ensoñado... Su pretensión: mutar lo oscuro por algo más claro. Su obcecamiento: la legibilidad. Su lógica: la de una ideología que se quiere encarnar, que aspira a convertirse en operacionalmente eficiente y lograr el milagro de una inteligibilidad absoluta. (14)

---

[27] "Como forma radical de espacio social que es, el espacio urbano no existe –no puede existir– como un proscenio vacío a la espera de que algo o alguien lo llene. No es un lugar donde en cualquier momento pueda acontecer algo, puesto que ese lugar se da / sólo en tanto ese algo acontece y sólo en el momento mismo en que lo hace. Ese lugar no es un lugar, sino un *tener lugar* de los cuerpos que lo ocupan en extensión, y en tiempo; como comarca rediseñada una y otra vez por las migraciones que la recorren y que dan pie a lo que Anne Cauquelin llamaba una 'armonía confusa'" (Delgado 13).

[28] In Delgado's opposition between the pre-established plan and the inpredictable life of the city streets there is a familiar Bergsonian distinction between the homogeneous space conceived by the intellect and a temporality that is essentially indivisible. See *Creative Evolution* and *Matter and Memory*. Delgado continues this critique in his recent work *La ciudad mentirosa* (Madrid: Catarata, 2007).

This is an essentially and at times explicitly Lefebvrian conceit to return to "everyday life" (Lefebvre 1947, 1961, 1981), to space not only as represented or conceived but as practiced and as lived. As Lefebvre clearly states in *The Production of Space*, "spatial practice is lived before it is conceptualized" (34). Thus between what Delgado, echoing Lefebvre's distinction, calls the "ciudad concebida," ultimately that of urbanists, and the "ciudad practicada" (2007: 11), that of lived spatial practices, there is, his work suggests, a Bergsonian difference of kind and not merely of degree. Just as in Lefebvre's tripartite model of spatial practice (1974: 33) and in Bergson's process philosophy, here, too, there is a dialectical relationship between thought and action, between ideas of space and the production of space. For Delgado, this dialectical relationship between thought and action (Lefebvre), between the realm of ideas and the realm of things, between matter and human consciousness (Bergson), is likewise not merely a question of urban space but rather a philosophical question involving perception as a whole. He writes: "En todos los casos –incluyendo sus expresiones en apariencia más infalibles, como la fotografía– se reproduce una relación dialéctica entre lo percibido, la percepción y lo plasmado, o entre la cosa apreciada, la sensación recibida y su transfiguración figurativa" (111). This dialectical relationship, in its attempt to acknowledge if not to reconcile perception and that which is perceived, recalls Bergson's writings on the connection of centripetal and centrifugal movements of the nervous system (*MM*) as well as his reconciliation of the supposed realm of purely inner and unextended experience with a purely extensive material world uninflected by consciousness.

In this context, Delgado's own reconciliation of inner and outer comprises a great testament to the work of both Bergson and Lefebvre. His effort amounts to a rejection of brute materialism –that is, of a materialism uninflected by consciousness. Just as Lefebvre hoped to join "representations of space" and "representational spaces" (1974: 33)–just as Bergson hoped to reconcile matter and memory (1896), just as Siegfried Kracauer sought to recapture the interior precisely through the exterior as presented on the silver screen (see chapter six of the present work; Kracauer 1960)–Delgado praises the exterior as the path to an important interiority. Anticipating the possible critiques of his ideas, he is forced to defend his position even as he articulates it: "Todo lo que antecede es una apología de lo exterior, lo que flota en la superficie –pero que no es superficial–, lo que se puede sentir, lo que surge o se aparece" (126). Just as Bergson railed against the untenable positions of both extreme realism and extreme idealism, neither is Delgado satisfied with the opposition of simplistic positions on complex concrete experience. Recalling this very struggle of Bergson's (most notable in *MM* 1896), he challenges both "el cientificismo estrecho y pacato" and "esa etnografía posmoderna policroma, esa suerte de fantasía objetiva narcisista que pretende –y consigue– disolver la antropología en la pura literatura ficcional" (125). In his insistence on a science more precisely attuned to reality (125), Delgado continues an essentially Bergsonian project. Although he was much maligned (wrongly) as an antiscientific idealist, Bergson was, the attentive reader will recall, an advocate of a certain kind of science which he envisioned as the necessary complement to philosophy, stating that "metaphysics cannot get along without the other sciences" (*CM*, 168).[29] As his eloquent essay on "The Philosophy of Claude Bernard" (*CM*, 201-08) demonstrates, his interest was methodological in nature.

---

[29] "To metaphysics, then, we assign a limited object, principally spirit, and a special method, mainly intuition. In doing this we make a clear distinction between metaphysics and science. But at the same time we attribute an equal value to both. I believe that they can both touch the bottom of reality. I reject the arguments advanced by philosophers, and accepted by scholars, on the relativity of knowledge and the impossibility of attaining the absolute" (37). Later, in the same work, Bergson continues to elaborate upon this idea: "Quite different is the metaphysics that we place side by side with science. Granting to science the power of explaining matter by the mere force of intelligence, it reserves mind for itself. In this realm, proper to itself, it seeks to develop new functions of thought. Everyone can have noticed that it is more difficult to make progress in the knowledge of oneself than in the knowledge of the external world. Outside oneself, the effort to learn is natural; one makes it with increasing facility; one applies rules. Within, attention must remain tense and progress become more and more painful; it is as though one were going against the natural bent. Is there not something surprising in this? We are internal to ourselves, and our personality is what we should know best.

Yet such is not the case; our mind is as if it were in a strange land, whereas matter is familiar to it and in it the mind is home. But that is because a certain ignorance of self is perhaps useful to a being which must exteriorize itself in order to act; it answers a necessity of life" (41).

And later still: "But if metaphysics demands and can obtain here an intuition, science has no less need of an analysis. And it is because of a confusion between the roles of analysis and intuition that the dissentions between schools of thought and the conflicts between systems will arise" (169). Bergson's view of science was in fact nuanced: "Modern science is neither one nor simple" (197).

The understanding that becoming is prior to being, thus that questions of method are prior to questions of being–that the method delimits the object–motivates Delgado to articulate a more complex understanding of the subjective than purely materialist approaches to the urban might suggest. He certainly distances himself from the idea of a bounded, fetishized (55) interior self that is unconnected with an exterior reality (54-55), and yet so did Bergson. The philosopher himself pointed out that there are two selves "(1) the fundamental self: (2) its spatial and social representation" (*TFW*, 231)–only the self that is reducible to categories is relevant to the machinelike regularity imposed by social life. Thus although he rejects a self-enclosed and thus untenable subjectivity, Delgado is intent to reconcile both extreme subjective and objective views into a complex understanding of the urban process. Consider this statement that undermines the classical nineteenth-century practice of the "objective" gaze of the armchair anthropologist: "El antropólogo, en este caso, trabaja sobre una realidad que le trabaja. Otra cosa es que se reconozca como pertinente esa querella que enfrenta en diversos frentes lo 'subjetivo' y lo 'objetivo' en las ciencias humanas y sociales, en una dicotomía cuyos términos son más que discutibles" (111).[30] This reconciliation of the subjective and the objective is no mere abstract philosophical diversion from supposedly "material" forces. As Harvey's *A Brief History of Neoliberalism* (2006) professes, contemporary capitalism has worked to construct a particular view of the individual, of the self, one that is more amenable to consumption. In doing this he implies that in practice there are aspects of subjectivity that are simply not (at present) useful to the capitalist machine. The connection between Delgado and Bergson is, then, only apparent once one has dispensed with the view that the name of Bergson is synonymous with interiority and subjectivity at the expense of the exterior. What is at stake is a process of differentiation and not the acceptance of one static category or another.

Delgado's position on differentiation is Bergsonian, not to men-

[30] A wonderful visual reinforcement of this idea occurs in the film *Kitchen Stories* (2004). Although Delgado does not reference this movie in his text, it would have fit in well since he incorporates films as illustrations in many other cases. Such films include Wayne Wang/Paul Auster's *Smoke* (73) and directors such as Ozu (121, 267), Pier Paolo Pasolini (81, 256), Resnais (78), Truffaut (266), Vertov (119, 120) and Billy Wilder (229) among others.

tion Deleuzian.[31] This position can be summed up in the concise statement that things are not in space, space is in things (Bergson 1889, Harvey 1996, also Hewitt 1974). Difference, understood as a relation, is not between things but *within* things. This understanding comes naturally from his understanding of the urban as mobile in nature, as multidimensional process that is constrained by rational design. This is to say that to talk about difference is at once to talk about two ways of conceiving it. The thing, for Bergson and Deleuze (1966), differs from itself. It is multiple. Nevertheless, there is the urbanist's conception of difference as a homogeneous and bounded thing that differs from other things through relations that are external and not internally constituted and that are thus things themselves. According to the first understanding, enigma, the multiple is constrained by the solid definition characteristic of our quotidian, intellectual view of things. The second understanding would have us reduce the multiple and heterogeneous nature of reality to an easily-digested abstraction. Delgado clearly opts for the first, criticizing the second for its mechanistic character. In the first, true difference is heterogeneity, multiplicity, whereas in the second, difference is a mere mechanistic system imposed on that multidimensional heterogeneous world. He writes:

> no son las diferencias las que generan la diversidad, tal y como podría antojarse superficialmente, sino que son los mecanismos de diversificación los que motivan la búsqueda de marcajes que llenen de contenido la voluntad de distinguirse y distinguir a los demás, no pocas veces con fines excluyentes. Una entidad clasificatoria cualquiera, es decir una unidad sobrepuesta definible por y en ella misma, no sirve tanto para alimentar la base de una clasificación, sino que, justo al contrario, constituye su producto, en otras palabras, no se clasifica porque hay cosas que clasificar, sino porque clasificamos que las podemos descubrir. No es la diferencia la que suscita la diferenciación, sino la diferenciación la que crea y deifica la diferencia. (2007: 200)

In this denunciation of the urbanist's conception of difference, Delgado's writings suggest a return to a chaotic protoplasm of the urban, what is, for Bergson, the brute fact of movement and change,

[31] Delgado is, in fact, quite attentive to the work of Deleuze (2007: 65, 118, 119, 121, 126, 221; also 1999: 60, 78, 79, 85, 116, 190, 209).

for Merleau-Ponty, the phenomenological priority given to enigma, for Benet, the zone of shadows that is the unfolding of temporality, and for Jacobs the sidewalk ballet. In this way, Delgado's *Sociedades movedizas* does not merely seek to outline the urban as a new concept for research but rather to signal the inadequacy of our overly-rational approaches to life, to urban life, whether they are historical, sociological, geographical, or anthropological in nature: "No hay una historia, ni una sociología, ni una geografía de lo irrelevante, de lo sobrante luego de haber acotado debidamente objetos de conocimientos sumisos al método, obedientes al discurso, dóciles al lenguaje" (2007: 83). This most recent work of Delgado's is best contextualized within the Bergsonian and Lefebvrian advances regarding the question of method.

The previous chapter dealt with the common goal of Bergson and Lefebvre's methodology and ended by suggesting that understood as a whole, Bergson-Lefebvre's critique of the spatialization of time characteristic of the intellect and the spatialization of time characteristic of capitalism called for a redoubled effort to engage the question of method, especially when faced with the moving nature of urban realities. In Delgado we see this same call. Whereas in *El animal público* (1999: 12)[32] he firmly established the need for a mobile anthropology in approaching the fluid and shifting nature of the urban, a call which he later echoed by incorporating Lefebvre's call for a rhythmanalysis (Delgado 2001: 36-41), in *Sociedades movedizas* he returns once again to this rejection of the classical traditions of research: "La sociología y la antropología clásicas se han centrado en las estructuras estables, en los órdenes más firmes y en los procesos positivos, siempre en busca de lo determinado y sus determinantes" (84). The approaches of these classical traditions, and of traditional analysis in general, infused as it has been with the designs of what Bergson called "intellect," has thus mistaken the temporal for the spatial, the dynamic for the static. Or, as Lefebvre suggests in his idea of rhythmanalysis (see chapter eight of the present work), it has privileged the hard-lines of analytical tools at the

[32] Delgado's urban anthropology as articulated in his *El animal público* was implicitly indebted to a strong tradition of anti-urbanism expressed by Lefebvre, the situationists (including Guy DeBord and Asger Jorn) and others who saw in urban planning the death of life on the streets. See also Jacobs, *The Death and Life of Great American Cities*.

expense of the blurred qualities and, Bergson would say, the enduring nature of temporal experience. A shared critique of intellect, of analysis, of stable structures at the expense of process, grows more intense and expands from Bergson through Lefebvre to reach Delgado. Ultimately, the solution to the problems of method engendered by these criticized approaches lies, still, in Bergson's idea of intuition.

Far from the mystical (in the pejorative sense) path (see chapter one of the present work) or a simplistic negation of existing material realities, intuition is a particular kind of self-awareness, one that highlights the imbrication of abstraction in perceived reality and, through a double movement, retraces the chain of static categories from which the intellect has distanced itself from reality to return to that concrete and complex reality itself. It is the intellect turned back upon itself. Where the intellect sees static poses, Bergson's intuition, Lefebvre's rhythmanalysis and Delgado's "antropología urbana" all see the brute fact of change, rhythm, and mobility. The question they all ask is one and the same, one which Bergson poses, to name just one place, in Introduction II of *The Creative Mind*:

> Thus perception, thought, language, all the individual or social activities of the mind, conspire to bring us face to face with persons, including our own, which will become in our eyes objects and, at the same time, invariable substances. How can we uproot so profound an inclination? How can we bring the human mind to reverse the direction of its customary way of operating, beginning with change and movement, envisaged as reality itself, and no longer to see in halts or states mere snapshots taken of what is moving reality? (70)

The answer is that this reversal is possible through the faculty of intuition, a faculty that has nothing at all to do with the "banking education" denounced by Paolo Freire (1970, 1998) and bell hooks (1994), something that is not teachable in the sense of being able to memorize a series of rules or principles in the abstract so as to later properly apply them to a shifting reality. Instead, "the faculty of intuition exists in each one of us, but covered over by functions more useful to life" (*CM*, 47). This is the faculty that obtains in the Greek concept "mētis," understood as a complex way of knowing applied to ever-shifting and unpredictable situations (see Detienne and Vernant 1978, Michel de Certeau 1984, James C. Scott 1998). Intuition asserts that complex processes require a complex method (Jacobs 1961, Lefebvre 1992). The purpose of the intellect, the physical brain as "the organ of attention to life" (*CM*) and thus as the organ of our virtual action on things, is opposed to all complexity. It proceeds from static and simple views, from what are necessarily abstractions, in order to quickly compose a plan of action. Even when its use is supposedly disinterested, its method is the same. The abstract categories through which perception operates, the selective use of memory which obtains in this process (Bergson *MM*), decompose a fluid and multivalent reality in order to stitch it back together again, simplifying it in the process. The reversal of this intellectual thought, what Bergson calls intuition, perhaps what the Greeks called "mētis," perhaps what some call skepticism, must trace itself back along its own lines.

Although this is ultimately a topic for another book, it is useful to close this one with a series of nine numbered points through which Bergson outlines what he means by intuition. These points are included as part of one of his most famous essays, "Introduction to Metaphysics" (1903), where he necessarily caters to the spatializing tendency of intellect as it obtains in language (see *CE*, 298-304). In these points there resound all the affirmations of Lefebvre and Delgado surrounding the mobile nature and complexity of urban life as well as the inadequacies of traditionally intellectual (Bergson) or analytical (Lefebvre) approaches to it. They equally recall Thomas Kuhn's *Structure of Scientific Revolutions* (1962) with its emphasis on sharp paradigm shifts at the expense of progressively mechanical evolution as well as the view of biology presented in Bergson's *Creative Evolution*.

> I. There is an external reality which is given immediately to our mind.
> II. This reality is mobility.
> III. Our mind [...] substitutes for the continuous the discontinuous, for mobility stability [...] It starts from the immobile and conceives and expresses movement only in terms of immobility.
> IV. The difficulties inherent in metaphysics, the antinomies it raises, the contradictions into which it falls [...] are due principally to the fact that we place ourselves in the immobile to watch for the moving reality as it passes instead of putting ourselves

> back into the moving reality to traverse with it the immobile positions.
> V. But it does not follow from the fact that we fail to reconstitute living reality with concepts that are rigid and ready made, that we could not grasp it in any other manner.
> VI. The truth is that our mind is able to follow the reverse procedure. It can be installed in the mobile reality, adopt its ceaselessly changing direction, in short, grasp it intuitively. But to do that it must do itself violence, reverse the direction of the operation by which it ordinarily thinks, continually upsetting its categories, or rather recasting them. [...] *To philosophize means to reverse the normal direction of the workings of thought.*
> VII. This reversal has never been practiced in a methodical manner; but a careful study of the history of human thought would show that to it we owe the greatest accomplishments in the sciences, as well as whatever living quality there is in metaphysics.
> VIII. The generative act of method lasts only an instant. That is why we so often take the logical apparatus of science for science itself, forgetting the intuition from which the rest was able to ensue. [...] Science and metaphysics thus meet in intuition. A truly intuitive philosophy would realize the unit so greatly desired, of metaphysics and science. [...] Its result would be to re-establish the continuity between the intuitions which the various positive sciences have obtained at intervals in the course of their history, and which they have obtained only by strokes of genius.
> IX. Let it be said that there is nothing mysterious about this faculty [of intuition]. [...] For one does not obtain from reality an intuition, that is to say, a spiritual harmony with its innermost quality if one has not gained its confidence by a long comradeship with its superficial manifestations. [...] But metaphysical intuition, although one can achieve it only by means of material knowledge, is an entirely different thing from the summary or synthesis of this knowledge. [...] In this sense, metaphysics has nothing in common with a generalization of experience, and yet it could be defined as the whole of experience. (*CM*, 188-200, original emphasis)

Intuition is no mere departure from the material world, nor is it a mere copy of the material world. It is, over all else, a reconciliation. It is a reconciliation of science and metaphysics, of disciplinary knowledge, of knowledge and life. In Delgado, this is an intuition that is more closely attuned to the movement of the living character of cities and urban life itself. This intuition critiques traditional method at the same time that it signals the importance of the enigma of the city, the heterogeneity of the urban, the primacy of movement over static poses, and ultimately the complex reconciliation of space and time. In *Sociedades movedizas*, smuggled into Delgado's work alongside Lefebvre's incisive and insightful critique, Bergson's philosophical effort to "dissolve into the Whole" (*CE*, 191) becomes fully modern and more relevant than ever to understanding the urban processes that shape today's cities.

CONCLUSION

STARTING from Deleuze's call for a "return to Bergson" (1966: 115) this book has argued both for the recognition of the philosopher's significant influence on Spanish letters in a historical sense and also for the relevance of his ideas to the methodological questions of film studies and urban studies today. Just as it is an error to see Bergson as merely a "philosopher of time," it should be apparent that Bergonism grapples not with some pure disembodied temporality, but instead with the key oppositions that structure contemporary life and interdisciplinary academic research. His topic was not time, but rather the relationship between time and space, mind and matter, consciousness and things, intuition and intelligence, and the dynamic and the static–in short, the movement of life itself.

In his direct influence on such important Spanish thinkers and novelists as Miguel de Unamuno and Juan Benet and his indirect influence on Pío Baroja and Belén Gopegui, Bergson left an indelible mark on Spanish letters that has been insufficiently acknowledged until now. Also, in its articulation of a complex methodology that would be more attuned to the process of life, Bergson's thought today appears more relevant than ever to the key problems of film studies and urban geography. His drive to focus on a moving reality and not merely representation supports the work of film theorists (Béla Balázs, Siegfried Kracauer, Peter Wollen, Pier Paolo Pasolini, Stephen Prince) who have challenged the primacy of film theories rooted in artistry, symbolism and montage alone. His emphasis on process has influenced many generations of urban theorists through Henri Lefebvre's debt to Bergsonism, unrecognized and unexplored until now. Through Spanish critic and anti-urbanist Manuel Delgado Ruiz, Bergsonism continues to directly and indirectly point to a more fluid, mobile and complex model of urban life than that which is put forth by developers who profit from the "spatialization of time" critiqued by Bergson through his condemnation of intellect.

The Bergsonian legacy is therefore one that underscores the complexity of the problems of our contemporary world. It is a legacy of reconciliation–of science and metaphysics, of knowledge as viewed from the perspectives of disparate disciplines, of thought and life. If scholarship is to approach the complex problems reframed by these reconciliations, it must do so by following the path of intuition outlined by Bergson in his philosophy. There is a difference in kind, and not merely in degree, he would say, between the intellect that sees movement only through its division into static poses and the intuition that grasps movement as a fluid reality. It is the intellect that compartmentalizes the world into things, and even into strictly delineated disciplines, which are the academic manifestation of those things. Intuition is what is required to open disciplines to one another and to recognize that each of them is but one face onto a multifaceted and complex problem that is the process of our increasingly urbanizing life.

APPENDIX: BERGSON'S ADDRESSES IN MADRID AT THE ATENEO ON MAY 2 AND 6, 1916

BERGSON'S lectures at the Ateneo in Madrid, Spain in 1916 took place in the chaotic context of World War I as part of a French diplomatic mission. From his first words on May 2nd he indicates that he holds Spain in great esteem: "...Great has been Spain's contribution to arms, to letters, to the sciences and also–permit me to say it–to philosophy." Because of his intent that philosophy be returned from the abstract realm of metaphysics, his goal that philosophy should place us in contact with the world and with each other, one notes no major difference in style between his written philosophical works and his speeches. As always he is clear and straightforward, placing communication with his audience first and foremost, believing that "Each philosophical idea, as subtle or as profound as it may be, can and should always be expressed in a tongue spoken by the whole world."

In the two speeches that follow, translated into English for the first time, there are constant allusions to the complex philosophical system, or perhaps it is better to say the complex escape from philosophical system, that he devoted his life's work to articulating. Having been delivered on May 2nd and May 6th, 1916, these two speeches thus occupy a crucial position in his larger oeuvre, a point midway between his first three major works, *Time and Free Will* (1889), *Matter and Memory* (1896) and *Creative Evolution* (1907), and his last work *The Two Sources of Morality and Religion* (1932). As such, they form a sort of bridge, both revisiting the ideas he previously explored and also anticipating their further extension.

The attentive reader will thus find references to the hallmarks of Bergsonian thought: the problem of freedom, the unity of conscious states and the indivisibility of movement (*TFW*); memories, aphasia and the nature of the past (*MM*); the creative will, the élan vital and the cinematographic illusion of intellect (*CE*); the shortcomings of psycho-physiological parallelism and the nature of the human soul (*ME*, 1919); and mystical thought and moral exaltation (*MR*). As in *Laughter* (1900), here, too, Bergson references the work of Cervantes. As in *The Meaning of the War* (1915), here we find a Bergson more attuned to the specific social conflicts of his surrounding world. In their breadth and depth, these speeches constitute an important summary of his life's contribution and his central concerns.

Yet, in tune with Bergson's contention that the old is always fused with the new, both lectures presented here, on "The Human Soul" and on "Personality," do not merely reiterate what has already been said or written. What is unique to these pieces is an attempt to delve further into the realm of personality, which although hinted at in *Time and Free Will* and later also in the *Two Sources of Morality and Religion*, achieves here a greater expression. In his exploration of personality he takes up case studies reported by William James and Doctor Azam that he has not explored in his major works. He ends his lecture of May 6th with an attempt to see personalities in the same way as nations. While certainly open to dispute, this approach itself resonates with the ideas of Spanish thinkers of the day: Ortega y Gasset's organicist understanding of *Invertebrate Spain*, or Ángel Ganivet's discussion of the psychological structure of Spain in his *Idearium español*. Over all else, these speeches serve as further documentation of his admiration for Spain and show just how far-reaching the effects of his philosophical revolution were. They also serve to further elucidate his own personality. Bergson comes across as humble, aware of the horrors of human existence and yet optimistic for a future guided by humanistic ideals.

THE HUMAN SOUL

CONFERENCE delivered at the Ateneo in Madrid on the 2nd of May, 1916, and transcribed stenographically by the weekly *España*.

PHILOSOPHY

...Great has been Spain's contribution to arms, to letters, to the sciences and also–permit me to say it–to philosophy. More than once I have heard it said modestly, all too modestly, to Spaniards, traveling in Paris, that Spain's contribution to philosophy has not been as considerable as its labor in other areas of culture. To this I reply: "That is not my opinion." Ah! If by philosophy one understands I know not what systematic construction of ideas piled on top of other ideas, like stones piled on top of other stones, in order to form an immense building, imposing yet nevertheless fragile, then Spain's participation in this philosophy may perhaps not be considerable. But this is not the conception of philosophy that reigns in the Latin countries, in general, nor in the Anglo-Saxon ones. Philosophy is not a great edifice built with abstractions; it should not be such. Philosophy is not an abstract study; there is nothing less abstract than philosophy. I will even say that, among all sciences, it is the only one that truly is not abstract. Each science focuses on one aspect of reality, that is to say, an abstraction; mathematics studies magnitude; physics heat, light, electricity, things that never exist separated from each other. But they are extracted, they are abstracted out of reality in order to be studied. Instead, the science that studies a concrete and complete reality, without the veils that cover it; the science that makes an effort to contemplate an integral and fundamental reality, this science is philosophy. For this reason there does not exist a study that requires less use of technical terms. It is not useful to resort to barbaric language. Each philosophical idea, as subtle or as profound as it may be, can and should always be expressed in a tongue spoken by the whole world.

Philosophy and Art

But if one understands philosophy in this way, how is Spain, so richly gifted in terms of artistic disposition, not to be equally gifted in terms of philosophy? Philosophy is not Art, but it shares with Art profound affinities. What is the artist? He is a man that sees better than others, because he observes reality fundamentally and with no veils. To see with the eyes of a painter is to see better than common mortals. When we observe an object, we are not accustomed to seeing it; because what we see are conventionalisms interposed between the object and ourselves; what we see are conventional signs that allow us to recognize the object and to distinguish it from another practically, for the convenience of life. But he who lights all these conventionalisms aflame; he who despises the practical utility and convenience of life and who makes an effort to see reality itself directly, without interposing anything between himself and it, he must be the artist. But he must also be the philosopher; with this distinction; that philosophy directs itself less toward external things than toward inner life, toward the soul.

Mysticism

And if we consider the question from this point of view, then Spain, the land of mysticism, is also the land of philosophy. Because the mystics–I refer to the great mystics, to those who were inspired–had a clear and direct vision of inner life. The mystic reaches deep down inside himself and even goes beyond himself; thus he discovers a world of things that other mortals do not even suspect. Of that world, discovered by the mystic, there is a part, undoubtedly, that only he can perceive; but there is another that the rest of us would be equally able to reach. You will tell me that the mystic is privileged. Without a doubt, the great mystics are inspired people, but what we call method is precisely a manner of bypassing inspiration, and an appropriate method must be exactly that which permits all of us unveiled contemplation, with direct vision, of the details of inner life.

The Sciences and Psychology

We are still far, very far from possessing this method. Philosophy thus conceived, as an intuitive study of the human soul, is a philosophy still in its infancy. We should not forget that our science is scarcely three or four centuries old. This science has dedicated itself, most of all, to the most urgent need: to the investigation of matter, whose knowledge is necessary to us in order to achieve the satisfaction of our necessities. First Astronomy was developed, later Physics, next Chemistry, and most recently Biology. Either inorganic matter or living matter was always the principal object of scientific preoccupations. Because of this, it happens that the study of the soul is quite far from the perfection that the other disciplines have achieved. But I must go even further: science, directing itself to material objects, has served to sever the spirit from the knowledge of the soul; because in the study of matter we acquire certain habits, from which we cannot detach ourselves, that obsess and alienate us. And when we turn our gaze toward the interior of the soul, we then see the soul materialized.

Determinism and Freedom

Speaking with greater precision, it is evident that matter is subject to necessity. In the material world everything happens inevitably. The material world, as science presents it to us, is an immense machine, a kind of clock, whose pieces interlock with each other perfectly; everything in it is mechanism. And when, with the habits of science, we consider man, we are necessarily compelled to perceive him as a mechanism implicated in other mechanisms, as a being that functions automatically. No freedom appears possible. It is true that common sense protests and that it has always protested against this idea of man as a kind of automaton. It appears evident to us that the will enjoys the power of choice. In this moment I am free, it appears, to turn toward the right or toward the left. Will it be toward the right? Will it be toward the left? I decide on the right. Here, according to all appearances, there is something incalculable, something totally unforeseeable; and as much as it is said and repeated to us that science, if it were correctly informed, would be able to calculate beforehand everything that happens in the world, this fact appears to elude calculation and foresight absolutely; just as it would be impossible to calculate an eclipse of the sun, if the moon, at the point of interposing itself between the sun and the earth, could say to itself: What am I going to do? Am I going to play a trick on the astronomer that is there waiting for me? Freedom, if it exists, is precisely that: the capability of fooling science that is waiting, the possibility of fooling mathematics in its aspiration to universality. That is what common sense says when it believes in the power to move itself freely. The will is precisely this power; it is the capability of introducing something, to all appearances, absolutely new into the world. And it is even more abundantly so, when that will of which we speak exercises its power, not only applying itself to simple movements, like turning toward the left or toward the right, but to true actions, to important acts; and moreover, when it occupies itself, no longer with creating movements or even actions, but–permit me the expression–with creating itself, with its own growth.

Creative Will

That is the will, a force capable of its own growth. Material forces exist in determined quantities. Of a material force there is no more than what is there, what it possesses: a fixed quantity. But the will possesses the marvelous virtue of being able to increase itself. From a little will more will can be made, much will can be made; with the ability to love one can learn to love. The spirit–spirit and will are almost one single thing–is the faculty of creation. Spiritual potency is a potency that can draw from itself more than that which it contains. I do not see that there can be another definition given of spirit. But–I persist as always rooted in the point of view of common sense–, is this not the reason for the spirit's existence, for the existence of the soul in the universe? It is a special power, destined to continue here creative action, destined to introduce into the world, where all would be calculable and foreseeable if it were up to matter alone, something foreign to calculation and foresight, something in truth absolutely new, a true creation.

Joy as a Sign of Creation

That is the goal and the sense of life. How can one fail to take note of it? Philosophers have sought a thousand definitions of the meaning of life, each one more artificial than the last. Nature has undertaken to offer us a very precise sign regarding the goal of life, a sign that indicates to us when this goal has been fulfilled; that sign is joy. I have not said pleasure, I have said joy.

Pleasure indicates that nature has satisfied its longing to maintain life; but it gives us no indication as to the direction that life takes or that it should take. Joy is a quite different thing. When joy is produced, we can be sure that life has accomplished in some measure its mission, and that the goal has been reached.

In true joy there is something of a triumph. Let us take this further, however, and we will see that wherever there is joy there is creation, and the more rich the creation, the more deep the joy. A mother that contemplates her child is joyous because she has the feeling of having created him physically, and moreover, morally. An industrialist, the boss of a workshop, experiences a similar joy. Can this be perchance because of the benefits he himself obtains? Without a doubt this satisfaction may coincide in part to the feeling that moves him. But this satisfaction is a pleasure more than it is a joy. True joy derives from the feeling that one has created something, that one has given impulse to something new, with movement and life. Let us consider those joys called superior, that of the wise man who has discovered a new truth, that of the artist who has given the world a great and beautiful work. It is commonly said that these joys derive in the main from the satisfactions of love proper, of fame and of the renown afforded by success. It is commonly affirmed that what the artist and the wise man are searching for is glory. I do not believe this. Glory is sought, applause and praise are solicited in exact proportion to the degree in which one is not sure of having hit the mark. One craves the approval of others in order to put oneself at ease. When the created work lacks the certain and undeniable trait of viability, when it is weak and premature, like a child born too soon, then the work's creator might want to surround it with solicitous concerns, to protect it through a kind of artificial incubator, strengthen it through the applause and admiration of others. But he who has absolute certainty–supposing such certainty is possible–of having created a viable and lasting work, hovers above glory; he is a creator, he knows it, he feels it, and the joy that he experiences must be something akin to divine joy.

But however noble this scientific and artistic creation may be, the creation of the man who is not a genius but rather a decent man is nobler still, and through the constant effort of his will he manages to bring into existence the character that he wished to have. This creation, gentlemen, that I call creation of oneself by means of oneself, is that which provides supreme joy and, in order to feel it, no exceptional gifts are needed; all that want to may achieve it.

Such are the appearances; and if we abide by appearances, by what common sense says, the human soul is effectively a power of creation, the faculty of introducing into the world something undetermined, something unforeseeable and absolutely new. Without spirit, all in the universe would be mechanism. Spirit is the capacity for continuously making the world grow, for making it grow morally.

The Principle of the Conservation of Energy

But perhaps one may reply to these affirmations in the following manner: freedom, choice, creation, all those are but words, all that is literature. Let us return to science. What does science say? You speak, for example, of the faculty that we have of moving toward the right, toward the left, as we may wish. But science tells us and shows us that this is impossible, given that, to be able to determine oneself freely, in order to choose, for example, between a movement toward the left or toward the right, it would be necessary to throw onto the scales, at a given moment, a certain quantity of energy. But we do not create anything; the principle of the conservation of energy affirms that in a given system, everything is, theoretically calculable beforehand. This pertains to that supposed faculty of realizing free and unforeseen movements.

Psycho-Physiological Parallelism

But not only should our outer movements be determined and calculable beforehand; so, too, should be our inner movements, the movements of our brain. The matter of which the brain is made is composed of elements, molecules, atoms, etc., that are in constant movement, and this movement is determined by the laws of mechanics. The solidarity between the soul that we spoke of and the brain is evident. It suffices to inhale chloroform for consciousness to fade. It suffices to ingest alcohol for consciousness to be exalted. A transitory intoxication subsequently modifies consciousness. A lasting intoxication, like that which probably constitutes the root of the great majority of mental illnesses, produces a permanent disorder of the spirit. The truth is that the soul, that supposed soul, is completely at the mercy of any cerebral accident whatsoever. Atomic and molecular movements take place in the brain, and to each of these movements there corresponds a state of mind. We know that damage to memory, for example, corresponds to perfectly determined damage to the brain; in this or that cerebral circumvolution, there lies the memory of the movements of the articulation of words; in yet another circumvolution, the memory of the sound of words; in another, the memory of the visual image of letters and words, etc…

There is more. It is probable, it is said, that in these circumvolutions of the brain memories are deposited like the images on photographic sheets or phonograms in phonographic discs. And study of the deterioration of verbal memory, as it is said, appears to establish and affirm this. And if memories are thus located in the brain, so it should be, too, with all states of consciousness, judgments, reasoning, feelings, decisions; such that, if we were to see through the skull to what happens in the brain and follow the dance that atoms and molecules execute; if, moreover, we were to possess the correspondence table that permitted us to translate each of those inner movements of the brain into a state of consciousness, we would be able to enter the person him or herself, and know better than him or herself what occurs in his or her consciousness; well he or she perceives no more than a small part of the intra-cerebral dance, whereas we would perceive the whole dance in all its phases.

This is what was said, in the name of science, during the time in which I was a student, and this is what is said many times even today, well the theory according to which the soul is limited to reproducing in another form what the brain does mechanically, is a theory still accepted today in the great majority of particularly detailed explanations. It is considered an evident fact, that to each state of consciousness there corresponds exactly a determined state of the brain, the latter being no more than a translation of the former in another language.

Consciousness in the Course of Evolution

However, let us examine the matter more closely. At once a thought comes to the aid of the mind that, for my part, I have not abandoned since the first time–many years ago–that I faced that theory of the parallelism between the brain and consciousness. This thought is quite simple. If consciousness were no more than what they say; if its role were limited to translating in its way what occurs mechanically in the grey matter of the brain; if consciousness were no more than a duplicate of matter, it would have disappeared from the world a long time ago, assuming that it had ever been produced. That which does not serve any purpose, the useless organ atrophies and disappears, and this we see in the very consciousness of movements, which diminishes and fades away as those movements become more automatic. Thus, if consciousness were merely a reproduction, in another form, of the molecular processes of the brain, it would have been extinguished a long time ago, or, better yet, it would never have appeared in the course of evolution. But consciousness exists; it serves some purpose and, consequently, is not limited to translating into another language what the brain does.

Will, Explosive Energy

Here is the first reasonable explanation that is given for the spirit. But against it it is alleged that the great laws established by science, the law of the conservation of energy, are opposed resolutely to the possibility that consciousness might do something and intervene in order to introduce a disturbance into movements subject to mechanical laws. But that law of the conservation of energy, that physical law that is invoked, how is it known to us? It becomes known through the observation of facts. It is a law taken from experience; it is a compendium of experiences. All those experiences, however, all those observations refer to facts in which the will does not intervene. But then one begs the question; one accepts, completely, that which is placed in question, when one extends that law to voluntary movements. If, then, the will were, precisely, capable of creating energy, then because of this, the principle of the conservation of energy would be applicable only to systems in which the will does not intervene. I should add that if, as is quite probable, the will is, effectively, capable of creating energy, this energy is reduced, in all likelihood, to a very small quantity. It is the creation of a spark that can produce great explosions, like the spark that ignites gunpowder. If we consider, if we examine the evolution of life and particularly that of the nervous system, it appears that nature has consisted of creating mechanisms disposed toward the most convenient mode of producing, in a given moment, enormous effects with a scant amount of energy, like the touch of a finger on the trigger of a shotgun. Voluntary movement is accomplished by means of a substance that is, in a certain sense, explosive, called glycogen, that is deposited in the nerves and, above all else, in the muscles. The muscle only awaits the spark to fire; the function of the will consists of igniting that spark, such that with a minimal creation of energy there may be developed a quantity of force as great as is desired. But to insist on this point would take us too far off course. It is enough to say that a general principle of physics cannot be invoked against human freedom, as has been done, given that that principle, like all principles, comes from experience, it is a compendium of experiences and these experiences, from which it comes, are facts in which the human will does not in any way intervene.

A Concealed Metaphysics

Many other considerations could be alleged against the thesis of a parallelism between matter and spirit. Of all of them one may be enough: and it is that that thesis exists, going on two or three centuries, in the history of the sciences and of philosophy, without having changed at all. A theory that remains unchanged is a theory that, the majority of times, does not follow the contours of experience. In effect: experience offers us new facts without ceasing, novel discoveries; and, when a theory remains fixed, there is a great probability that it is a mere construction of intelligence and not a datum of experience. As a matter of fact: it is easy to discern that that theory of parallelism is an outdated metaphysics. Born in the 17th century, obtained by prolonging and exaggerating the philosophy of Descartes, that theory later passed from philosophy to today's science. This is well understood; it is to be expected that science could, and even should, make use of such a theory, because science aspires to foresee and to calculate. The data of the spirit, the data of the soul, are resistant to measurement. Because of this, science, from its beginnings, has attempted to substitute for the soul and for the spirit, something susceptible to calculation. It was discovered that the brain, evidently, plays a considerable role in mental life; and as only the brain could be subject to the methods of science, it was agreed to consider it as the equivalent of all mental life. But this is a mere convention, and the moment has arrived to search for what the human soul really is.

Outline of the Problem

If we, then, leave to one side those theories that, upon first glance, appear to be scientific, but that in reality are no more than a metaphysics disguised in scientific clothing; if we consider directly the facts without prejudice, we arrive at very different conclusions. Some time ago now–some 30 years–the idea occurred to me, it must have also occurred to others, to see what the data say, both the normal and the abnormal data, when they are contemplated with no previous decision made and outside of any preconceived hypothesis. Is it correct, for example, that the deficiencies of the spirit and the study of brain lesions lead us to the conclusion that the spirit is the simple translation, in the language of consciousness, of what occurs in the brain? With great amazement I took notice first that it was necessary to eliminate all the supposedly observed data that were not related to memory. Neither for judgment nor for reasoning, nor even for any other function of the spirit, is there one datum that establishes solidarity–in the sense of absolute parallelism–between the state of consciousness and the state of the brain. One must, therefore, disregard all the data that are not data of memory; and I do not need to say that I also leave to one side sensations and movements, given that the brain is, surely, an organ of sensations and of movements.

Conservation and the Evolution of Memories

There remain the phenomena of memory, particularly that of the memory of words. The only cases in which we can be certain that lesions of the spirit correspond to determined lesions of the brain, are the cases of deficiencies of verbal memory, cases of aphasia, as they are commonly called. From this the conclusion is reached that different memories are located in different points of the brain, and that memories are stored in the brain; but if memories can be stored in the brain, other states of consciousness will also be able to correspond exactly with cerebral states. Well then: a study of the phenomena of aphasia undertaken over many years; an investigation of the phenomena of lesions of verbal memory, the only function of consciousness, I repeat, in which the thesis of parallelism finds the beginnings of a proof, has provided me with knowledge of something unexpected, and it is precisely that the deficiencies of verbal memory, studied without prejudice, lead us to the conclusion that it is impossible that memories are really stored or inscribed inside the brain. That which the brain does, that which cerebral circumvolution in this case, does, is something quite distinct: it serves to incite the appearance of the memory of words; it allows us to evoke, in a useful moment, the desired memory; but its function is limited to that. The evocation of memory is not, in any way, its conservation. I will not enter in the detail of the proofs that may be presented to sustain this thesis. I will only cite the most evident, the one which jumps to mind.

The Grammatical Order of Aphasia

In every case, even the most serious, of verbal memory loss, a given word can always return. A strong emotion or a profound excitation is enough. Would this be possible if the lesion had reached the memory itself? No. The lesion has reached only the faculty of evoking or of attracting verbal memories. Another fact that also calls itself to attention, is the following: in the cases of progressive aphasia, when the deficiency is growing incrementally, it has been observed that the words that are lost first are the proper nouns, next the common nouns, later the adjectives, and, last, the verbs. The deficiency follows a grammatical order. From this peculiarity there surged an argument, in appearance quite a strong one, in favor of the localization of memories in the brain. It was said that memories must occupy, in a certain way, successive layers in the interior of the relevant circumvolution; the deficiency would then consume these layers little by little. A minor detail was forgotten, however, which was that the deficiency could begin at any given point of the circumvolution, move in any given direction, and, nevertheless, the memories would disappear always, always in the same order. How was this to be possible, if the memories themselves were progressively attacked? But the truth is that the lesion has attacked the function of attracting, of evoking memories; such that once this function is disturbed, the memories lost first are those which are most difficult to evoke: proper nouns. Common nouns follow, which are the most difficult to evoke among the remaining memories; later adjectives and, last, verbs, which are the most easily evoked. Interjections, it is true, still remain. But interjections are never forgotten.

The Brain, Organ of Pantomime

And why is a verb more easily evoked than an adjective, and an adjective than a noun? Here we reach the essential point. A verb expresses an action, and action can be sketched out, outlined, imitated by the body. Adjectives can not be the object of this type of pantomime, except by means of a verb, and nouns by means of an adjective; such that, examining things closely, we see that the brain does not store memories, instead it serves to incite their return to consciousness, permitting us to internally imitate this or that action, and sketch out, initiate through faint movements, the attitude of this or that activity.

If we examine other functions of the spirit, we arrive at analogous conclusions. The function of the brain, judging by the study of psychological data and certain cerebral lesions, is not, in any way, that of producing inner movements that are then translated into consciousness. The function of the brain and of the nervous system in general, but particularly of the brain, is that of facilitating for us a type of mimicry, externally and even internally, of our thought; that of internally representing for us those movements of mimicry; in such a way that we might define the brain from this point of view–only from it, given that the brain has other functions–as an organ of simple pantomime. Whoever might, as we were saying before, see through the skull and follow the inner movements of the brain, would not know more than a minimal part of our mental life. He would know of the life of the spirit only that which a deaf person would perceive of a symphony, upon seeing the movements of the baton, or of a tragedy or a comedy that which someone attentive only to the movements, gestures, and comings and goings of the actors on the stage would understand. That is the function of the brain: to activate internally the life of the spirit. But that mimicry, that pantomime has an enormous importance, because it places our soul in contact with life, through it we adapt to reality, through it the spirit responds with appropriate reactions to whatever situations present themselves. The brain might be defined, not as the organ of thought, but as the organ of thought's attention to life.

The Relation between the Brain and the Spirit

By means of the brain our thought adheres to life and latches onto the act to be realized. Suppose that one or another part of the brain is damaged. What occurs?: it is found in the same state as that of a boat, tied to the port, if the ties are undone or cut. The boat comes and goes at the mercy of the waves. He who might want to explain all the lesions of judgment, of reasoning, of the states of the soul caused by cerebral lesions; he who might want to seek in the disorder of this or that cerebral movement the explanation of this or that disorder of the spirit, proceeds in no other way than that of the philosopher who, upon seeing the boat drift without direction, searches for the explanation of the movements of the craft in the details present in the broken rope. Certainly, it is because the rope has been broken that the boat drifts; but the detailed explanation of what happens to the boat will never be found in the rope. In a similar fashion, it is because there are cerebral lesions that there are mental lesions; but the study of the cerebral lesion will never explain the unique peculiarities of the mental disorder. Every error–I do think that it is a matter of error–of the doctrine of parallelism lies here. The explanation that I propose, rests, evidently, on a study of the phenomena of aphasia and of the deficiencies of memory, from which come conclusions that might appear paradoxical for the time in which they were presented. In that time there predominated a theory of aphasia and, in general, of mental-cerebral parallelism, that the entire world accepted as dogma. But today, the presently defended thesis appears less paradoxical, given that the studies and efforts of one of out greatest neurologists, M. Pierre Marie, and that of his students, have come to show that it is necessary to profoundly modify the ideas that are accepted on this point. It is easy to see that every day research tends to orient itself in this direction.

The Return of the Past

Well then: from all this we should reach the conclusion that the activity of the brain consists of placing the spirit in communication with reality; it is an organ that obliges the spirit to pay attention to reality. But for precisely this reason it is also an organ that limits the life of the spirit. To live with the brain and with the mind at the same time, is to live a more narrowly defined life. This is evident in the operation of memory. There are some data that appear to indicate that all memories are conserved and that we forget nothing. All of you know what is said of those who drown, of those who are hanged and yet who have been revived. They say that in the space of a few seconds, or even less than a mere second, they have perceived and reviewed the totality of their past existence down to the tiniest detail. And it is easy to see that it is not asphyxiation that causes this phenomenon, the same case has been produced equally in people who have not been on the brink of dying of asphyxiation. A mountain climber, for example, who tumbles on the edge of a precipice, can also have this vision of the past; a soldier, around whom bullets are raining, can experience this same panoramic vision. Examples are being cited, one in particular, during the course of this war, even when the fight leaves little leisure time for psychological study. There are also cases of sudden conversion in which this elastic trip through the past is likewise produced. Can one talk about asphyxiation in all these cases?

Selection of Memories

No, the truth is that our past survives with all its integrity. I lack sufficient time to explain the reason for this persistence; but, in a general way, we all feel that the past is that which exists most; the past is unerasable and indestructible. It survives in each one of us at each instant, and it weighs over us in each instant. All of our memories are there; but in normal time we cannot nor should we perceive them. We should not perceive them, because our purpose is active function in life; life and action, however, always face forward. We cannot nor should we take a glance backward. The brain has as its mission precisely to direct our gaze forward, and from the treasure of past memories to let only those with relevance to the present situation, immanent action, pass through. At most, some others manage to secretly join with the former and pass through as contraband. But let there set in some incident that turns our attention from life; let there take hold a sudden disinterest in life. Then the entire past rushes forth into the present and appears to us in the most minute detail. Thus, then, the brain, whose role is to permit the evocation of useful and pertinent memories, serves also as containment for and obstacle to the rest, and obliges them to remain in obscurity. This double function of the brain, in memory, is also that which it realizes in the whole of mental life. The brain is an organ of spiritual limitation, due to the continual attention that we place on life.

Consequences: The Survival of the Soul

If we study this conclusion, there result a good number of consequences, of serious consequences. I do not refer only to those consequences relevant to pure science in the study of mental deficiencies. Since it has marched in this direction, it has been seen that many mental deficiencies should be explained in a manner rather different from the current one; not by the appearance of a new element that sets in, but by the suppression of that obstacle that our inner life encounters continuously in the necessity to limit itself to action. I will not speak of these consequences of a scientific nature. There are others of a moral nature. Among them I will not insist too much on one that is perhaps the most important of all: the matter of the survival of the soul. This is a problem that has always worried philosophers, it is clear, and one to which philosophy has always responded in a vague and hypothetical way. If it is resolved with the light of faith, one arrives, from the perspective of religion, at a moral certainty. But if the matter is considered from the point of view of science and of philosophy, it will never be able to reach anything other than vague and problematic hypotheses, reasoning that is always open to attack by other reasoning. Without a doubt these reasonings have value, and those which conclude in favor of the survival of the soul have a superiority, which would be easy to prove, over those others whose conclusion is rather the opposite. But reason opposes reason and, in matters of fact, there is no certainty more absolute than experimental certainty, that which comes from observation. Well then: if we accept for one instant that thesis, which prevailed for a long time as scientific, and according to which each state of consciousness corresponds exactly to a cerebral state, the latter being a mere translation of the former, then a disappearance of the soul after death is likely, given that the brain decays. But suppose that experience establishes–and each time it continues to establish in a more solid manner–that what happens in the brain, does not represent more than a minimal part of mental life; that from now on the spirit finds itself, to put it thus, unhinged from the brain, to which it adheres only to the degree necessary to concentrate its attention on life; then, once the brain is suppressed, the spirit subsists just as it was: less limited perhaps, more independent, with a total, a complete, memory of the past. And although the proof of this thesis may not yet be complete, it will become progressively more complete and, of course, one thing may now be said, and it is that in this problem, the obligation of proof falls not upon those who affirm the survival of the soul, but upon those who deny it. Because the only reason that we have to deny the survival of the soul, is that we see the brain decay just like the rest of the body. But this reason loses all its value, if it is established that the spirit, in great measure, is independent of cerebral function.

Consequences: Moral Exaltation

This is a serious consequence, I think, for humanity. There is another. I am convinced that, starting from a philosophy of this kind, and following it through all its results, one can manage to transform, to transfigure daily life. Once we are pointed in that direction, and placed on that track, we may become aware of that independence, that partial unhinging of the spirit and the body, and the conviction thus acquired will be like an illumination of our inner life and of all our experience. I was talking of the joy of the artist and of the emotion that he feels upon contemplating reality directly, without interference. But we can give ourselves that pleasure, that joy, not only through shapes and colors, but rather through all the incidents, even the most trivial incidents of daily life. The consciousness that we acquire of our spiritual existence is intensified, and whereas the artist is privileged–not all who aspire to be artists may become artists–, on the contrary, one does not need a special disposition to arrive at this state of mind: it is enough to have gone through the required reflections, to have given oneself the necessary education.

The Spirit of Sacrifice in Present-Day France

I foresee that, as philosophy advances in this direction, a true spiritual renovation of humanity will be forged. I do not doubt that the sign of this new life will come from the Latin countries, because they were not the ones who invented those theories that systematically deny freedom and the creative force of the spirit. Idealism constitutes the basis of their nature. Permit me to tell you that that idealism is, especially, the basis of the spirit of France. That which is called the *awakening* of present-day France, the sprouting of all our spiritual activities, has brought much surprise. There are those who have wondered at that boundless spirit of sacrifice that reveals itself in our country, and of which it would not be easy to give an idea. It can be said that everyone has made sacrifices before. I have seen men who have lost everything in this war, and they have not complained. I have seen mutilated men without arms, without legs, and they have not complained. I have seen blind men, almost children, condemned to spend their, perhaps long, lives in darkness, and they have not complained. I have seen fathers, mothers who have lost a child, two children, three children; they did not cry. This immense spirit of sacrifice, where does it come from? Is it something altogether new? Do you believe that similar energies might, in effect, be created in a flash, in an instant? No, no. If you were to go to France, you would have the same impression. You would not see grand gestures, you would not hear grand declarations. If you were to go to the front, you would see a simple and calm courage: the courage of men who, knowing that they defend a lofty ideal, an ideal of justice and of humanity, have been transported, through thought, to that ideal, which is eternal, and who, participating from that moment of their eternity on, no longer worry about the rest and go to their death, to a certain death, with a feeling of supreme tranquility. That is what you would see.

The Philosophy of Spirit

Tomorrow, when the spirit has triumphed; when the spiritual forces to which I referred before have revealed their creative force; when they have opposed the most formidable material preparation that the world has seen–military preparation, industrial preparation–equal and superior forces, truly improvised–they were forced to improvise–, but forces that are literally creations of moral and spiritual breath, tomorrow I say, a great gust of spirituality will pass through the world, and, then, I am sure that it will be proven, not only by way of the data of which I was speaking, abnormal data, normal data, scientific data, not only by way of those data, but through others, through action and not through speculation; tomorrow, the creative potential of spiritual forces will be proven, and it will be established, I hope, by that double method and on that double base, philosophy, whose general lines I have wanted to trace here, even if imperfectly, and that I would call, if you will permit it, the philosophy of spirit.

PERSONALITY

CONFERENCE delivered at the Ateneo in Madrid on the 6th of May, 1916, and transcribed stenographically by the weekly *España*.

In the previous conference, that you did me the honor of listening to with such kind-hearted attention, I tried to show the relative independence of the soul with respect to the body. I do not claim that in the present state of things, here in the world, the soul might think, feel, desire independently of the body; consciousness is not unhinged from the body to that degree. Neither do I sustain that mental deficiencies are not cerebral deficiencies. But I tried to establish that the thesis, according to which consciousness is no more than a type of duplicate of cerebral activity, and that it is limited to illuminating the movements of nerve matter, that that thesis, even when it is presented as scientific, is not in reality anything other than a metaphysical hypothesis, a metaphysics that is unconscious of itself. The worst way to be metaphysical is without knowing it. This occurs in the theory of parallelism. It is a metaphysics disguised as science. The idea that states of consciousness amount to phosphorescence that illuminates the trail of the corresponding cerebral phenomena, this idea has not been proven by the data.

THE SPIRIT AND THE BRAIN

If we consider the known facts and those only, if we study without prejudice the mental lesions that we know correspond exactly to determined cerebral lesions–I am referring to those that concern the different classes of verbal memory–, if we then examine the conclusions that immediately are presented, we find that the brain must be, regarding thought and the soul's activity, an organ that outlines or sketches out the actions that are implicit in each of our states of consciousness, an organ that consequently carries the inner rhythm of spiritual life, an organ that allows the spirit to be introduced into things, to influence them, initiating in advance the immanent act. The brain fixes the attention of the spirit upon material realities and, at the same time, limits the spirit, places blinders on it, like those worn by horses to prevent them from looking to the side and obliging them to face forward. The brain does us this favor, which is at the same time to impose on us a sacrifice. It closes off the horizon to the right and to the left, and most of all makes it impossible for us to look backward. But, in exchange, we are able to concentrate our gaze on the object in front of us; the purpose of life is, before all else, action.

The Frame and the Picture

I would like, ladies and gentlemen, to continue this study today, treating the matter of the human personality. The diversity of people is wondrous, as rich as the diversity of physiognomies, and not unrelated to the diversity of physiognomies. The physical personality influences the moral personality to a certain degree. It does not determine it; a given moral personality does not correspond necessarily to a given physical personality, just as a frame does not necessarily correspond to a given picture. But just as it is not possible to put just any picture in a frame, but only those pictures that have the dimensions and the shape of the frame, thus too a given physical personality cannot be fitted with just any moral personality. Many moral personalities are possible with a physical one, with a given physiognomy, but not just any personality.

Virtual Personalities, Art, the Creation of Living Persons

It would be very interesting to show how, over the course of our existence, many possible moral personalities are presented, how they enter in competition and concurrence, and how our life must choose between them. We soon choose one, in order to modify it little by little, to see it progress, and, at times, recede. Our moral life is thus a choice and a creation. It is curious to see how, in infancy most of all, this multiplicity of virtual moral persons appears. In this, childhood is much more rich than maturity. We smile when we see a mother in awe with admiration for her child, as if before a wondrous being. She perceives in the child an infinity of things, and she is right, all these things really are in him. Hope is always more complete, it is always more dense than reality, because reality chooses and hope is the appearance, in a given moment, of many equally possible futures. Let us suppose that the most brilliant, the most complex of all these is realized; it will be necessary to sacrifice the others, and many, many virtualities will have been lost forever. The same thing occurs in the passage from childhood to maturity. As we advance in life, we toss aside many possible personalities. And the creative temperament of the poet, of the dramatic author, of the great novelist, is it not a kind of prolongation of infancy in maturity, a prolongation reduced in this case to the realm of imagination? A Cervantes, for example, is a creator of characters: Don Quijote, Sancho Panza–excuse my pronunciation–, and a thousand other characters who live and act. How has he created them? Arranging and recomposing known fragments? But through this mosaic labor he will never manage to create a living being. It is life that begets life, and all of these living beings have come from the very life of the poet, of the novelist. They are the poet himself, they are Cervantes himself, just as he might have been, the lives that he might have lived, if he had lived fifty lives instead of but one. All these existences that are virtually included in his unique existence, Cervantes has realized them, he has borne them of himself, he has projected them outward, and thus here are the created characters. How many more things might be said analyzing thus the different moral personalities that exist, that coexist in each one of us, and comparing them with the physical personalities that we defined the previous day! But this will not be the subject of the present talk.

The Metaphysical Problem and the Psychological Problem of Personality

I have seen, ladies and gentlemen, that you have been paying such a great and vivid attention to the most difficult matters of philosophy, that I would like to direct your attention to and retain it on the difficulties presented by problem of personality. Thus I will take advantage–and I confess that in this there is something of an egoism on my part–, thus I will take advantage of the few minutes that I have left to spend with you. I would like, then, in those brief instants, to condense the greatest number of things possible. I will discuss the philosophical, metaphysical problem of personality; and then the psychological problem, in its most confusing aspect. I hasten to add that of these two problems, there is one, the one that has captured the interests of philosophers since antiquity, that appears to me false, and if I discuss it, it will be as an example, to make clear how and on what grounds some of the greatest difficulties that have demanded the attention of philosophy are false. Then I will return to the second problem that refers not to fictions, but to realities.

The Unity of Conscious States

What is the metaphysical problem of personality? It is the following. How is a personality something unique? When our consciousness turns its gaze inward, what does it perceive? A state of mind, another state of mind, and then another, and so on successively, ideas, sensations, judgments. All these states, however, sustain each other, they join together and constitute that which each one of us calls a person. How is this possible? What is the link that connects all of these discontinuous states with one another? Speaking with more precision, there is, as it is said, a succession of conscious states in time, and to link all of them together something is needed; what is there that will do this? When our consciousness turns to look inward, what it finds is always a state, and yet, there must be something other than the states of the soul to unite, to join together the links of the chain.

The Two Personalities

Here is the problem that, without having been formulated explicitly, has captured the attention of philosophers since antiquity, since Plotinus and even–without their having been conscious of it–since Aristotle and Plato. The solution adopted by philosophers, by metaphysicians, since Plotinus, is more or less this one: there are two personalities, one, which is the real, true person, situated in eternity, outside of time, and then the other, the whole series of the conscious states that follow each other and unfold in time. This second personality is nothing other than a shadow or projection of the first in time. If we take the example given by Plotinus himself, we will say that on one side there is the true Socrates, the eternal Socrates, who inhabits a region beyond time, and on the other side, the Socrates that is born, lives and dies, who develops over time, and who is, if I am permitted the phrase, no more than the copper coin of the true Socrates, undivided and indivisible, like the golden shield. This solution must appear strange, extraordinary; but it is the one imposed when it is accepted that the person is a collection of conscious states. If conscious states are conceived as a kind of dust that spreads throughout time, nothing will be able to unite those specs of dust, and it must be supposed that in all likelihood there is something from which these specs are issued, a unity equivalent to this multiplicity. This solution has changed over the centuries. We find it again in Liebnitz, and, in another form, in Spinoza; but always as two personalities: one in eternity, and another in the temporality, the latter being the development of the former. This lasts until Kant, who accepts also that our personality, as apprehended by consciousness, is a series of discontinuous states, but understanding that an eternal unity, non-temporal, like that supposed by metaphysicians, is something that our consciousness cannot perceive, and who, convinced, moreover, of the existence of that unity, reaches the conclusion that our consciousness, our faculty of knowledge, cannot reach it.

The Cinematographical Illusion of Discontinuity

This is the metaphysics of the matter, and, certainly, one would have to accept the Kantian solution, as have many others, if in effect consciousness were presented to us as a series of discontinuous states of the soul, in constant succession. But that discontinuity is an illusion, one analogous to that which, for example, a cinematographer, conscious of himself, would have if he were to take a series of instantaneous photographic stills of a movement, and if, upon later contemplating the series of immobile photographs, he were to reach the conclusion that the moving scene is no more than the sum of immobilities. But with those immobilities, our cinematographer, friend of metaphysics, would try in vain to explain how continuity, whole and undivided from movement, could exist, and he would imagine one philosophical theory after the other until the moment in which a Kantian came to prove to him the impossibility of knowing the intimate and ultimate reality of things.

Movement

Consciousness apprehends our personality in quite another way. It is a continuity of movement, a continuity of change. Here we reach the root of the fundamental, metaphysical problem, the matter of how movement and change must be considered. I think, for my part, that the greatest difficulties accumulated by philosophers, the greatest problems, the unsolvable matters of metaphysics, come from having considered movement from the perspective of immobility, or, more clearly, from not having understood that change and movement are found at the root of all reality. We are accustomed to believing that immobility is a more real and fundamental thing than movement. It pleases us to think that immobility is given first, and that movement comes later; we always begin by supposing something immobile, and that movement happens later in that immobile *quid*. Nevertheless, let us look more closely. We will see that what is real in the world is not immobility but rather movement. That which we call immobility is no more than a peculiar case of mobility. In this instant I say that this table is immobile; but I know very well that it is in movement, dragged by the earth, in its orbit around the sun, and by the sun, in its movement toward the constellation Hercules.

Immobility: Two Movements

There is nothing immobile in the world. What do we mean by immobility? When we are traveling on a train, and another train moves in the same direction as ours, with the same velocity, on a parallel track, we say that that train is immobile in relation to ours. Well, that is all there is in immobility. Immobility is the coexistence of two movements. But if that is so, movement is a more simple thing than immobility, for we can produce one single movement, but if we remain immobile, that means we produce at least two movements. Immobility is, then, the composite, and movement the simple. Thus the metaphysician who wants to place himself in truth, to avoid difficulties and contradictions, and, let us say it frankly, the absurdities toward which one is quickly driven, that metaphysician must ground himself in movement and not in immobility. It is necessary to start there. But all of our mental habits are oriented in the opposite direction. It always seems to us that immobility is given first, and that movement comes later. Why? It is simple. Our intelligence is not made for metaphysics; our intelligence is made for action, for practical life. And what are the objects over which our action exercises itself with ease? They are immobile objects; that is, those that are found, with respect to ourselves, in the same situation as that of the moving train with respect to another train that is moving in the same direction, with an identical velocity. And thus that unique situation–it is no common and ordinary thing that two trains move in such a manner–, that situation, in sum, which is exceptional, but of supreme utility for our action on things, is elevated to the category of a privileged situation. It certainly is from the perspective of action, but it lacks all speculative value. Yet, even in the moment in which we speculate, we seek to ground ourselves in the immobile, and we want movement to be posterior to stillness. We would be happy to affirm that movement is no more than a series of immobilities, a series of positions.

The Arguments of Xeno of Elea: The Arrow

All of metaphysics has grown out of the absurdities that follow from this way of considering things, because the origin of metaphysical speculation lies in the arguments of Xeno of Elea against movement. This philosopher, upon formulating his well-known four proofs against movement, contributed to the birth and growth of metaphysics. But Xeno's arguments do nothing else–even though Xeno did not see this–than prove the contradictions that are produced when immobility is considered to be something more simple than movement. The most simple of these four arguments is the third, designated as the arrow. Let us contemplate an arrow, shot from a bow from one point to another, during one moment of the trajectory covered. In this moment it is immobile; in order to be in movement, it must occupy at least two positions, and, accordingly, these two moments are those which are missing; but if we only take one moment, the arrow is during this instant immobile. In each moment of the trajectory the arrow is, then, immobile; thus it is such during the whole trajectory. Thus, then, the arrow is immobile while it is moving… and movement is a contradiction.

Indivisibility of Movement

Xeno would be correct–many refutations have been sought and I think that none is definitive–if immobility were more simple than movement. But the truth is that, when the arrow shot from point A comes to land in point B, that movement from A to B is absolutely indivisible. Mathematicians, it is clear, have a supreme interest in considering the matter in a different way, and in supposing that movement is divisible. But, in reality, it is a simple and indivisible act. But it occurs that we may, by means of the imagination, place ourselves in movement along with the arrow and follow identically its movement, in the same direction and at the same velocity; we can place ourselves, in other words, in the situation of the trains that I mentioned before. We may, then imagine, by means of the coexistence of both movements, as many immobilities as we may wish, and thus we have what we call positions, the series of positions of the arrow. In reality there are no such positions; if the arrow were to be truly in one place, it would stop there and would have to recover its motor force, in which case we would find ourselves before two movements, instead of one. I cannot begin to examine the subtleties of the question. Movement is, truly, a totally indivisible thing.

Achilles and the Tortoise

The other arguments of Xeno might be explained and refuted in the same way. Permit me but two words regarding the most famous of all, that of Achilles and the Tortoise. Achilles, he of the quick legs, runs after the tortoise. He will never catch it. Why? When Achilles has reached the point that the tortoise has just left behind, the tortoise will have moved some distance. When Achilles has crossed the interval that separates him from the tortoise, as he will have needed some amount of time to traverse that interval, the tortoise will have advanced some distance; and, thus, every time Achilles reaches the tortoise, the latter will have already abandoned the spot where it just was. Achilles will never, then, reach the tortoise, according to reason. And yet, he reaches it. I know very well that mathematics purports to resolve that argument of Xeno; and, indeed, it is enough to set the problem up through equations; a simple equation of the first order determines the point where Achilles reaches the tortoise. But to proceed in this way is to accept what is in question, it is to presuppose that there is, surely, a point of coincidence. But the point is, precisely, to know if this point exists, and how, imitating the movement of Achilles, placing ourselves in his position, to put it thus, we might exhaust that infinity. The metaphysicians have sought many answers; the philosophers, too. I think that none of them has been conclusive. It appears to me that the only way of knowing how Achilles manages to reach the tortoise would be–it is so simple that the metaphysicians have not stumbled upon it–, it would be, I say, to interview Achilles and ask him how he does it. Achilles would then answer: "Xeno wants that, in order to reach the tortoise, I first go to the point that the tortoise has just left behind; then, that from this point that I go to the next spot that the tortoise has just left, and so on successively. This is how Xeno proposes that I walk and run. But I move in another manner. I begin with one step, and then another. My steps are indivisible, and after a few of them I surpass the tortoise. I have reached it." In order to be convinced by these affirmations of Achilles, it is enough to understand that movement, as a phenomenon that is produced between two points of rest, is an indivisible thing.

Inner Life as a Continuous Movement

I have taken a circuitous route in order to reach this conclusion: that our psychological life, that our inner life is something whole and totally indivisible, precisely because it is change and movement. If we consider our inner experience from the moment that we are born until the moment we die, and even beyond, all of it, all that movement is absolutely like that of Xeno's arrow: it is an indivisible leap that takes time, all the time that one might want, but indivisible still. Any divisions we would introduce into it will be false. Our conscious life is a stream, it has the continuity of a current that begins at the moment of birth and never ceases. It is an indivisible movement, even though it occupies an indefinite duration. We trace that movement with our consciousness, and our consciousness, moved by the same movement as our inner life, finds itself, with respect to that inner life in the same relationship as the two trains I mentioned before. Thus our consciousness, turning inward, perceives a state of the soul, and then another, and then another. It is content to introduce discontinuity into our inner life. The philosopher comes along, who, faced with this discontinuity, asks himself where the unity might come from. But as the discontinuity he has found is false, so too the unity that he tries to reestablish is false. From here there may arise as many doctrines as are desired, just like what occurs when the intellect moves within the false, and those doctrines are contradictory, each with the others. This continues until the day in which a philosopher like Kant comes along and proclaims that reality cannot be known. But reality is there, right before us, within reach of everyone. Common sense resolves the problem by not posing it. The unity of the person pertains to inner life itself, as an undivided continuity, and needs not be sought in any other place, outside of time or in the unknowable. It is manifest with perfect clarity in the continuity of inner life if the uncertainties falsely introduced by the metaphysicians are pushed to one side.

The Great Political Errors

What I have just said about inner movement and immobility, seems to me to be not merely important from the point of view of metaphysics. I have spoken of the illusions and errors of metaphysics. But the great majority of the illusions and errors of psychology, and even sociology and politics themselves, stem from them. Immobility is commonly taken as natural, as given, and change, movement, appears as something exceptional and accidental, like an abnormality. But, in reality, change and movement are what is normal. The great political errors almost always stem from not having started from this fact: that reality moves and is constantly moving. One reasons that a person, that a town, is and will always be what it has been. Once labeled and defined, we imagine it in a certain way, and we think that it must remain the same. But in reality, the name and the definition are labels stuck on something that changes, and whoever wants to tackle and influence the direction that reality takes, must, through an effort of imagination, of insight, place himself at the heart of this movement and accept change into his thinking. This is how the future must be anticipated.

The Psychological Problem. The Effort to be a Person

But let us leave behind this general problem of movement and of change; let us leave behind too the problem of the unity of the person in its metaphysical aspect, and let us turn to the psychological aspect of the question.

In a certain sense, it is also the problem of the unity of the person which occupies psychology. But in a very different sense. It is a matter of knowing what those ruptures, what those supposed breaks of personality that are produced in some exceptional states, mean. We were saying that consciousness, upon looking inside the spirit, was perceiving the indivisible flow of inner life. But experience seems to suggest that many times that flow is interrupted, and the continuity of interior life in broken into chunks independent from one another. I am referring to those phenomena of dissociation, of doubling of the personality.

But first I would like to call your attention to the special character of that movement of inner life that we have just mentioned. There is no need to consider that indivisible movement that animates consciousness from birth until death, and beyond; there is no need to fancy it, I say, a simple movement that is produced with no effort. We should note that it is unique to man. Only man is a personality. Only he forms an indivisible continuity of his inner and conscious life. My dear and eminent friend mister Edmond Perrier, was speaking to us regarding the intelligence of animals, and was making us realize that that intelligence is quite superior to what many people think. In fact, we are far from having done justice to animals. But if we consider, not intelligence in particular, but rather the totality of the inner life of the animal, it is very problematic–we cannot see into the inner conscious life of the animal, and, thus, we are only permitted hypotheses–, it is very doubtful that animals have the feeling of continuity in their inner lives, from the beginning until the end of their run, if I can express myself in these terms. The animal is conscious of itself, it is clear. It has a certain memory. But I imagine that even the most intelligent of animals, a dog, a monkey, an elephant, does not develop an inner life similar, in its movement, to the movement of the arrow, that goes without stopping from one point to another, rather, the animal passes, from the beginning until the end, through a series of movements in which stops are inserted. The superior animal would like to have a personality, and it makes an effort to attain one. But it seems as if in order to let that flow of inner life pass, without interruption, it would be necessary to continually maintain a compressed storage of energy. The animal would not have enough strength to accomplish this; the storage would be depleted immediately. Man, on the other hand, manages to continually leave his resources compressed, and yet the flow of his conscious life passes continually without breaking apart into pieces. This is hard work, it represents an exhausting effort. It is very tiring to be a person, just as it is very tiring to remain upright and walk on two legs. In order to adopt this attitude an exhausting effort has been necessary, an effort that is perhaps costing us more than it appears. Well then: we apprehend that fatigue that is experienced in order to be a person, we perceive it directly in the supposed doubling of the personality.

Dissociations of the Personality

I do not believe in dissociations of the personality; I don't think that a personality can break apart into pieces like glass. Yet the facts are there, they must be interpreted. But in order to interpret them one must keep in mind that effort, that fatigue, that exhaustion that results from being human. The cases of doubling, of supposed dissociation of the personality, exhibit that exhaustion, they allow us to feel it, and once it is felt, we are better able to comprehend the strange phenomenon. I lack, unfortunately, sufficient time to examine one by one all the necessary cases of doubling. I will limit myself, then, to two examples. We will first take a simple example, a light case of dissociation, and then a complicated example, a very serious case. If in both cases the explanation is enough and gives a good account of the facts, it will be very probable that it serves equally for intermediate cases.

I am going to read you the description of the case that is most simple and most undemanding, in my opinion, that is known in the annals of pathology. This case has been studied in an insightful way by the great American psychologist William James in his *Principles of Psychology*. It is found described from page 392 of the first tome. I have translated the corresponding pages, and I will read them to you quickly.

The Case of William James

"On the 27th of January, 1883, the Reverend Ansell Bourne, a protestant pastor, withdrew 550 dollars from a bank in the city of Providence (United States); he paid a few bills, and got on a trolley car. This is the last incident that he remembers. He did not return home that day, and nothing was heard of him for two months. His disappearance was announced in the dailies, and, as there were suspicions of some kind of foul play, the police were notified, who then undertook an investigation with no result. But on the 14th of May–two months later–, in the city of Norristown, in Pennsylvania, a man who had until then claimed to call himself Brown, who had rented a small store stocked with stationery, confections and fruits, and who had calmly devoted himself to his small business, without his life amounting to anything extraordinary, woke up in the morning in a fright, calling for the people in the house and asking them where he was. He claimed to call himself Bourne; he said that he was absolutely unfamiliar with Norristown; that he knew nothing of business, and that the last thing he remembered–which seemed to him to be yesterday–was having withdrawn money from the bank. He did not want to believe that two months had passed. The people in the house thought him insane, as did the doctor who was called to see him. But when Providence had been telegraphed, confirmation of his assertions was obtained; his nephew came looking for him, put his business affairs in order, and took him home. It goes without saying that Bourne never had the slightest contact with business. Nevertheless, the shop-keeper Brown's neighbors declared that he had not appeared the least bit eccentric to them, and that he was considered a well-put-together man, a little taciturn. He went many times to Philadelphia to replenish his stock. He prepared his own food; he went regularly to church, and once, in a prayer-meeting, he had given an address that went over well."

A Study of the Case

I have already said, that William James has studied this case, and, in fact, pleaded with the Reverend Bourne that he let himself be hypnotized. As was to be expected, Bourne once again turned into Brown and no longer knew Bourne... He had heard, he said, of a certain Bourne, a pastor, but neither did he know him nor had he come in contact with him. In the presence of Mrs. Bourne he stated that he had never met her. William James had the idea of asking him, once he became Brown again, for explanations about his flight, in order to know what had happened, but he couldn't get anything out of him, except this–very important in my estimation–. "There was trouble over there and I wanted rest." Let us remember this phrase: *I wanted rest.* William James asked him how he explained that existence of Brown that had been inserted in his life as a whole. James wanted to know how he saw the two extremities of that existence, and all that he could glean was this sentence: "I am all hedged in and I cannot get out at either end."

To sum it up, it appears that there are two different personalities: the normal personality of Bourne and a certain personality Brown, which manifested itself one day, lasted two months, disappeared and then reappeared artificially in the hypnotic state. William James tried to fuse both personalities through a series of hypnotic practices. As was to be expected, he could not manage to do so. Here is his conclusion: "Mr. Bourne's skull still covers two distinct personal selves."

Explanation of the Case. Memories

But, are there, in reality as William James says–he is a great psychologist, but in this matter perhaps he has not directed his attention toward the necessary point–, are there two distinct personalities? To talk of two personalities is to talk of two beings whose memories are completely different and absolutely independent. Is it true that one of the two subjects, the second one, Brown, has lost the memories that the other had? Let us examine the matter more closely. The subject Brown could orient himself in the midst of the objects that surround him, he could distinguish a table from a house. He had, then, conserved all the material memories of the objects that the subject Bourne possessed. He spoke the same language as Bourne: English; all the memories relevant to language, then, remained for him. These memories are quite numerous. What, then, was he lacking? He was lacking his personal memories, those memories that, gathered over time, constitute the history of a person.

Exhaustion and its Cure

It is those memories which require effort to be conserved in the spotlight of consciousness, given our physical composition. It is like a stock that must be maintained compressed. Well then, our subject could not, without a doubt, realize that effort. This is how those memories are lost. What has happened? I was saying that the sentence "There was trouble over there and I wanted rest," is that which provides the clue as to the difficulty and the solution of the problem. In fact: in a period of great decline, of that intense loss of energy that comes, most of all, from a multitude of tasks and different people monopolizing the attention, bringing it and carrying it in a thousand different directions, there usually arises a great exhaustion, a type of mental partitioning of the personality. Who has not happened, in that situation, to think: "Ah, if I could flee, hide myself in some corner where no one knows me and where I don't know anyone, in which I don't know myself, in which I am immersed in novelty like a kind of eternal fountain of youth!" This is an idea that cuts across our spirit like a shooting star, it is a fantasy;

it is clear that we are not going to stop to consider it, and, even though we might want to, we would never do so. One can escape, flee, forget about everyone, but no one can forget himself at will. But suppose that the person imagines himself threatened by a serious mental sickness, by a complete disorganization of the spirit, as a consequence of that great expense of energy. Well then, nature possesses what the ancients called the *vis medicatrix*, a capacity to resist and defend itself against sickness. Nature carries out what we cannot achieve, and nature can provide us with that rest that we cannot give ourselves at will, that which would consist of forgetting ourselves. Nature will give us vacations of one or two months; she will tell us: "Take that needed rest, forget yourself." Because of this, in a case like this one, nature imposes upon the person a forced rest, during which the person lives and dreams a simplified life, a life from which all the memories that constitute our normal personality are absent, memories that are too burdensome given the scarce resources possessed by that normal person. Thus, this is not a case of doubling or dissociation of the personality. There is but one personality: the normal personality.

But then, as an effect of this excessive exhaustion, this person, forgetting himself, lapses into the somnambulist's dream, simplifying himself in order to rest and recover until the day in which, returning to find himself, he once again adopts his normal state. In the case studied by William James, there is not, then, a break nor a splitting of the personality.

The Case of Doctor Azam

Nor do I think that this is true in the second case, an extreme one that I will not, due to lack of time, explain in great detail. It is the famous case of Félida, observed by Doctor Azam of Bordeaux. This is the most studied and most complete case that we have, given that Doctor Azam's observation started in 1858, and was still ongoing in 1882, close to thirty years afterward, when Doctor Azam published his book *Double Consciousness and Personality*. The observation had spanned, then, a long period of time, and had been carried out by a psychologist of the first order. Here is the case:

It concerned a person named Félida, who, at the age of fourteen, was seized by the incidents whose description follows. She falls asleep; the periods of sleep can last, at first, ten minutes. But, as long as this phenomenon repeated itself, that period of sleep diminished, until it lasted no more than a few seconds, and, finally, one or two instants. What happens after this, such a brief period of sleep? Félida wakes up in a state that Doctor Azam has called second state, in opposition to the normal state, that he calls first state. But the extraordinary thing is that, in that second state, Félida comes and goes, she devotes herself to her tasks as is customary, whereas in the first state she is totally unaware of what has occurred in the second state. Once she wakes up and returns to the first state, termed normal, she has lost all memory of what has happened in the second state. Thus, all first states are completely unaware of what happens in the second states. But let us note this last point well; the opposite is not true, and in the second state, Félida remembers, not only what has happened in the previous second states, but also what has happened in the first states. At the beginning, the totality of the second states made up no more than a tenth of Félida's life; but, as she advanced in age, they increased; they constituted a third, a half, three-fourths of it. When Doctor Azam published his book, the second state had completely taken over her personality, eliminating the first state.

Here there are, then, as it is said, two different personalities. It would be very interesting, and even entertaining, to review this case in all its details. The first state is unaware of what the second state does. In each state, Félida is, in all else, intelligent, with no trace of mental disorder. But her character is not the same in the two states. In the first state, called normal, she has more of a sad character, and her health leaves something to be desired. In the second state, her character is calm and sociable, and her health is good. But the strange and curious thing is that, upon waking from the second state, she returns to things, exactly, at the point in which they were left upon leaving the first state. The interval of time that has passed doesn't count. If she had met someone while in the second state, she would not recognize him in the first state. Félida has some children; but she has had all of them in the second state; such that in the first state she does not know where they have come from. She suspects it, however, and, moreover, knowing of her duality of states, manages, by means of astute questions, to figure out, perfectly, in the first state, what must have happened in the second state. She asks questions of the people around her regarding what she has done, just as one would seek to understand the actions of another person, and thus she manages to reconstitute, approximately, the events that must have occurred.

Explanation of the Case

Here we have a typical case of that supposed rupture or fragmentation of the personality. Well then: my opinion is also, in this case, that if it were to be examined closely one would see that the personality is absolutely indivisible. What has happened is this. We are told that the first state is normal, and that the second state is abnormal. But remember that, in the first state, Félida forgets what has happened in the second state; while in this second state she remembers everything that has happened in herself and in the first. But then I say: Why not call the second state normal? Why not consider the first state, the one poorly-designated as normal, as an abnormal state, as a state reached by constricting the normal personality with the aim of allowing it to rest? As the person lacks the sufficient energy to sustain himself while conserving all his memories, he needs unencumber himself once in a while.

I will not get into details; but here is what must have occurred. At age fourteen, when the personality is growing and becoming more complicated, Félida cannot maintain that mental exhaustion that often goes unnoticed by the greater part of people, but that is real and profound. Thus, after a certain period of time, having lived this new, wider, more developed life over the course of a few weeks, perhaps months, she has returned, unexpectedly, to the previous existence, to that which preceded her puberty. Upon returning to this existence, the doctor that is watching over her has mistaken this existence for the normal state. But it was not: it was an abnormal state achieved by an impoverishment of her new life. Thus, whenever the exhaustion becomes too great, the personality lapses into a kind of somnambulist's sleep, in which it forgets a part of itself. This sleep is called the first, or normal state; but, in reality, it is abnormal, and it lasts until the rest is sufficient for the person to return to his normal state. In all other respects, as he advances in age, his health improves. The so-called abnormal state, which is in reality normal, gains ground and ends up completely taking over. We will say that Félida is cured, as one might be cured in similar cases; that is, with the constant danger of a relapse.

Thus I explain this case, supposing that there is no break of personality. But these cases make us see that, in order for a personality to exist, it is necessary to expend energy; and the supposed splitting of the personality is no more than a trick of nature so that the individual might take a break from that effort that, if it becomes too prolonged, would run the danger of causing more serious disorders. What we call symptoms of illness, are, many times, no more than symptoms of treatment, or, at least, of the effort to cure. This occurs in the cases of mental illnesses and, probably also, in many physical illnesses.

Creation and Life

I have directed your attention, gentlemen, to this problem of the personality and, primarily, on its movement. How many things might now be said regarding the aim of that movement! Because the personality does not move only for the sake of moving, but rather to do, to create. Conscious life is a perpetual creation, the creation of acts, by means of which novelty is introduced into the world, and into one's inner self, reconstituting itself, without ceasing, in what should be the most ample, the most beautiful form. Conscious life, personal life, is, evidently, in the entire organized world, that which occupies the most sublime position. I cannot go into the details of life in general as I imagine it; but I see in the immense effort of life from its origins, from the time in which it is no more than a simple mass of protoplasm until the moment in which it becomes the human organism; I see in this evolution of life an enormous effort to achieve something, whose idea predates the beginning: the constitution of the human personality, of the creative personality.

I imagine every day–not only our planet, but also the others that gravitate in space–as a material mass, through which a stream has been thrown. This stream passes through a tunnel, to put it that way, and reappears later, in broad daylight, and in the moment and at the point of its reappearance, the human personality manifests itself charged with introducing novelty and creation into this material world that, without it, would be pure mechanism and brute necessity. In the beginning, then a great artist who creates the world, and later, as he desires, other minor artists that continue his work and are also creators; through a long process involving organic material, each day more docile and malleable, they continue the work of divine creation.

Respecting the Person

This is what people are; and as humanity has undertaken to comprehend, better each time, what people are, as it has undertaken to define, better each time, the relation that mediates between those creative forces and God, as it has undertaken to understand, better each time, what there is of the sacred in the person, it has ended up taking full stock of itself and proclaiming the inviolability of the person. Each conscious being, each moral person is surrounded, for us, by a kind of aura that makes him sacred. Each person is protected by an immaterial wall that we call rights, and, luckily, today we are already accustomed to considering the rights of the person as inviolable.

National Personalities. Two Opposing Theories

But still we might–and I will finish–consider one last matter: that of knowing if only human beings, individuals, are persons, or if the societies that they constitute, through their agglomeration, are not also or might not become people, when they reach a certain degree of maturity. For my part, I do not hesitate in affirming it. When a society has grown and matured, when it has managed to take full stock of itself, it is a person. When a society has traditions, laws, institutions that condense its past and that play the same function in it as memory in the individual, it is a person. A society that has its own form, its own character, and which imposes that form and that character on the acts that it realizes, it is a person. A society that modifies itself, disfigures itself, reforms itself, betters itself, creating for itself a kind of new character, is a person. A society that develops that character in a certain preferred direction, and which in that way plays a special role in the world, and fulfills a perfectly determined mission, is a person.

It matters little whether the nation is big or small. Does an individual stop being a person because he is small in stature? A nation can be small, and in certain cases, this does not prevent its soul from being great; just as in a small individual body there may reside a great soul, the same occurs in a compact social body. A society is a person, and it has, as does a person, inviolable rights. This is, I think, the conclusion that is reached–I can do no more than point it out–in the development of the aforementioned idea and considering the society that is conscious of itself, society with its traditions.

In opposition to this thesis, to this doctrine, there arises another that says: No, societies are not people; individuals are people, societies are not; nations are not comparable to people who have inviolable rights. There is justice, but only concerning the relationships of individuals in the State, not concerning the relationships of some States with others. A State has no responsibilities toward another State; it has no responsibilities outside of those to itself, and all those responsibilities amount to just one: to be strong, to make itself stronger every day. From which it follows, primarily, that force is the only measurement–between States, of course–, the equivalent and substitute of Rights, and the stronger a State is, the more reasons it has to exist and subsist. Consequently, if a small nation lacks the necessary force to defend itself, neither will it have the right to exist: it will subsist only due to the tolerance of larger nations. From which it follows, likewise, that nations are not linked through their pacts, nor obligated, each with the others, by their word, as are individuals. Pacts exist, but they express only a certain state of equilibrium between the forces that confront each other in a given moment; when that equilibrium is modified, the pact, which was no more than the documentation of that equilibrium, is, in fact, virtually broken; it will break, in fact, if one of the two parties has an interest in breaking it.

I cite both theses, I describe them, I do not judge them, I do not appraise them: I do no more than document that they oppose one another. And I also document that they have been, the one and the other, formulated by philosophers and statisticians. The second one, primarily elaborated by recent German theorists, is the development of a few ideas of the great philosopher Hegel. This thesis has been put into practice, since Hegel, in conditions that that philosopher had not, perhaps, entirely foreseen.

After having defined both theses, I might say–I am speaking as a philosopher, without considering politics–I might say what given ideal each of them entails, what hope they hold for the future of humanity.

Two Contrary Ideals

Let us consider the first, according to which nations are people. Thus the ideal humanity, that we will not realize tomorrow, no matter what occurs, but which might be realized in a matter of years or of centuries, the ideal humanity will be a group of nations, all of which, large or small, strong or weak, each one with its own mission and destiny to fulfill in the world, will work on that mission, and thus, thanks to the introduction of the greatest possible variety of national characters into the world, will develop in it the greatest possible amount of riches and moral beauty, through the agreement of nations, working, cooperating together, in an organic way, as living beings. This is like the different parts of an organism understanding each other, developing themselves freely and spontaneously and coming together in the harmony of the group, giving to this group the greatest beauty and the greatest riches.

In the second conception–I am simply analyzing–there is another implicit ideal. This, too, must be recognized in fairness, it is the ideal of a humanity unified, not immediately; it could be later, although perhaps this ideal is in a hurry to be realized as soon as possible. It is the ideal of a unified humanity, but through other means; if, then, it is true that for a nation force is the only measure and the sign of its right, a nation that might have, for example, enough military and industrial force to stand up to the other great nations, and, thus, to the rest of the world, that nation would have the right–and I will even say that it would have the responsibility–of imposing its dominion and its organization upon the entire world. And from this there would come another unification quite different from the first, a unification that would not spring from the consent of nations, each developing its own personality and individuality, but rather, on the contrary, from a kind of compulsion that would impose upon the whole of humanity a type of mechanical conformity. This would be also a unity, but–it is necessary to say it–an abstract, poor, empty unity, the unity of a machine, and not the harmonious and fecund unity of life.

Here there are the two theses that are face to face; once again I am formulating them; I do not appraise them: I philosophize.

Witness, now, after the philosophy, a little psychology.

The Wasted Sacrifice

In our most recent conversation, to wrap everything up, I was speaking to you of the moral state of France. I was saying to you that it is a France that has said yes, in advance, to all of the sacrifices, whatever they might be: sacrifice from each man of whatever he possesses, sacrifice of his life, sacrifice–that which is most serious–of the lives of his children; France has said yes to all of these sacrifices. And now we may ask ourselves: Why? What is the profound, inner reason for which, at the present hour, there is no Frenchman who is not prepared to calmly, silently make those sacrifices? The reason is that every Frenchman–I am analyzing a state of the soul, not appraising it–every Frenchman feels and believes, believes fundamentally that it is not merely a matter of the fate of France alone. Alas!, this would be sufficient enough to defend the country; there is no sacrifice too great to make for her; but perhaps that sacrifice would not take that form, that extraordinary form of which I will try to give you right now, from the point of psychology, a more precise idea; that would not be enough. It is that, moreover, every Frenchman has the feeling that this is not merely a matter of the fate of France alone, but rather–I make it known, I do not judge it–, he believes it is a matter that concerns all of humanity. A crossroads, a forking has been reached, in which two roads are possible, each one of which leads to one or another of the two systems of humanity's unification; at the end of one, unification in richness, in abundance, in moral exuberance, in the exuberance of life; at the end of the other, poverty, drought, I will almost say death.

I will say right away that if every Frenchman has opted without hesitation for the first ideal, whatever may happen, it is because every Frenchman has said to himself that if the other is realized, life will no longer be worth living. Such is the feeling of all of the French, from the wise man, the philosopher who reflects, to the most humble worker, to the peasant. You can enter the cabin of a peasant and ask him: you will see, if you guide the conversation properly–because they are ideas that present themselves to consciousness at times in a clouded and vague form–, you will see that therein lies the wellspring of this truly extraordinary state of the soul.

The State of the French Soul

And, to conclude, I was telling you that I would try to define this state of the soul with the greatest precision; but I do not know if I will be able to achieve this, because I have not found, in the psychological literature, a description of states comparable to it; but if a distant analogy could be enough, I would say that the state of the soul that best approximates this one is the state of the soul of those great mystics of which I spoke to you even yesterday. Mysticism is not necessarily a violent state; it is not necessarily enlightenment and ecstasy. The great mystics have passed through that state, but they have not remained in it, and beyond those states, beyond the vision of God, they have found what I will call contact with God, a state in which, having returned to themselves, coming, going, attending to their most humble tasks, they feel, wholly transformed, transfigured. It was God that was in them, he was working through them as if through an instrument.

I am far from the idea of identifying the state of the French soul with this mystical state; but I will say that of all the known states it is that which most closely approximates it.

There is nothing more tranquil than present-day France, nothing more virtuous; each attends to his tasks. The greatest sacrifices are made almost without being conscious that they are made; but it is that there is like an inner fire that lifts France up, and that bequeaths something immense, something formidable, that stirs France, and with it (I think) all of the peoples who are not its enemies, all of the peoples with which it feels fraternally united, and it feels, it believes, it knows that it will save its brothers by saving itself.

Here is the state of its soul; I do not appraise it, I analyze, I perform a simple psychological analysis.

And with this simple analysis I conclude, ladies and gentlemen, thanking you for the sustained attention that you have lent to this talk. In my name and in the name of my companions I make known to you our lively and very sincere feelings of gratitude for this atmosphere of sympathy in which we have felt of course continually immersed; of this we will carry with us a lasting, I can even say, an unforgettable memory.

REFERENCES

Aguirre, J. M. "La voz a ti debida: Salinas y Bergson." *Revue de Littérature Comparée* 52 (1978): 98-118.

Aitken, Stuart & Leo Zonn, Eds. *Place, Power, Situation, and Spectacle: A Geography of Film.* Maryland: Rowman and Littlefield Publishers, 1994.

Alberich, José. *Los ingleses y otros temas de Baroja.* Madrid: Alfaguara, 1966.

Amenábar, Alejandro, dir. *Abre los ojos.* Perf. Eduardo Noriega II, Penélope Cruz and Chete Lera. Sociedad General de Televisión (Sogetel), S.A., 1997.

Anderson, Benedict. *Imagined Communities: Reflections on the Origin and Spread of Nationalism.* London: Verso, 1983.

Antliff, Mark. *Inventing Bergson: Cultural Politics and the Parisian Avant-Garde.* Princeton: Princeton UP, 1993.

Arendt, Hannah. *The Human Condition.* Chicago: University of Chicago Press, 1958.

Ares Montes, José. "'Camino de perfección,' o las peregrinaciones de Pío Baroja y Fernando Ossorio." *Cuadernos Hispanoamericanos* 267 (1972): 481-516.

Arocena, Carmen. *Víctor Erice.* Madrid: Cátedra, 1996.

Arocena, Luis A. *Unamuno, sentidor paradojal.* Buenos Aires: Emecé Editores, 1981.

Balázs, Béla. *Theory of the Film. Character and Growth of a New Art.* Trans. Edith Bone. New York: Dover Publications, Inc., 1970.

Barja, César. "Pío Baroja." *Libros y autores contemporáneos.* New York: G. E. Stechert, 1935. 299-359.

Barnard, G. William. "Vital Intuitions: Henri Bergson and Mystical Ethics." *Crossing Boundaries: Essays on the Ethical Status of Mysticism.* Eds. G. William Barnard, Jeffrey John Kripal. New York: Seven Bridges Press, 2002. 309-360.

Baroja, Pío. *Obras completas*, 8 vols. Madrid: Biblioteca Nueva, 1946-51.

———. *Las horas solitarias.* 1918. Madrid: Caro Raggio, 1982.

———. *Camino de perfección: (Pasión mística).* 1902. Madrid: Caro Raggio, 1993.

———. *El árbol de la ciencia.* 1911. New York: Las Américas, n.d.

———. *El dolor: Estudio de psico-física.* 1896. Salamanca: Real Academia de Medicina de Salamanca, 1980.

———. *Las noches del Buen Retiro.* 1933. Barcelona: Tusquets, 1999.

———. "Literatura y bellas artes." *El modernismo visto por los modernistas.* Ed. Ricardo Gullón. Barcelona: Labor-Guadarrama [Colección Punto Omega], 1980. 75-81.

———. "La defensa de la religión." *Juventud, egolatría.* Madrid: Caro Raggio, 1920. 30.

Barthes, Roland. *The Eiffel Tower and Other Mythologies*. Trans. Richard Howard. New York: Hill and Wang, 1979.

Batchelor, R. E. *Unamuno Novelist. A European Perspective*. Oxford: The Dolphin Book Co. Ltd., 1972.

Bayón Martín, Fernando. "*El sol del membrillo*, de Víctor Erice: anatomía de un sueño." Euskonews & Media (2000a). www.euskonews.com/0092zbk/gaia9202 es.html. Accessed 08 Oct 2008.

———. "*El sol del membrillo*. La realidad que habita la imagen." *Ikusgaiak* 4 (2000b): 117-34. Accessed online at www.clubcultura.com/clubcine/sol_membrillo/f_bayon.pdf on 08 Oct 2008.

Bello Vázquez, Félix. *Pío Baroja: El hombre y el filósofo*. Salamanca: Universidad de Salamanca, 1993.

Benet, Juan. *Volverás a Región*. 1967. Barcelona: Destino, 1997.

———. *Una meditación*. 1969. Madrid: Alfaguara, 1990.

———. *Herrumbrozas lanzas*. 1983-85. Madrid: Alfaguara, 1999.

———. *La inspiración y el estilo*. 1966. Barcelona: Seix Barral, 1970.

———. *El ángel del Señor abandona a Tobías*. 1976. Madrid: Taurus, 2004.

———. *Del pozo y del Numa*. Barcelona: La Gaya Ciencia, 1978.

———. "Un extempore." *Puerta de tierra*. 1969. Valladolid: Cuatro, 2003. 69-88.

———. *Return to Región*. Trans. Gregory Rabassa. New York: Columbia UP, 1985.

———. "¿Qué fue la Guerra Civil?" 1976. *La sombra de la guerra*. Madrid: Taurus, 1999. 21-141.

Benito y Durán, Angel. "San Agustín y Bergson: la conciencia psicológica punto de partida de metafísicas divergentes." *Agustinius* XIV (1969): 95-134.

Benjamin, Walter. "The Author as Producer." *Understanding Brecht*. Trans. Anna Bostock. London: NLB, 1973. 85-101.

Bentov, Itzhak. *Stalking the Wild Pendulum*. New York: E. P. Dutton, 1978.

Benson, Ken. "La poética de Juan Benet y sus implicaciones pragmáticas." *Salina: revista de la Facultat de Lletres de Tarragona* 7 (Dec. 1993): 79-88.

Bergson, Henri. *Duration and Simultaneity*. 1922. Ed. Robin Durie. Manchester: Clinamen Press, 1999.

———. *El alma humana. Precedido de un estudio de Manuel García Morente*. Trans. Manuel García Morente. Madrid: Biblioteca "España", 1916.

———. "Bergson en la Residencia." *Residencia* 2 (1926): 174-76.

———. *Quid Aristoteles de loco senserit*/Aristotle's Concept of Place. Trans. J. K. Ryan. *Studies in Philosophy and History of Philosophy* 5 (1970): 13-72.

———. *Time and Free Will. An Essay on the Immediate Data of Consciousness*. 1889. Trans. F. L. Pogson, M.A. Mineola. New York: Dover, 2001.

———. *The Two Sources of Morality and Religion*. 1932. Trans. R. Ashley Audra & Cloudesley Brereton with the assistance of W. Horsfall Carter. Garden City, NY: Doubleday & Co., Inc. 1935.

———. *Matter and Memory*. 1896. Trans. Nancy Margaret Paul and W. Scott Palmer. London, G. Allen & Co., Ltd.; New York, Macmillan Co., 1912.

———. *Mind-Energy*. 1919. Trans. H. Wildon Carr. London: Macmillan and Co. Ltd, 1920.

———. *Creative Evolution*. 1907. Trans. A. Mitchell. Mineola, New York: Dover Publications Inc., 1998.

———. *The Creative Mind*. 1934. Trans. Mabelle L. Andison. NY: Citadel Press, 2002.

———. *The World of Dreams*. New York: Philosophical Library, 1958.

———. *The Philosophy of Poetry: The Genious of Lucretius*. Ed., trans. and in part recast by Wade Baskin. New York: Philosophical Library, Inc., 1959.

Bergson, Henri. *The Meaning of the War: Life and Matter in Conflict*. Introd. H. Wildon Carr. New York: Macmillan, 1915.

———. *Ecrits et paroles*. Paris: Presses Universitaires de France, 1957-59.

Bernard, Claude. *Introduction to the Study of Experimental Medicine*. 1865. Trans. Henry Copley Greene, introd. Lawrence J. Henderson, foreword I. Bernard Cohen. New York: Dover, 1957.

Bhattacharya, Abhoy Chandra. *Sri Aurobindo and Bergson: A Synthetic Study*. Gyanpur: Jagabandhu Prakashan, 1972.

Birdwhitsell, Ray. *Kinesics and Context*. Philadelphia: U of Pennsylvania Press, 1970.

Bistis, Marguerite. "Managing Bergson's Crowd: Professionalism and the Mondain at the Collège de France." *Historical Reflections/Reflexions historiques* 22.2 (1996): 389-406.

Blanco Aguinaga, Carlos. *El Unamuno contemplativo*. Barcelona: Editorial Laia, 1975.

Blasco, Pedro. "El PSOE critica los constantes anuncios del cierre del Parque del Retiro." *El Mundo*. 01 Febuary 2000.

Blunt, Alison. "Cultural Geographies of Migration: Mobility, Transnationality and Diaspora." *Progress in Human Geography* 31.5 (2007): 684-94.

Boas, George. "Bergson (1859-1941) and His Predecessors." *Journal of the History of Ideas* 20.4 (1959): 503-14.

Bohm, David. *Wholeness and the Implicate Order*. 1980. London & New York: Ark, 1983. London; Boston: Routledge & K. Paul, 1980.

———. *Thought as a System*. London; New York: Routledge, 1994.

Boyer, Christine M. "The Return of Aesthetics to City Planning." *Society* 25.4 (1988): 49-56.

Brennan. Gerald. *The Spanish Labyrinth*. 1943. Cambridge: Cambridge UP, 1960.

Brenner, Neil. *New State Spaces: Urban Governance and the Rescaling of Statehood*. Oxford: Oxford University Press, 2004.

Brown, Michael. "Reconceptualizing Public and Private in Urban Regime Theory: Governance in AIDS Politics." *International Journal of Urban & Regional Research*, 23.1 (1999): 70-87.

Bunge, W. W. and R. Bordessa. *The Canadian Alternative: Survival, Expeditions and Urban Change*. Toronto: University of Toronto Press, 1975.

Burunat, Silvia. *El monólogo interior como forma narrativa en la novela española (1940-1975)*. Madrid: José Porrúa Turanzas, 1980.

Burwick, Frederick and Paul Douglass, eds. *The Crisis in Modernism: Bergson and the Vitalist Controversy*. Cambridge: Cambridge UP, 1992.

Campbell, Jan. *Psychoanalysis and the Time of Life: Durations of the Unconscious Self*. New York: Routledge, 2006.

Čapek, Milič. *Bergson and Modern Physics: A Reinterpretation and Re-evaluation*. Dordrecht, Nijhoff, 1971.

Cardwell, Richard A. "Los 'borradores silvestres', cimientos de la obra definitiva de Juan Ramón Jiménez." Peñalabra 20 (1976): 3-6.

Carter, Erica. "Béla Balázs, *Visible Man, or* the *Culture of Film* (1924)." Trans. Rodney Livingstone. *Screen* 48.1 (Spring 2007): 91-108.

Castaneda, Carlos. *The Teachings of Don Juan; a Yaqui Way of Knowledge*. Berkeley, University of California Press, 1968.

Certeau, Michel de. *The Practice of Everyday Life*. Berkeley: University of California Press, 1988.

Cheever, John. "The Swimmer." *The Swimmer and The Death of Justina*. New York, N.Y.: Caedmon, 1981.

Chevalier, Jacques. *Henri Bergson*. 1928. Trans. Lilian A. Clare. New York: AMS Press, 1969.

Clarke, David B., ed. *The Cinematic City*. New York: Routledge, 1997.

Clavería, Carlos. "Notas sobre la poesía de Antonio Machado." *Hispania* 28.2 (1945 May): 166-83.

Cobb, Carl W. *Contemporary Spanish Poetry (1898-1963)*. Boston: Twayne, 1976.

Cockburn, Jacqueline. "Gifts from the Poet to the Art Critic." *Crossing Fields in Modern Spanish Culture*. Eds. Federico Bonaddio and Xon de Ros. Oxford: Legenda, European Humanities Research Center, University of Oxford, 2003. 67-80.

Commisso, Sandra. "Empezó la obra de remodelación de la estación de trenes de Retiro." *Clarín* 26, Oct. 2000.

Compitello, Malcolm. "*Volverás a Región*, the Critics and the Spanish Civil War: A Sociopoetic Reappraisal." *The American Hispanist* 4.36 (May 1979): 11-20.

———. "The Paradoxes of Praxis: Juan Benet and Modern Poetics." Ed. Roberto C. Manteiga, David Herzberger & Malcolm Alan Compitello. *Critical Approaches to the Writings of Juan Benet*. Hanover and London: University Press of New England, 1984. 8-17.

———. "Región's Brazilian Backlands: The Link Between *Volverás a Región* and Euclides Da Cunha's *Os Sertões*." *Hispanic Journal* 1 (1980): 25-45.

———. "Benet and Spanish Postmodernism." *RHM*, XLIV (1991): 259-72.

———. "From Planning to Design: The Culture of Flexible Accumulation in Post-Cambio Madrid." *Arizona Journal of Hispanic Cultural Studies* 3 (1999): 199-219.

———. "Recasting Urban Identities: The Case of Madrid 1977-1997." *Arachne* 2.1 (2002): no pagination. Web Site: arachne.rutgers.edu.

García de la Concha, Víctor. *Historia y crítica de la literatura española*. Vol. 7. Barcelona: Editorial Crítica, Grijalbo, 1984.

Cresswell, Tim. *On the Move: Mobility in the Modern Western World*. London: Routledge, 2006.

Cresswell, Tim and Deborah Dixon, eds. *Engaging Film: Geographies of Mobility and Identity*. Lanham, Maryland: Rowman and Littlefield, 2002.

Danks, Adrian. "Come Towards the Light: The Films of Víctor Erice." *Senses of Cinema* (2003) www.sensesofcinema.com/contents/directors/03/erice.html.

Dear, Michael. *The Postmodern Urban Condition*. Oxford; Malden, Mass.: Blackwell, 2000.

Iglesia, Alex de la. dir. *El día de la bestia*. Perf: Alex Angulo, Armando de Razza, Santiago Segura. Sogetel S.A., 1995.

Deleuze, Gilles. *Bergsonism*. 1966. Trans. Hugh Tomlinson & Barbara Habberjam. NY: Zone Books, 2002.

———. *Cinema I: The Movement-Image*. 1983. Trans. Hugh Tomlinson & Barbara Habberjam. Minneapolis: University of Minnesota Press, 2003a.

———. *Cinema II: The Time-Image*. 1985. Trans. Hugh Tomlinson & Robert Galeta. Minneapolis: University of Minnesota Press, 2003b.

———. *Desert Islands and Other Texts 1953-1974*. Ed. David Lapoujade. Trans. Michael Taormina. Los Angeles; New York: Semiotext(e), 2004.

———. *Foucault*. Trans. Seán Hand. Foreword Paul Bové. Minneapolis; London: University of Minnesota Press, 1998.

———. *Pure Immanence: Essays on a Life*. Intro. John Rajchman. Trans. Anne Boyman. New York: Zone Books, 2001.

Deleuze, Gilles and Félix Guattari. *A Thousand Plateaus: Capitalism and Schizophrenia*. Minneapolis: University of Minnesota Press, 1987.

Delgado Ruiz, Manuel. *El animal público*. Barcelona: Anagrama, 1999.

Delgado Ruiz, Manuel. *Memoria y lugar: El espacio público como crisis de significado*. Valencia: Ediciones Generales de la Construcción, 2001.
———. "Espacio público." (29 mayo 2006) *El País*. Web Site: www.elpais.com.
———. *Sociedades movedizas: pasos hacia una antropología de las calles*. Barcelona: Anagrama, 2007.
Detienne, Marcel and Jean-Pierre Vernant. *Cunning Intelligence in Greek Culture and Society*. Sussex: The Harvester Press Ltd., 1978.
D'Lugo, Marvin. "The Geopolitical Aesthetic in Recent Spanish Films." *Postscript* 21.2 (2002): 78-89.
———. *The Films of Carlos Saura: The Practice of Seeing*. Princeton: Princeton UP, 1991.
Dodson, George Rowland. *Bergson and the Modern Spirit: An Essay in Constructive Thought*. Boston: American Unitarian Association, 1913.
Douglass, Paul. *Bergson, Eliot and American Literature*. Lexington: UP of Kentucky, 1986.
Drinkwater, Judith. "'La soledad de las islas': Towards a Topography of Identity in Belén Gopegui, *La escala de los mapas*, and Juan José Millás, *La soledad era esto*." *The Scripted Self: Textual Identities in Contemporary Spanish Narrative*. Warminster, England: Aris & Phillips, 1995. 99-113.
Durie, Robin. "Introduction." In Bergson, Henri. *Duration and Simultaneity*. 1922. Ed. Robin Durie. Manchester: Clinamen Press, 1999. v-xxiii.
Egea, Juan F. "Poetry and Film: *El sol del membrillo* and *Los amantes del círculo polar*." *Hispanic Review* 75.2 (2007): 159-80.
Ehrlich, Linda C. "Interior Gardens: Víctor Erice's 'Dream of Light' and the 'Bodegón' Tradition." *Cinema Journal* 34.2 (Winter 1995): 22-36.
———. *An Open Window. The Cinema of Víctor Erice*. Lanham: Scarecrow Press, 2000.
Elden, Stuart. *Understanding Henri Lefebvre: Theory and the Possible*. London; New York: Continuum, 2004.
———. "Rythmanalysis: An Introduction." In Henri Lefebvre, *Rhythmanalysis*, Trans. Stuart Elden and Gerald Moore. London; New York: Continuum, 2006. vii-xv.
———. "Politics, Philosophy, Geography: Henri Lefebvre in Recent Anglo-American Scholarship." *Antipode* 33.5 (2001): 809-25.
Elliot, Hugh S. R. *Modern Science and the Illusions of Professor Bergson*. London: Longman's Green & Co., 1912.
El Mundo. "El Parque del Retiro se cerrará por las noches a partir del verano." 12 Apr. 1998.
Elosegui Itxaso, María. *Lo físico y lo mental en Bergson*. Valencia: NAU Llibres, D.L., 1990.
Eoff, Sherman H. *The Modern Spanish Novel*. New York: New York UP, 1961.
Erice, Víctor. *El sol del membrillo* [*Dream of Light*]. Perf. Antonio López García, Enrique Gran, María Moreno. Rosebud Films, S. L., 1992.
———. "Writing Cinema, Thinking Cinema..." Trans. Carlos Morrero. *Rouge* 4 (1998): no pag. Accessed online at www. rouge.co.au/4/html on 23 Sept 2008.
Esteban, Rafael. "El Ayuntamiento cerrará El Retiro por la noche por motivos de seguridad." *El Mundo*. 17 Aug. 1998.
———. "Aprendiendo a restaurar los monumentos." *El Mundo*. 10 Jan. 2001.
Fernández, Pelayo H. "La teoría de la novela realista de Ortega y la teoría de lo cómico de Bergson." *Cuadernos del Sur* 14 (1981): 173-82.
———. "Bergson y Pérez de Ayala: Teoría de lo cómico." *Cuadernos Americanos* 248.3 (1983): 103-09.
———. "Pérez de Ayala y Bergson." *Boletín del Real Instituto de Estudios Asturianos* 41.1 (1987): 143-83.

Ferrater Mora, José. *Cuestiones disputadas: Ensayos de filosofía.* Madrid: Revista de Occidente, 1955.

———. *Ortega y Gasset: Etapas de una filosofía.* Barcelona: Seix Barral, 1957.

———. *Unamuno: Bosquejo de una filosofía.* Madrid: Alianza, 1985.

Fiddian, R. W. "Unamuno-Bergson: A Reconsideration." *Modern Language Review* 69.4 (Oct 1974): 787-95.

Flaxman, Gregory, ed. *The Brain is the Screen: Deleuze and the Philosophy of Cinema.* Minneapolis: University of Minnesota Press, 2000.

Flewelling, Ralph Tyler. *Bergson and Personal Realism.* New York and Cincinnati: The Abingdon Press, 1920.

Flint, Weston and Norma Flint. *Critical Guides to Spanish Texts: Pío Baroja Camino de perfección (Pasión mística).* London: Grant & Cutler with Tamesis Books, 1983.

Flusty, Steven. *Building Paranoia: The Proliferation of Interdictory Space and the Erosion of Spatial Justice.* West Hollywood, CA.: Los Angeles Forum for Architecture and Urban Design, 1994.

Fónagy, Ivan. "Why Iconicity." *Form Miming Meaning: Iconicity in Language and Literature.* Ed. Max Nänny and Olga Fischer. Amsterdam: John Benjamins Publishing Company, 1999. 3-36.

Font, Domènec. "En el curso del tiempo." www.domenecfont.net/Textos/Erice.doc. Accessed 08 Oct 2008.

Ford, Larry. "Sunshine and Shadow: Lighting and Color in the Depiction of Cities on Film." *Place, Power, Situation and Spectacle: A Geography of Film.* Eds. Stuart Aitken and Leo Zonn. Maryland: Rowman and Littlefield Publishers, 119-36.

Fox, E. Inman. "Baroja y Schopenhauer: *El árbol de la ciencia.*" *Revue de Littérature Comparée* 37 (1963): 350-59.

Foucault, Michel. *Discipline and Punish.* 1975. New York: Penguin Books, 1978.

———. *The Order of Things: An Archaeology of the Human Sciences.* New York: Vintage, 1994.

Fraser, Benjamin. "Madrid's Retiro Park as Privately-Public Space & the Spatial Problems of Spatial Theory." *Journal of Social and Cultural Geography* 8.5 (2007a): 673-700.

———. "Manuel Delgado's Urban Anthropology: From Multidimensional Space to Interdisciplinary Spatial Theory." *Arizona Journal of Hispanic Cultural Studies* 11 (2007b): 57-75.

———. "Unamuno and Bergson: Notes on a Shared Methodology." *Modern Language Review* 102.3 (2007c): 753-67.

———. "A Snapshot of Barcelona from Montjuïc: Juan Goytisolo's *Señas de identidad*, Tourist Landscapes as Process and the Photographic Mechanism of Thought." In *Spain is (Still) Different: Tourism and Discourse in Spanish Identity.* Eds. Eugenia Afinoguenova, Jaume Martí-Olivella. Lexington: Rowman & Littlefield Publishers Inc., 2008a. 151-84.

———. "Toward a Philosophy of the Urban: Henri Lefebvre's Uncomfortable Application of Bergsonism." *Environment and Planning D: Society and Space* 26.2 (2008b): 338-58.

———. "Baroja's Rejection of Traditional Medicine in *El árbol de la ciencia.*" *Bulletin of Spanish Studies* 85.1 (2008c): 29-50.

———. "The Difference Space Makes: Bergsonian Methodology and Madrid's Cultural Imaginary through Literature, Film and Urban Space." Dissertation, Department of Spanish and Portuguese, University of Arizona, 2006a.

———. "The Space in Film and the Film in Space: Madrid's Retiro Park and Carlos Saura's *Taxi.*" *Studies in Hispanic Cinemas 3.1* (2006b): 15-33.

Fraser, Benjamin. "On Mental and Cartographic Space: Belén Gopegui's *La escala de los mapas*, Bergson and the Imagined Interval." *España Contemporánea 18.1* (2005): 7-32.

Freire, Paolo. *Pedagogy of the Oppressed*. 1970. Trans. Myra Bergman Ramos. New York: Continuum, 1989.

———. *Teachers as Cultural Workers. Letters to Those Who Dare to Teach*. Trans. Donaldo Macedo, Dale Koike and Alexandre Oliveira. Boulder: Westview Press, 1998.

Fuentes, Carlos. *Aura*. 1962a. México, D.F.: Ediciones Era, 1977.

———. *La muerte de Artemio Cruz*. 1962b. México, Fondo de Cultura Económica, 1970.

Fuoto, Abby. "A Critique of Margaret Newman's *Health as Expanding Consciousness*." Unpublished manuscript.

Galison, Peter. *Einstein's Clocks, Poincaré's Maps*. New York; London: W. W. Norton, 2003.

García Blanco, Manuel. *En torno a Unamuno*. Madrid: Taurus, 1965.

García Delgado, José Luis. "La economía española durante el franquismo." *Temas para el debate*. 1995. Web Site www.vespito.net/historia/franco/ecofran.html.

García Morente, Manuel. *La filosofía de Henri Bergson*. 1917. Selection and Introduction by Pedro Muro Romero. Madrid: Espasa-Calpe, 1972.

———. *Escritos desconocidos e inéditos*. Eds. Rogelio Rovira y Juan José García Norro. Madrid: Católica, 1987.

Ghirardo, Diane. "The Absence of Presence: The Knickerbocker Residence and the Fate of Nonelitest Architecture." 1997. *Judging Architectural Value*. Ed. William S. Saunders, Introd. Michael Benedikt. Minneapolis; London: University of Minnesota Press, 2007. 165-71.

Gil, Mateo, dir. *Nadie conoce a nadie*. Perf. Eduardo Noriega II, Jordi Mollà and Natalia Verbeke, Warner Sogefilms S.A., 1999.

Gillies, Mary Ann. *Henri Bergson and British Modernism*. Montreal & Kingston: McGill-Queen's University Press, 1996.

Gingerich, Stephen D. "Returning to the Originary Enmity of Philosophy and Literature: Juan Benet's *Del pozo y del Numa (Un ensayo y una leyenda)*." *Revista de Estudios Hispánicos* 38 (2004): 317-40.

Glendinning, Nigel. "The Philosophy of Henri Bergson in the Poetry of Antonio Machado." *Revue de Littérature Comparée* 36 (1962): 53-70.

González, Josefina. "Tecnología y Arcadia en *Volverás a Región*: Un contraste descriptivo." *Hispania* 78.3 (Sept. 1995): 456-62.

González Bedoya, Jesús. *Teoría del hombre de Bergson: Fundamentación gnoseológica de su dimensión moral*. Madrid: Facultad de Filosofía y Letras de la Universidad Complutense, 1976.

González Umeres, Luz. *La experiencia del tiempo humano: de Bergson a Polo*. Pamplona: Servicio de Publicaciones de la Universidad de Navarra, 2001.

Gopegui, Belén. *La escala de los mapas*. Barcelona: Anagrama, 1993.

———. *Tocarnos la cara*. Barcelona: Anagrama, 1995.

———. *La conquista del aire*. Barcelona: Anagrama, 1998.

———. *Lo real*. Barcelona: Anagrama, 2001.

———. *El lado frío de la almohada*. Barcelona: Anagrama, 2004.

Goytisolo, Juan. *Señas de identidad*. 1966. Madrid: Alianza, 1999.

Grafton, Anthony. *The Footnote: A Curious History*. Cambridge: Harvard UP, 1997.

Graham, John T. *A Pragmatist Philosophy of Life in Ortega y Gasset*. Columbia and London: University of Missouri Press, 1994.

Greenberg, Joseph H. "On Language Internal Iconicity." *Syntactic Iconicity and Linguistic Freezes: The Human Dimension*. Ed. Marge E. Landsberg. Berlin: Mouton de Gruyter, 1995. 57-63.

Grogin, R. C. *The Bergsonian Controversy in France 1900-1914*. Calgary: University of Calgary Press, 1988.

Grosz, Elizabeth. *Volatile Bodies: Toward a Corporeal Feminism*. Bloomington: Indiana UP, 1994.

———. *Space, Time and Perversion: Essays on the Politics of Bodies*. New York: Routledge, 1995.

———. *Architecture from the Outside: Essays on Virtual and Real Space*. Cambridge, Mass.: MIT Press, 2001.

———. *The Nick of Time: Politics, Evolution, and the Untimely*. Durham and London: Duke UP, 2004.

———. *Time Travels: Feminism, Nature, Power*. Durham and London: Duke UP, 2005.

Guerlac, Suzanne. *Thinking in Time: An Introduction to Henri Bergson*. Ithaca and London: Cornell UP, 2006.

———. "The 'Zig-zags of a Doctrine': Bergson, Deleuze, and the Question of Experience." *Pli: The Warwick Journal of Philosophy* 15 (2004): 34-53.

Gunn, J. Alexander. *Bergson and His Philosophy*. London: Methuen & Co., 1920.

Gunter, Pete A. Y., ed. *Bergson and the Evolution of Physics*. Knoxville: University of Tennessee Press, 1969a.

Gunter, Pete A. Y. "Introduction." *Bergson and the Evolution of Physics*. Knoxville: University of Tennessee Press, 1969b. 3-42.

Guy, Alain. "Ortega y Bergson." *Revista de Filosofía* 7 (1984): 5-19.

Habermas, Jurgen. *The Structural Transformation of the Public Sphere: An Inquiry into a Category of Bourgeois Society*. Cambridge, Mass.: MIT Press; Cambridge, England: Polity Press, 1989.

Hanna, Thomas, ed. *The Bergsonian Heritage*. New York and London: Columbia UP, 1962.

Hannam, Kevin, Sheller, Mimi and Urry, John. "Editorial: Mobilities, Immobilities and Moorings." *Mobilities* 1.1 (2006): 1-22.

Harvey, David. *The Urban Experience*. Baltimore: Johns Hopkins UP, 1989.

———. *The Condition of Postmodernity*. Cambridge, MA & Oxford, UK: Blackwell, 1990.

———. *Justice, Nature and the Geography of Difference*. London: Blackwell, 1996.

———. *Spaces of Hope*. Berkeley: California UP, 2000.

———. "Afterword." *The Production of Space*. Henri Lefebvre. Trans. Donald Nicholson-Smith. Oxford, OX, UK; Cambridge, Mass., USA: Blackwell, 1991. 425-434.

———. *Spaces of Capital*. Edinburgh: Edinburgh UP, 2001.

———. *A Brief History of Neoliberalism*. Oxford: Oxford UP, 2006.

Hatzenberger, Antoine. "Open Society and Bolos: A Utopian Reading of Bergson's 'Final Remarks.'" *Culture and Organization* 9.1 (2003): 43-58.

Havard, Robert G. "Antonio Machado's Knowledge of Bergson Before 1911." *Neophilologus* 67.2 (1983): 204-14.

———. "The Reality of Words in the Poetry of Pedro Salinas." *Bulletin of Hispanic Studies* LI (1974): 28-47.

Herman, Daniel J. *The Philosophy of Henri Bergson*. Washington, D.C.: University Press of America, 1980.

Hernández, José. "Juan Benet, 1976." *Modern Language Notes* 92.2 (Mar. 1977): 346-55.

Hernández García, Gabriela. *La vitalidad recobrada: un estudio del pensamiento ético de Bergson*. México, D.F.: Facultad de Filosofía y Letras, Universidad Nacional Autónoma de México, 2001.

Herrero, Gerardo, dir. *El principio de Arquímedes*. Perf. Marta Belaustegui, Roberto Enríquez, Blanca Oteyza, Alberto Jiménez. Alta Films, S.A. 2004.

———. *Las razones de mis amigos*. Perf. Marta Belaustegui, Sergi Calleja, Joel Joan. Alta Films, S.A. 2000.

Herzberger, David. "The Emergence of Juan Benet: A New Alternative for the Spanish Novel." *The American Hispanist* 1.3 (1975): 6-13.

Hewitt, Paul. *Conceptual Physics: A New Introduction to Your Environment*. Boston, Mass.: Little, Brown, 1974.

Higginbotham, Virginia. *Spanish Film under Franco*. Austin: University of Texas Press, 1988.

hooks, bell. *Teaching to Transgress. Education as the Practice of Freedom*. New York and London: Routledge, 1994.

Hopkins, Jeff. "Mapping of Cinematic Places: Icons, Ideology, and the Power of (Mis)representation." *Place, Power, Situation, and Spectacle: A Geography of Film*. Eds. Aitken, Stuart C. and Leo E. Zonn. Maryland: Rowman and Littlefield Publishers, 1994. 47-65.

Hutcheon, Linda. *Narcissistic Narrative: The Metafictional Paradox*. Waterloo, Ont.: Wilfred Laurier University Press, 1980.

Iglesias, Carmen. *El pensamiento de Pío Baroja: Ideas centrales*. México: Antigua Librería Robredo, 1963.

Ilie, Paul. *Unamuno: An Existential View of Self and Society*. Madison, Milwaukee, and London: University of Wisconsin Press, 1967.

Iriarte, Joaquín. "El místico gesto de Bergson." *Razón y Fe: revista hispano-americana de cultura* 160 (1959): 25-38.

Izuzquiza Otero, Ignacio. *La arquitectura del deseo*. Zaragoza: Secretariado de Publicaciones de la Universidad de Zaragoza, 1986

Jacobs, Jane. *The Death and Life of Great American Cities*. 1961. New York: Vintage, 1992.

Jakobson, Roman. "Quest for the Essence of Language." *Diogenes* 51 (1965): 21-37.

Jakobson, Roman and Linda Waugh. *The Sound Shape of Language*. Bloomington: Indiana University Press, 1979.

Jalón, Mauricio. "Epílogo." Juan Benet. *Puerta de tierra*. Valladolid: Cuatro, 2003. 160-64.

James, William. *The Principles of Psychology*. New York: Henry Holt, 1890.

Jarmusch, Jim, dir. *Night on Earth*. Perf. Gena Rowlands, Winona Ryder, Armin Mueller-Stahl, Giancarlo Esposito, and Isaach De Bankolé. Fine Line Features, 1992.

Jessop, Bob. "Narrating the Future of the National Economy and the National State: Remarks on Remapping Regulation and Reinventing Governance." Ed. George Steinmetz. *State/Culture: State-Formation After the Cultural Turn*. Ithaca & London: Cornell UP, 1999. 378-405.

———. *State-Theory: Putting the Capitalist State in its Place*. Cambridge: Polity, 1990.

Johnson, Roberta. *Crossfire: Philosophy and the Novel in Spain, 1900-1934*. Lexington: The University Press of Kentucky, 1993.

Jongh-Rossel, Elena de. "La Institución Libre de Enseñanza, el joven Unamuno y la pedagogía." *Hispania* 69.4 (dec. 1986): 830-36.

Jordan, Barry. "The Spanish Film Industry in the 1980s and 1990s." *Contemporary Spanish Cultural Studies*. Eds. Barry Jordan and Rikki Morgan-Tamosunas. London: Arnold, 2000. 179-92.

Kennedy, Ellen Lee. *"Freedom" and "The Open Society": Henri Bergson's Contribution to Political Philosophy*. New York & London: Garland Publishing, Inc., 1987.

Kinder, Marsha. "Documenting the National and its Subversion in a Democratic Spain." In *Refiguring Spain: Cinema, Media, Representation*. Ed. Marsha Kinder. Durham: Duke UP, 1997. 65-98.

Kitchin, Rob and Dodge, Martin. "Rethinking Maps." *Progress in Human Geography* 31.3 (2007): 331-44.

Koch, Gertrud. "Béla Balázs: The Physiognomy of Things." Trans. Miriam Hansen. *New German Critique* 40 (1987): 167-77.

———. "Rudolf Arnheim: The Materialist of Aesthetic Illusion: Gestalt Theory and Reviewer's Practice." *New German Critique* 51 (Autumn 1990): 164-78.

Kolakowski, Leszek. *Bergson*. Oxford: Oxford University Press, 1985.

Kovács, András Bálint. "The Film History of Thought." Flaxman, Gregory, ed. *The Brain is the Screen: Deleuze and the Philosophy of Cinema*. Minneapolis, University of Minnesota Press, 2000. 153-70.

Kracauer, Siegfried. *Theory of Film: The Redemption of Physical Reality*. 1960. New York; Oxford: Oxford University Press, 1968.

Kuhn, Thomas. *The Structure of Scientific Revolutions*. 1962. Chicago: University of Chicago Press, 1970.

Kumar, Shiv K. *Bergson and the Stream of Consciousness Novel*. Westport, CT: Greenwood Press, 1962.

———. "Bergson's Theory of the Novel." *Modern Language Review* 56 (1961): 172-79.

———. "Bergson's Theory of the Novel." *Modern Fiction Studies* 6 (1960): 325-36.

Lacey, A. R. *Bergson*. New York & London: Routledge, 1989.

Lacy, Allen. *Miguel de Unamuno: The Rhetoric of Existence*. The Hague & Paris: Mouton & Co., 1967.

Landeira Brisson, Mary Jo T. "The Presence of Henri Bergson in Antonio Machado." Dissertation. UNC, Dept. of Romance Literatures, 1979.

Lane, Harlan. *The Mask of Benevolence*. 1992. New York: Vintage, 1993.

Lapsley, Rob. "Mainly in Cities and at Night." *The Cinematic City*. Ed. David B. Clarke. New York: Routledge, 1997. 186-208.

Larra, Mariano José de. "¿Quién es el público y dónde se encuentra?" 1832. *Mariano José de Larra: artículos*. Barcelona: Noguer, 1975: 173-80.

Latham, Alan & Derek McCormack. "Moving Cities: Rethinking the Materialities of Urban Geographies." *Progress in Human Geography* 28.6 (2004): 701-24.

Lawlor, Leonard. *The Challenge of Bergsonism: Phenomenology, Ontology, Ethics*. London; New York: Continuum, 2003.

Lefebvre, Henri. *The Production of Space*. 1974. Trans. Donald Nicholson-Smith. Oxford, OX, UK; Cambridge, Mass., USA: Blackwell, 1991a.

———. "The Right to the City." 1968. Ed. & Trans., E. Kofman & E. Lebas. *Writings on Cities*. Oxford: Blackwell, 1996. 63-181.

———. *Rhythmanalysis*. Trans. Stuart Elden and Gerald Moore. London; New York: Continuum, 2006.

———. *Critique of Everyday Life, Vol. 1*. 1947. Trans. John Moore. London; New York: Verso, 1991b.

———. *Critique of Everyday Life, Vol. 2*. 1961. Trans. John Moore. London; New York: Verso, 2002.

———. *Critique of Everyday Life, Vol. 3*. 1981. Trans. Gregory Elliott. London; New York: Verso, 2005.

———. *The Urban Revolution*. Trans. Robert Bononno. Minneapolis: University of Minnesota Press, 2003.

———. *The Survival of Capitalism*. London: Allison & Busby, 1973.

Le Roy, Edouard. *The New Philosophy of Henri Bergson*. Trans. Vincent Benson. New York: Henry Holt & Co., 1913.

Libet, Benjamin & David Ingle, Steve J. Heims, reply by Oliver Sacks. "'In the River of Consciousness': An Exchange." *The New York Review of Books* 51.6 (April 8, 2004): 84-85.

Linstead, Stephen. "Organization as Reply: Henri Bergson and Causal Organization Theory." *Culture and Organization* 9.1 (2003): 95-111.

Linstead, Stephen & Mullarkey, John. "Time, Creativity and Culture: Introducing Bergson." *Culture and Organization* 9.1 (2003): 3-13.

Loewy, Hanno. *Dialógus a dialógusról/Dialogue on Dialogue*. Budapest: Athenäum, 1913.

———. "Space, Time, and 'Rites de Passage': Béla Balázs's Paths to Film." *October* 115 (Winter 2006): 61-76.

Loncke, Filip and Quertinmont, S. "Spatial Structure as a Syntactical or a Cognitive Operation: Evidence from signing and nonsigning children." In *Syntactic Iconicity and Linguistic Freezes the Human Dimension*, Ed. M. Landsberg. Berlin: Mouton de Gruyter, 1995. 343-49.

Longhurst, C. Alex. "Kant in Baroja: *El árbol de la ciencia* and *The Critique of Pure Reason*." *Bulletin of Spanish Studies* LXXXVIII.3-4 (2005): 529-48.

———. "The Turn of the Novel in Spain: From Realism to Modernism in Spanish Fiction." Ed. Anthony H. Clarke. *A Further Range. Studies in Modern Spanish Literature from Galdós to Unamuno*. Exeter: University of Exeter Press, 1999. 1-43.

Lorand, Ruth. "Bergson's Concept of Art." *British Journal of Aesthetics* 39.4 (1999): 400-15.

Lorimer, Hayden. "Cultural Geography: Worldly Shapes, Differently Arranged." *Progress in Human Geography* 31.1 (2007): 89-100.

Lotman, Iuri. *Semiotics of Cinema*. Ann Arbor: University of Michigan Press, 1976.

Machado, Antonio. *Campos de Castilla*. Ed. Geoffrey Ribbans. Madrid: Cátedra, 2003.

———. *Los complementarios*. Ed. Manuel Alvar. Madrid: Cátedra, 1980.

Madanipour, Ali. *Design of Urban Space: an Inquiry into a Socio-spatial Process*. Chichester: Wiley, 1996.

———. *Public and Private Spaces of the City*. London: Routledge, 2003.

———. "Multiple meanings of space and the need for a dynamic perspective." In Madanipour, A., Hull, A. and Healey, P. (eds.), *The Governance of Place*. Aldershot: Ashgate, 2001. 154-68.

Maher, Jane. *Seeing Language in Sign: The Work of William C. Stokoe*. Washington D.C.: Gallaudet University Press, 1996.

Mahoney, Elisabeth. "'The People in Parentheses': Space Under Pressure in the Postmodern City." *The Cinematic City*. Ed. David B. Clarke. New York: Routledge, 1997. 168-85.

Manteiga, Roberto C. "Time, Space, and Narration in Juan Benet's Short Stories." Ed. Roberto C. Manteiga, David Herzberger & Malcolm Alan Compitello. *Critical Approaches to the Writings of Juan Benet*. Hanover and London: University Press of New England, 1984. 120-36.

Marcus, Laura. "'A New Form of True Beauty': Aesthetics and Early Film Criticism." *Modernism/modernity* 13.2 (2006): 267-289.

Marías, Julián. *Miguel de Unamuno*. Barcelona: Editorial Gustavo Gili, 1968.

Marker, Chris, dir. *Le joli mai*. Cast: Chris Marker, Yves Montand, Simone Signoret. Sofracima, 1963.

Marston, Sallie. "The Social Construction of Scale." *Progress in Human Geography* 24.2 (2000): 219-42.

———. "What's Culture Got to Do With It?: A Response to Jakobsen and Van Deusen." *Political Geography* 23.1 (2004): 35-39.

Martínez Bonati, Félix. *La ficción narrativa: (su lógica y ontología).* Murcia. Secretariado de Publicaciones, Universidad de Murcia, 1992.

Martín-Santos, Luis. *Tiempo de silencio.* 1961. Barcelona: Seix Barral, 1997.

Marx, Karl. *Grundrisse.* Harmondsworth: Penguin Publishers, 1973.

Massey, Doreen. "Philosophy and the Politics of Spatiality: Some Considerations." In *Power-Geometries and the Politics of Space-Time.* Heidelberg: Dept. of Geography, University of Heidelberg, 1999. 27-42.

Maxwell, Donald R. *The Abacus and the Rainbow: Bergson, Proust, and the Digital-Analogic Opposition.* New York: Peter Lang, 1999.

McNamara, Patrick. "Bergson's 'Matter and Memory' and Modern Selectionist Theories of Memory." *Brain and Cognition* 30 (1996): 215-31.

Medem, Julio, dir. *Los amantes del Círculo Polar.* Perf: Najwa Nimri and Fele Martínez. SOGECINE, S.A., 1998.

Merleau-Ponty, Maurice. *Phenomenology of Perception.* 1945. Trans. Routledge & Kegan Paul. London & NY: Routledge, 2004.

———. *The Primacy of Perception.* 1964. Ed. James M. Edie. Trans. James M. Edie et al. Evanston: Northwestern UP, 2000a.

———. *The Prose of the World.* 1964. Ed. Claude Lefort. Trans. John O'Neill. Evanston: Northwestern UP, 2000b.

———. *The Visible and the Invisible.* 1973. Ed. Claude Lefort. Trans. Alphonso Lingis. Evanston: Northwestern UP, 2000c.

———. *Sense and Non-Sense.* 1948. Ed. & Trans. Hubert L. Dreyfus & Patricia Allen Dreyfus. Evanston: Northwestern UP, 1982.

Mermall, Thomas. "Ortega y Bergson: Un paralelo sociológico." *Revista Canadiense de Estudios Hispánicos* 13.1 (1988): 134-42.

Merrifield, Andy. *Henri Lefebvre: A Critical Introduction.* New York; London: Routledge, 2006.

Meyer, François. *La ontología de Miguel de Unamuno.* Madrid: Gredos, 1962.

Mitchell, Arthur. *Studies in Bergson's Philosophy.* Lawrence: University of Kansas Press, 1914.

Mitchell, Don. *Cultural Geography: a Critical Introduction.* Oxford: Blackwell, 2000.

———. *The Right to the City: Social Justice and the Fight for Public Space.* New York: The Guilford Press, 2003.

Mitchell, Tim. "Society, Economy, and the State Effect." *State/Culture: State-Formation After the Cultural Turn.* G. Steinmetz, Ed. Ithaca & London: Cornell UP, 1999. 76-97.

Moon, H. Kay. "Alejandro Casona and Henri Bergson." *Spanish Thought and Letters. Pensamiento y Letras en la España del siglo XX.* Eds. Germán Bleiberg and E. Inman Fox. Nashville: Vanderbilt University Press, 1966. 345-59.

Moore, F. C. T. *Bergson: Thinking Backwards.* Cambridge: Cambridge UP, 1996.

Morrow, Carolyn. "An Analysis of 'Poema de un día': The Philosophy of Bergson in Machado's Concept of Time." *Romance Notes* 2 (1961): 149-53.

Moss, Richard. *The I That is We.* Millbrae, CA: Celestial Arts, 1981.

Mullarkey, John. *Bergson and Philosophy.* Edinburgh: Edinburgh UP, 1999a.

Mullarkey, John, ed. *The New Bergson.* Manchester: Manchester UP, 1999b.

Mumford, Lewis. *Technics and Civilization.* New York: Harcourt Brace and Co., 1934.

Muñoz-Alonso López, Gemma. *Bergson (1859-1941).* Madrid: Ediciones del Orto, 1996.

Muro Romero, Pedro. *Filosofía, pedagogía e historia en Manuel García Morente.* Sevilla: Instituto de Estudios Giennenses, Consejo Superior de Investigaciones Científicas, 1977.

Murphy, Timothy S. "Beneath Relativity: Bergson and Bohm on Absolute Time." *The New Bergson*. Manchester: Manchester UP, 1999. 66-81.

Nabokov, Vladimir. *Ada; or, Ardor: A family chronicle*. New York: McGraw-Hill, 1969.

Nelson, Esther W. "Narrative Perspective in *Volverás a Región*." *The American Hispanist* (May 1979): 3-6.

Newman, Margaret. *Health as Expanding Consciousness*. New York: National League for Nursing Press, 1999.

———. "The Pattern that Connects." *Advanced Nursing Science* 24.3 (2002): 1-7.

———. "Prevailing Paradigms in Nursing." *Nursing Outlook* 40.1 (1992): 10-14.

Nozick, Martin. *Miguel de Unamuno*. New York: Twayne Publishers Inc., 1971.

Olkowski, Dorothea. "Flesh to Desire: Merleau-Ponty, Bergson, Deleuze." *Strategies* 15.1 (2002): 11-24.

Olmedo Moreno, Miguel. *El pensamiento de Ganivet*. Madrid: Revista de Occidente, 1965.

Orlock, Carol. *Inner Time: The Science of Body Clocks and What Makes Us Tick*. Secacus, NJ: Carol Publishing Co., 1993.

Orringer, Nelson R. "Juan Benet a viva voz sobre la filosofía y el ensayo actuales." *Los Ensayistas* 8-9 (March 1980): 59-65.

Ortega, José. *Ensayos de la novela española moderna*. Madrid: José Porrúa Turanzas, 1974.

Osegueda, Raúl. *El Problema de la Libertad y Personalidad en la Temática Bergsoniana*. Guatemala: Universidad de San Carlos, 1949.

Ouimette, Víctor. *Reason Aflame: Unamuno and the Heroic Will*. New Haven and London: Yale UP, 1974.

Papanicolau, Andrew C. & Pete A. Y. Gunter, eds. *Bergson and Modern Thought: Towards a Unified Science*. Chur, Switzerland: Harwood Academic, 1987.

Parenti, Michael. *The Sword and the Dollar: Imperialism, Revolution, and the Arms Race*. New York: St. Martin's Press, 1989.

Pasolini, Pier Paolo. *Heretical Empiricism*. Ed. Louise K. Barnett. Bloomington: Indiana University Press, 1988.

Pearson, Keith Ansell. *Philosophy and the Adventure of the Virtual: Bergson and the Time of Life*. London: Routledge, 2002.

Pedraza Jiménez, Felipe B., and Rodríguez Cáceres, Milagros. *Manual de literatura española. VIII. Generación de fin de siglo: Introducción, líricos y dramaturgos*. Tafalla: Cénlit, 1986.

———. *Manual de literatura española. IX. Generación de fin de siglo: Prosistas*. Tafalla, Cénlit: 1987.

Pereda Barona, Tina. "Una lectura bergsoniana de la memoria en la poesía de Rafael Alberti." *Letras Peninsulares* 15.1 (2002): 43-54.

Pérez, Janet. "Tradition, Renovation, Innovation: The Novels of Belén Gopegui." *ALEC* 28.1 (2003): 115-138.

———. "The Rhetoric of Ambiguity." Ed. Roberto C. Manteiga, David Herzberger & Malcolm Alan Compitello. *Critical Approaches to the Writings of Juan Benet*. Hanover and London: University Press of New England, 1984. 18-26.

Pérez-Firmat, Gustavo. *Literature and Liminality: Festive Readings in the Hispanic Tradition*. Durham: Duke UP, 1986.

Perkins, Claire. "Cinephilia and Monstrosity: The Problem of Cinema in Deleuze's *Cinema* Books." *Senses of Cinema* 8 (2000): no pagination.

Philo, Chris, & Kearns, Gerry. "Culture, History, Capital: a Critical Introduction to the Selling of Places." Eds. Chris Philo & Gerry Kearns. *Selling Places. The City as Cultural Capital Past and Present*. Oxford: Pergamon, 1993. 1-32.

Piccioto, Robert S. "Meditaciones rurales de una mentalidad urbana: El tiempo,

Bergson y Manrique en un poema de Antonio Machado." *La Torre: Revista de la Universidad de Puerto Rico* 12 (1964): 141-50.

Pilkington, A. E. *Bergson and His Influence: A Reassessment*. Cambridge: Cambridge UP, 1976.

Pope, Randolph D. "Benet, Faulkner, and Bergson's Memory." Ed. Roberto C. Manteiga, David Herzberger & Malcolm Alan Compitello. *Critical Approaches to the Writings of Juan Benet*. Hanover and London: University Press of New England, 1984. 111-19.

Power, Carl. "Freedom and Sociability for Bergson." *Culture and Organization* 9.1 (2003): 59-71.

Prince, Stephen. "The Discourse of Pictures: Iconicity and Film Studies." *Film Theory and Criticism, 5th ed.* Eds. Leo Braudy and Marshall Cohen. Oxford: Oxford UP, 1999. 99-117.

Pullman, Bernard. *The Atom in the History of Human Thought*. Trans. Axel Reisinger. Oxford: Oxford University Press, 1998.

Quirk, Tom. *Bergson and American Culture: The Worlds of Willa Cather and Wallace Stevens*. Chapel Hill: UNC Press, 1976.

Reynaud, Alain. *La Géographie entre le mythe et la science: Essai d'épistemologie*. Reims: Institut de Géographie, 1974.

Ribbans, Geoffrey. "Introducción." Antonio Machado. *Campos de Castilla*. Madrid: Cátedra, 2003. 11-88.

Richardson, Nathan E. "Youth Culture, Visual Spain, and the Limits of History in Alejandro Amenábar's *Abre los ojos*." *Revista Canadiense de Estudios Hispánicos* 27.2 (2003): 327-46.

Richardson, Robert D. *William James. In the Maelstrom of American Modernism*. Boston/New York: Houghton Mifflin, 2006.

Rivero, José. "Juan Benet: proyecto y cartografía." *Cuadernos Hispanoamericanos* 651-652 (Sept.-Oct. 2004): 147-54.

Robertson, Sandra. "Life is a Virtual Dream: Amenábar Reading Calderón." *Cine-Lit 2000: Essays on Hispanic Film and Fiction*. Eds. & Introd. George Cabello-Castellet, Jaume Martí-Olivella & Guy H. Wood. Corvallis: Oregon State UP: 2001. 115-24.

Rogers, Martha E. *An Introduction to the Theoretical Basis of Nursing*. Philadelphia: Davis, 1970.

Rosenzweig, Roy. *Eight Hours for What We Will: Workers and Leisure in an Industrial City, 1870-1920*. Cambridge: Cambridge University Press, 1983.

Roura Roca, Jaime. "La etapa barcelonesa de Eugenio D'Ors." *Actas del III Seminario de Historia de la Filosofía Española*. Salamanca: Ed. Universidad de Salamanca, Departamento de Historia de la Filosofía y de la Ciencia, 1983. 355-64.

Rulfo, Juan. *El llano en llamas*. 1953. México: Fondo de Cultura Económica, 1973.

Russell, Bertrand. *The Philosophy of Bergson*. London: Macmillan & Co. Ltd., 1914.

Sabater Morant, Ricardo J. Carlos. "Aproximación a la personalidad de Azorín." *Anales Azorinianos* 3.1 (1986): 293-97.

Sacks, Oliver. "In the River of Consciousness." *The New York Review of Books* 51.1 (January 15, 2004): 41-44.

Sánchez Barbudo, Antonio. "Una experiencia decisiva: La crisis de 1897." *Miguel de Unamuno*. Ed. Antonio Sánchez Barbudo. Madrid: Taurus, 1974. 95-122.

Sánchez Venegas, Juana. "Origen común y desarrollo divergente en Bergson y en Ortega." *Pensamiento: revista trimestral de investigación e información filosóficas* 41 (1985): 57-67.

Santayana, George. *Winds of Doctrine: Studies in Contemporary Opinion*. New York: Charles Scribner's Sons, 1926.

Sator Ros, Alejandro Esteban. *Bergson: vida y muerte del hombre y de Dios*. Barcelona: Herder, 1975.

Saura, Carlos, dir. *Taxi*. Perf. Ingrid Rubio, Carlos Fuentes II, Ángel de Andrés López and Eusebio Lázaro. Columbia TriStar Films de España S.A., 1996.

———. *La caza*. Perf: Ismael Merlo, Alfredo Mayo, José María Prada. Elías Querejeta S.L., 1965.

———. *El jardín de las delicias*. Perf: José Luis López Vázquez, José Nieto, Julia Peña. Elías Querejeta S.L., 1970.

———. *Ana y los lobos*. Perf: Geraldine Chaplin, Fernando Fernán Gómez, José María Prada. Elías Querejeta S.L., 1972.

———. *La prima Angélica*. Perf: José Luis López Vázquez, Fernando Delgado, Lina Canalejas. Elías Querejeta S.L., 1973.

———. *Cría cuervos*. Perf: Geraldine Chaplin, Mónica Randall, Ana Torrent. Elías Querejeta S.L., 1975.

Saussure, Ferdinand. *Course in General Linguistics*. London: Duckworth, 1983.

Scharfstein, Ben-Ami. *The Roots of Bergson's Philosophy*. New York: Columbia UP, 1943.

Scherer, Klaus and Paul Ekman. *Approaches to Emotion*. Hillsdale, N.J.: Lawrence Erlbaum Association, 1984.

Scorsese, Martin, dir. *Taxi Driver*. Perf. Robert de Niro, Cybill Shepard. Columbia, 1976.

Scott, James. *Seeing Like a State: How Certain Schemes to Improve the Human Condition Have Failed*. New Haven: Yale UP, 1998.

Sedwick, Frank. "Maxims, Aphorisms, Epigrams and Paradoxes of Unamuno." *Hispania* 38.4 (Dec 1955): 462-64.

Seguin, Jean-Claude. *Historia del cine español*. Trad. José Manuel Revuelta. Madrid: Acento, 1999.

Shaviro, Steven. *The Cinematic Body*. Minneapolis: University of Minnesota Press, 1993.

Shields, Rob. *The Virtual*. London: Routledge, 2003.

Simonsen, Kirsten. "Bodies, Sensations, Space and Time: The Contribution from Henri Lefebvre." *Geografiska Annaler, Series B: Human Geography* 87.1 (2005): 1-14.

Sinclair, Alison. *Uncovering the Mind: Unamuno, the Unknown and the Vicissitudes of Self*. Manchester: Manchester UP, 2001.

Smith, Richard G. "World City Typologies." *Progress in Human Geography* 27.5 (2003): 561-82.

Sobejano, Gonzalo. *Nietzsche en España*. Madrid: Editorial Gredos, 1967.

———. *Novela española de nuestro tiempo (En busca del pueblo perdido)*. 1970. Madrid: Mare Nostrum, 2005.

Soja, Edward W. *Thirdspace. Journeys to Los Angeles and Other Real-and-Imagined Places*. Oxford: Blackwell, 1996.

Sontag, Susan. "Against Interpretation." 1964. *Against Interpretation and Other Essays*. Dell Publishing Co. Inc., 1969. 13-23.

Staeheli, Lynn. Publicity, Privacy, and Women's Political Action. *Environment and Planning D* 14 (1996): 601-19.

Steinmetz, George. "Introduction: Culture and the State." *State/Culture: State-Formation after the Cultural Turn*. Ed. George Steinmetz. Ithaca & London: Cornell UP, 1999. 76-97.

Stephen, Karin. *The Misuse of Mind: A Study of Bergson's Attack on Intellectualism*. New York: Harcourt, Brace & Company, Inc., 1922.

Stewart, J. McKellar. *A Critical Exposition of Bergson's Philosophy*. London: Macmillan & Co., 1911.

Stone, Rob. *Spanish Cinema*. Harlow, England; New York: Longman, 2002.
Styhre, Alexander. "Knowledge as a Virtual Asset: Bergson's Notion of Virtuality and Organizational Knowledge." *Culture and Organization* 9.1 (2003): 15-26.
Suances Marcos, Manuel A. *Los fundamentos de la moral en Bergson*. Madrid: Facultad de Filosofía y Letras de la Universidad Complutense, 1974.
Teilhard de Chardin, Pierre. *The Phenomenon of Man*. 1955. New York: Harper, 1959.
Testa, Daniel P. "Baroja ante Santa Teresa: Lectura e intertextualidad en *Camino de perfección*." *Santa Teresa y la literatura mística hispánica*. Madrid: Edi-6, 1984. 801-06.
Thorns, David. *The Transformation of Cities: Urban Theory and Urban Life*. Houndmills, Basingstoke, Hampshire: Palgrave, 2002.
Tilly, Charles. "Epilogue: Now Where?" *State/Culture: State-Formation After the Cultural Turn*. G. Steinmetz, Ed. Ithaca & London: Cornell UP, 1999. 407-19.
Tobler, Walso. "Three Presentations on Geographical Analysis and Modeling." www.geodyssey.com/papers/tobler93.html. Accessed on 08 Oct 2008.
Torrecilla, Jesús. "Lo moderno como modelo: el concepto equívoco de fuerza en *Camino de perfección*." *Hispanic Review* 64.3 (1996): 337-58.
Torrente Ballester, Gonzalo. *Literatura española contemporánea (1898-1936)*. Madrid: Afrodisio Aguado, no date.
Tristán, Rosa M. "SOS Racismo denuncia la presión policial a los inmigrantes en El Retiro." *El Mundo*. 15 Aug. 1998.
———. "Escasos resultados del aumento de la presión policial en El Retiro." *El Mundo*. 29 Aug. 1998.
Tuñón de Lara, Manuel. "Antonio Machado y la Institución Libre de Enseñanza." *Ínsula* 344-45 (1975): 7, 20.
Turiel, Pedro. *Unamuno: El pensador, el creyente, el hombre*. Madrid: Compañía Bibliográfica Española, 1970.
Turner, David G. *Unamuno's Webs of Fatality*. London: Tamesis Books Limited, 1974.
Turner, Graeme. "Cultural Studies and Film." *Film Studies: Critical Approaches*. Eds. John Hill and Pamela Church Gibson. Oxford: Oxford UP, 2000. 193-99.
Turner, Victor. *The Ritual Process: Structure and Anti-Structure*. 1969. New York: Aldine de Gruyter, 1995.
Unamuno y Jugo, Miguel de. *Del sentimiento trágico de la vida*. New York: Las Américas Publishing Company, n.d.
———. *En torno al casticismo*. Madrid: Alianza Editorial, 2000.
———. *Amor y pedagogía*. 1902. Madrid: Alianza Editorial, 2004.
———. "Cientificismo." *Mi religión y otros ensayos breves*. Madrid: Espasa-Calpe, [1907]1978. 132-39.
———. "Verdad y vida." *Mi religión y otros ensayos breves*. Madrid: Espasa-Calpe, [1907]1978. 16-22.
———. *Niebla*. 1914. 6th ed. Buenos Aires: Espasa-Calpe, 1950.
———. *San Manuel Bueno, mártir y tres historias más*. 5ª ed. Madrid: Espasa-Calpe, 1963.
———. "Recuerdo de Don Francisco Giner." *Obras completas*. Ed. Manuel García Blanco. Vol. 3. Madrid: Escelicer, 1968.
———. "Gramática y otras cosas." *Obras completas*. Ed. Manuel García Blanco. Vol. IV. Madrid: Escelicer, 1968. 289.
Urry, John. *Sociology beyond Society: Mobilities for the 21st Century*. London: Routledge, 2000.
Uscatescu, Jorge. "Bergson y la mística española." *Folia Humanistica* 29.323 (1991): 465-82.

Valdés, Mario J. and María Elena de Valdés. *An Unamuno Source Book: A Catalogue of Readings and Acquisitions with an Introductory Essay on Unamuno's Dialectical Enquiry*. Toronto: University of Toronto Press, 1973.

Valli, Clayton and Ceil Lucas. *Linguistics of American Sign Language: An Introduction*. Washington D.C.: Clerc Books/Gallaudet University Press, 2000.

Van Gennep, Arnold. *Rites of Passage*. 1909. Trans. Monika B. Vizedom and Gabrielle L. Caffee. Chicago: Chicago UP, 1960.

Vázquez Montalbán, Manuel. *Los mares del sur*. 1979. Barcelona: Planeta, 1997.

Vidal Domínguez, María Jesús. "Estudio de circulación urbana: el barrio del Retiro (Madrid)." *Estudios Geográficos* 49 (1988): 421-43.

Voloshinov. *Marxism and the Philosophy of Language*. New York: Seminar Press, 1973.

Watson, Sean. "Bodily Entanglement: Bergson and Thresholds in the Sociology of Affect." *Culture and Organization* 9.1 (2003): 27-41.

Waugh, Linda and Madeleine Newfield. "Iconicity in the Lexicon and its Relevance for a Theory of Morphology." *Syntactic Iconicity and Linguistic Freezes: The Human Dimension*. Ed. Marge E. Landsberg. Berlin: Mouton de Gruyter, 1995. 189-221.

Waugh, Patricia. *Metafiction: The Theory and Practice of Self-Conscious Fiction*. London; New York: Methuen, 1984.

Wheeler, Olive A. *Bergson and Education*. Manchester: Cloister Press, 1922.

White, Hayden. *The Content of the Form: Narrative Discourse and Historical Representation*. Baltimore: John Hopkins University Press, 1987.

Williams, Raymond. "The Future of Cultural Studies." 1986. In *Politics of Modernism: Against the New Conformists*. London: New York: 2007. 151-62.

Wollen. Peter. *Signs and Meaning in the Cinema*. 3rd ed. Bloomington: Indiana UP, 1972.

Wood, Guy H. "Una aproximación cartográfica a *Herrumbrosas lanzas*." *España Contemporánea* 6.2 (1993): 7-18.

Wyers, Frances. *Miguel de Unamuno: The Contrary Self*. London: Tamesis Books Limited, 1976.

Young, Arthur M. *The Geometry of Meaning*. San Francisco: Robert Briggs, 1976a.

———. *The Reflexive Universe: Evolution of Consciousness*. San Francisco: Robert Briggs, 1976b.

Zaragüeta, Juan. *La intuición en la filosofía de Henri Bergson*. Madrid: Espasa Calpe, 1941.

Zubizarreta, Armando F. *Tras las huellas de Unamuno*. Madrid: Taurus, 1960.

Zunzunegui, Santos. "Lo viejo y lo nuevo. La reinvención de la tradición cinematográfica en el final del siglo XX." *Letras de Deusto* 25.66 (1995): 59-74.

INDEX

NORTH CAROLINA STUDIES IN THE ROMANCE LANGUAGES AND LITERATURES

I.S.B.N. Prefix 978-0-8078-

Recent Titles

AN EARLY BOURGEOIS LITERATURE IN GOLDEN AGE SPAIN. *LAZARILLO DE TORMES, GUZMÁN DE ALFARACHE* AND BALTASAR GRACIÁN, by Francisco J. Sánchez. 2003. (No. 277). *-9280-7.*

METAFACT: ESSAYISTIC SCIENCE IN EIGHTEENTH-CENTURY FRANCE, by Lars O. Erickson. 2004. (No. 278). *-9282-3.*

THE INVENTION OF THE EYEWITNESS. A HISTORY OF TESTIMONY IN FRANCE, by Andrea Frisch. 2004. (No. 279). *-9283-1.*

SUBJECT TO CHANGE: THE LESSONS OF LATIN AMERICAN WOMEN'S *TESTIMONIO* FOR TRUTH, FICTION, AND THEORY, by Joanna R. Bartow. 2005. (No. 280). *-9284-X.*

QUESTIONING RACINIAN TRAGEDY, by John Campbell. 2005. (No. 281). *-9285-8.*

THE POLITICS OF FARCE IN CONTEMPORARY SPANISH AMERICAN THEATRE, by Priscilla Meléndez. 2006. (No. 282). *-9286-6.*

MODERATING MASCULINITY IN EARLY MODERN CULTURE, by Todd W. Reeser. 2006. (No. 283). *-9287-4.*

PORNOBOSCODIDASCALUS LATINUS (1624). KASPAR BARTH'S NEO-LATIN TRANSLATION OF *CELESTINA*, by Enrique Fernández. 2006. (No. 284). *-9288-2.*

JACQUES ROUBAUD AND THE INVENTION OF MEMORY, by Jean-Jacques F. Poucel. 2006. (No. 285). *-9289-0.*

THE "I" OF HISTORY. SELF-FASHIONING AND NATIONAL CONSCIOUSNESS IN JULES MICHELET, by Vivian Kogan. 2006. (No. 286). *-9290-4.*

BUCOLIC METAPHORS: HISTORY, SUBJECTIVITY, AND GENDER IN THE EARLY MODERN SPANISH PASTORAL, by Rosilie Hernández-Pecoraro. 2006. (No. 287). *-9291-2.*

UNA ARMONÍA DE CAPRICHOS: EL DISCURSO DE RESPUESTA EN LA PROSA DE RUBÉN DARÍO, por Francisco Solares-Larrare. 2007. (No. 288). *-9292-0.*

READING THE *EXEMPLUM* RIGHT: FIXING THE MEANING OF *EL CONDE LUCANOR*, by Jonathan Burgoyne. 2007. (No. 289). *-9293-9.*

MONSTRUOS QUE HABLAN: EL DISCURSO DE LA MONSTRUOSIDAD EN CERVANTES, por Rogelio Miñana. 2007. (No. 290). *-9294-7.*

BAJO EL CIELO PERUANO: THE DEVOUT WORLD OF PERALTA BARNUEVO, by David F. Slade and Jerry M. Williams. 2008. (No. 291). *-9295-4.*

ESCAPE FROM THE PRISON OF LOVE: CALORIC IDENTITIES AND WRITING SUBJECTS IN FIFTEENTH-CENTURY SPAIN, by Robert Folger. 2009. (No. 292). *-9296-1.*

LOS *TRIONFI* DE PETRARCA COMENTADOS EN CATALÁN: UNA EDICIÓN DE LOS MANUSCRITOS 534 DE LA BIBLIOTECA NACIONAL DE PARÍS Y DEL ATENEU DE BARCELONA, por Roxana Recio. 2009. (No. 293). *-9297-8.*

MAPPING THE SOCIAL BODY. URBANISATION, THE GAZE, AND THE NOVELS OF GALDÓS, by Collin McKinney. 2009. (No. 294). *-9298-5.*

ENCOUNTERS WITH BERGSON(ISM) IN SPAIN: RECONCILING PHILOSOPHY, LITERATURE, FILM AND URBAN SPACE, by Benjamin Fraser. 2009. (No. 295). *-9299-2.*

When ordering please cite the *ISBN Prefix* plus the last four digits for each title.

Send orders to: University of North Carolina Press
P.O. Box 2288
Chapel Hill, NC 27515-2288
U.S.A.
www.uncpress.unc.edu
FAX: 919 966-3829